A Variorum Edition of

The Works of Geoffrey Chaucer

Volume II   The Canterbury Tales

Part Seven   The Summoner's Tale

Paul G. Ruggiers and Daniel J. Ransom

General Editors

The Variorum Edition

Part Seven
The Summoner's Tale

Here bygynneth the Somonours tale

Lordynges ther is in yorkshyre as I gesse
A merssh contree called holdernesse
In which ther wente a lymytour aboute
To preche and eek to begge it is no doute
And so bifel that on a day this frere
Hadde preched at a chirche in his manere
And specially abouen euery thyng
Excited he the peple in his prechyng
To trentals and to yeue for goddes sake
Therwith men myghte holy houses make
Ther as diuyne seruice is honoured
Nat ther as it is wasted and deuoured
Ne ther it nedeth nat to be yeue
As to possessioneres that mowen lyue
Thanked be god in wele and habundaunce
Trentals seyde he deliuereth from penaunce
Hir freendes soules as wel olde as yonge
Ye whan that they been hastily ysonge
Nat for to holde a preest ioly and gay
He syngeth nat but o masse in a day
Deliuereth out quod he anon the soules
Ful hard it is with flesshhook or with oules
To been yclawed or to brenne or bake
Now spede yow hastily for cristes sake
And whan this frere hadde seyd al his entente
With qui cum patre forth his wey he wente
Whan folk in chirche hadde yeue hym what hem leste
He wente his wey no lenger wolde he reste
With scrippe and tipped staf ytukked hye
In euery hous he gan to poure and prye
And beggeth mele and chese or ellis corn
His felawe hadde a staf tipped with horn
A peyre of tables al of yuory
And a poyntel polysshed fetisly
And wroot the names alwey as he stood
Of alle folk that yaf hem any good

A Variorum Edition of The Works of Geoffrey Chaucer

Volume II
The Canterbury Tales

Part Seven

Edited by John F. Plummer III

University of Oklahoma Press : Norman and London

Library of Congress Cataloging-in-Publication Data

Chaucer, Geoffrey, d. 1400.
    The summoner's tale / edited by John F. Plummer III.
        p.   cm — (A variorum edition of the works of Geoffrey
    Chaucer ; v. 2. The Canterbury tales ; pt. 7)
    Includes bibliographical references (p.) and indexes.
    ISBN 0-8061-2744-9
    I. Plummer, John F. (John Francis), 1944–   .   II. Title.
    III. Series: Chaucer, Geoffrey, d. 1400. Works. 1979 ; v. 2.
    IV. Series: Chaucer, Geoffrey, d. 1400. Canterbury tales (Norman,
    Okla.) ; pt. 7.
    PR1866.R8   1983 pt. 7
    [PR1868.S]
    821′.1 s—dc20
    [821′.1]   94-38951
                                                       CIP

The paper in this book meets the guidelines for permanence and durability of the Committee on Production Guidelines for Book Longevity of the Council on Library Resources, Inc. ∞

To Anne

Qu'el mont ne truis si bele ne si sage

Contents

The Summoner's Tale

Illustrations

General Editors' Preface

A Variorum Edition of the Works of Geoffrey Chaucer is a collaborative effort of forty-two medievalists whose chief interest is the work of Geoffrey Chaucer and his time. Originally projected exclusively as a commentary upon the entire canon of Chaucer's poetry and prose, the *Variorum Chaucer* was expanded in 1979 to include a series of facsimiles representing the tradition upon which subsequent editors of the printed editions of his work have based their texts. Thus the *Variorum Chaucer* rests upon the two great foundations of text and commentary.

I

The facsimile series, the prime support for the various texts provided by the *Variorum Chaucer*, was inaugurated in 1979 with the publication of the facsimile of the Hengwrt manuscript (Peniarth 392D) of *The Canterbury Tales*. The series was begun with this particular manuscript on the obvious ground that it was our base manuscript for *The Canterbury Tales* and that the treatment of *The Canterbury Tales* was the part of the project that initially commanded our greatest attention. An explanation of the reasons for the choice of the Hengwrt manuscript as base text is given in the introductions to the publication, along with a full description of the manuscript by A. I. Doyle, Keeper of Rare Books and Reader in Bibliography, University Library, Durham; and M. B. Parkes, Tutor in English Language and Lecturer in Palaeography, Keble College, Oxford. In brief, with reliance upon the Hengwrt manuscript as the base text for *The Canterbury Tales* and with the provision of a running comparison between the transcribed Hengwrt and Ellesmere manuscripts, the *Variorum Chaucer* returns to the sources from which virtually all modern editions of *The Canterbury Tales* have emanated.

Reliance upon the Hengwrt manuscript as a base text does not free the editors of *The Canterbury Tales* from the survey of the manuscript tradition, but rather places each under the obligation to survey both the manuscripts and the printed editions, emending in the light of both sources. The practices that govern the treatment of *The Canterbury Tales* generally set the norms for the establishment of the text for the other parts of the Chaucer canon.

Other parts of the facsimile series include Tanner 346 (*The Legend of Good Women, The Book of the Duchess, The Parliament of Fowls, Anelida and Arcite*); Bodley 638 (*The Legend of Good Women, The Book of the Duchess, The Parliament of Fowls, The House of Fame, Anelida and Arcite*); Pepys Library 2006 (*The Legend of Good Women, The Parliament of Fowls, The House of Fame, Anelida and Arcite, The Tale of Melibee, The Parson's Tale, Chaucer's Retraction*); Trinity R.3.19 (*The Legend of Good Women, The Parliament of Fowls, The Monk's Tale*); St. John's College L.1 Cambridge (*Troilus and Criseyde*); and Morgan 817, *olim* Campsall (*Troilus and Criseyde*).

II

The commentary series is built upon a model evolved over many years: critical and textual introductions, newly established texts for the poems, collations providing evidence both of the manuscripts and of the printed editions, textual and explanatory notes, and bibliography. It is our conviction that so full an apparatus will constitute a summary of the commentary, both textual and evaluative, that has accumulated over the past six hundred years, as well as afford a starting point for future scholarship.

It should be noted that the textual apparatus, melding evidence from both manuscripts and printed editions, will enable the user of the *Variorum Chaucer* to see at a glance the changes through which the various Chaucer texts have passed over the course of six centuries.

III

The *Variorum Chaucer*, when complete, will follow the plan here offered provisionally:

Volume   I: *The Canterbury Tales: A Facsimile and Transcription of the Hengwrt Manuscript* (and the facsimiles listed above; seven parts)

Volume   II: *The Canterbury Tales* (twenty-five parts)

Volume   III: *Troilus and Criseyde* (three parts)

Volume   IV: *The Vision Poems* (*The Book of the Duchess, The House of Fame, The Parliament of Fowls, The Legend of Good Women*) (four parts)

Volume   V: *The Minor Poems* (two parts)

Volume   VI: *The Prose Treatises* (two parts)

Volume   VII: *The Romaunt of the Rose*

Volume   VIII: *History of the Printed Editions*

IV

The collational system of the Variorum Edition is, of course, related to that of John M. Manly and Edith Rickert (*The Text of the Canterbury Tales*, 8 vols.,

1940). That relationship and an explanation of the Variorum approach to Manly and Rickert's work are presented in some detail in our Preface to *The Miller's Tale* (volume 2, part 3, of the Variorum Edition, the first of *The Canterbury Tales* to be published) and *The Physician's Tale* (volume 2, part 17, of the Variorum Edition). Hence no restatement is required here. Similarly, the rationale for the conservative modern punctuation supplied for all texts of *The Canterbury Tales* is provided in those prefaces.

PAUL G. RUGGIERS
DANIEL J. RANSOM
General Editors

Norman, Oklahoma, 1995

Preface

Late in 1984 my colleague Emerson Brown asked me if I would be interested in sharing responsibility for the Variorum Chaucer fascicle of *The Summoner's Prologue and Tale*, specifically taking on the textual portion (text, collations, textual notes and introduction). My first acknowledgement of debt must therefore be to Emerson. Also my second, for when in August of 1987 I had finished the textual work, Emerson, still busy with another major project, suggested that I take responsibility for the critical material as well. For the original confidence he showed in me, for his constant encouragement and support, for generously sharing his time and wisdom (and his personal copy of the *MED*), my heartfelt gratitude.

Thanks to Paul Ruggiers, for bringing to my aid his apparently limitless knowledge of matters textual, for his patience and his helpfulness in all matters, to Dan Ransom for many services and especially for sharing his experience in managing the sheer weight of details which accompany collating, and to Lynne Hunt Levy for her splendid work in checking the accuracy of my collations.

For financial support of this project I would like to thank the University Research Council of Vanderbilt University and the National Endowment for the Humanities.

For kind and patient scholarly assistance I must thank the staff of the British Library; the Bodleian, particularly the staff of the Duke Humphries Reading Room; the Folger Shakespeare Library; and the Inter-library Loan staff of the Jean and Alexander Heard Library of Vanderbilt, who demonstrated truly remarkable invention and determination in helping me amass the materials needed for the volume.

Nashville, Tennessee   JOHN F. PLUMMER III

A Brief Guide to the Use of This Edition

The Introduction comprises a history of critical commentary on and a textual history of *The Summoner's Prologue and Tale*. The Critical Commentary gathers all substantive criticism and appreciation of *Prologue and Tale* from the earliest (1635) through the bibliography for 1986 published in *Studies in the Age of Chaucer* in 1988. The Textual Commentary presents the manuscripts and printed editions used in preparing this edition, and seeks to describe the historical development of this text. The Textual Commentary includes as well a Table of Correspondences showing the relations among the base-manuscripts and Caxton's first edition.

The text itself, as is described further at the end of the Description of Printed Editions, is based on the Hengwrt manuscript, very conservatively emended; light punctuation is introduced in conformity with Variorum practice, along with modernization of punctuation and capitalization. The letters *i, j, u, v* are printed according to modern usage, and *þ* is printed as *th*. Accompanying the text are Collations (which retain original spelling) showing all substantive variants from this edition of the ten base-manuscripts and twenty-one printed editions, and melded Textual and Critical Notes. The volume also includes a Bibliographical Index and a General Index.

Abbreviations and Sigils

ABBREVIATIONS OF CHAUCER'S WORKS

Note: Following Manly's lead, to permit the scholar the widest latitude of reference, abbreviations are provided suited to specific reference needs; for example, *Monk-Nun's Priest Link* as well as *The Nun's Priest's Prologue*; *Second Nun-Canon's Yeoman Link* as well as *The Canon's Yeoman's Prologue*; and *Knight-Miller Link* as well as *The Miller's Prologue*.

ABC	*An ABC*
Adam	*Adam Scriveyn*
Anel	*Anelida and Arcite*
Astr	*A Treatise on the Astrolabe*
Bal Compl	*A Balade of Complaint*
BD	*The Book of the Duchess*
Bo	*Boece*
Buk	*The Envoy to Bukton*
CkT, CkP, Rv-CkL	*The Cook's Tale, The Cook's Prologue, Reeve-Cook Link*
ClT, ClP, Cl-MerL	*The Clerk's Tale, The Clerk's Prologue, Clerk-Merchant Link*
Compl d'Am	*Complaynt d'Amours*
CT	*The Canterbury Tales*
CYT, CYP	*The Canon's Yeoman's Tale, The Canon's Yeoman's Prologue*
Equat	*The Equatorie of the Planets*
For	*Fortune*
Form Age	*The Former Age*
FranT, FranP	*The Franklin's Tale, The Franklin's Prologue*
FrT, FrP, Fr-SumL	*The Friar's Tale, The Friar's Prologue, Friar-Summoner Link*
Gent	*Gentilesse*
GP	*The General Prologue*
HF	*The House of Fame*
KnT, Kn-MilL	*The Knight's Tale, Knight-Miller Link*
Lady	*A Complaint to His Lady*
LGW, LGWP	*The Legend of Good Women, The Legend of Good Women Prologue*
ManT, ManP	*The Manciple's Tale, The Manciple's Prologue*

Mars	*The Complaint of Mars*
Mel, Mel-MkL	*The Tale of Melibee, Melibee-Monk Link*
MercB	*Merciles Beaute*
MerT, MerE-SqH	*The Merchant's Tale, Merchant Endlink-Squire Headlink*
MilT, MilP, Mil-RvL	*The Miller's Tale, The Miller's Prologue, Miller-Reeve Link*
MkT, MkP, Mk-NPL	*The Monk's Tale, The Monk's Prologue, Monk-Nun's Priest Link*
MLT, MLH, MLP, MLE	*The Man of Law's Tale, Man of Law Headlink, The Man of Law's Prologue, Man of Law Endlink*
NPT, NPP, NPE	*The Nun's Priest's Tale, The Nun's Priest's Prologue, Nun's Priest Endlink*
PardT, PardP	*The Pardoner's Tale, The Pardoner's Prologue*
ParsT, ParsP	*The Parson's Tale, The Parson's Prologue*
PF	*The Parliament of Fowls*
PhyT, Phy-PardL	*The Physician's Tale, Physician-Pardoner Link*
Pity	*The Complaint unto Pity*
Prov	*Proverbs*
PrT, PrP, Pr-ThL	*The Prioress's Tale, The Prioress's Prologue, Prioress-Thopas Link*
Purse	*The Complaint of Chaucer to His Purse*
Ret	*Chaucer's Retraction [Retractation]*
Rom	*The Romaunt of the Rose*
Ros	*To Rosemounde*
RvT, RvP	*The Reeve's Tale, The Reeve's Prologue*
Scog	*The Envoy to Scogan*
ShT, Sh-PrL	*The Shipman's Tale, Shipman-Prioress Link*
SNT, SNP, SN-CYL	*The Second Nun's Tale, The Second Nun's Prologue, Second Nun-Canon's Yeoman Link*
SqT, SqH, Sq-FranL	*The Squire's Tale, Squire Headlink, Squire-Franklin Link*
Sted	*Lak of Stedfastnesse*
SumT, SumP	*The Summoner's Tale, The Summoner's Prologue*
TC	*Troilus and Criseyde*
Th, Th-MelL	*The Tale of Sir Thopas, Sir Thopas-Melibee Link*
Ven	*The Complaint of Venus*
WBT, WBP, WB-FrL	*The Wife of Bath's Tale, The Wife of Bath's Prologue, Wife of Bath-Friar Link*
Wom Nob	*Womanly Noblesse*
Wom Unc	*Against Women Unconstant*

MANUSCRIPTS

Collated Manuscripts

Hg	Hengwrt, National Library of Wales, Aberystwyth (now Peniarth 392D)
El	Ellesmere, Henry E. Huntington Library, San Marino, California (now 26.C.9)
Ad³	Additional 35286, British Library (Ashburnham Appendix 125)
Cp	Corpus Christi 198, Corpus Christi College (Oxford)
Dd	Cambridge University Dd.4.24, Cambridge University Library
Gg	Cambridge University Gg.4.27, Cambridge University Library
Ha⁴	Harley 7334, British Library
He	Helmingham, Princeton University Library
La	Lansdowne 851, British Library
Pw	Petworth, Petworth

Manuscript Employed to Supplement He (Where He is Out)

Ne   New College D.314, New College (Oxford)

The manuscripts were collated from films provided by the Variorum Chaucer, with the following exceptions: Hg was collated from the Variorum facsimile; Ne at the Bodleian; and Ad³ and La at the British Library.

Other Manuscripts Cited by Manly and Rickert

Constant Groups (as cited by Manly and Rickert)

a	Cn Dd	*En²*	En² Ll¹
b	He *Ne*	*En³*	En³ Ad¹
c	Cp La Sl²	*Lc*	Lc Mg
d	Dl *En²* Ha² *Lc Pw Ry²* Sl¹	*Mc*	Mc Ra¹
Ad³	Ad³ Ha⁵	*Mm*	Mm Gl
Bo¹	Bo¹ Ph²	*Ne*	Ne *Cx¹*
Cn	Cn Ma	*Ps*	Ps Ha¹
Cx¹	CX¹ Tc²	*Pw*	Pw *Mm* Ph³
Dd	Dd *En¹*	*Ra²*	Ra² Ht
En¹	En¹ Ds	*Ry²*	Ry² Ld²

Individual Manuscripts

Ad¹	Additional 5140, British Library
Ad²	Additional 25718, British Library
Bo¹	Bodley 414, Bodleian Library
Bo²	Bodley 686, Bodleian Library
Bw	Barlow 20, Bodleian Library
Ch	Christ Church (Oxford) 152

Cn	Cardigan (now University of Texas Humanities Research Center MS 143)
Dl	Delamere (now Takamiya MS 32)
Do	Douce d.4, Bodleian Library
Ds	Devonshire
En[1]	Egerton 2726, British Library
En[2]	Egerton 2863, British Library
En[3]	Egerton 2864, British Library
Fi	Fitzwilliam Museum (Cambridge) McClean 181
Gl	Glasgow Hunterian 197 (U.1.1), Glasgow University Library
Ha[1]	Harley 1239, British Library
Ha[2]	Harley 1758, British Library
Ha[3]	Harley 7333, British Library
Ha[5]	Harley 7335, British Library
Hk	Holkham 667
Ht	Hatton Donat. 1, Bodleian Library
Ii	Ii.3.26, Cambridge University Library
Lc	Lichfield Cathedral 2
Ld[1]	Laud 600, Bodleian Library
Ld[2]	Laud 739, Bodleian Library
Ll[1]	Longleat 257
Ln	Lincoln Cathedral 110 (A.4.18)
Ma	Manchester Eng. 113 (John Rylands Library)
Mc	McCormick (now University of Chicago 564)
Me	Merthyr fragment (National Library of Wales)
Mg	Pierpont Morgan 249
Mm	Mm.2.5, Cambridge University Library
Nl	Northumberland
Ox	"Oxford fragments": John Rylands Library Manchester 63 (two leaves); Rosenbach 1084/2 (eleven leaves), Rosenbach Collection, Philadelphia
Ph[2]	Phillipps 8136 (now Bodmer Library, Geneva, Switzerland)
Ph[3]	Phillipps 8137 (now Rosenbach 1084/1)
Pl	Plimpton, Columbia University Library
Ps	Paris, Bibliothèque nationale fonds anglais 39
Py	London, Royal College of Physicians 13
Ra[1]	Rawlinson poet. 141, Bodleian Library
Ra[2]	Rawlinson poet. 149, Bodleian Library
Ra[3]	Rawlinson poet. 223, Bodleian Library
Ry[1]	Royal 17.D.15, British Library
Ry[2]	Royal 18.C.2, British Library
Se	Selden Arch. B.14, Bodleian Library
Si	Sion College Arch. L. 40.2/E.23, London
Sl[1]	Sloane 1685, British Library

Sl²   Sloane 1686, British Library
Tc¹   Trinity College (Cambridge) R.3.3
Tc²   Trinity College (Cambridge) R.3.15
To   Trinity College (Oxford) Arch. 49

PRINTED EDITIONS

(In chronological order; for complete citations of editions later than SP³, see the Bibliographical Index. Bodleian and British Library shelf marks are given for those editions collated in those libraries; CX¹, WN, PN², TH², and ST were collated from microfilm copies published by University Microfilms [Ann Arbor, Michigan].)

CX¹   William Caxton, [*The Canterbury Tales*], 1478 [1476]. *STC* 5082.

CX²   William Caxton, [*The Canterbury Tales*], 1484 [1482]. *STC* 5083. BL G.11586.

PN¹   Richard Pynson, [*The Canterbury Tales*], 1492. *STC* 5084. Bodleian Douce 218.

WN   Wynkyn de Worde, *The boke of Chaucer named Caunterbury tales*, 1498. *STC* 5085.

PN²   Richard Pynson, *Here begynneth the boke of Caunterbury tales / dilygently and truely corrected / and newly printed*, 1526. Pt. 3 of an edition of the works. *STC* 5086.

TH¹   William Thynne, *The workes of Geffray Chaucer newly printed / with dyuers workes whiche were neuer in print before*, 1532. *STC* 5068. Bodleian Douce C Subt. 19.

TH²   William Thynne, *The workes of Geffray Chaucer newlye printed, wyth dyuers workes whych were neuer in print before*, 1542. *STC* 5069.

TH³   William Thynne, *The workes of Geffray Chaucer newly printed, with dyuers workes whiche were neuer in print before*, 1545 [1550]. *STC* 5071. BL 644.m.1.

ST   John Stow, *The workes of Geffrey Chaucer, newlie printed, with diuers addicions, whiche were neuer in print before*, 1561. *STC* 5075 [mistakenly labeled 5076 in the University Microfilms reproduction].

SP¹   Thomas Speght, *The Workes of our Antient and lerned English Poet, Geffrey Chaucer, newly Printed*, 1598. *STC* 5077. Bodleian Vet. Alc.13.

SP²   Thomas Speght, *The Workes of Ovr Ancient and learned English Poet, Geffrey Chaucer, newly Printed*, 1602. *STC* 5080. Bodleian A.2.5 Art Seld.

SP³   Thomas Speght, *The Works of our Ancient, Learned, & Excellent English Poet, Jeffrey Chaucer*, 1687. *STC* C3736. Bodleian L.2.23 Art.

UR   John Urry, *The Works of Geoffrey Chaucer*, 1721. Bodleian C 6.2.Jur.

TR   Thomas Tyrwhitt, *The Canterbury Tales of Chaucer*, 1775.
WR   Thomas Wright, *The Canterbury Tales of Geoffrey Chaucer*, 1847–51.
SK   Walter W. Skeat, *The Complete Works of Geoffrey Chaucer*, 1894.
RB¹   F. N. Robinson, *The Complete Works of Geoffrey Chaucer*, 1933.
MR   John M. Manly and Edith Rickert, *The Text of the Canterbury Tales*, 1940.
RB²   F. N. Robinson, *The Works of Geoffrey Chaucer*, 2d ed., 1957.
PR   Robert A. Pratt, *The Tales of Canterbury, Complete, Geoffrey Chaucer*, 1974.
RI   Larry D. Benson, et al., *The Riverside Chaucer*, 1987.

OTHER ABBREVIATIONS

Books

DNB   *Dictionary of National Biography*, edited by Sir Leslie Stephen and Sir Sidney Lee. London: Oxford University Press, 1917–.

MED   *Middle English Dictionary*, edited by Hans Kurath et al. Ann Arbor: University of Michigan Press, 1952–.

OED   *Oxford English Dictionary*, edited by James A. H. Murray et al. Oxford: Clarendon Press, 1884–1928. Rev. ed. 12 vols., 1933. *A Supplement to the Oxford English Dictionary*, edited by R. W. Burchfield. 4 vols. Oxford: Clarendon Press, 1972–86.

PL   *Patrologia Cursus Completus . . . Series Latina*, edited by J.-P. Migne. 221 vols. Paris, 1844–65.

STC   *A Short-Title Catalogue of Books Printed in England, Scotland, and Ireland, . . . 1475–1640*, first compiled by A. W. Pollard and G. R. Redgrave [1926]; 2d ed., revised and enlarged by W. A. Jackson, F. S. Ferguson, and Katharine F. Pantzer. 2 vols. London: Bibliographical Society, 1976–86.

       A Short-Title Catalogue of Books Printed in England, Scotland, Ireland, Wales, and British America . . . 1641–1700, compiled by Donald Wing. 3 vols. New York: Columbia University Press, 1945–51. 2d ed. New York: Modern Language Association, 1972–.

Journals

AnM   *Annuale Mediaevale*
CE   *College English*
ChauN   *Chaucer Newsletter*
ChauR   *Chaucer Review*
CLS   *Comparative Literature Studies*
E&S   *Essays and Studies*

EIC	*Essays in Criticism*
ELH	*ELH: A Journal of English Literary History*
ELN	*English Language Notes*
ES	*English Studies*
JEGP	*Journal of English and Germanic Philology*
JNT	*Journal of Narrative Technique*
MissFR	*Mississippi Folklore Register*
MLN	*Modern Language Notes*
MLQ	*Modern Language Quarterly*
MLR	*Modern Language Review*
MP	*Modern Philology*
MS	*Mediaeval Studies*
N&Q	*Notes and Queries*
NM	*Neuphilologische Mitteilungen*
PBA	*Proceedings of the British Academy*
PMLA	*PMLA: Publications of the Modern Language Association of America*
PQ	*Philological Quarterly*
RUO	*Revue de l'Université d'Ottawa*
SAC	*Studies in the Age of Chaucer*
SB	*Studies in Bibliography: Papers of the Bibliographical Society of the University of Virginia*
SFQ	*Southern Folklore Quarterly*
SP	*Studies in Philology*
SSF	*Studies in Short Fiction*
TSL	*Tennessee Studies in Literature*
TSLL	*Texas Studies in Literature and Language*
UMS	*Unisa Medieval Studies* (Pretoria)
UMSE	*University of Mississippi Studies in English*
UTQ	*University of Toronto Quarterly*

Other Abbreviations

AV	Authorized Version
bef.	before
BL	British Library
corr.	correct *or* correction
CV	Corpus of Variants (MR 6.174–240)
del.	deleted
diff.	different
EETS	Early English Text Society
e.s.	extra series
eras.	erasure *or* erased
Lat.	Latin

ME	Middle English
ModE	Modern English
MS., MSS.	Manuscript, Manuscripts
n.	note
n.s.	new series
OE	Old English
OF	Old French
om.	omitted
ON	Old Norse
o.s.	original series
RR	(Guillaume de Lorris and Jean de Meun) *Le Roman de la Rose*
SATF	Société des anciens textes français
spur.	spurious
s.v.	sub verbo
trans.	transposed

Part Seven
The Summoner's Tale

Introduction

CRITICAL COMMENTARY

George Lyman Kittredge's characterization of Chaucer's *Summoner's Prologue and Tale*—"an incomparable satire on begging friars, worked up on the basis of a trivial and sordid fabliau" (1915:192)—encapsulates fairly well the mixture of positive response and discomposure heard from several centuries' worth of readers. Few indeed have failed to respond to the tale's deft characterization, narrative pace, dramatic dialogue marked by natural speech rhythms, and of course the satire: "incomparable" has not been judged too strong a commendation. On the other hand, few have been the readers who have shown no embarrassment at all, felt no need to explain or apologize for what Kittredge called the "sordidness" or "triviality" of the tale. This ambivalence has been assuaged but not entirely erased by the discovery in recent years that *The Summoner's Prologue and Tale* is saturated with allusions to contemporary theological-political issues. The consensus of the years is clearly that, on the grounds of advancing and intensifying the satire, the tale is well worth whatever sordidness the gentle reader might encounter, and in this century there is a growing consensus that the material in Chaucer's handling is, if not polite, not really trivial either. The tradition of reading the tale as ultimately earnest if not entirely serious begins quite early, as is evident in the eighteenth-century "modernizations" which highlight (while over-simplifying) Chaucer's satirical energies so as to depict him as a kind of proto-Protestant. More modern critics see in *The Summoner's Prologue and Tale* a bitter satire on clerical abuse directed against those who had fallen from the higher ideals of medieval Christianity (and Franciscanism in particular), in which view Chaucer's object was essentially conservative. Another group of twentieth-century readers which sees more of earnest than game in the tale (or at least game in the service of earnestness) takes it not as a defense of a conservative vision of the Church but as an exposé of the material bases and financial goals of that Church. There are equally those modern critics who argue that in *The Summoner's Prologue and Tale* Chaucer is at his most ludic, that in effect Kittredge is right to call the tale "trivial," and that to seek in it moral norms is to engage in serious misprision in the service of the personal ideals of modern critics. Curiously then—or perhaps not—discussion of this, surely the least likely of Chaucer's tales to be called philosophical, has consistently given rise to central questions about Chaucer's conception of himself as an artist, about his view of his art and of its place in the world.

The survey of commentary on *The Summoner's Prologue and Tale* which follows opens with a rehearsal of the speculation and research focused on possible sources, analogues, and inspirations (e.g. jokes, paintings) for the text. Most of the early and some of the more modern commentary on *The Summoner's Prologue and Tale* is essentially evaluative rather than explanatory in nature. This kind of commentary has been particularly important for *The Summoner's Prologue and Tale*, given its scatological quality; the question has been raised often enough whether the tale had sufficient redeeming qualities to be worth reading at all. Answers to this and related questions are clustered below under "Evaluations." Especially because *The Summoner's Prologue and Tale* and *The Friar's Tale* are linked so effectively, beginning with the exchange between Summoner and Friar in *The Wife of Bath's Prologue*, much important criticism has addressed the relation between *The Summoner's Prologue and Tale* and other tales, especially *The Friar's Tale* and *The Wife of Bath's Tale*. Much of this commentary has been dominated by the question of who tells the better tale, or who dominates the conflict between Friar and Summoner. These and other discussions are reported below under "Relationship to Other *Canterbury Tales*." The relation between the tale and teller for *The Summoner's Prologue and Tale* has been a fruitful area of discussion; many readers have clearly been ill at ease with the Summoner himself while admiring his tale. The degree to which Chaucer intended the tale to be perceived as the product of the Summoner's narrative skill, learning, (odious) personality and moral character has been the focus of a debate reported below under "Appropriateness of the Tale to the Teller." Irony is so important in *The Summoner's Prologue and Tale* that one might logically assign almost any of the commentary to that section; the justification for isolating a few essays under this heading is their importance in focusing further discussion specifically on the ironies of the tale. The subjects taken up by the commentary found below under "Thematic Issues" is quite varied, though more than half concerns itself with characterizing the moral failures of the Summoner and his protagonist Friar John. Probably the most influential work on *The Summoner's Prologue and Tale* in terms of re-adjusting the focus of further discussion and demonstrating Chaucer's penchant for combining learning with laughter is that gathered below under "*The Summoner's Prologue and Tale* and Anti-fraternalism"; a subtitle for this section might well be "and Other Parodies of Learned Traditions and Iconography," as the range of materials which has been proposed as the object of Chaucer's parody in *The Summoner's Prologue and Tale* is quite remarkable. As suggested above, *The Summoner's Prologue and Tale* has emerged as perhaps (with the grudging exception of *The Miller's Tale*) the most lunatic combination of *sentence* and *solas* in the whole of *The Canterbury Tales*. The proportions of that mix, and Chaucer's intentions in this parodic manipulation, are the subject of the debate gathered under "Authorial Intention, Serious or Comic," which concludes the survey.

Sources and Analogues

The investigation of sources and analogues for *The Summoner's Prologue and Tale* has been a vigorous exercise and has historically broken into separate discussions of what might be called the tale's three plots, viz., the infernal vision of *The Summoner's Prologue*, the main *Summoner's Tale* story of the "infelicitous gift," and the concluding story of the division of the fart. Sources have also been sought for the exempla which play such an important role in the sermon Friar John gives Thomas on the sin of wrath. These exempla aside, there are no clear sources for *The Summoner's Prologue and Tale*, and only distant analogues. The discussion of sources and analogues which follows will be structured along the lines given above.

The Summoner's Prologue

Those who have sought the inspiration or source of the Prologue in its visionary aspect have pointed to a number of texts, classical and medieval; for example, Jephson (Bell 1855:2.102) adduces the descent of Ulysses and Æneas "into the infernal regions," but Spencer (1927:177) argues that Chaucer's description of hell and purgatory show little if any influence of the classical underworld, and is instead "entirely dependent on the convention of infernal description . . . prevalent in Chaucer's day." Bede's stories of the visions of St. Furseus and of a monk called Drythelm in *Ecclesiastical History* 3.19 and 5.12 (ed. King 1930:1.415–25 and 2.253–69) are mentioned by Jephson and SK (n. to 1676); SK adduces further the vision of hell in the Life of Saint Guthlac (ed. Colgrave 1956:100–107) and of purgatory in *The Revelation to the Monk of Evesham* (ed. Arber 1869:19–98) and the various accounts of *Saint Patrick's Purgatory* (see e.g. Zander, ed. 1927:4.24 and Horstmann, ed. 1887:204–20). SK suggests the influence of 2 *Cor.* 12.4 on such visions, and further notes the long descriptions of hell in *Cursor Mundi*, ll. 23195–23350 (ed. Morris 1874) and the *Pricke of Conscience*, ll. 6464 ff. (ed. Morris 1863). For the possible influence of *Saint Patrick's Purgatory* on the *Tale* itself, see Explanatory Note to lines 1730–31. Hertzberg (1866:623) draws on Warton (1774: section xxvii) to adduce various analogues, including a story told by Matthew Paris in his *Chronica Major*, of a certain Turkhill taken on a tour of hell by St. Julian (ed. Luard 1872-83:2.497–511).

As for the imagistic quality of *The Summoner's Prologue*, early discussion (e.g. Lindner 1888:171, Lounsbury 1892:2.119, Kittredge 1892:21, Kaluza 1893:237, Skeat 1894:5.330, Fansler 1914:164–65, and Brusendorff 1925:411) focuses on the connections—if any—between *The Summoner's Prologue* 1690–91 and *Rom* 7575–76: "For thou shalt for this sinne dwelle / Right in the devils ers of helle." (See further in note to lines 1690–91.) While the *Rom* author might be alluding to or remembering specifically *The Summoner's Prologue* in his translation of *RR* (thus Lounsbury and RB), there is wide-spread suspicion though little hard evidence that the image of Satan's fundament as the site of punishment for errant clerics was widespread before Chaucer. SK (3.452) suggests that the story was "probably a current joke"; Brusendorff holds that "the story is probably pretty nearly as old and as wide-spread as the Church it satirizes," and Kittredge (1892:21) says that "such stories . . . were in the air."

And on the walls too: as RB puts it, "the same repulsive conception is also represented in ecclesiastical art." Spencer (1927:196–97) and others point to the *Last Judgement* fresco in the Camposanto at Pisa, now generally attributed to Francesco Traini (mid-fourteenth century), which in its depiction of hell shows an enormous Satan ingesting, digesting, and excreting sinners. Giotto's *Last Judgement* (ca. 1306) in the Arena Chapel at Padua also shows an outsize Satan ingesting and excreting sinners while crushing others in his hands. Either of these Satans appears large enough to hold, if not twenty-thousand friars, at least hundreds. PR (p. 295) adds to this list the *Last Judgment* of Giusto di Menabuoi in the Parish Church of Viboldone, near Milan, and he reproduces the image of Satan from Traini's fresco (p. 296). He suggests the real possibility that Chaucer might have seen the Traini: "when Chaucer travelled from Genoa to Florence in 1373, the most famous sight to be seen in Pisa was the Camposanto . . . and its walls in the process of being covered with frescoes by Tuscan artists." Other Italian examples of this remarkably stable iconographic tradition include a fresco of hell by Tadello di Bartello, in the Collegiate Church of San Gimignano, dated about 1320 (reproduced in Hughes 1968:32) in which Satan, who is eating and defecating sinners, bears on his lower abdomen the features of a second face, of which his anus is the mouth. A fourteenth-century painting of the Bolognese school (Bufalmacco?) of Heaven and Hell, currently in the Pinacoteca Museum in Bologna, and reproduced in Cavendish (1977:15), shows the angels and saints of heaven surrounding Christ, the Father, and the Virgin, and in the lower third the damned. Central in hell, in a direct line beneath the divinity, squats Satan, chained, who with both hands holds and chews one unfortunate while he excretes another, head-first, into a group which includes at least one bishop. This Satan also has a "nether visage." The later (ca. 1410) painting of hell in the Chapel of San Petronio in Bologna by Giovanni da Modena shows exactly the same iconography, including the second face; in this case many of those who appear to have undergone ingestion and to have collected beneath Satan's legs wear crowns, and the group is marked by a banner reading *superbia*. Baird (1969:105–06) suggests that the best pictorial representation of the punishments of hell "closely connected with the private parts of Satan" is Hieronymus Bosch's Hell section of the *Garden of Delights*, which he feels was probably influenced by Tundale's Vision of Hell (ed. Friedel and Meyer 1907). Baird also cites as relevant the thirteenth century Mechthild de Magdeburg, whom he cites as linking Satanic ingestion with the Summoner's sin of greed: "He [Satan] gulps down the greedy man because he always wants more. But then when he has swallowed him, he comes out of him again behind . . . and at many an hour will he stuff himself and his maw gapes wide." Ross (1972:82–83) notes that the image "persisted long after Chaucer," and reproduces a woodcut dated 1545, attributed to Lucas Cranach the Elder, which shows a pope and cardinals issuing from a female demon's (according to Ross, Satan's) rectum, being "born," according to the text accompanying the figure (reproduced in Ross 1972:83 and with the text in Hughes 1968:230). There is also a wood-cut showing the "Italian" iconography complete with the Satanic anus-mouth conflation in the Louvre (reproduced in Cavendish 1977:104). Wright (1844:35) suggests the direct influence of Tundale's vision on *The Summoner's Prologue*, but Spencer (1927:196) argues that in Tundale's vision, "where the souls of monks and canons are swallowed and digested by a hideous beast, and then expelled, . . . the beast is not Satan, nor are the souls permanent inhabitants of his posterior." Clearly enough, *The Summoner's Prologue* stands athwart a deep and vigorous medieval tradition of scatalogical eschatology; none of these images or texts can make a claim to be an exclusive source or particular inspiration for the vision of *The Summoner's Prologue*, and indeed, taken together their collective testimony is that the notion of Satan's rectum as the most hideous of *loci inferni* was very commonplace indeed in Chaucer's lifetime.

It is Tatlock (1914:143) who first points out that "a story does exist of which this cannot be quite independent," specifically the thirteenth-century tale told by Caesarius of Heisterbach of a Cistercian monk who, carried to heaven and wondering that he saw none of his fellow Cistercians there, was comforted by the Virgin, who revealed a countless number of them beneath her mantle (ed. Strange 1851:2.79–80; trans. Scott and Bland 1929:1.546). But while Tatlock suggests that "Chaucer's jape has every appearance of being a vulgarization of this," Brusendorff (1925:411 n. 3) argues the other way round, that Caesarius's text is "a pious set-off to this vulgar jape, and not the origin of it," and Curry (1923:253), followed by Schless (1984:194–95), is more persuaded that Chaucer had in mind *Inferno* 34, which describes Satan's position at the base of hell. The point where Dante and Virgil, climbing down Satan's back, reverse themselves to turn upwards, ascending his legs toward the Mount of Purgatory, "is, of course, the center of the universe," writes Curry, "but it seems quite likely that Chaucer—in the person of a Somnour—is for the time being one of the 'grosser sort' who associates the curious 'point,' the lowest hell, with that part of Satan's body which figures in the Somnour's joke." Spencer (1927:197 n.), however, finds it "difficult to believe that Dante had anything to do with Chaucer's description." Fleming (1967:95–107), echoed by Giaccherini (1980:136–37) and others, holds with Tatlock, and argues for a rich relationship between *The*

Summoner's Prologue and the Benedictine vision of Maria Misericordia, showing how it came to be appropriated during the thirteenth and fourteenth centuries by the Dominicans and Franciscans, and put to use especially in the service of their lay confraternities. The Summoner's parodic version of the image would thus be a particularly offensive anti-fraternal blow. Fleming (1967:95 n. 2) also notes the vague parallel to *The Summoner's Prologue*, what might be "the echo of a tradition," in a Lollard exegesis of Isaiah 9.15: "*Rome* is the very Nest of Antichrist. And out of that Nest cometh all his Disciples. Of whom Prelates, Prestes, and Monkes are the Bodye, and these pylde Fryers are the Tayle which covereth his most fylthye Part." Though he offers no specifics, Olson (1986:229) suggests that *The Summoner's Prologue* is "in parody of Spiritualist rhetoric stationing dead friars next to God in heaven or in His side or representing dead enemies directly chastised by Christ and St. Francis."

In sum, the evidence suggests that the image of punishment by confinement in Satan's rectum at the base of hell was available to Chaucer as a commonplace; the image of Maria Misericordia was also available and indeed widely known. The notion of combining these two images, or perhaps of adding the motif of "discovery of a special place reserved for a class" to the infernal image, and thus inverting the image of Maria Misericordia, is very likely Chaucer's own inspiration.

The Gift

The central plot of *The Summoner's Tale* has customarily been regarded as an instance of the motif of the "satiric legacy." Benson and Anderson (1971:339) remark that the motif is "at least as ancient as the biblical theme of Jacob and Esau," though they admit that in that story the roles of trickster and dupe are reversed from *The Summoner's Tale*. Hart (1941:275) remarks that these "testaments, in which good things were bequeathed to friends, ill things to enemies, were not uncommon in folk literature. These were easily parodied and readily became an instrument of satire"; both Benson and Anderson and Hart point to Child (1882–94:1.143–44), who lists a number of instances of the motif in many languages, taken from ballads. The assumptions underlying this characterization of *The Summoner's Tale* remain, however, largely unexamined: it has not been explained, for example, why Thomas's ironic gift should be seen as a legacy when nothing suggests that he is near death. Indeed, Thomas explicitly says (lines 2129–30) ". . . and somewhat shal I yeve / Unto youre holy covent *whil I lyve.*" In the examples of ironic legacies gathered by Child, the legacy is bequeathed by a dying or condemned person, and the relationships among the characters are quite unlike those in *The Summoner's Tale*.

Tyrwhitt (TR 4.155), Hart, Benson and Anderson, and others believe that such a story as the one Chaucer tells must have had wide circulation in the oral tradition, noting that Jean de Meun was said to have perpetrated a trick upon the Jacobin friars in Paris wherein he promised them a great legacy in return for burial within their church, specifying that the chest containing the gift was not to be opened until after his interment. The chest turned out to contain lead; a version of the story is given in Méon (1814:1.57–63) and Le Grand D'Aussy (3d ed., 1829), the latter cited in Furnivall (1872–87:144). Düring (1883–86:3.446–47) and Benson and Anderson (p. 340) note that a similar story is told of Til Eulenspiegel and the town council of Möln. Benson and Anderson also offer (pp. 360–61) from Til Eulenspiegel the analogue of "How Howglas Deceived his Ghostly Father," in which a sick man offers a priest a pot half-filled with excrement covered over with a little money. He warns the priest not to be hasty or reach in too deep, but of course the priest grips "a great handful," and finds his hand "all tobeshitten." Wlislocki (1889) offers several analogues from Hungarian stories of the eighteenth and nineteenth centuries, but Benson and Anderson point out that these appear to be based upon *The Summoner's Tale*, and to be "unexpected examples of [Chaucer's] far-ranging influence rather than testimony to the tradition on which he drew" (p. 340).

The most extensive parallel story is the fabliaux *Le dis de le vescie a prestre* ("The Tale of the Priest's Bladder") by Jacques de Baisieux; the parallelism between this text and *The Summoner's Tale* was noted as early as 1859 by E.-G. Sandras (pp. 237–38), who claims indeed that Chaucer worked directly from the fabliaux, "imitating several passages faithfully"; Skeat likewise (SK 3.452–53) appears to treat Jacques' fabliau as a source of *The Summoner's Tale*, speaking of Chaucer's having transferred the scene from Antwerp to Holderness. Dempster (1932:45) is more cautious, but feels that the setting of the fabliau in Antwerp argues for a northern provenance, and "a fabliau of the North had especially good chances of reaching our poet, either in England or in the course of his many journeys on the Continent." I reproduce here Skeat's summary of *Le vescie*:

> A Priest, dwelling near Antwerp, a wise man and a rich, falls ill, and is about to die. He sends for his dean and his friends, to dispose of his property. Two Jacobin friars come to visit him and to beg. The Priest explains that all his property is settled. The friars insist on the merit of giving to them above all others, and are very importunate. At last, to quiet them, he tells them he will leave them a jewel for which he would not take a thousand marks; and their Prior must come next day, to learn where the jewel is kept.
>
> Next day, five of the friars again visit the Priest, but leave the Prior at home. The Priest says he will only reveal the secret in the presence of the Sheriffs and the Mayor, who are duly sent for. On their arrival, the Priest explains all about the cupidity and importunity of the two friars, and how, in order to get rid of them, he promised to give them something which he valued very much. He then reveals the secret, that the jewel is his own bladder; and the Jacobins retire crest-fallen.

Le vescie is printed by Furnivall (1872–87:135–47) and Hart (1941:275–86), both of whom see it as an analogue to rather than a source of *The Summoner's Tale*. Furnivall, commenting on Sandras' claim about Chaucer's "faithful imitation" remarks (p. 136 n. 2) that "M. Sandras often indulges in gammon," and the claim is equally dismissed by Düring (1883–86:3.447), who observes that Chaucer had no need of a French source when such stories were available in oral form at his front door. Hart (p. 277) adds that the Sandras claim is "manifestly, an overstatement." Hart urges the excellence of Jacques' story, and rather surprisingly argues against Chaucer's knowing *Le vescie* on the grounds that *The Summoner's Tale* lacks irony: "had he encountered the character of the Priest, had his attention been called to the possibilities for irony in speech and situation, he would surely have developed them in the *Summoner's Tale*. . . . But he had other fish to fry: the Summoner must tell a tale at the expense of a Friar; the character of the Friar must then be the important matter, not the plot, not the character of the sick man; and not irony, which, in any case, had just been exploited in the *Friar's Tale*" (pp. 276–77). Benson and Anderson (p. 340) quote this argument from Hart and agree that *Le vescie* is not Chaucer's direct source, concluding that the fabliau is "best read simply as an example of how another very talented fourteenth-century poet used the same themes as Chaucer employed in his 'Summoner's Tale.'" Craik (1964:117–18) likewise contrasts the essential dramatic irony of the Tale of the Priest's Bladder, irony arising from the "contrast between the priest's intended bequest and the friars' great expectations," with Chaucer's tale. Whereas in the first case the tale ends immediately after the revelation of the nature of the gift, in *The Summoner's Tale* "only twenty lines separate the sick man's proposal of a gift from the astonished friar's angry reception of it. The gift is a surprise to us, as well as to the friar" (p. 118), and Chaucer consequently adds a *coda* to his story. Richardson (1970), however, takes issue with Hart's judgment, arguing that *The Summoner's Tale* "depends upon irony for its effect," and that the irony is "typically Chaucerian: it owes nothing to the French analogue" with its "simple irony of situation [created] by having a day elapse between the dying priest's promise that he will give the friars a 'jewel' and the revelation that this gift is really his bladder. . . . The gift itself, however, has no ironic relevance to the friars' previous begging, and the only irony of speech in the tale appears in what the priest says at the moment when he reveals the nature of the 'jewel.' . . . Chaucer's irony is far more subtle, and the purpose it serves is essentially more serious, even though his fabliau is much more vulgar" (p. 157–58).

Heist (1950:252–53) is also critical of Sandras, and complains of Chaucerian studies that "if a written analogue, however remote, existed, it is unhesitatingly set down as Chaucer's source," singling out particularly the argument that Chaucer worked directly from *Le vescie* to create *The Summoner's Tale*; he remarks further that Hart (1941) appears only grudgingly to admit the likelihood of a source in the oral tradition for *The Summoner's Tale* "for sheer lack of a plausible literary source."

Pearcy (1974) has challenged the status of *Le vescie* as analogue. He dismisses as superficial the chief similarities of the proposed analogues (the gift offered by the sick figure to an acquisitive religious figure) and seeks instead the deep structure of such stories, which is to be found in the logical fallacy that triggers the comic conclusion. *Le vescie* and its analogues employ a fallacy or sophistry that "consists in supposing the universal validity of the premise that things are worth more than what one would not accept for them in exchange" (pp. 108–09). In *Le vescie*, the priest says he would not take a thousand marks for the object he intends to bequeath the Jacobins. By contrast, the logical error in the story of Howglas and its structural analogues is the fallacy of the consequent, "in which it is falsely assumed that if A implies B, then B implies A" (p. 110), e.g., if Howglas' pot is full of money he would urge the priest not to grip deeply; therefore the warning implies that the pot is full of money. The logical fallacy of *The Summoner's Tale* itself, Pearcy argues, is the fallacy of the *accident*, in which the dupe reasons that if something shares accidental qualities with something of value (e.g., being hidden in privitee) then it too must be valuable. As Craik (1964:127) puts it, "the dark ambiguity of Thomas's words, and his insistence on an oath that the gift shall be shared equally among all the friars, suggest to the friar that he will get something of great value." Other texts, like the fabliau *Boivin de Provins*, feature this fallacy, but such stories as that of Jean de Meun and Til Eulenspiegel are closer to *The Summoner's Tale*, Pearcy says, for "these anecdotes, like the Summoner's Tale, use the *accidens* fallacy in the sense that the benefactors argue from the fact that a chest full of money would be offered as a bequest and would be heavy to the notion that the heavy chests bequeathed to them are therefore full of money" (p. 112).

Tupper (1915c:260) points out that "Chaucerians have not remarked that the *motif* of the Summoner's Tale bears a superficial likeness to that of the sixth story of Bandello's first book. . . ." It must be admitted that the likeness is quite superficial: Bandello's story (ed. Ferrero 1974:147–55) tells of a sick man, his wife, and a Dominican friar. The wife seeks the Dominican's aid in persuading her husband to confess his sins, particularly sodomy. Since the Dominican is a genuinely holy man, the husband in fact guilty of the said sin, the wife genuinely concerned, and the story features no gift or deception, it is hard to see what could be made of the comparison.

Biblical sources have also been proposed for some of the non-narrative features of *The Summoner's Tale*. Clark (1976a) and Haskell (1976) argue for the relevance of the story of Doubting Thomas and Thomas of India (the same person) in *The Summoner's Tale*. Haskell argues that the name Thomas, the discussion of church building, the mention of the square (l. 2090), and St. Thomas's disdain for gold all contribute to suggest "an ironic inversion" of the St. Thomas the Apostle story (pp. 61–62). Clark's argument is similar, though more highly articulated. He sees Thomas and Friar John as sharing the double (Doubting Thomas / of India) identity of the saint. Chaucer's parody of Thomas of India in

Friar John is "bitterly ironic," for while Thomas of India "spread Christianity to the outer regions of the known world, Friar John spreads greed and hypocrisy throughout Yorkshire" (pp. 168–69). The "groping" scene (2119–51) parodically inverts the scriptural and legendary accounts of Thomas's probing of Christ's wounds (pp. 170–74). This set of allusions fits, then, with the Pentecostal imagery which concludes *The Summoner's Tale*: "Both scenes involve divine appearances to the apostles in closed rooms after the Resurrection. . . . the two episodes provide the theological underpinnings of the Christian Church" (p. 174), and these parodies provide us with a norm against which to judge the friar, reminding the audience that "although churchmen may be crooked, the Church is straight" (p. 175). See further in note to lines 2140–48.

Lancashire (1981), who accepts the importance of the Pentecostal parodies argued by Levitan and Szittya (see below, "*The Summoner's Prologue and Tale* and Anti-fraternalism"), seeks to develop further biblical parody. John alludes pointedly to Moses and Elijah, claiming to be their spiritual heir. Thomas's rude gift is in response to such claims: "If Jankin's cartwheel suggests Pentecost, Thomas' first gift recalls the events in the lives of Moses and Elijah that Pentecost fulfills" (p. 18). Moses' conversations with God and reception of the Law on Sinai, and Elijah's theophany on Horeb were commonly taken as figures of Pentecost. In *The Summoner's Tale*, John plays the part of Moses and Elijah, and Thomas that of God: "like Moses and Elijah at Sinai, John does endure a fast (at Thomas' house) in Lent, and at its end is rewarded by a 'break-fast' gift of 'speech' (the fart) from his benefactor. Because John perverts all virtue in the law-giver and the prophet, the Friar gets a profane parody of the mysteries spoken by God at Sinai" (p. 20). Lancashire quotes the depiction in Exodus 33.18–23 of God's description to Moses of what he will see: "And it shall come to pass, while my glory passeth by, that I will put thee in a clift of the rock, and will cover thee with my hand while I pass by: And I will take away mine hand, and thou shalt see my back parts; but my face shall not be seen." Lancashire suggests that it is these "back-parts" of God and the "clift of the rock" which, in a very carnal reading of Exodus, the Summoner uses parodically as he describes John's exploration of the "clift" in Thomas's backsides. "The loud broken wind from Thomas' 'cleft' perhaps distorts scatologically, as if in a 'demoniac's' mind, the thunder and trumpet call announcing God's first descents on Sinai, but more probably the perversion concerns the great godless wind that shatters the rocks when God passes by another 'cleft,' Elijah's cave [3 (AV 1) Kings 19.11–12]" (p. 25). See further in notes to 1885–93, 1890, and 1894–1901.

Alford (1984) sees a comic and telling parallel between the "groping" scene and two other Old Testament scenes, Genesis 24.1–4, which tells how Abraham instructs his servant Eliezer to place his hand under Abraham's thigh and swear not to take a wife for his son Isaac from among the daughters of the Chanaanites, and Genesis 47.29, where Jacob asks his son Joseph to promise, while holding his hand in similar fashion, not to bury him in Egypt. Exegetical commentary on the story of Abraham and his servant casts further ironic light on the failures of Friar John's pastoral ministrations (pp. 202–03).

Finally, under the heading of non-narrative sources must be mentioned the vast materials of the anti-fraternal tradition, the influence of which on *The Summoner's Prologue and Tale* is documented by a variety of hands, most notably Williams (1953 and 1960), Fleming (1966, 1967 and 1983), Levy (1966), Levitan (1971) and Szittya (1974 and 1986). Fuller treatment of Chaucer's use of these materials may be found under the heading of "*The Summoner's Prologue and Tale* and Anti-fraternalism" below.

The Division

Brewer (1984*a*) and Green (1987) both suggest that the inspiration for *The Summoner's Tale* may have been centered in the episode which concludes it, like the punch-line of a joke or riddle. Brewer points out Chaucer's evident interest in arithmetic in *The Summoner's Tale* and elsewhere, and wonders whether he had in mind a parody of an arithmetic handbook, perhaps one like the *Liber Abaci* written by the Italian Leonardo Fibonacci, whose method was to use examples (word-problems) with titles like "The man who went to Constantinople to sell three pearls," "The two ships which sailed together," and "Finding the equivalence of bad money and good." "Any of these," writes Brewer, "might be the titles of stories by Chaucer," and he suggests others: "'How to have your cake and eat it' (*The Reeve's Tale*); 'How to divide a fart into twelve equal portions' (*The Summoner's Tale*); 'How to turn good money into bad' (*The Canon's Yeoman's Tale*). It is quite significant, he concludes, that "there are no extant literary analogues for the last two examples. Their origin perhaps lies in the arithmetical conditioning of the travelling salesman's purely oral repertorie" (Brewer 1984*a*:118).

Green agrees with Pearcy that Jacques de Baisieux's story has been over-rated as a close parallel to *The Summoner's Tale*, and points out that the element of the division of the fart has not been accounted for in discussions of sources. He argues that "a very precise literary (or rather quasi-literary) parallel for this motif exists in a courtly collection of riddles and verbal games preserved in a manuscript from northern France of about 1470 (Chantilly, Musée Condé MS 654)," and quotes (1987:25):

Demande.

Comment partiroit on une vess en douze parties?

Response.

Faittes une vesse sur le moieul d'une roe, et douze personnes ayent chascun son nez aux xii trous, et par ainsi chascun en ara sa part.

> (*Question*:
>
> How can one divide a fart into twelve parts?
>
> *Answer*:
>
> Make the fart in the middle of a wheel, with twelve people, each with
> his nose in the twelve holes, so that each shall thus get his share.)

While Green recognizes the real possibility that the French riddle may itself have been inspired by *The Summoner's Tale*, he notes that farts are prominent in this riddle collection. Seventeen of the 550 riddles have to do with farting, and another is "specifically concerned with a problem of division: 'Comment pourroit on partir une vesse en deux?' (How can one divide a fart in two?)," from which evidence he argues that an ancestor of the joke might have provoked *The Summoner's Tale* (p. 26).

As with *The Summoner's Prologue*, the inversion of specific iconographic imagistic traditions have recently been put forward as possible inspirations for the imagery of Jankyn's *divisio flatus*. According to Levitan (1971:236), who made the initial discovery in 1965, "what appears as a merely ribald anecdote is, in fact, a brilliant and satirical reversal of the descent of the Holy Ghost at Pentecost." He argues that the wagon-wheel in *The Summoner's Tale* is inspired by the iconographic tradition of representing—in manuscript illuminations and church paintings—the Apostles at Pentecost grouped circularly, as around a wheel, to receive the grace of the Holy Spirit; and he offers and reproduces a number of highly suggestive examples. Levy (1966:55) is also persuaded that representations of Pentecost in art lie behind *The Summoner's Tale*: "the Squire's solution . . . represents a rather precise parody of one of the iconographic devices used to represent the descent of the Holy Spirit upon the Apostles—the actual use of a wheel with twelve spokes, the recipients placed at the furthest point of each of the spokes, and the source of inspiration at the hub, the center of the wheel—though the general description would suggest the scene of Pentecost whether or not one were familiar with this representation."

Wentersdorf (1980:254) suggests that Chaucer might also have had in mind the common representation of the twelve winds of heaven, "sometimes represented iconographically as a cartwheel, with each wind depicted as a face blowing along one of the spokes towards the hub," and cites an example from a twelfth-century English manuscript of Bede's *De natura rerum* (printed in Donald Howard 1976:204, fig. 11). Most recently, Wright (1988) has suggested that Chaucer's inspiration might have been the argument used by Lady Philosophy in Boethius' *De consolatione philosophiae* (Book 2, prose 5) in which she illustrates the impossibility of dividing earthly wealth evenly by contrasting riches to sound, which is heard simultaneously and with equal strength by all auditors (pp. 5–6). Jankyn's wheel might also, Wright argues, have been suggested by Boethius' image of Fortuna's wheel or his discussion of the propagation of sound in concentric waves in *De institutione musica* (p. 5). See further in notes 2255 and 2259, and below under *"The Summoner's Prologue and Tale* and Anti-fraternalism."

The Exempla

Root (1906:250–51) suspects that a version of the "Tale of the Priest's Bladder" might have existed which contained both the gift and the suggestion of its division, but assumes that "the long hypocritical predication with which Friar John favors the bed-rid churl, and the perfect life-likeness of the scene, are Chaucer's original addition." Without denying Chaucer's originality in constructing the scene, commentators have noted that Chaucer's reading did make a contribution to this section of *The Summoner's Tale*. Scholars as early as Tyrwhitt (1775:4.276) have recognized of course that the ultimate source of several of the exempla and exemplary figures in John's sermon against wrath is Seneca's *De Ira*. The "irous potestate" whose story occupies lines 2017–42 is found in *De Ira* 1.18.3–6 (ed. Bryan and Dempster 1941:286–87), and his story is also told of Emperor Heraclius in the *Gesta Romanorum*, ch. 140 (ed. Oesterley 1872; 1963:494–95), as TR (note to line 7600), Brunet (1858:311), SK and others note. The story of Cambyses (lines 2043–2071) is found in *De Ira*, 3.14.1–6 (ed. Bryan and Dempster 1941:287), and Herodotus 3.34–35 (ed. Godley 1920-30: 2.45–47); the story of irascible Cyrus (lines 2079–84) and his "destruction" of the river Gyndes is told in *De Ira*, 3.21.1–3 (ed. Bryan and Dempster 1941:287) and in Herodotus 1.189 (ed. Godley 1920–30:1.235–237). TR, WR, and SK note that Mandeville tells this story of the Euphrates (Mandeville 1919–1923:25). Lange (1938:80) claims that Mandeville (1919–1923:27)—and only he—calls the river *Gyson*, and therefore would seem to have influenced Friar John's anecdote; but Magoun (1953:119) explains that *Gysen* is a medieval version of the name *Gyndes* and not evidence of the influence of a particular author.

Chaucer appears actually to have used, however, not Seneca but the *Communiloquium Sive Summa Collationum* of John of Wales (or some text very similar to it), as Pratt (1966) demonstrates. The *Summa* is "a mosaic of several thousand quotations, chiefly from the Bible and . . . classical, patristic, and mediaeval writers" (Pratt 1966:619–20), designed, according to its introduction, to facilitate the preaching of the gospel to all ranks of men. The version of *The Summoner's Tale* anecdotes found in the *Communiloquium* is in each of the above mentioned instances closer to Chaucer's than is Seneca's. As Pratt puts it, "the 'irous' friar, lecturing old Thomas on the wickedness of Wrath, took his exempla from the friars' conversation book of the day, apparently putting this compendium to the very use for which John of Wales had intended it—morality at the dinner table and in the home" (p. 639); indeed, "when Chaucer mimics the preachers' style, he follows the preachers' method and goes to the friars for material and guidance." See the notes to lines 2017, 2043, 2079, 2080, and 2086–88 for further details.

Other sources have been proposed as well. Landrum (1924) makes a case for Chaucer's independent use of the Vulgate, and makes of *The Summoner's Tale* a bulwark to her argument: she counts twenty-three scriptural allusions or references, some of which he might have garnered from his *Parson's Tale* materials, and some from Jerome or Innocent. But, she argues, Chaucer can claim fifteen as his own. "They are not at all recondite, to be sure; neither are they exceptionally familiar" (p. 96). Chaucer's source of some scriptural allusions—Lazar and Dives in line 1877, 1 Timothy 6.8 in lines 1881–82, Moses in lines 1885–93, Elijah in line 1890, Aaron in lines 1894–1901, Adam in lines 1915-17, and James 1.22 in line 1937—was apparently Jerome's *Epistola Adversus Jovinianum* (cf. note to line 1929), as Koeppel (1891*a*) and Tupper (1915*b*) were first to observe. Fleming (1965) argues that Chaucer's ironic use of *Placebo* in line 2075 was inspired by the *Roman de Favel*. For the evidence and interpretations see the Explanatory Notes to the specific passages. Makarewicz (1953:223–24) suggests that Chaucer developed *The Summoner's Tale* as an exemplum on the contrast between the ideal and the real in response to his reading of Augustine's commentary on Psalm 40 (*PL* 36.460).

The Date of The Summoner's Prologue and Tale

The date of *The Summoner's Prologue and Tale* has not been the object of serious study. Koch (1890:79) appears to date it with the rest of Group D in the 1390's, but says nothing specific. The consensus, largely unstated, appears to be that *The Summoner's Prologue and Tale* is a product of *The Canterbury Tales* years when Chaucer was at his peak of narrative skill.

Modernizations and Avatars

In 1717 John Gay published in his *Poems on Several Occasions* "An Answer to the Sompner's Prologue of Chaucer" (ed. Dearing 1974:1.198–200). Though subtitled "In imitation of Chaucer's style," the poem has, unsurprisingly, nothing of Chaucer's manner. It would appear that the jesting and scatological quality of *The Summoner's Prologue and Tale* triggered Gay's "Answer." He refers specifically to the site of friars in hell—"But lo! the Devil turned his erse about, / And twenty thousand Freers wend in and out. / By which in *Jeoffrys* rhiming it appears, / The Devils belly is the hive of Freers" (lines 5–8)—and he weaves his joke around that topos: An empty house deep in the woods is widely rumored to be haunted; a grey friar from a nearby abbey, unafraid of goblins, decides to spend the night there in hopes of seeing some apparition, or discovering gold, or determining that the house is not haunted and might be purchased, cheap, by the abbey. Insofar as Chaucer is being imitated in spirit here, it is his reputation as both anti-cleric and proto-Protestant that shows through most clearly in several passages: the friar comes to the house armed with ". . . candle, beades, and holy watere, / And legends eke of Saintes, and bookes of prayere" (lines 33–34). These talismans are combined with prayer (an *ave marye*, of course), and the crossing of all the holes and chinks of the house, down to the key-hole of the door, to keep out demons. "Ne was there not a mouse hole in thilke place, / But he y-crossed hath by God his grace; / He crossed hath this, and eke he crossed that, / With *benedicte* and God knows what" (lines 41–44). All in vain, however, for as soon as the friar falls asleep, Satan appears, rolls the friar on his belly and "[thwacks] him sore," declaring "Thou didst forget to guard thy postern door. / There is an hole which hath not crossed been: / Farewel, from whence I came I creepen in" (lines 64–66). Reversing and "topping" Chaucer's infernal vision, Gay concludes that "If Devils in hell bear Freers in their erse, / On earth the Devil in Freers doth ydwell; / Were there no Freers, the Devil mought keep in hell" (lines 68–70).

In 1733 a modernized version of *The Summoner's Tale* by a Mr. Grosvenor (according to Spurgeon [1925:3.iv.86], a pseudonym for Eustace Budgell) appeared under the title "The Whimsical Legacy: A Tale" in volume 2 of Budgell's *The bee, or Universal Weekly Pamphlet*, pp. 1020-25. This text, as noted by Bowden (1987:295), was reprinted as "The Comic Gift: or, The Sumner's Tale, Imitated from Chaucer" in *The Universal Spectator*, edited by Henry "Stonecastle" [pseudonym for Baker], 3d ed., volume 2 (1756), pages 197–202; and as "The Whimsical Legacy. In Imitation of the Sumner's Tale in Chaucer" in *The Mery Droll, or Pleasing Companion* (London: C. Parker, 1769), pages 84-90. It also appeared with George Ogle's modernization of *The Summoner's Prologue*, in Ogle's *The Canterbury Tales of Chaucer, Modernis'd by several Hands*, this time titled "The Farmer and the Fryar: or, *The Sumner's Tale*" (1741:3.127–42). This compilation was reprinted in 1742 and again, by William Lipscomb, in 1795; Lipscomb's alterations to the work did not affect the renditions of *The Summoner's Prologue and Tale*.

Ogle's *Summoner's Prologue* is a straightforward if uninspired "modernization," though one obvious change is that the Friar is allotted 30 lines in which to expand upon his remarks in *The Friar's Tale* 1645–64 on the pains of hell and the repentance of summoners. The tale proper, as observed by Lounsbury (1892:3.191–92), is only a third the length of Chaucer's story and, as Grosvenor himself states, "cannot properly be called a translation." It omits the friar's sermon and house-to-house begging, opening at the point where he enters Thomas's house. The wife's complaint about Thomas's irascibility and her announcement of the death of the child are both omitted, along with the friar's claimed "vision" and his sermon on wrath. The character of the friar is much coarsened (e.g., "Sick lay the host, the Fryar growl'd a Pray'r," and ". . . the sneering Priest reply'd, more sure to speed" [1741:3.133]). The wife is made into a silly flirt responsive to the friar's flattery: "The sweetly simpring Dame new Pleasure found, / With greedy Ear imbib'd the flatt'ring Sound: / Prink'd up her Tucker, ev'ry Charm she try'd, / And by her little Arts reveal'd her Pride" (1741:3.134) and she "tripp'd in" and "Swift tripp'd . . . away, and seem'd to fly, / Brisk as a Colt, and jolly as a Pie" (1741:3.135). Thomas, on the other hand, is made much more cynical, openly hostile from the beginning of the visit. To the friar's initial claims of superiority for his order, Thomas replies

> . . . I have been told,
> The whole Pursuit of Priesthood is for Gold.
> Thus some have said; this I myself aver,
> I'm not a Jot the better for their Pray'r:
> To Monk, To Fryar, and to Priest I've giv'n;
> All were Divine Ambassadors from Heav'n.
> But late, alas! I found this Truth confest,
> The Man that gives the Least, succeeds the Best.
> (Ogle 1741:3.136)

And as the friar finishes his plea for money, the narrator observes ". . . ah! th'Harrangue no convert gains; / Thomas the same gruff churlish Wight remains: / So daring impious, that he thought the Fryar / A canting Hypocrite, a fawning Liar" (1741:3.138). In sum, the Augustan adaptations of *The Summoner's Tale* suggest that those writers read the tale as rather more simple-mindedly anti-clerical than most modern readers would judge it.

In the twentieth century, as Raizis (1969) has shown, the satirical portrait of the begging friar in *The Summoner's Tale* influenced Nikos Kazantzakis's novel *The Fratricides* (Kazantzakis 1954:11), providing a comic moment in a novel otherwise wholly bleak. Kazantzakis's first notice of *The Summoner's Tale* is found in his travel journal *England* (Kazantzakis 1941:124–28). See further in notes to lines 1746–53 and 1761.

Survey of Criticism

Evaluations

As the eighteenth-century imitations and modernizations noted above suggest, *The Summoner's Prologue and Tale* has never been without its admirers; though many early writers have forborn to discuss it in detail, and though the tale has often been judged to be indelicate, it has almost always been allowed brilliance as well. The ebb and flow of response to the tale may best be viewed by taking up separately (as far as such separation is possible) first those responses which are primarily negative and second those which are quite positive.

Negative Response or Acknowledgment of Coarseness.   Godwin (1804:4.188) writes that *The Summoner's Tale* is "exceedingly offensive for the clownish joke with which it is terminated," but adds that it is "equal in its opening and preparatory circumstances to any satirical narrative that was ever penned." In comparing *The Summoner's Tale* with Jacques de Baisieux's fabliau, Sandras (1859:238) remarks that one sees in it a feeble seed brought to fruition by genius, and he feels the speech of the friar is a chef-d'oeuvre capable of comparison with a page from Molière; he also feels, however, that only the first half of the tale is "readable." Kirby (1953) draws our attention to some letters of Theodore Roosevelt containing remarks on *The Summoner's Prologue and Tale* which show the future president to be equally repelled. In a letter written in 1892 to Thomas Lounsbury to congratulate him on the publication and good reception of *Studies in Chaucer*, Roosevelt offered the opinion that the "prologue to the Sompnour's tale, and the tale itself . . . are very nearly indefensible. There are parts of them which will be valuable to the student of the manners of the age simply from the historical standpoint, but as literature I don't think they have a redeeming feature" (Kirby 1953:35). Similarly, in a letter written soon after to British diplomat Cecil Arthur Spring Rice, Roosevelt complains, "I must say I think [Chaucer] is altogether needlessly filthy—such a tale as the 'Sompnour's' for instance is unpardonable, and indeed unreadable" (p. 36).

Kittredge (1915:192) refers to the "basis" of *The Summoner's Prologue and Tale* as "a trivial and sordid fabliau." Kennard (1923:16) complains that the "dénouement of the tale may not be told. . . ," and that it is "the humour of stableboys and swineherds." For Cowling (1927:170) *The Summoner's Prologue and Tale* lacks the "pith and point" of *The Friar's Tale*. Though he praises its characterization, its realistic dialogue, and in general its "excellent realism," he declares that the tale "fails to convince," not because of its improbability, or because of the digression on anger, but rather because "to temper the intolerable coarseness of the climax, Chaucer carried on the tale too long, and belabours the friar more than he deserved. Jenkin's suggestion of the cartwheel is unsavoury and unnecessary" (p. 170). Manly (1928:323) explains that he prints only lines 1665–73 and 1709–1850 of *The Summoner's Prologue and Tale* because of the "vulgarity" of the rest. Donaldson (1958), though finding the tale "hilariously funny" (p. 917), also omits it from his first edition; he does, however, include it in the second (1975) edition.

Engel (1931:68–70) holds *The Summoner's Prologue and Tale* at arm's length, avoiding any treatment of the "coarse trick," and seeing the tale as "weak in dramatic plot"; but he admits that it shows "strength, sense, and unity because of its satire." Sedgwick (1934:293), allowing that the Summoner gives as good as he gets in his dispute with the Friar, dismisses the tale as a stable-boy story, "impossible except to extreme youth, and yet there are admirable Chaucerian lines in it." According to Chute (1946:279), "the story itself is worthless, but it gives Chaucer an opportunity to make a beautiful little sketch of a begging friar in action." Schlauch (1956:266) dismisses the text as "anecdotal," a "loosely organized diatribe against friars, with a number of vivid if malodorous illustrations of their greed." Corsa (1964) finds *The Summoner's Prologue and Tale* one of Chaucer's "most morally mirthful tales" (p. 187), but she adds that its vulgarity "could be considered even by the pilgrims (and Chaucer's audience) a questionable violation of taste and manners." Edwin Howard (1964:145) deplores the "genuinely bad taste" of *The Summoner's Prologue*, and Whittock (1968:138) declares that the crux of the tale is "very coarse indeed. Nor does the narrative have the energy and fast-moving plot that redeem the coarseness of *The Miller's Tale*. Chaucer seems bent on giving the nastiness its full weight and not on playing it down." Braddy (1969) severely condemns *The Summoner's Prologue and Tale* as "Chaucer's most offensive writing" (p. 127), and he is "gagged" by the concluding episode, a "discreditable sort of filth, Chaucer at his worst" (p. 137).

Donald Howard (1976:257) also appears to find *The Summoner's Prologue and Tale* rather beyond hope, referring to it as "pre-adolescent filth," noting the "absurd conundrum" about the division of the fart, and judging it "childish," "primitive," and showing the Summoner's grossness, his "anal aggression," which operates at an "infantile level." In response, Alford (1984:198 n. 4) remarks that "as 'criticism' this is not really very helpful. No one doubts the Summoner's 'grossness.' The more important question—as in the case of the Miller or Pardoner— concerns the ways in which the tale transcends the moral failure of its teller." Owen too has little interest in the story; he feels its issues are trivial, and "only the satire against clerical abuse and hypocrisy raises it above the level of the typical fabliau" (1977:167). Indeed, "none of the three stories [of the D-Group] would have a chance for the prize, and only the Friar's has any real distinction as narrative art" (p. 168).

Positive Response.   The earliest critical response I have found to *The Summoner's Tale* is in a 1635 volume entitled *Amorvm Troili et Creseidae: Libri duo priores Anglico-Latini*, Sir Francis Kynaston's Latin translation of books 1 and 2 of Chaucer's *Troilus and Criseyde* (Kynaston 1635). Among the congratulatory epigrams, apostrophes, and supplementary dedicatory materials by various hands which head the volume is a twenty-line poem by one Samuel Evans, who expresses the hope that Kynaston will complete his translation of *Troilus and Criseyde* and then undertake to render *The Canterbury Tales* into Latin. The final eight lines of the poem focus on the division of the fart in *The Summoner's Tale* (text in Spurgeon 1925:1.i.211):

> But aboue all the *famous Legacie*
> Amongst the Couent dealt, so Legally,
> Where twelue diuide the As, and everyone
> Hath part *withouten Defalcation.*
> And all in Latine, surely when the Pope

Shall heare of this and all the sacred Troupe
Of Cardinalls peruse the Worke, theyle all
In generall Councell mak't Canonicall.

As so often in the sixteenth and seventeenth centuries, Chaucer is here being pressed into the service of Protestant raillery, his own satire read not merely as anti-clerical but as foresightedly anti-Papist.

Warton (1774:2.362) remarks that "in the clas [sic] of humorous or satirical tales, the *Sompnour's Tale*, which exposes the tricks and extortions of the mendicant friars, also has . . . distinguished merit." Hertzberg (1866:623) avers that in even greater measure than *The Friar's Tale*, *The Summoner's Tale* offers fine and piquant characterization that is rarely matched and never surpassed in the other Canterbury tales. Ten Brink (1883–96:1.164), referring to Thomas's revenge only obliquely as a "dirty trick," feels that Chaucer "treated the coarse subject with ingenious freedom, and at the same time with the highest artistic tact, and has presented a ludicrous farce through the medium of high style comedy. In psychological observation, clear outline, and characteristic miniature painting, joined to a strong application of local coloring and comic power, the Tale may be compared with Chaucer's best." Düring (1883–86:3.446) speaks of the tale's "rare artistry," and calls it the "most true-to-life and piquant" illustration of anti-fraternal satire. While admitting that "some readers . . . will be offended at the coarseness of the *Summoner's Tale*," Root (1906:251) adds that it is "not in the least vicious. So callous is the wretched friar of the tale in his miserable hypocrisies, that he needs a coarse insult by way of discipline. Indeed, the outspoken frankness of the conclusion comes as a positive relief after the sanctimonious pretenses of the friar." Root also finds "admirable" the characterization of *The Summoner's Tale*, especially the portrait of the wife and of course the hypocrisy of the friar. Legouis (1910; 1913:189) similarly praises Chaucer's portrayal of individuality, finding *The Summoner's Tale* the most characteristically Chaucerian of his tales in that respect, and noting in particular "the presentation of the mendicant Friar, his wheedling ways, his familiar manner, his oratorical efforts to extort money. . . ." Legouis feels that the "coarse joke"— "the *raison d'être* of Jacques de Baisieux's *fabliaux*"—"is here but the conclusion of a study of character, wonderful for its thoroughness and abundance of comic effects" (p. 189). Ewald (1913:79–81) and Meyer (1913:104–06) also praise the ironic, humorous characterization. Manly (1926a:97) refers to the "matchless humour" of *The Summoner's Prologue and Tale*, and Curry (1926:53) calls the tale an "unsavory but cleverly told story."

Chapman's 1929 essay on Chaucer's attitude towards preaching touches several times but always obliquely upon *The Summoner's Tale* to praise the friar's oratory. Dempster (1932:45) like many others sees Chaucer's interest as being "not so much in the story itself as in a striking portrait of a hypocritical and covetous friar. . . ." She praises his development of the ironies potential in the plot as he found it (presuming it to be something like the Priest's Bladder), especially the addition of the sermon against wrath which terminates so wrathfully. Lowes (1934) praises the tale's dialogue—"unmatched for its revelation of character. . . . No one who reads with ear as well as eye . . . can fail to catch the subtly characterized inflections of the Friar's voice" (p. 244)—and the tale's characterization: "The greatest of Chaucer's portraits within the body of a tale is the Friar . . . as described in the first two hundred and fifty lines or so of the narrative. I doubt if, within its compass, it has its match in English" (p. 229). Patch (1939:217) accords *The Summoner's Prologue and Tale* only a few words, characterizing the satire, without elaboration, as "more in the manner of Horace than of Juvenal or Persius, in that of Fielding rather than that of Thackeray." Like many others, Shelly (1940) is full of praise for *The Summoner's Tale's* vividness of character, the "real heart of the story" (p. 107), and is particularly taken by the wife: "I have no doubt that in winter she knitted [the friar] socks and mufflers" (p. 253), and the lord of the manor, "a village Sir Thomas Browne" (p. 254). In Jankyn's witty solution of the problem in division, and the company's delight in it, Shelly suggests we may see "the germ of those humorous modern stories in which the omniscient butler or the very superior gentleman's gentleman answers all the questions" (p. 254). Lawrence (1950:69) also finds the characterization of the friar admirable, and Speirs (1951:149) marks *The Summoner's Tale* along with *The Friar's Tale* as "great comic art." Brewer (1953:164) remarks that the tale "evokes the interiors of yeoman's cottage and lord's hall with the warmth and solidity, the familiar intimacy, of the Dutch interiors of Teniers," while Schaar (1955:225) notes the characterization through action. Ruggiers (1965:107–08) is specific in his praise, calling *The Summoner's Tale* *"psychologically* one of Chaucer's richest stories. The depiction of the deteriorating composure of the friar ranks with the portrayal of the Canon's Yeoman, and invites favorable comparison with those of the Wife of Bath and the Pardoner. . . . More than any other story of the pilgrimage it invites acting out so that the vividness of the character and its truth to life can be grasped." Lawlor (1968:123) singles *The Summoner's Prologue and Tale* and *The Miller's Tale* out as Chaucer's best fabliaux; the two "have never, in their own kind, been equalled. Realism can never be the same again." In a similar vein, Wagenknecht includes *The Summoner's Tale* friar among "the greatest characters in English literature before Shakespeare . . . ," arguing that ". . . Chaucer creates them as a dramatist would have created them by permitting them to talk themselves alive" (1968:5). Knight (1973:75) likewise admires the "tremendous flow of Chaucer's poetry [which] has made it sound as if real fourteenth century people, of differing characters, are talking." Brewer (1984c:213) makes a similar point, remarking that while the friar's character is "only a broad sketch . . . the amount of self-revelatory speech given to him etches in the few lines very deeply." O'Brien (1990:2) objects that such readings are mistaken, that the characters of lord and squire "serve as markers for a play of discourses rather than as 'reifiable' characters."

Thro (1970) admires particularly the humor of the concluding episode, comparing it in its "gratuitously creative" quality to the comic machinery of the *Miller's Tale* or *Shipman's Tale*. "This posing of a creative exercise and its fantastically imaginative solution appear, because they are in excess of plot requirements, to be dictated by Chaucer's enthusiastic delight in mental gymnastics" (pp. 97–98); Brewer (1984c:213) agrees, calling the episode a "remarkable illustration of what can only be called [Chaucer's] scientific, and specifically his arithmetical interests. No other poet in English could have invented such a story."

Kean (1972:89) singles out for notice the scene at the local court which concludes the tale, which she takes as showing us the reaction of an internal audience and indicating "the way in which [Chaucer] intends his own audience to react." The tale, she feels, succeeds with both internal and external audiences "by the sheer perfection in virtuosity of each of the participants," the friar "a prince among his kind," Thomas who provokes "maddened astonishment at his brilliant improvisation," and Jankyn, whose solution is "even more outrageous than the original insult" (p. 90). Mehl (1973; 1986:187–88) remarks upon the great breadth of effect and material in the story. The "explosive point . . . is a particularly happy and convincingly motivated combination of uninhibited farce and discursive rhetoric. . . . A wealth of theological thought and religious didacticism has been incorporated and put to the service of pointed satire whose domestic realism recalls the fabliaux of the Miller and the Reeve and whose timeless vitality needs very little explanation."

Havely (1975:23) praises the dramatic quality of *The Summoner's Prologue and Tale*, arguing that with its two short scenes serving as prologue and epilogue to the main one at Thomas's house, its paucity of straight narrative outside of "stage-directions," and vibrant dialogue, it could be produced as a play. He notes too that Friar John varies his tone "from stage to stage" during the tale, "threatening in his trentals-sermon . . . wheedling in his doorstep-manner . . . chatting roguishly with Thomas's wife . . . preaching solemnly to Thomas . . . on his knees pleading pathetically, on his feet spluttering threats" (p. 24). Burlin (1977) also praises the tale's structure, the "framing" of the central scene by "two panels of ingenious iconographic parody" (p. 166) in which "the commonplaces of antifraternal satire are realized in repulsive icons of irrepressible 'subtiltee / And heigh wit' . . ." (pp. 166–67).

Working out the relevance and appropriateness of excremental imagery for a story of the debasement of fraternal spirituality, Fleming holds the fart to be a "multi-faceted icon of delightful versatility. Superficially indelicate, it is in fact one of Chaucer's most delicate strokes, as excrement the appropriate reward of mendicant cupidity, as *flatus* the perfect vehicle for the burlesque Pentecost at the end of the poem" (1983:17). On this point see further in notes to lines 2103 and 2149–51.

Relationship to Other Canterbury Tales

Relationship to The Friar's Tale.   Especially for those who emphasize the "dramatic" reading of *The Canterbury Tales*, the most important relationship involving *The Summoner's Prologue and Tale* is that which it has with *The Friar's Tale*. Of particular interest has been the question of who "wins" the quarrel, though in recent years the issue seems to be losing its appeal.

Coghill (1949; 1967:122) writes that the Friar wins the battle of the tales: the Summoner lacks the wit of the Friar, his weapon is "the bludgeon, not the rapier . . . or perhaps a blunderbuss, loaded with filth. He was at home in ordure. . . . His scattered attack has none of his adversary's educated concentration." Preston (1952:248) suggests that Chaucer conceived of the conflict as a game of skill and delicacy, in which qualities the Friar is clearly superior, but ". . . when the Summoner comes forward with unexpectedly brilliant mimicry, the Friar's victory is by no means certain." It is perhaps unfair to admit the testimony of someone who writes essentially only on *The Friar's Tale*, but Beichner's essay (1961) arguing that the Friar impales the Summoner on the horns of a dilemma does address the question and is influential. "If [the Summoner] retaliates, he will appear more and more unrepentant and stupid, like the summoner of the *exemplum*. If he remains silent, he will have to swallow his boast of the *Prologue* to best the Friar, and he will give the impression that he is repenting of prior evil ways. In either case the Friar will appear to win" (p. 376). Bowden too feels Huberd wins the battle, having told a story which "condemns summoners more emphatically than the *Summoner's Tale* condemns friars" (1964:60).

Lumiansky (1953:140) calls the contest a draw: "each has openly attacked the other with a skillful story suited to its teller's character. . . . In the exchange, however, the Friar proved far less harshly acrimonious than the Summoner, a difference stemming perhaps from the different demands of their professions." Richardson (1975) too sees the contest as having no winner, arguing that Chaucer worked to make the contest result in a draw: "His entire treatment of the Friar and the Summoner is so fraught with parallels and balances that the question of a victor seems ultimately to defy solution" (p. 227). Externally the two are opposites, but at base they are moral equals, and "this situation of external difference masking internal likeness is beautifully duplicated in the stories that the rivals tell," for ". . . the structural patterns of the tales are identical" (p. 229). This structure has five parts: 1) an initial description of the culpable protagonist, 2) the encounter with the eventual punisher, 3) an extended, one-sided dialogue, 4) one event, followed by 5) a second event triggered by something the protagonist has said (p. 230). "Thus . . . the two stories follow exactly the same structural pattern even though they differ considerably in externals and in total effect" (p. 231). Both tales too, Richardson says, feature a "mixture of perceptiveness and self-revelation in characterizing the opponent" (p. 233); for example, the wrath exhibited by Friar John has more to do with the Summoner than the Friar. Indeed, "the specific characteristics that initiate the retribution are those of the narrator rather than the rival" (p. 234) in both *The Summoner's Prologue and Tale* and *The Friar's Tale*. Richardson concludes that the quarrel has all the qualities modern readers would call psychological projection, so that the narrators exhibit "rather striking accuracy in depicting each other's moral degeneracy while simultaneously revealing their own defects . . ." (p. 235). Donald Howard (1976:257) is impatient with the entire exchange: "It is impossible to say whether the Friar or the Summoner comes off worse in the clash. The angry outburst ends in a silly quibble."

Donaldson (1958:917) appears to give the decision to the Summoner, noting that Friar Huberd "makes a tactical mistake" in suggesting at the conclusion of his own tale that he could "really dazzle" his audience if he chose to display all his learning. The Summoner, argues Donaldson, seizes upon this posture to "destroy Hubert's pose of superiority." By the end of *The Summoner's Tale* "all the friar's intellectual pretensions have been laid low by an ignorant churl and a flippant young squire. It is significant that Chaucer permits the Summoner to have the last, devastating word in the quarrel. The Friar's degradation begins when he becomes involved in a quarrel with so low a fellow as the Summoner, and it is completed when he is permitted no rebuttal to the Summoner's scurrility. This is the harshest judgment visited by the author on any pilgrim except the Pardoner."

Another critic who awards the bout to the Summoner is Baker, who feels that the Friar unwittingly reveals vulnerable parts of his character in *The Friar's Tale*, after which "Chaucer joyously leaves him to the Summoner, who then descends upon [him] with his own weapons and drives him from the field" (1962:40). The Summoner of course has "the advantage of speaking second, and thus having the counter-punch. . . ." For Levy (1966:46) "the supposed ineffectuality of *The Summoner's Tale* is belied by the pilgrim-friar Huberd, who apparently becomes enraged at the Summoner's portraiture because the characterization has so accurately hit the mark. . . ." The Summoner himself is so visibly filled with wrath, however, that the tale's moral point "backfires" upon him as well (Levy 1966:58).

Zietlow (1966) takes the question of who wins the contest as central to his study. For him, the Summoner wins the battle by exposing Friar John, and by extension Huberd, as hypocrites and by demonstrating that he, unlike *The Friar's Tale*'s summoner, is shrewd, controlled, perceptive. Both Friar and Summoner are rascals, Zietlow argues, but the Summoner makes no attempt to conceal his rascality, and is outraged at Huberd's social acceptability which allows him to thrive. Lindahl (1987:146) makes much the same point, arguing that *The Summoner's Tale* is meant to suggest the idea that "'dainty' theft is even more reprehensible than the fictional summoner's coarse cruelty." The character of Friar John, says Zietlow, is intended to suggest Friar Huberd, greedy, imperceptive, self-impressed; ". . . parasitic hypocrites consort in public with their superiors, not with their equals or inferiors—they are friendly with franklins, not with pardoners" (p. 16). Friar John has several opportunities to redeem himself in the course of *The Summoner's Tale*, or at least to avoid catastrophe, but, relying on an over-estimation of his persuasive skills and rhetorical powers, he blunders first into the fart and then its public consideration. The donation itself "bears some resemblance to the climax of the Friar's Tale. In both cases the issue is the giving of something, and in both cases the action results from the confusion of intention and profession" (Zeitlow 1966:9). Whereas Friar John, like the summoner of *The Friar's Tale*, is too obtuse to recognize Thomas's anger, Thomas himself knows the friar "will stoop to the grossest kind of physical grasping for the sake of gain as surely as the fiend [of *The Friar's Tale*] knows that the summoner will sell his soul for a frying pan" (p. 10).

Zietlow deals in some detail with the friar's sermon on wrath, particularly its "comic incoherence and inconsistency," which he takes to be indicative of the friar's "moral and intellectual obtuseness" (p. 10). He argues further that the concluding sermon of *The Friar's Tale*, which he feels is inappropriate on several grounds as a conclusion of the exemplum of the summoner and the fiend, is parodied in Friar John's sermon on wrath: "Thus the long sermon in the *Summoner's Tale* is appropriate both as illustration of the offensive garrulity of friars and as a comic parody of the *Friar's Tale*" (p. 15). A similar argument is made about the concluding "gloss" to *The Friar's Tale* by Carruthers (1972:210): "the Friar's gloss is clearly an attempt to elevate his tale into a general exemplum for the company. But in the process, he also covers over his true intention—to get back at the pilgrim-Summoner." Zietlow makes clear that his defense of the summoner is intended as a corrective only, not as praise. The summoner is offensive, and "has nothing to lose by creating offence, because he has little to hide. Unlike his opponent, he never contrives to 'make his English sweete upon his tonge.' His goal is to show that the Friar is, beneath the surface, as gross and obscene as he himself obviously is" (p. 17). But though he succeeds admirably in destroying Huberd, the summoner is none the less "despicable for his malice . . . , devilishly, fiendishly, maliciously powerful. . . . Even though we feel the justice of his exposure, we see the malignancy and egotism of his motive" (p. 19).

Lawlor (1968) disagrees with those who see the Summoner as driven out of control by his anger. His story is "delivered with no less self-possession than the Friar's" (p. 120); in fact "anger has stimulated in the Summoner a wonderfully heightened awareness" (p. 121). Though initially clearly shaken by *The Friar's*

Tale, the Summoner recovers, and "never in the upper reaches of 'flyting' have game, set and match been so comfortably won, after so unpromising a start" (p. 123). Burlin too feels the Friar is the loser in the exchange of insults, if for no other reason than that there is no adequate defense against the Summoner's "double-barreled riposte of anal anecdotes" (1977:165). Owen (1977) sees the Friar of the pilgrimage as having "precisely the position of the character in the Summoner's story before he is enlightened by the angel: he has an exhaustive knowledge of the pains of hell, along with a smug delight in his own immunity. The story quickly dispels his illusions of immunity" (p. 163). Owen also regards the Summoner as winning the "battle of the interjections" (in reference to the Friar's interruption at line 1761) and finds the satire "devastating and beautifully articulated" (p. 164). Knight (1973:75–76) finds it a "grand irony" that the Friar's tale told of a summoner is less witty and subtle than *The Summoner's Tale*, which offers "genuine satire on the friars through its verbal brilliance." Cooper (1983:132) would award the round to the Summoner on points, for ". . . the Summoner's Tale numerically surpasses the Friar's even more decisively than the Reeve's does the Miller's. The Friar dispatches a single summoner to Hell; the Summoner gets a whole convent of friars, thirteen in all, ranged around his wheel."

In recent years the relationship between *The Friar's Tale* and *The Summoner's Prologue and Tale* has been explored in ways not connected directly to the "dramatic" reading, and thus less concerned with who tells the better tale. Carruthers (1972), for example, explores the thematics of glossing, spirit and letter, in the two tales. "The Friar is a glossator by trade, and being hypocritical, a false glossator. The Summoner reduces all things to a literal level, refusing to see any higher truth. The Friar seeks to deny the letter, the Summoner to deny the gloss" (p. 209). Carruthers emphasizes the directness of the Summoner in comparison to the Friar: while the latter "takes his whole tale to get summoners to hell, the Summoner starts with friars there" (p. 212). The Summoner's descriptions are more concrete than those of *The Friar's Tale* and the main characters are named, again in contrast to *The Friar's Tale*. While the wit of *The Friar's Tale* is ironic, depending on "unseen or unstated meanings concealed beneath the surface," the wit of *The Summoner's Prologue and Tale* is dependent upon puns (e.g. "ferthyng," "fundement," "ars-metrik"), "a literal type of wit. . . . Even the tale's gloss, Jankyn's explication of Thomas's text, is wholly material, a matter of applied science" (p. 213).

Allen and Moritz (1981) see a variety of connections between *The Summoner's Tale* and *The Friar's Tale*, centered on the notion of gifts and giving (*beneficium*), an idea "at the very heart of the ordering process of medieval society" (p. 155). Summoners, they argue, live by bribery, friars by gifts. *The Friar's Tale* concludes with a gift sincerely given to the devil, and Thomas's gift to John is the point of *The Summoner's Tale*; in the epilogue Jankyn receives a gift of a gown-cloth from his lord (p. 155). Another pattern linking *The Summoner's Prologue and Tale* and *The Friar's Tale* is "a diptych pattern . . . involving five elements" (p. 156). In *The Friar's Tale* summoners are defined, and in *The Summoner's Prologue and Tale* friars; a society is next formed, in *The Friar's Tale* between demon and summoner, in *The Summoner's Tale* between John and Thomas and his wife; third there is a discussion of doctrinal points, the nature of demons in *The Friar's Tale* and the nature of glossing, prayer, and wrath in *The Summoner's Tale*; fourth is "a two-part exemplum which poses a problem," the two curses in *The Friar's Tale* and the fart and its division in *The Summoner's Tale*; finally, the problems are solved: the Summoner places friars definitively in hell, and Jankyn solves the problem of division (pp. 156–57). Lacking in each of these diptychs is, of course, the central panel, *in bono*, which would demonstrate the proper understanding and use of *beneficium*, but this panel of truth and value is implied, "literally absent but ironically present . . ." (p. 157). Fleming (1967) also sees *The Friar's Tale-Summoner's Tale* sequence as forming "a kind of grotesque literary diptych on the subject of the orders of justice [the summoner] and mercy [the friar]" (p. 106). Later he adds (1983:9) that "the one tale [is] a picture of God's justice corrupted, the other a tableau of His grace prostituted; each with its scriptural ironies and iconography; each with its '[biter]-bit' climax." Further, "in the *Friar's Tale* the villain of the piece is eventually caught in the trap of his own literalism; the same thing happens in the *Summoner's Tale* . . ." (1983:17). *The Summoner's Tale* "plunges deeper [than *The Friar's Tale*] and raises more frightening questions about the very practicability of penance administered by 'vessels of mercy' who are really vessels of wrath . . ." (1983:19).

Cooper (1983:131) sees *The Friar's Tale* and *The Summoner's Tale* as linked through certain themes. The two pilgrims share the vices of avarice, anger, and drunkenness, and condemn themselves in attacking each other. The protagonists in both tales receive a reward other than that sought, and both tales "use the motif of brotherhood in a way that turns its conventional associations inside out" (p. 131). Friar John, like *The Friar's Tale* summoner and the knight in *The Wife of Bath's Tale*, is trapped by an oath; *The Friar's Tale* and *The Wife of Bath's Tale* had "worked out their plots through speeches expressing intention," and the climax of *The Summoner's Tale* features sincere, though non-verbal communication. Because it has no semantic content, Friar John fails to find a satisfactory gloss for the fart as text (p. 132).

Rogers (1986:59) sees the concluding episode of *The Summoner's Tale* as a link to, a kind of gloss on, *The Friar's Tale*. Two tentative explanations of Thomas's action are offered: the lady sees him as foolish, mad (lines 2206–09), "in a manere frensye," while the lord sees him as possessed (lines 2221, 2240), "demonyak." Interestingly, these are two explanations frequently offered to explain the actions of the summoner in *The Friar's Tale*, whose "decision" to go to the devil has been seen as an act of stupidity or of absolute corruption (p. 60).

Jankyn's empirical solution resolves the issue, showing that Thomas is neither irrational nor possessed, but clever. "The Summoner's tale shows us . . . that we can understand evil without invoking the categories of the irrational and the demonic. Simple human hypocrisy . . . and the perversion of the intellect by wrath are sufficient to account for the evil . . ." (p. 61).

Wetherbee (1989:66–67) argues that "one of the main points of Chaucer's pairing of the two" tales is to show the Summoner to be "healthier in his imaginative life than the Friar" and hence to "portray the triumph of [the Summoner's] instinctual good will." Whereas *The Friar's Tale* proffers "cold authoritarianism" and "harsh criticism," *The Summoner's Tale*, "richer and more humane," achieves through humor a "far more effective satire" (pp. 62–63).

Knapp (1990:56–59) finds a link between *The Friar's Tale* and *The Summoner's Tale* in that each offers a critique of fraternal claims to special knowledge of spiritual realities. Friar Huberd insinuates through the demon's remarks in his tale that he knows something of hell; Friar John pretends to spiritual knowledge that comes to those who fast and pray. O'Brien (1990:12) suggests that the tales are joined by an interest in a different sort of knowledge: "The scientific quest shapes [their] plots . . . : in both, the climax occurs when the curious poser of the question, the descendant of Bacon and Grosseteste in search of 'God's privities,' discovers the answer, and particularly one that depends on the senses rather than authority."

Relations to Group D as a Whole.   Huppé (1964:201–09) works toward seeing both *The Friar's Tale* and *The Summoner's Tale* as responding to the Wife of Bath, the wife in *The Summoner's Tale* echoing Alice's carnality, and the friar echoing her self-serving interest in glossing scripture. East (1977) argues that the D Group is "a debate about debates, a disputation about academic disputations," beginning with the Wife of Bath's challenge to authority in the opening words of her prologue. The dispute about the relative value of experience and authority continues in *The Friar's Tale* as the summoner questions the "authoritative" fiend about hell, who assures him that he will soon know the answers to all such questions through his own experience. In *The Summoner's Tale*, one encounters "what must be the most impossibly abstract scholastic question of all time: how to divide a fart equally into thirteen *distinctiones*. . . . *Auctoritee* is of no help, but there remains *experience*. Jankyn solves the problem 'By preeve which that is demonstratif'" (p. 81). Thus in the D-Group the questions move from the concrete (how many times may Alisoun marry), through the abstract (what is the material and formal nature of fiends?) eventually to "evaporate into airy nothing," while the solutions or answers to the questions become increasingly less theoretical and more concrete, relying increasingly on experience (p. 81).

Owen (1977:168) finds Group D "the most thoroughly dramatic" of the fragments, for "each of the tales expresses the personality of the teller, and the first and third have at times a special idiom associated with the teller." Wasserman (1982) finds the unity of the fragment in its concern for Platonist-Aristotelian questions of signification and understanding, the Wife of Bath and Summoner being Aristotelians and the Friar a Platonist. The Summoner begins by mocking, in *The Summoner's Prologue*, the "visionary experiences of Dante who is specifically invoked in the fiend's final comments in the *Friar's Tale* . . . , [presenting] a scatological answer to the eschatological attack of the Platonist" (p. 82). The Summoner further disputes with the Friar by inverting some of *The Friar's Tale* imagery. Whereas the Friar had satirized Aristotelian multiplicity "by telling the tale of a greedy summoner who foolishly vows to extort twelve pence from a widow who would rather have her neck broken than yield up a single penny" (p. 84), Friar John argues for a whole coin rather than a twelfth of one. "The Aristotelian thus desires the multiple twelve pence. The Platonist wants a single coin while rejecting the twelfth part as a worthless fragment of the whole" (p. 84). Jankyn, finally, proves the Platonic ideal of indivisible unity to be a fiction (p. 85).

Fleming (1983:9) speaks of the "thematic drift" of Group D, arguing that Chaucer explores therein "a number of the most cherished Pauline metaphors of nature and grace: the old and the new, the letter and the spirit, vessels of wrath and vessels of mercy." Alford sees a "pervasive concern throughout" the fragment for the relation between letter and gloss, marked by a steady erosion in decorum (1984:197). The Wife of Bath perverts both letter and spirit to suit her desires, the Friar follows on with a tale of a summoner "blind to the spirit," and the Summoner concludes with a tale of a friar slain by the letter (pp. 197–98).

Voss (1985) sees rhetoric, or language more generally, as the controlling theme of Group D, *The Wife of Bath's Tale* demonstrating the power of the spoken word, *The Friar's Tale* turning on the efficacious curse, and *The Summoner's Tale* demonstrating that the preaching of Friar John is nothing but broken wind (p. 16).

Patterson (1987:484–88) sees the D Group as appended to *The Man of Law's Tale*, and he regards the sequence B¹D (Fragment II–Fragment III) as parallel with the structure of Group A. Each series begins with a tale by a representative of the dominant culture who is rebutted in some fashion by the subsequent taleteller. In Group D, Patterson suggests, *The Summoner's Tale* fulfills the function that *The Cook's Tale* seems intended to perform at the end of Group A, each portraying a "churlish world of mockery and retaliation." Both the Cook and the Summoner, Patterson observes, are diseased. But the tale of the Cook, who "derives from the threatening urban proletariat," remains incomplete because its political implications would have been dangerous. The Summoner, by contrast, represents "the apparatus of social control imposed upon medieval society by the Church," and his tale reduces "peasant energy, however potentially threatening, . . . to a playful manipulation of the images of the official culture that leaves the realities firmly in place."

Hornsby (1988:89) writes that the tales of the D Group all "center on pledges of faith and deal with the consequences of pledging one's faith on promises to perform unspecified acts." So viewed, the concluding episode at the lord's manor is "a type of courtroom scene where the performance of the pledge of faith is outrageously enforced." Cooper (1989:181) observes that *The Wife of Bath's Prologue* like *The Summoner's Tale* parodies the "processes of scholastic debate."

Relationship to The Parson's Tale.   Koeppel (1891*b*:44) is the first to note that a number of passages in *The Summoner's Tale* are shared with *The Parson's Tale*. Others to make this point are SK (notes on lines 2007–10 and 2075), Merrill (1962:346), Boyd (1967:66 on "Placebo" in line 2075), Ruggiers (1965:105), Patterson (1978:368–69 on lines 2094–98), Crowther (1980), Lawler (1980:160–61), and Shaw (1984:9–10). Fleming (1983) takes the exposition of wrath in *The Parson's Tale* to be a "telling internal referent for Fr. John's venal charade of a call to penance" (p. 12).

Appropriateness of the Tale to the Teller

In general, those who have seen *The Summoner's Prologue and Tale* as particularly appropriate to the Summoner as narrator have found least in it to praise, while those who have seen it as sophisticated have either tacitly or explicitly assigned its artistry to Chaucer.

To begin with questions of content, Lumiansky (1955:140) sees the repellent Summoner and his repellent narrative as well matched. Of *The Summoner's Prologue* one may say that "both the vulgarity of the anecdote and the free expression of animosity towards the Friar come naturally from the mouth of this diseased and embittered scoundrel," while there is about *The Summoner's Tale* proper "the same ugly air that surrounds the Summoner himself." For Lumiansky even the humorous device suggested by the lord's squire at the end of the tale has its unattractive aspects. Huppé (1964:201) too finds a match between teller and tale, the "Summoner's venomous retaliation [having] about it the odor of his sewer-like mind," while "the basis of his tale, its plot, is simply nasty and nastily simple—like the Summoner himself." Corsa (1964:186) feels "no surprise that the Summoner's tale depends for much of its comedy upon coarse and open vulgarity," given that he is "the most obviously repulsive pilgrim." Ruggiers (1965:100) also sees *The Summoner's Prologue and Tale* as "an intimately revealing outgrowth of the character and personality" of the Summoner, who "by comparison with his adversary the Friar, . . . comes off as considerably more vulgar, and perhaps even more depraved." Whittock finds *The Summoner's Prologue* in particular to "exempli[fy] the Summoner himself, his malice suddenly flying forth, then withdrawing again within his unpleasing person" (1968:138). Benson (1980:71) along with numerous others notes that the Summoner ironically condemns himself: ". . . pointing out the hypocrisy of the friar's preaching wrathfully against the sin of wrath, [he] is also guilty of the same sin. . . ."

As regards narrative technique or voice in *The Summoner's Tale*, confusion has sometimes marked attempts to link it to the Summoner's character. Coghill (1949; 1967:122) sees multiple possibilities: when the Summoner's friar "enters upon his long sermon to Thomas . . . he seems to lose grip. . . . Thus the Summoner's lack of art is a sign of art in Chaucer, for it is fitting that a Summoner should be less intelligent than such a Friar as Hubert was. And yet it may be that the Summoner was trying to put into the mouth of the Friar in his story a parody of what might normally be expected of a Friar, and that the sermon is deliberately ill-constructed." Yet again, ". . . what the Summoner can do best is neither parody nor sermoning, but building up a picture of country life. . . . with an artistry that is Chaucer's rather than the Summoner's" (p. 123). Subsequent critics consider whether the success and/or failure of the tale should be attributed to the Summoner and therefore taken as part of his characterization. Owen (1955:22) sees *The Summoner's Tale* as appropriate to the Summoner's character, and judges it a mixed performance: the Summoner's anger takes control of his story telling, ". . . furnishing and then subverting the central theme of his tale, and impelling him to carry his victim through the denouement of Thomas's gift to the ridiculous anticlimax of its imagined division at the wheel." Baker (1962) sees a contrast between *The Friar's Tale* which is "sly, oily, and insinuating, and the Summoner's, crackling and obscene, but extremely well told" (p. 40), and sees the Summoner himself as "a rather rough but extraordinarily witty man, and though unlearned by the standard of the friars, possessed of at least enough '*questio quid juris*' learning to suit his purpose here" (p. 41).

Merrill attributes the puzzling length and (for some readers) tedium of the friar's sermon on wrath to the Summoner's intention to satirize his foe Huberd: "The sermon is clumsy if for no other reason than the fact that it covers too many subjects" (1962:344), including abstinence, alms-giving, patience, anger, and alms-giving again. The emphasis, Merrill argues, is on wrath because the Summoner feels this to be Huberd's personal weakness, already demonstrated in his tale's preamble. "Anger forms the framework upon which the whole quarrel has been carefully developed, since both tales are instigated by the wrath of their narrators" (p. 346). Oddly then, despite its aesthetic shortcomings, the digression on anger in *The Summoner's Tale* "acts as an authoritative moral text—a text against which the anger of Huberd and the Summoner is measured," for "in spite of the satiric elements, Friar John's sermon is doctrinally sound" (p. 346).

Corsa (1964) credits the Summoner with being "a master of characterization, inspired into brilliance, perhaps, by his aroused hostility" (p. 188), and concludes that "scurrilous the Summoner on the pilgrimage may be, but he has told a moral tale without once violating the consistency of his own character" (p. 190). Craik (1964:125–26) argues that the inept use of examples and the rambling character of the sermon on wrath is not the Summoner's, or Chaucer's, but friar John's. Owen (1977:165) blames the sermon's poor construction on the Summoner's own anger and pursuit of his enemy. The "speech is thus not a lapse on Chaucer's part from the dramatic situation" (1977:165). Again, as the Summoner angrily tells tales of angry men, the "aesthetics of the situation, already compromised by the earlier veerings from the sermon's function in the tale, give way to the satisfying release of the flesh-quaking passion" (1977:166). Gardner (1977:281) simply sees the Summoner as brilliant as well as malicious.

Ruggiers (1965:101) allows that *The Summoner's Prologue and Tale* "seems to belie the anti-intellectual nature of its teller," but he reminds us that the same must be said of *The Miller's Tale* and *The Reeve's Tale*, not to mention *The Wife of Bath's Tale*. "In short," Ruggiers concludes, "even if we may cavil that the Summoner knows much that the *General Prologue* denies him, we must approve the depiction of the friar within the tale, in whom such knowledge is exquisitely apt. The foreign tags, the stock of *exempla*, all flow from the lips of an educated man who desecrates and abuses his intellectual gifts" (p. 101).

Levitan (1971), concluding his argument for an elaborate and learned parody of Pentecostal iconography in *The Summoner's Tale* (see "*The Summoner's Tale* and Anti-fraternalism" below), makes explicit a distinction probably implicit in much of the foregoing discussion: "For the summoner who tells the tale, Jankyn's jest is probably nothing more than a surface-ribaldry; for the poet behind the fictional teller, the proposal contains a highly sophisticated and formally perfect thrust at the inversion of the Holy Spirit among the corrupt friars" (p. 244). Mehl (1973; 1986:187) also notes that the parody of the friar, marked by such "devastating accuracy and rhetorical competence [is] hardly credible in this vulgar narrator; similarly, the concluding part, with its pseudo-learned mock-debate is not exactly in tune with his coarse narrative style. The exuberant rhetoric of the satire," however, "is evidently more important here than strict psychological consistency. . . ." Havely (1975:24) agrees that the range of knowledge displayed in *The Summoner's Tale* is beyond the Summoner's intellectual level; he notes that the Summoner is in any case not a prominent narrator, and he senses that Chaucer's goal was to fashion an "imaginative satire on greed . . . rather than to tailor it exactly to the character of the teller." Nevertheless, "something of his violent, talkative and highly-coloured character can be seen reflected not only in the earthiness of the *Tale's* plot, but also in the vividness of its dialogue and descriptive language" (p. 25). Knight (1973:76) feels that the narrator "sounds more like Chaucer himself." Howard, who finds little to praise in *The Summoner's Tale*, attributes what little value it has, the anti-fraternal satire, to Chaucer: "This is unimpersonated artistry: the gross Summoner isn't capable of such satiric deftness" (1976:257). Burlin (1977:164–65) sees the angry energy of the attack as appropriate to the angry Summoner, but finds that the "artfully refined portrait of the unctuously pomp-ous friar . . . exceeds the realistic capacities of the teller," and he feels Chaucer, "while carefully insisting on the dramatic propriety of the performance, . . . has invested the *Summoner's Tale* with a surprisingly generous artfulness. . ." (p. 167).

Recent work has tended to move away from concerns for "dramatic" reading decorum. Martha Fleming (1984), for example, insists that the narrative voice of *The Summoner's Prologue and Tale* is not the furious Summoner's, "not that of a man out of control with anger" (p. 90), nor is the narrative voice that of a man whom drunkenness reduces to Latin "or for whom ire calls forth the outburst of the prologue . . ." (p. 95). The tale reveals the Summoner's character, she ar-gues, not by being told angrily but by unveiling his wrathful nature as he projects his own sins upon the Friar (pp. 96–97), a point also raised by Rich-ardson (1974). Brewer (1984c) also sees no attempt to suggest personality through the tale; the "central incident" may fit the Summoner's character, but "the varied interest of the subject matter, the subtlety of attitude, in no way correspond to, or express his personality" (p. 211). Indeed, Lawton (1985:97) notes that in Chaucer's "quytyng" tales, "where we might most expect a dra-matically developed narratorial *persona*, we are given hardly anything. The nar-ratorial voices of the Friar's and Summoner's Tales are utterly neutral."

Pearsall similarly remarks that the anger dramatized in the opening of *The Summoner's Prologue* is "not converted into an angry or distempered story"; rather the tale is "coolly and wittily observed" (1985:222; cf. 1986:140, the story "is not vile and reeking of the sewer, but cool, witty, and precisely judged"). By the time we reach the division of the fart, the Summoner is "virtually forgotten" (1985:222). Further, "the narrator . . . resumes unperturbed after the Friar's interruption (1761), with no addition of malice . . . , indeed with no apparent malice at all" (1985:223). Despite "a kind of absurd aptness" in assigning the tale's matter to the Summoner, Pearsall continues, it would be "dreary" to press the argument as Huppé does (1964:201), for the "witty and indecent word-play" of the tale is "quite in Chaucer's normal vein, . . . and the whole tale is told with cool urbanity" (p. 223). Pearsall (p. 227) thus finds unpersuasive arguments like those of Owen (1977), Coghill (1949), and Merrill (1962) about the tale's shape and quality as indicative of the Summoner's anger or lack of art.

Arguing that the social consciousness of Chaucer's art is consistent across tales told by different characters, Aers (1986a) feels that in *The Summoner's Prologue and Tale* "there is no plausible case for maintaining that the tale's poetic idiom and critical intelligence is a naturalistic projection carefully designed for the simple-minded, semi-literate 'harlot' of the *General Prologue*" (p. 41). So too Knight (1986:106) sees the story as having, like *The Friar's Tale*, "a considerable degree of autonomy from its violent teller." Cooper (1989:180) also regards the psychological link between tale and teller as "minimal once its coarseness and its antifraternalism have been acknowledged: the style of telling, its procedure by indirection, the skill with which the damning portrait of the unctuous friar John is developed, are qualities of the tale, not the teller." Wetherbee (1989: 66–67), however, reads the tale as an expression of the Summoner's healthy "imaginative life" and "instinctual good will."

Rhetoric

Though Manly (1926a:107) lists *The Summoner's Tale* among those *Canterbury Tales* "in which the rhetorical devices do not occupy more than 1 per cent of the text," Shain (1955:242) finds extensive use of "secular rhetoric," including balance (lines 1872–74, 1877–78), contrast (line 1979), play on words (lines 1916–17), a Latin pun (line 1934), a rhetorical question (lines 1935–38), similes (lines 1930–38), a typical rhetorical listing (lines 1907–10), and "an example of the I-won't-say-anymore-but-I-could formula." Baker (1962) also points to rhetorical devices, especially exempla and exemplary figures, noting that though Manly may be right, one can demonstrate the importance of this "one per cent" in both *The Friar's Tale* and *The Summoner's Tale* by noting especially the ironic contrasts set up between the exemplary figures to which Friar and Summoner allude (pp. 35–36). Knight (1973:73–74) notes several tropes in Friar John's sermon, including *frequentatio* (lines 1906–10), *apostrophe* (lines 1927 and 1963–66), and *repetitio* and *compar* (lines 1963–66).

Irony.　Birney's 1960 article on "Structural Irony" in *The Summoner's Tale* opens a new line of inquiry, or at least a new focus. Rather than treating the tale primarily as the expression of the Summoner's character and his goal of vituperating the Friar, Birney seeks to reveal the tale's own inner cohesiveness shaped by its "rich texture of ironic foreshadowings, ambiguities and reversals" (p. 205). Both *The Summoner's Tale* and the analogous Tale of the Priest's Bladder, Birney argues, are stories "based upon dramatic irony, upon expectation monstrously and comically frustrated. Throughout, Chaucer keeps this denouement in mind, and most of his apparent digressions in the interests of framework satire will be seen, on a second reading, to be contributions to this central irony" (p. 206). Birney is the first (excepting Grosvenor in Ogle 1741) to see Thomas as entirely aware of Friar John's hypocrisies: "he is that dangerous man, a gull whose gullibility has run out" (p. 208), and if he does not send the friar packing immediately it is only perhaps because he is apathetic, "lacking passion or plan to rid himself of this useless visitor" (p. 209). The wife too is perhaps not as naive as earlier readers assumed, and "it is highly unlikely that the friar's hasty attempt to pretend that he knew of their bereavement all along would pacify her, even if she were still gullible enough to believe it" (p. 211). Birney also seeks to adjust somewhat our understanding of the friar. In addition to being wholly insincere, he is also insensitive and blundering, and ". . . like so many of Chaucer's clerical rogues . . . he deceives partly by compulsion, and on such a huge scale that eventually he deceives himself in the process of undeceiving others" (pp. 221–22).

MacDonald (1966), focusing on Chaucer's use of monitory elements in *The Summoner's Tale*, also sees the friar as inept: though he is a "professional manipulator of proverbs, *sententiae*, and *exempla* whose technique has been polished by years of diligent practice," he makes a "series of comically fatal errors that identifies him with John [of *The Miller's Tale*] and other naive comic types" (pp. 461–62). In the same year Zietlow defends the Summoner by arguing that he creates in his tale a protagonist-dupe who reminds us of Friar Huberd: "he presents us with a friar who is unable to control a situation because, ironically enough, he shares the failings of the Friar's summoner: he is greedy, imperceptive, and insensitive to others" (1966:7).

Given these understandings of character, then, Birney senses a growing tension, emotional and gastric, as the tale progresses: "The friar does not bore *us*, he is too fascinating a rogue, and our ox is not gored, our capon's throat is not cut, but he is unwittingly yet inexorably producing in Thomas, through the protracted stuffing quality of his monologue, an indigestion of words, a swelling of unreleased wrath, to add to the tabour-tight swell of the sick man's belly" (p. 212). These ironies are deepened, of course, by the friar's insistence on the virtues of abstinence, the "empty womb," and lean belly. The twisting and malaprop arguments of the friar's sermon on wrath also figure in the pattern of irony, revealing the friar's worldliness, hypocrisy and insensitivities, as does of course his consuming wrath following the receipt of Thomas's gift, and his inarticulateness before the lord of the manor. The suppressed amusement of the lord's household, and Jankyn's "diabolically plausible solution" complete the humiliation of the friar and the pattern of irony.

Adams (1962) follows Birney with another study of *The Summoner's Tale*'s ironies, noting such ironic patterns as problems of distribution versus concentration (masses, farthyngs, farts) and patterns of anal word play wrought against the background of the anal *Summoner's Prologue*. The structure of the tale is built upon standardized criticisms of friars, but these are always dramatized rather than named. Adams emphasizes the ironic role of the lord in the conclusion. By pretending to be sympathetic, by implying (in treating the "impossible" division as the problem) that the friar is impervious to simple insult, and that the insult is removed once the logical problem is "solved," he gives the jest "a second life" (pp. 131–32).

Thematic Issues

In an exchange which became almost as heated as that between Summoner and Friar, Tupper (1914, 1915c, 1916) and Lowes (1915) argue repectively for and against the proposition that "Wrath in its general aspect is represented by the Friar-Summoner Tales" (Tupper 1914:112). Tupper's argument incorporates both *The Summoner's Prologue and Tale* and *The Friar's Tale*, and indeed *The Canterbury Tales* as a whole. He sees *The Friar's Tale* as illustrating "the Cursing phase of Wrath," while *The Summoner's Tale* presents the anger of Thomas, the "boar-like frenzy of the friar," and the friar's sermon against ire, which last, Tupper notes, owes something to *The Parson's Tale* 534 and 564; Tupper also sees as significant the wrath of the Summoner himself (1914:112–13). Lowes attacks not the self-evident importance of wrath in *The Summoner's Prologue and Tale* but Tupper's desire to see the tale as essentially a reflex of a scheme for portraying each of the Seven Deadly Sins in *The Canterbury Tales*. Hence Lowes stresses the importance for *The Summoner's Tale* of other sins, such as gluttony, pointing to the excursus or sermon against gluttony in lines 1873–1941 and the passage in lines 1915–17 cited from Jerome's *Adversus Jovinianum*, which is used by the Pardoner in his attack against gluttony (*PardT* C 508ff.), and the inclusion of the exemplum on Cambyses (lines 2043–78), "an *exemplum* against Drunkenness as well as Wrath" (1915:281). Tupper replies (1916) that Lowes places too much emphasis upon the theme of gluttony, refusing to see it as integral to the Summoner's character (as he feels wrath is); he does not, however, address Lowes's observation (1915:280–81) that *GP* 626, 634–36, and 649–51 depict the Summoner as "both a glutton and a lecher."

Robinson (RB[1], p. 751; RB[2], p. 650) finds that Tupper's system of assigning to each pilgrim a particular Deadly Sin, which the pilgrim both incarnates and condemns in his tale, "breaks down when applied to the whole series of tales." Tupper (1940) reiterates his argument (for *The Summoner's Tale* on pp. 519–20 and 525). Particular elements of the debate are cited in Explanatory Notes to lines 1873–1941 and 1915–17. Severs (1964), among others, points to other failings besides wrath in the friar's character; he particularly notes the significant echoing in *The Summoner's Tale* 2184–88 of Matthew 23.8–11: "Despite the Friar's familiarity with the passage . . . he fails to live by it"; and he reveals his failures: "Gluttony, Wrath, Pride, and Hypocrisy." Robertson argues (1962:331) that the friar represents hypocrisy. Ruggiers (1965:105) on the other hand finds the friar's many faults ("hatred, slander, hypocritical counsel, lying, subtle flattery, reproachful chiding, and ceaseless criticism") to "add up to wrath itself" as it is described in *The Parson's Tale*.

Levy (1966:56–57) connects the prominence of wrath as an idea in *The Summoner's Tale* with the parody of Pentecost which he sees underlying Jankyn's wagon-wheel (see note 2255 and below under *"The Summoner's Prologue and Tale* and Anti-fraternalism"): rather than being inspired by grace and love to preach with eloquence, the friars are in fact "kindled with wrath by the diabolic afflatus, the flameless fumes designed to defile their hearts, animate them with hatred. . . ." Fleming (1967:105–06) connects the notion of wrath in *The Summoner's Prologue and Tale* with its antidote, mercy, arguing that the tale suggests Ephesians 2.3–5: "'We were by nature the children of wrath, just like the others,' says St. Paul. 'But God, who is rich in mercy . . . has revived us together with Christ.' . . . The Latin text, of course, reads *misericordia* for 'mercy,' . . . For the antidote to *ira* is *misericordia*. . . ." Thus *The Summoner's Prologue*'s inversion of the vision of *Maria Misericordia* is an emblem of both Friar and Summoner's refusal of mercy and immersion in wrath. Fleming develops this argument further in 1983, pp. 9–10: "the first theme of the tale is wrath, the second, the merciful grace of penance." Arguing against "roadside-drama" readings, he finds the angry outburst from the Summoner "thin fare, deficient in motivation, false in pitch" if considered only dramatically, and argues instead for seeing it as "an arresting icon of wrath" (p. 10). The Summoner and Thomas are both "children of wrath," and both are urged to repent, which is sound advice; "but is it practical for a world in which the children of wrath themselves have usurped the machinery of mercy?"

Whittock sees the friar as exemplifying "all the deadly sins" (1968:136), but sees his "most fundamental sin" as blasphemy (p. 139). Gardner (1977:281) finds wrath to be one of the tale's two major motifs, and impurity, "the failure to subjugate the desires of the flesh," the other. He adds (pp. 281–82) that the idea of the (corrupted) tripartite soul is another organizing feature, in that all levels of the friar's soul are corrupted. Haskell (1976:58) argues for the centrality of wrath in *The Summoner's Tale*, but adds that the sin is given two faces, and embodied in two characters, and as it passes from one (Thomas) to the other (John), it changes its character from righteous indignation to self-destructive wrath. See further in note to line 1825.

Martha Fleming (1984) argues that while it is self-evident that wrath is the theme of *The Summoner's Prologue and Tale*, beginning with the dramatization of the Summoner's wrath and continuing through the exempla of angry men in Friar John's sermon, wrath is not commonly found among the sins attributed to friars in anti-fraternal writings, and the Summoner is the only one "consumed by his wrath" (p. 96). Finally, she feels, the anger that the tale both dramatizes and is about tells us of an angry Summoner. The advice (lines 2086–88) not to associate with an angry man applies to Friar Huberd, who was unwise to provoke one, and to the other pilgrims as well. Shaw, on the other hand, argues that the sermon of wrath is a projection of John's own anger: he is angry at Thomas's division of his donations, and projects his own anger onto Thomas (1984:9).

One of the more important issues raised by *The Summoner's Tale* is Chaucer's attitude towards exegesis, or in the terms of the story, "glosing." Among modern critics, Bloomfield (1958:80 n.), Carruthers (1972), and Besserman (1984:65–66) are less certain than Robertson (1962:331–32) and Fleming (1966:694 and 1983:18) of Chaucer's earnestness on this question. Carruthers, like several other readers, notes the ambivalence of the term itself during the period of *The Canterbury Tales* (see further in note to line 1793). Brewer remarks without elaboration that Friar John's glosing "causes us to remember Chaucer's own contemptuous attitude to 'glosing'" (1984c:212). Besserman (1984:66) points out that while the idea that the letter kills and the spirit gives life was "unchallenged orthodoxy" in Chaucer's lifetime, at least for Wycliffites "this first premise of exegesis was no guarantee of true piety. . . . As one Wycliffite document puts it: 'These be the arms of Antichrist's disciples against true men: *And the letter slayeth'*." Besserman adds that not only does Friar John in *The Summoner's Tale* clearly pervert glossing in the service of personal gain, but the Parson also takes a stand (*ParsP* 31–36) against glossing. Glossing had such a bad name in Chaucer's lifetime, argues Besserman, that it is not frivolous to question Chaucer's respect for it. The Parson's use of Scripture is "faultless" while Alice of Bath's literalist distortions obviously abuse Scripture. But while most of these distortions "are easily corrected by putting the verses or fragments of verses she quotes back into their context, . . . the friar's false *glosynges* are not so easily exposed," and suggest a serious concern for "abuses of biblical authority" (p. 69).

Cooper (1983:132) and Alford (1984) observe that *The Wife of Bath's Tale* and *The Summoner's Tale* are joined by an interest in text and glossing (e.g., D 1–2 and 346–47). Alford notes in particular Friar John's cavalier regard for the literal, and the way in which both fart as text (unglossable) and the concluding episode represent the revenge of the letter. Once John has told the company the nature of the insult, including the requirement that the gift be equally divided, "immediately everyone puts his mind to thinking how to divide the gift and thus help the Friar to keep his promise. This, of course, is not what the Friar meant at all" (p. 201).

Hanning (1985) explores a kind of "language game," textual harassment, in *The Wife of Bath's Tale* and *The Summoner's Tale*, arguing that in both tales people are depersonalized, treated as texts, in order to be undercut. The Wife and Friar John, "two consummate text-torturers," are reduced to the status of texts, "and thus 'glossed' into submission or disrepute" (p. 5). John invites this depersonalization in describing his order (lines 1920–23) as a "living gloss" upon the Sermon of the Mount. The mock-Pentecostal solution of the problem in division "turns against the scoundrelly friar his own weapon, the self-serving biblical gloss" (pp. 12–13), and Jankyn's linking of friars and farts (lines 2281–84) reminds us of the *Prologue*.

Focusing on medieval ideas about language, Holley (1980) explores what she sees as a gap between words and intentions in *The Summoner's Tale*. Whereas in medieval thought the Incarnation demonstrated the perfect fit of word and meaning, the Summoner describes a friar "who, not allegorically this time but literally, attempts to make word flesh for his own profit—and fails" (p. 41).

Boucher (1986) takes up the theme of language to contrast the strategies and expectations of Chaucer and Boccaccio—late medieval, "post-nominalist" writers—with those of Dante, for whom it was still possible to see poetry as a gloss upon the Word of God, and the poet as prophet. Such confidence had undergone extensive erosion by the fourteenth century, and both Boccaccio and Chaucer see language as ambiguous. Boccaccio's tale of Frate Cipolla, like *The Summoner's Tale*, depicts a world in which language has escaped the restraints of dogma to create artificial, fictional, often parodic versions of official thought and images, which versions are "not exactly blasphemy" (p. 215). While critics have not attempted to make of Boccaccio a fourteenth-century Dante, Boucher argues, exegetically oriented critics have sought to paint Chaucer as a poet-theologian. But the puns, glossing, and general thematizing of the problematics of language, including the "quintessential empty signifier of the fart," suggest a more playful intention, a desire to "exploit the gap between reverence and blasphemy" (p. 219).

Considering the matter in terms of authority versus experience, Cooper (1989:181) writes: "Thomas's gift refutes the claims of verbal authority as decisively as Samuel Johnson's kicking of a stone refuted Berkeley. The whole medieval cosmos of the Word—text, gloss, narrative, moral, authority, and the rest—are reduced to the semantics-free broken air of Thomas's gift." Knapp (1990:58) observes that several words in the tale, including "groping" (of consciences and clefts) and "fundament" (foundation or anus) are "brought into raucous verbal contention" and occupy a "dialogically agitated" atmosphere such as Bakhtin describes.

A relatively recent development in writing on *The Summoner's Prologue and Tale* is an attentiveness to social issues that the tale might be said to raise. Havely (1975:22–23) notes a broadening of the issues as the story concludes: "by the end of the *tale* . . . the friar has not only been paid out by someone of a class that he usually exploited, but he has also been ridiculed by members of a class that he had been accustomed to depend upon. This widening of the social setting in the final scene gives additional force to the conclusion of the summoner's attack on friars, and could also amount to an encouragement—an appeal even—to the educated people and the 'gentles' among Chaucer's pilgrims and in his audience to join in the laugh against them." Also focusing on the end of the tale, Lawlor (1980:74) feels that "the Summoner's lord and lady express a harmony in their town which the friar has disrupted"; he asserts that "the end of the Knight's Tale and the end of the Summoner's Tale are the two major un-ironic expressions, outside of the Parson's Prologue and Tale, of community and harmony in the poem."

Aers (1986*a*) too sees the text as addressing social concerns. He takes in earnest the friar's statement that "an odious meschief" (line 2190) has been done to himself and the church: "What many scholarly teachers and readers of Chaucer tend to overlook is that the 'odious meschief' which subverts the self-images and authority of 'hooly chirch' is Chaucer's art itself" (p. 45). *The Summoner's Tale* calls attention, Aers argues, to the material basis of orthodoxy, including the penitential and purgatorial doctrine (pp. 38–39). As for the issue of glosing, "the poet sets the crucial issue of interpretation within a context where the power and self-interest of the clerical corporation is foregrounded as a basic determinant. . . . [The] poet makes explicit the material dimensions and consequences of an official spiritual practice. He discloses that the version of charity taught from the clerical pulpit, with the clerical apparatus of 'glosynge,' serves the material self-interest of clerical glozers and the corporation which employs them" (pp. 39–40). In another essay from the same year, Aers urges again an attentiveness to Chaucer's depiction of "social and institutional contexts" which generated theories of allegory; Chaucer demonstrates, he suggests further, that the friar's exegetical activities serve his and his fellow churchmen's material interests (1986*b*:61–62).

In another Marxist reading, Knight (1986) insists that *The Summoner's Tale*, like *The Friar's Tale*, is "a starting point for a powerful analysis of socio-economic reality and change . . ." (pp. 108–09). The friar of the tale is cash-oriented, as his "litany of coinage" at lines 1963–65 suggests. At the end, as the feudal lord enjoys the wit of his churl and the proposal of his squire to employ the "non-financial device of a cartwheel," the "world of collective feudal relations and rural objects closes in around the cash-based friar who has developed into an ogre of the exchange economy" (p. 107). (Cf. Wetherbee [1989:66]: "the several ranks of society [act] in concert to repudiate friarly pretension.") Patterson (1987:488) believes that the lord has a rather different view of his churl's cleverness: "Taken aback by signs of mental power in a creature thought to lack the capacity, the lord is intrigued but finally retreats into typical defamations: the churl is either foolish ('nyce') or crazy ('a demonyak')."

O'Brien (1990:20) diverges from Knight's reading in yet another way: he argues that "Chaucer *identifies* the individualistic ogres of the exchange economy, the friar and the summoner, with the manorial figures, the lord and his squire," and "rather than conservatively and protectively activating 'the old world social force' against the friar, Chaucer exposes that force as having departed from the moral vision, with its discourse of measurement and description." Wallace (1990:233), on the other hand, supports Knight's view; he regards the friar's importunings as a "direct attack on the structure of feudal society," and he finds that that society "succeeds in expelling the outsider who threatens its own internal equilibrium." On the subject of class antagonism, Lindahl (1987:147) notes that "Chaucer's most successful practitioners of class warfare, the Miller and Summoner, both use that ultimate expression of man's animal nature to dispel the feigned gentility of would-be nobles."

Yet another strain of commentary finds witchcraft in *The Summoner's Prologue and Tale*. Baker (1961) argues that *The Friar's Tale* and *The Summoner's Tale* are linked through the "Summoner's allusions to the tradition associating friars in general with sorcery and witchcraft" (p. 33). Though most evidence linking friars and witchcraft post-dates Chaucer, Baker argues that "there existed in the popular imagination as early as the Fourteenth Century the traditional association of friars with the dark arts" (p. 34); moreover, the place assigned to friars in hell and Thomas's fart are comic allusions to the *osculum infame* or *osculum in ano* associated with witchcraft (p. 35). Another critic to find the demonic at work in *The Summoner's Tale* is Haskell (1971), who argues that the invocation of "Saint Simon" in line 2094 can only refer to Simon Magus, associated in medieval legend with the anti-Christ and witchcraft. Friars were "not infrequently used as medieval symbols for the devil" (p. 220), the devil is mentioned several times in *The Summoner's Prologue and Tale*, and it is set in March, influenced by Mars, "the planet of wrath and of the devil" (p. 221). Seizing upon the mention of the cat in line 1775, Rowland (1971) argues for a demonic reading of *The Summoner's Tale*: ". . . the cat was generally recognized as a demonic animal" (p. 71), and "by taking the cat's place [on the bench], the Friar . . . may suggest that he is a substitute for the demonic powers with which the cat, by long tradition, is invested" (p. 73). She adds that the number of friars in a *covent* was the same as the number of witches in a coven. Furthermore, "the Devil is said to flee in dismay from human flatulence" (p. 72), and in farting Thomas may be seeking to rid himself of the Devil in the form of the friar or perhaps to expel the cause of his own demonic disorder (pp. 72–73). Jungman (1980) notes that Chaucer uses the word *covent* eleven times in *The Summoner's Tale*, and argues that the word refers "not just to the friar's 'convent' but also to a witches' 'coven'" (pp. 20–21). While admitting that the historical, lexical, and textual evidence is very thin, he uses Baker's arguments (1961) and concludes that Jankyn's reference to the thirteen-membered *covent* in lines 2255–61 shows that "a friar is really a witch" (p. 22). Using references to "scatological exorcism" in classical and renaissance texts, the "idea that the breaking of wind was efficacious against evil influences, mortal or spiritual," Wentersdorf (1980:251) argues that Thomas's fart "underscores the teller's intention that his fictional friar be regarded as an embodiment of the devil, to be exorcized in whatever manner is available" (p. 253). He makes the same argument in passing in his study of *figurae scatologicae* found in Gothic manuscripts (Wentersdorf 1984:9).

In a curious essay exploring the metaphysical and eschatalogical issues of flatulence in Chaucer's writings, Bowen (1959) suggests that the flatulator is the natural man, and that the flatulatee is the fop. *The Summoner's Tale* brings quantum theory to mind in its description of Thomas's taut belly, wherein the "laying up of a quantum" precedes "a single, though possibly extended, articulation" (p. 20). It may be, he argues, that the "current distaste for flatus and flatus discussion has contributed to the current lack of popular interest in Chaucer" (p. 22).

In an article seeking to account for the structure of *The Canterbury Tales* in terms of zodiacal signs, Rutledge (1973) assigns *The Summoner's Prologue and Tale* to Capricorn, dominated by Saturn, associated with death and destruction. *The Summoner's Prologue and Tale* "abounds with strange images of death" (p. 133); Saturn is also associated with ill will, of which *The Summoner's Prologue and Tale* provides "myriad examples" (p. 134); Saturn's subjects enjoy drinking, and "there are a series of intoxicated individuals" in *The Summoner's Tale*; finally, Capricorn's symbol is the goat, and the story includes three mentions of cheese, "a product that might have been made with goat's milk" (p. 135).

Benson (1980) explores the role of gesture in *The Summoner's Tale*, writing that "the static, expository quality of the tale calls attention to the stage business, the methods Chaucer employs to get his characters placed in a particular sequence," adding that "almost all of the action and stage business in the tale bear the significance of gesture" (p. 71). Gallacher (1986) argues that the tension between medieval ascetic and medical views of disease is dramatized in *The Summoner's Tale*. While physicians would prescribe Galen's advice, a moderate diet and emotional calm, the friar, a spokesman for the "ascetic" position, recommends to Thomas fasting and sorrow for his sins. The Summoner, depicting the churchman as hypocrite, clearly sides with the physicians, but his own physical and moral maladies suggest that he would profit from less food and more attentiveness to his sins. Kendrick (1988:68) offers an Oedipal reading of the tale that takes the friar as "father" and "master," and Thomas as his spiritual son: "Thomas's fart is a symbolic castration of the friar, a deflation of his masculine pride, and that is how the friar takes it."

Andreas (1990) offers a Bakhtinian reading. The genre of grotesque or carnivalesque, he writes, provides a category within which all the diverse elements of *The Summoner's Tale* can be fully appreciated: its demystified, comic perspective on hell and damnation, the hypocritical *sermon joyeux* of the friar, the gross parodies of apostolic motifs from the New Testament and of sacred Christian ceremonies such as Pentecost and Whitsunday, the lambasting of the new scholastic and scientific learning, the pervasive anal character of the tale and its teller, and finally, the comic scapegoating of a figure of clerical authority" (p. 139). Carnivalesque texts re-enact sacred time and space, but in collapsed, deflated and domesticated forms "rehabitable and manageable by common folk" (p. 141), and it is appropriate that the two main scenes of the tale are played domestically, in Thomas's room and at the lord's table.

Holley (1990:100) studies Chaucer's construction of narrative boundaries and the measurable, concluding that "the space of the tale contains edges and entrances that lead to the center, where we see geometric demonstration for measuring force in organized space—the space beneath the devil's tail, the space of Thomas's bed, and finally the organized space of wheel and spokes." O'Brien (1990:13) finds numerous references to scientific questions of Chaucer's day, especially questions of scientific procedure, demonstration, and proof, and disputes over the relative value of authority (often represented by Augustine) versus experience (represented by Aristotelian practices). Questions of "division," parodied in the concluding episode, were highly disputed in Chaucer's day at Oxford, with Mertonians like Bradwardine arguing with Aristotle that *continua* "were composed only of divisibles" while others argued the opposite. See further in note to line 2231.

The Summoner's Prologue and Tale *and Anti-fraternalism.* As mentioned above in "Sources and Analogues," it is clear that Chaucer drew heavily from anti-fraternal writings in the construction of *The Summoner's Prologue and Tale.* Williams (1953) is the first to bring the evidence together and to assess its implications. While the harshness of Chaucer's criticism of friars in *The Summoner's Prologue and Tale* and in *The General Prologue* had previously been attributed either to the general degradation of the four orders by the late fourteenth century or to Chaucer's observations of particular "unlovely" friars, Williams argues that "what Chaucer did . . . was merely to give artistic form to the most important of the charges against the friars" (p. 513) made by writers from William of Saint Amour in his *De periculis novissimorum temporum* through Jean de Meun in *RR* to Richard FitzRalph, chancellor of Oxford, archbishop of Armagh and primate of Ireland, and Wyclif just before and in Chaucer's day. The friars' aspirations to evangelical poverty, their interest in preaching and hearing confessions, and their interest and activities in learning were the three qualities most often criticized in the attacks of their enemies, as Williams shows.

The controversies began early in the second half of the thirteenth century, with the division of the Franciscans themselves over whether to follow Francis's rule of poverty fully and literally—the position of the Spirituals—or to compromise with the world to the extent of, for example, allowing gifts to the order with the understanding that all such property belonged to the Church, which held it for their use—the position of the Conventuals—an argument adumbrated in the decretal *Exiit qui seminat* of Nicholas III in 1279. The conflict between the two wings remained quite deep, even after the re-affirmation of

Nicholas's decretal in Clement V's *Exivi de Paradiso* in 1312. John XXII demanded obedience from the Spirituals under threat of excommunication, and burned four intransigents in 1318 as heretics. The internal dispute invited external criticism, and in particular the writings of the Spiritual Franciscans attacking their less strict brothers furnished ammunition to anti-fraternal writers in general (Williams 1953:502, Fleming 1966:691–92).

The second point of controversy, that which provoked the attacks of various secular orders, was the movement that has come to be called Joachism, after Joachim of Fiore (ca. 1132–1202), whose highly influential writings argued that history is tri-partite: first, the Old Testament dispensation under the Law and the Father; second, the age of the New Testament dispensation under the Son, which was to last until about 1260; and third, the age of contemplation, under the Holy Ghost. "This last age would see the rise of new religious orders destined to convert the whole world and to usher in the 'Ecclesia Spiritualis'" (Cross and Livingston 1974:740). Accordingly, a Spiritual Franciscan named Gerard of Borgo San Donnino sought, in 1254, to declare a new Gospel, the "Eternal Evangel," which consisted of excerpts of Joachim's works and which was to replace the Old and New Testaments. The friars, according to the thinking of many Spirituals, would be the leaders of the new age, as befitting their status as imitators of the poverty of Christ and the disciples. These pretensions provoked quite outraged response from a number of quarters, the locus classicus being the *De periculis* of William of St. Amour mentioned above; and the controversy was still on the boil in Chaucer's day, as is demonstrated by the translation from Latin into English of FitzRalph's *Defensio Curatorum* by Chaucer's contemporary, Nicholas Trevisa. Further, as Williams puts it, "the agitation aroused by FitzRalph's sermons had scarcely died down when a new attack on the friars was launched by Wyclif, who took over the principal charges of William of St. Amour and of FitzRalph and added some of his own" (p. 504). Chaucer's satire shows no peculiarly Wycliffite qualities, however, says Williams, and it would be "a mistake to use Wycliffite documents to illustrate Chaucer's friar" (p. 504).

Specific instances of Chaucer's dramatizing the accusations of these anti-fraternal texts are found throughout the Explanatory Notes. Suffice it to say here that Chaucer focuses on those vices (shameless begging, usurpation of parochial duties, pretensions of learning, and hypocrisy) most often attacked in the anti-fraternal tradition. Robertson (1962:249) agrees with Williams on the importance of the anti-fraternal texts to an understanding of *The Summoner's Prologue and Tale*, writing indeed that it is "little more than a compendium of charges which had been leveled at friars ever since the first protests of William of St. Amour, skillfully adapted to the purposes of a narrative."

From the connection of *The Summoner's Prologue and Tale* to this learned tradition Fleming (1966) draws an important implication: "It is too easy to dismiss the poem as merely a *fabliau* or a 'merry tale'—though it is undoubtedly that in part. In fact the *Summoner's Tale* is a work of some intellectual pretensions and achievement, a poem with roots deep in a rich and diverse tradition, echoing the scatology as well as the eschatology of antifraternalism" (p. 700). He argues that Chaucer made considerable use not only of the simply anti-fraternal work of seculars and their sympathizers but also the writings of Franciscan Spiritualists whose works, "praising the zeal of Saint Francis and the first friars, defending the literal integrity of the Rule, and (by implication) condemning the 'revisionism' of the Coventuals, were in wide circulation in the fourteenth century" (p. 691). Much of the humor of *The Summoner's Tale*, Fleming argues, arises from Chaucer's juxtaposition of Friar John against the idealism of the Franciscan Rule, which had itself become "a potent weapon in the hands of the friars' enemies, who used it in polemics against mendicants of all orders" (p. 691); a position reiterated by Olson (1986), who points to such Spiritualist writings as the *Fioretti* or *Little Flowers*, which "emphasize the four features of Franciscan life parodied in the Summoner's Tale" (p. 226). For example, on the friar's glossing and self-serving citation of scripture, Fleming (1966:695) cites the controversies over the glossing of the Franciscan Rule by the Conventuals which led to the dilution of the notion of spiritual poverty. Arguing against any attempt (especially that of Manly 1926*b*) to find an "original" for Friar John, Fleming locates his character in the anti-fraternal tradition, and attributes his convincingness to Chaucer's "genius for clothing traditional iconographic types with a realistic human nature . . ." (p. 690). The friar's appeal for money in aid of building and library preservation may be traced to commonplace criticisms contrasting contemporary fraternalism with Francis's ideals; and even the fart, traditionally understood as "an obscene *fabliau* element in keeping with the coarse nature of the tale's narrator . . . , can be explained quite as convincingly in the light of the ideals of mendicant poverty" by which money in any form was regarded as no better than excrement (p. 698).

Levy (1966) and Levitan (1971) seek to show that Chaucer incorporated a specifically Pentecostal parody into *The Summoner's Tale*, Levitan apparently making the discovery initially. As Levy puts it, *The Summoner's Prologue and Tale* contains "a pattern of biblical parody which informs the whole tale and concentrates the Summoner's attack on. . . . the Friar's claim that friars have a special divine grace that sets them apart from and makes them superior to all other clergymen" (pp. 46–47). The most wild-eyed of such fraternal claims were of course the apocalyptic speculations of Joachimite Franciscans which provoked the initial attack of William of Saint Amour. Williams (1953:501) summarizes: "as the Old Law had been superseded by the New, so the New was now to be superseded by the 'Eternal Gospel.' The friars, particularly the Franciscans, were the forerunners of this third age, as John the Baptist had been of the second." "The point of the heresy for the friars," as Levy (1966:48) puts it, "was that they were the inheritors of the age of the Eternal Gospel, the era of the Holy Ghost, and they therefore claimed special grace in their teachings and practices as specially inspired by the Holy Ghost." The Summoner, eager to attack this particular claim, constructs "a magnificent parody of the theme of the Feast of Pentecost" (p. 52) in Jankyn's cartwheel-based division of the "gift" which the friar in fact receives. The parody is based upon the centrality of circular, wheel-like imagery in medieval depictions of Pentecost. This parodic inversion of the inspiration of the Apostles by the divine wind of the Holy Ghost "has been carefully prepared for, and most of the other central images and puns, which superficially seem only to be casual jokes, lead up to a final image. . . ." (p. 55); *The Summoner's Prologue* joke about the devil's arse, and the pun on "fundement" in line 2103 fit together: the pun reminds us of Satan's "fundement" and antici-pates the final scene, in which the lord of the village assumes Thomas must have been demonically "inspired" to have posed this insolubilium, "and the ultimate suggestion is that the Friar's special gift of inspiration, his gift of wind, does not derive from the Holy Spirit at all, but rather from the original source, the *develes ers*" (p. 56).

Levitan finds specific Joachimite qualities in *The Summoner's Tale*, including John's fantastic claims of spiritual worth and, referring to *Rom* 7165–86 where the followers of Joachim are so styled, the name John itself (pp. 237–38). *The Summoner's Tale* parodies the Pentecostal imagery of Acts 2.1–4 in a variety of ways, including the inversion of the "diverse tongues" given the apostles to spread the Gospel: "Friar John uses *his* 'divers tongues' for purposes of affecta-tion and nasty humour," including the latinate joke on *eructavit* and the several French phrases. The cartwheel imagery is tied to friars first through Dante's *Paradiso* 10–12, which cantos feature friars (Thomas, Francis, Bonaventura) in heavenly glory. At the beginning of canto 12, the wheel image mutates into turning millstones. "The millstones revolve horizontally, while Jankyn's wheel . . . is a kind of static parody of these paradisial 'wheels of friars.' The explicitly sweet music emanating from these turning wheels on which several friars are placed . . . is perhaps parodied in the 'stynk' and 'soun' wending along the twelve spokes of Jankyn's single and motionless wheel" (Levitan 1971:241–42). The wheel is also tied to Pentecostal iconography as found in architecture and manuscript illuminations, several of which Levitan reproduces.

To the foregoing, Szittya (1974) adds that *The Summoner's Tale* is marked by a pattern of biblical allusions which had become "rhetorical commonplaces in the literature (both polemical and fictional) of the [mendicant] controversy," noting that ". . . allusions to the exegetical commonplaces of the controversy establish patterns and expectations which not only heighten the comedy but . . . provide a thematically important principle of unity in the tale" (p. 21). Szittya points to the allusions to Moses and Elijah as suggesting Chaucer's anticipation of the eventual Pentecostal parody, for these Old Testament figures were commonly taken as types of the Pentecostal theophany (pp. 24–27). As for the connection between friars and Pentecost, Szittya argues that Levitan reaches needlessly far in seeing Friar John as a Joachimite, for the General Chapter of the Franciscans was held every third year at Pentecost, as stipulated in the Rules of 1221 and 1223, and there is some evidence that Francis had in mind the Round Table of Arthurian legend as a pattern (he called his friars "my Round Table knights"), while the Pentecostal feast has "symbolic connection with the apostles, whose life [Francis] strove so devoutly to imitate" (pp. 28–29). Indeed, Szittya argues, the series of biblical allusions made by the narrator, the characters, and the friar himself, which associates Friar John with the apostles, is "one of the most significant thematic patterns which unifies the tale . . ." (p. 30). These allusions (along with further commentary in the relevant Explanatory Notes) are in lines 1816–22, 1970–73 (note 1973), 1974–80 (note 1980), 2184–88, and 2195–96 (note 2196). In sum, "Chaucer's establishment of the broad apostolic pattern, when pegged to biblical verses that were centers of controversy in the antifraternal dispute, was designed to call into the mind of the reader those very arguments that were more often advanced against the friars" (p. 45).

Clark argues (1976*b*) that the Pentecostal parodies in *The Summoner's Tale* are perhaps connected with the controversy, contemporaneous with Chaucer's adulthood, over the friars' opposition to an English translation of the Bible. Clark takes as evidence certain "antifraternal tracts which look back to the polyglottism of Pentecost as justification for the translation of the Bible into English" (p. 48). In several of these texts, emphasis falls upon the word *wit*, a term used to suggest linguistic and spiritual power available at Pentecost and available too in the efforts to translate the Bible. Chaucer uses *wit* "in two revealing contexts" in *The Summoner's Tale* (p. 54), viz. at line 1789 in reference to the "symple wit" of Friar John, and at line 2291 in reference to the "heigh wit" of Thomas. Although the tale contains no overt reference to the controversy, the uses of "wit" and the friar's "blatant manipulation of sacred text" (p. 56) suggest that the issue was on Chaucer's mind. Besserman (1984) similarly feels Chaucer was "engaged by the issues" debated by the two camps. While *The Summoner's Tale* makes clear his opposition to a fraternal monopoly on biblical interpretation, the ideas of the Wife of Bath may on the other hand also suggest a Chaucerian skepticism about lay ownership of translated Bibles (pp. 69–70).

Havely (1983) examines the question of motives in Chaucer's anti-clericalism by comparing his and Boccaccio's treatment of friars. Though noting (p. 255) that *The Summoner's Prologue*—with its "friar making a visionary pilgrimage through hell," and with its "bizarre form of the *contrapasso*"—might be viewed as an allusion to the *Inferno*, he feels neither Chaucer's nor Boccaccio's friars are importantly indebted to Dante. Rather, both are heavily indebted, as others have argued, to the antifraternalism flowing from William of St. Amour through French vernacular poets, especially Jean de Meun and Rutebeuf. As for real friars and Chaucer's possible attitudes towards them, we have far less specific information about Chaucer's contact with contemporary friars than Boccaccio's. The Dominicans were privileged within the English royal households of Chaucer's day, holding the post of confessor to the king from Henry III to Richard II (p. 256). Noting that Richard paid 40 shillings for a sermon preached by a Dominican at Christmas 1395 and offered a convent a noble of gold with frankincense and myrrh at the feast of the Epiphany, Havely remarks that "the poet's account of his own poverty in the final stanza of the *Complaint to his Purse* may perhaps gain further ironic poignancy, especially when he ruefully explains that: 'I am shave as nye as any frere'" (p. 256). The Carmelites were patronized by John of Gaunt, and "both he and the first two kings of the House of Lancaster employed them as confessors" (p. 257); they were also highly successful and active preachers. "Some, indeed, gained bishoprics as a direct result of their prowess in this field, and it is perhaps not without relevance . . . that Friar John, whose sermons in *The Summoner's Tale* seek more obviously material rewards, should associate himself at one point [ll. 2115–17] with the Carmelite Order" (p. 257). The Austin friars were perhaps most important as a link with Italy, Italian Austin friars coming to study at Oxford.

Chaucer was of course not alone among English poets in criticizing the friars. Havely notes that *Peres the Ploughman's Crede, Wynnere and Wastoure, Piers Plowman*, and Gower in the *Mirour de l'Omme* all attack the friars' building campaigns, as Chaucer does in Friar John's appeal to Thomas. For both Boccaccio and Chaucer, however, the chief interest appears to have been the commerce in words between laymen and friars. Boccaccio seems particularly intent to parody the educational mission of the friars—the parody based on a genuine lay appetite for sermons and devotional materials, especially among the friars' "third orders." Chaucer seems similarly engaged in *The Summoner's Tale* as he shows a friar proud of his learning successively outwitted by Thomas, teased in learned or mock-learned terms by the lord, and "utterly befooled" by squire Jankyn (p. 263). In fact the form of *The Summoner's Prologue and Tale* itself might represent a judgement upon the friar who seeks to gain through his *exempla*: "The pilgrim-Friar has attempted to discredit the Summoner by means of a neatly devised 'game', which he retrospectively seeks to incorporate as an *exemplum* within a piously homiletic design. With typically violent contempt for such tactics, however, the Summoner in effect turns the Friar's whole procedure inside out and traps the mendicant sermon, *exempla* and all, within the framework of his (and Chaucer's) 'game'" (p. 264). Both Chaucer and Boccaccio may have regarded the friars as competitors, "rivals for the ear of the educated laity" (p. 264), and Chaucer and Langland may have felt the parallelism between "frere faytour" and other purveyors of fables, including—potentially—themselves, condemned by the Parson (*ParsP* 31–34), who quotes Paul to Timothy so as to connect fabulists with Paul's false teachers, an image important in anti-mendicant satire.

Hanning (1986:14), who agrees with Fleming that *The Summoner's Prologue* is a parody of the Maria Misericordia, adds that the Summoner's imagery there depicts friars as the devil's fart; and, reminding us that the entrance to hell in drama and illustration was a gaping mouth, he argues that "the devil's fart must be understood as a cosmic inversion and perversion of the *Verbum Dei*." Wetherbee (1989:65–66) suggests that by reducing spirituality to belching and flatulence, each "a by-product of overindulgence," and by associating such wind with the friar's own preaching, the tale dismisses "the excesses of the fraternal orders . . . as bearing no functional relation to the life of the body of the Church."

Authorial Intention, Serious or Comic. From early on, many critics have suggested that *The Summoner's Prologue and Tale* raises serious issues, includes earnest in its game; certainly the discoveries of the allusions to learned controversies show that it is a text upon which Chaucer lavished a good deal of energy. But whether his purposes were primarily comic or primarily serious, and if serious then about which issues, continues to be debated.

The nature of the tale's comedy is articulated very differently by Ruggiers (1965, 1976) and Pearsall (1985, 1986). Ruggiers includes this tale among Chaucer's darker comedies, those in which "the comic retreats from light-heartedness before the weight of truly serious considerations" (1976:200). He argues also that Chaucer's ironic tales divide rather sharply into those he calls "Plautine," in which "the subject matter is the outwitting of convention and propriety by instinct and craft," and whose plots "advance the triumph of youthful folly . . . over the normative forces in the world" (Ruggiers 1965:144), and those like *The Summoner's Prologue and Tale* that he calls "Aristophanic." These—for example the tales of the Canon's Yeoman, the Friar, the Pardoner, and the Summoner—"are studies in vice deliberate, rampant, self-conscious" (p. 145). These tales are "unmaskings," and "describe ugly actions in the process of raising questions about the kind of society that allows them" (1976:196).

Pearsall (1985:170), makes a different assessment: *The Friar's Tale* and *The Summoner's Tale* "are satirical only from the point of view of their deliverers and not according to any normative values expressed through the narrative. . . . Both tales . . . pay conventional tribute to the victim's wickedness, but reserve their main ammunition for his stupidity. They are not morally normative satirical tales, except through the ironic reconstructions we may choose to place on them, but tales told within the framework of the assumptions common to all these comic tales, namely that the important thing is survival and the preservation of the maximum range of opportunities for the satisfaction of appetite."

Further, Pearsall feels that Chaucer created the Summoner and the feud with the Friar precisely to be free to write "unconstrained by the tyrannies of moral satire" (p. 224). In 1986 Pearsall reiterates his views, holding that the satire of *The Summoner's Prologue and Tale* and *The Friar's Tale* is "made part of a mutual exchange of abuse and thereby pushed away from any authoritative moral centre. The wickedness of summoners and friars remains the theme of the two tales, respectively, but not their *point*" (p. 127); he argues further that "moral outrage at what they describe each other as doing is a proper preliminary response, but it is swallowed up in laughter, since what the narrators try to do is to prove not that their victims are knaves but that they are fools" (p. 139). Again, Pearsall feels that the conclusion of the tale overwhelms moral notions, and that Chaucer ". . . seems to prefer complicity with the world of his creatures to moral criticism" (p. 141).

Historically, more critics seem to have been inclined to view the tale as at least partially serious in intent. As early as 1906, Root praises the humor of *The Summoner's Tale*, but finds serious implications as well: a comparison of the antics of Friar John to the ideals of St. Francis and St. Dominic leads him to see in the tale "more of tragedy than of comedy" (p. 252). Fleming (1967:95) argues of *The Summoner's Prologue* that "Chaucer's burlesque humor should not disguise the seriousness and urgency" that mark both *The Summoner's Prologue and Tale* and *The Friar's Tale*. Indeed, the question of which pilgrim, friar or summoner, tells the better or more devastating tale (see "Relationship to *The Friar's Tale*," above) is for Fleming ultimately trivial "in light of the moral urgency which the poems generate. . . . We have in these two tales an agonizing *tableau* of the profound spiritual crisis of late medieval Christendom, an episode in the sickness unto death of the old world: two very 'mery' tales indeed!" (p. 106). While attributing the nastiness of *The Summoner's Prologue and Tale*, especially the *Prologue*, to the character of the Summoner himself, Whittock (1968:138) feels that "the Summoner's personal malice against the Friar becomes submerged in the popular hostility. . ." (p. 136), and further that "behind the social satire, there is more than a hint of another dimension, of truly eschatological things. A firm sense of an ordained moral order is partially embodied in the poem, and gives greater weight to the social criticism" (p. 138).

In an article which addresses directly the issue of Chaucer's earnestness in *The Summoner's Prologue and Tale*, Fleming (1983) reiterates his position that the tale is as serious as it is satirical, "that, indeed, Chaucer uses anticlerical polemic as a means of advancing a deep religious argument grounded in conservative belief" (p. 5). Offering more evidence of the debt of *The Summoner's Prologue and Tale* to the materials of the mendicant-secular controversies of the thirteenth and fourteenth centuries, Fleming once more criticizes "dramatic" readings, which seek to explain the tale in terms of the Friar-Summoner antagonism, and readings that take the tale as historically realistic: "this friar is 'typical' only if viewed as a caricature of the stage and not as a type from the street. . . . [He is] a purpose-ful and schematic literary caricature. Fr. John is a perfect pseudoapostle" (p. 8). Fleming is not satisfied by the assessment of those who focus on the humor of *The Summoner's Prologue and Tale*, who offer "demonstration of cleverly arranged ironies and verbal schema"; such readings, he feels, make it "curiously difficult to locate the center of the tale" and render "the shape of the narrative . . . unsatisfyingly anecdotal" (p. 11). Whereas comic readings do not take into account the sheer bulk of the friar's sermon to Thomas, Fleming takes this scene to be a tableau, a "picture" of the exhortation to penance, "a grotesque picture, of course, but [one that] fits fluently into the tale's iconographic schedule, where it occupies a central place" (p. 11). Indeed, though it is often called a digression, the sermon, in terms of the friar's ostensible reason for visiting, is "the first episode in the poem which is really to the point . . . ; as he begins to preach repentance, [John] comes to the center of the tale and to the heart of fraternal idealism" (p. 14).

Fleming makes a similar point in 1984, arguing that Chaucer was in fact familiar at first hand (not just through such intermediaries as the *Romance of the Rose*) with William of St. Amour's *De periculis novissimorum temporum*, and that *The Summoner's Tale* has "as its very foundation . . . the specialized tradition of scriptural exegesis associated with the ascetical texts of the mendicant contro-versy . . ." (p. 185). In sharp contrast with Mehl (1973; 1986:187–88) who, as noted earlier, sees in *The Summoner's Tale* a "wealth of theological thought and religious didacticism" but finds it to need "very little explanation," Fleming argues that "one can no more understand the strategies of *The Summoner's Tale* without reading the *De periculis* than one can understand the Wife of Bath without reading Jerome against Jovinian" (pp. 185–86).

Focussing on the image of the dead son, Allen (1987) also argues for "serious-ness beyond the buffoonery" in *The Summoner's Tale*. John does nothing to help Thomas and his wife cope with the death of their child. He offers the mother a sentimentalized fiction, and in speaking to Thomas, "unwittingly recalls the boy's death" (p. 6) as he inadvertently uses the word "sonne" in line 2113. In his stale and hackneyed response to the family's grief, John reveals another spiritual and fraternal failure.

TEXTUAL COMMENTARY

The Textual Tradition of The Summoner's Prologue and Tale

The affiliations of the manuscripts for *The Summoner's Prologue and Tale* (*SumPT*) are described in MR 2.227–42. In general the results of the work done for the present edition corroborate MR's description, though some clarification of their analysis can be offered. The groupings of the manuscripts are complex and shifting, but the essential facts, subject to qualification, are these:

1. Hg and El through line 1991 form a group with Bo² and *Bo¹*; after that point El splits off.
2. Ha⁴ is effectively independent, though perhaps going back ultimately to an *a–b** manuscript.
3. *a* and *b* form another group.
4. *cd* begins *SumPT* as a group and then splits into *cd*²* and *d*¹* after line 1734.

Two particularly interesting features may be noted: first, the apparent sharing of an exemplar by Hg and El from line 1665 to about line 1991 and the subsequent shift in affiliation of El after that point; and second, the splitting of group *cd** into two, *d*¹* (represented among the base-group manuscripts by Pw) and *cd*²* (represented by Cp and La). As MR put it, "the details are so complicated that they can best be set forth in connection with the study of each group" (2.227).

In fact, though the details are complicated enough, the MR presentation in volume 2 is more confusing than it needs to be, and it would be well to keep the central issues in mind while working through some details. MR state the case accurately, if not clearly: "The groupings of the MSS are fairly stable in the body of the tale (1735–2158), although there is much mixture and incomplete grouping caused in large part by [contamination] and editing. Before 1735 and after 2158 marked changes in the grouping are clearly recognizable" (2.227). *SumP* occupies lines 1665–1708, and *SumT* itself lines 1709–2294. *SumP* and *SumT* do not have separate textual histories; the points of shifting alliances noted by MR and confirmed by my collations do not coincide with the seam between *SumP* and *SumT*. What might be thought of as "the concluding episode," however, lines 2159–2294, the visit of the friar to the lord of the manor and the solution to the problem of the division of the fart, is not found in a number of manuscripts (including Pw), and the shifting at this point could be considered as coinciding with a narrative seam in the tale. It is remotely possible that the *d*¹* ancestor never contained the "final episode" and might represent an early version of *SumT*, but, as will be seen, this is unlikely.

To begin with the most important manuscripts, in *The Friar's Prologue and Tale* El and Hg join together for the first time, and this conjunction continues into *SumP* and through about line 1991 of *SumT*. As MR put it,"through 1991, . . . aside from the editorial efforts in El, Hg and El are not very different in quality; from 1991 the difference is enormous" (2.239). The divergence of the two manuscripts can be seen quite clearly in this fact: 21 of the 101 variants of El from the text of this edition occur in lines 1665–1988, while 77 variants occur in lines 1994–2294. That is, three-quarters of the El variants occur in the second half of the text. The Hg–El relationship will be explored below, in the description of Hg; and the nature of the post-1991 affiliations of El will be examined in the description of El.

The splitting of *cd** into *d**[1] (En[2] Fi–Nl Ha[2]–Sl[1] Pw–Ph[3] Ra[2] and the related Hk–*En*[3]–*Ry*[2]) and *cd**[2] (*c*–Bw–Ld[1]–Mm–Se Ad[2]–Ht–*Lc*–*Mc*) is a more complex phenomenon. It might in fact be more accurate to speak of a shattering of than a split in the *cd** group in *SumPT*, and the usefulness and meaningfulness of the MR groups *d**[1] and *cd**[2] becomes increasingly questionable as one sifts the evidence. In outline form, MR hold that

    I.   *cd**[2] and *d**[1] are together through line 1734 but apart beginning about line 1743.

    II. *d**[1] and *cd**[2] continue as two separate groups through line 2158.

    III. At line 2158 several members of *d**[1] break off: "The most striking fact about the *d**[1] group is that it is held together primarily by the absence of 2159–2294 in their ancestor. The lines are still missing in Fi Pw–Ph[3] Ra[2] Sl[1] Hk–*Ry*[2]" (MR 2.228–29).

My collation strongly supports the first of these claims: Cp La and Pw agree in 21 variant readings in lines 1665–1734, while in the same stretch of text Cp and La agree without Pw only twice (at lines 1671 and 1686; further, in line 1671 Pw corrected to read as Cp and La). Soon after this point the strong link among the three breaks down: Cp and La continue together, in 133 agreements without Pw in lines 1754–2153 (Pw ends after line 2158), while Cp, La, and Pw agree 30 times, mostly by obvious convergent variation in readings shared with other unrelated manuscripts.

My work can provide no evidence for or against the continuation of *d**[1] as a separate group in *SumT* after line 1743 for the simple reason that only Pw among the base-group manuscripts is a member of *d**[1]. The evidence for the continuation of *cd**[2], represented by Cp and La, is strong: they continue in 186 shared variants after line 1743, showing more coherence as a pair than any other pair of base-group texts save He and CX[1].

Pw does indeed break off after line 2158, at which point some of the other members of *d**[1] pick up the remainder of *SumT*, according to MR (2.228–29), but as none of them are base-group manuscripts the reader interested in that subject is directed to the MR account. The MR claim that "it is, then, impossible to doubt that [the common ancestor of] *d**[1] was without D 2159–2294, the final episode of the tale" (2.229) seems reasonable. They present two possible explanations: "either [the common ancestor of] *d**[1] had lost two folios (136 lines) or *d**[1] represents an earlier and unfinished form of SuT." For two folios to amount to 136 lines, they would obviously be written 34 lines to the folio side. But as we will see, 34's will not add up correctly for the loss presumed at the beginning of *SumP*.

A few pages later (2.242), MR attack the problem again, with slightly different ideas: "the puzzle of the split of the usual *cd** group of MSS and the indubitable facts that the two parts are textually together for one leaf at the beginning of the tale and that [the common ancestor of] $d*^1$ lacked two leaves at the end cannot be solved by purely textual evidence." In truth, they do not believe it indubitable that the $d*^1$ ancestor lacked two leaves at the end. As they say themselves, "on the one hand, the last episode of the tale may have been lacking originally in the MS; on the other hand, it may have been lost. If [the common ancestor of] $d*^1$ were a MS of 70 lines to a leaf, SuT would occupy a quire of nine leaves, and the loss of the outside sheet and the extra leaf would necessitate supplying the text of the first leaf and supplying or suppressing the final episode" (2.242). The numbers in this analysis work better than the first, though there is still a slight problem. If the question is to be resolved in terms of mechanical loss, one must face the fact that no regular number of lines per folio will yield the correct number of lines to account perfectly for the Pw text, as the contradictory suggestions of MR show. If *SumPT* in $d*^1$ was made up of 70 lines per leaf, it would indeed require nine leaves to accommodate its 630 lines. The loss of an outer sheet and one singleton at the end would remove lines 1665–1734 from *SumP*, which fits perfectly with the textual evidence of Cp, La, and Pw. But at the end, the text would break off at line 2154, which can hardly have been true, for Pw and the other defective manuscripts break off after line 2158 (and then add 4 spurious lines), and if the lines 2155–58 had been picked up from a complete exemplar then why not the rest of *SumT*? On the other hand, if the text were ruled in 36's, *SumP* would break off at line 1736, which still fits what we know of the shift in affiliations at that point, and *SumT* would break off at line 2168, after the Pw breakoff point at line 2158. The scribe would see that his exemplar was defective and, presumably unable to eek out the text from another source, back up looking for a convenient breakoff point, with which he was luckily provided in line 2158; there is no other point between lines 2158 and 2169 where the story could be stopped except after line 2159, which would awkwardly break a couplet. Such an explanation remains tentative, of course, all the more so because it presumes that the $d*^1$ ancestor began *SumP* at the first line of the first leaf and ended *SumT* at the last line of the last leaf, which may not have been the case. Granted that assumption, however, the hypothesis does fit the facts.

MR twice (2.229, 2.242) refer the reader to their chapter "Early and Revised Versions" (2.495–519) for evidence in favor of the view that the $d*^1$ *SumT* represents an early authorial version of the text. The promise implied in these references was unfortunately not kept; nothing is said of the subject in that chapter save the bare notice that Fi (among other $d*^1$ manuscripts) lacks the lines in question. Furnivall (1868:24) thinks the $d*^1$ version represents an early draft of *SumT*, but Brusendorff (1925:134 n. 1), for reasons he does not explain, considers this idea "of course impossible," and argues rather that this is the only section of *The Canterbury Tales* "which seems ever to have been suppressed out of consideration for the Church," a matter of omitting "the most offensive part about the Friar." He considers that the omission could not have been accidental, because the last of the spurious lines ("ffor we were almost at þe toun" in the Pw version) is a corruption of line 2294. As the preceding paragraphs suggest, it is not necessary to believe that the Pw version of *SumT* represents an earlier draft or a censored version, though as MR say, the issue cannot be settled on purely textual evidence. The four lines after line 2158 that Pw shares with the other manuscripts which break off short can with absolute confidence be rejected as spurious, and *SumT* without those four lines lacks any kind of closure; so if the Pw text represents a stage in the development of *SumT*, it would have to be thought of as a draft, not a version, for Chaucer could not have allowed it to circulate without some conclusion, however perfunctory, beyond "And forth he gooth with a ful angry cheere." If the manuscript evidence does not settle the issue, it does at least provide a reasonable explanation of the Pw (d^{*1}) text as it stands. Kane (1984:226) saw the early version theory as a justification by MR of their system of classifying manuscripts, but it seems likely, given the number of casual references at widely scattered points and the self-contradictions (see, for example, MR's note to line 1993 [3.467], which includes the wholly gratuitous comment, "When Chaucer added the final episode [lines 2159–2294], he may have failed to note the change made by the scribe") that the provisional statements about the revision theories were simply never adequately revised.

MR conclude that the *a*, *b*, *cd*^{*2} groups are related in *SumPT* as follows: *a* and *b** are said to be affiliated after line 1734 (MR 2.236), while *a*–Ln–*b** and *cd*^{*2} "share enough errors to establish the double group" (2.237). Obviously, the second claim can only have been meant in reference to lines 1734–2294.

a and *b** from line 1734: Dd and He share 98 variants in *SumPT*, Dd and CX^1 101, a not inconsiderable number. Many of these no doubt represent coincidence, and MR signal only a fraction of them in their evidence. Of most interest are perhaps those in lines 1820 (but it is an error shared by *c* and others), 1840, 1850, 1949, and 2156, and the transposition of lines 1963–64.

1820   **Cristen]** *om.* Cp Dd He La+ CX^1
1840   **softe]** white Dd He+ CX^1–TR
1850   **wolde nat telle]** nold han told Dd He+ CX^1–TR
1949   **Crist]** god Dd He+ CX^1–PN^2
2156   **this]** swich Dd He+ CX^1–PN^2

The testimony of the base-group manuscripts alone is insufficient for a thorough assessment of the validity of the MR claim for *a*–*b** affiliation, though it does not contradict it. It is important, however, not to give the impression that Dd and He–CX^1 present roughly equivalent texts. In the aggregate the *b* text is atrocious, the *a* (as Dd represents it), quite good indeed.

a, *b*, and *cd*^{*2}: Dd, He, Cp, and La share only 20 variants in *SumPT*, which, numerically at least, casts doubt on the MR claim that "it seems clear that *a*–Ln–*b** and *cd**[2] are together, and that *d**[1] is not with them" (2.237). In fact, one wonders what motivated MR to argue for this "double group," and what "together" means in such a claim. The evidence is not only thin, it is visibly strained. Four of the 5 instances in which my collations agree with the 14 readings MR offer as evidence of this group are uniformly dismissable as accidental convergence:

    1828   on} ouer Cp Dd Ha[4] He La+ CX[1]–WR RB[1] RB[2] RI
    1848   ye be} þat ye be Cp Dd Ha[4] He La+ CX[1]–PN[2] UR–WR
    1946   thee send} s. t. Cp Dd He La+ CX[1]–PN[2] UR
    2148   there and heere} h. a. t. Cp Dd He La Pw+ CX[1]–UR

According to my reading of the variants, these manuscripts are simply not together in the remainder of the cases MR adduce. In defense of the MR argument, our lemmata sometimes differ in ways which obscure the evidence they would offer, and Dd, the base-group *a* manuscript, is "away from the group occasionally, either because it is higher on the line or because it is independently corrected" (2.236), but even with "irregularities disregarded" (2.237), and allowing for the superiority of Dd to the other *a* manuscripts, the evidence is fatally weak, and one wonders that the argument was felt to be worth making.

To summarize the outlines of the textual tradition of *SumPT*, until about line 1991, Hg and El are together and provide excellent text; after line 1991 El's affiliation with *cd* manuscripts lessens its value considerably. There is strong evidence for the following lines of affiliation among the other manuscripts: *c* (Cp and La) throughout, *d**[1] (Pw) with them through line 1734, afterwards away from them and breaking off after line 2158; *a* (Dd) is with *b* (He CX[1]) after line 1734 often enough to suspect remotely shared ancestry. Further notes on affiliation are to be found under the descriptions of individual manuscripts.

Evidence of the Glosses

The glosses to *SumT* offer little evidence about manuscript affiliation except for the relationship between El and Ad[3] in lines 1880, 1882, 1968, 1973, 1989, 2017, and 2243. The extent of the sharing of glosses between those two manuscripts (also Ra[1] and Tc[2]; see MR 3.504) is too great to be accidental, and suggests borrowing from El to Ad[3], either directly, as MR imply (3.504, speaking of *WBT*) or through a non-extant intermediary. The evidence for textual affiliation between El and Ad[3] is found in the Collations and in the Table of Correspondences and is discussed under the description of El below, but suffice it to say here that the evidence of affiliation is remote, and if the Ad[3] scribe had El in his hands it was after he had already copied the text. The glosses and headings are as follows:

1794 Litera occidit et cetera El

1880 Melius est animam saginare quam corpus El Ad[3]

1882 Victum et vestitum hiis contenti sumus El Ad[3]

1884 de oracionibus et Ieiunijs El

1968 Omnis virtus vnita forcior est seipsa dispersa El Ad[3]

1973 Dignus est operarius mercede et cetera El Ad[3]

1989 Noli esse sicut leo in domo tua euertens domesticos tuos opprimens subiectos tibi El Ad[3]

1999 Nota bene Gg

2017 De quodam potestate Iracundo El Ad[3] (*in text*); Of an Irous potestat Gg

2243 The wordes of the lordes Squier and his keruere / for departynge of the fart on twelue El (*in text before line* 2243) Ad[3]

2294 quod Wyttoun Dd

From the point of view of content, the glosses are uninteresting, largely simply restating the text (the exception being the scribal signature in Dd at line 2294), and there is no reason to connect any of them with Chaucer himself.

Order Among The Canterbury Tales

While *SumPT* itself presents no difficulties or testimony on the question of tale order in *The Canterbury Tales* (it is found in "all relatively complete MSS except Dl" [MR 2.227] and linked to *WBT* and *FrT* to form the D Group in all but one of these, Hk), it is nevertheless involved in certain questions about the construction of the Hengwrt manuscript, and thus by extension in the tale order debate. *SumPT* occupies folios 78*v* to 86*v* in Hg. It commences on the lower third of 78*v* and is followed by a blank ruled leaf (folio 87). Group D follows immediately after A, and is followed in turn by *MkPT*, *NPPT*, and *ManPT*. MR's description (1.14, 267) of the second quire of the tale is partly in error, and is corrected by Doyle and Parkes (1979:xxviii), who reason that the blank ruled leaf noted above suggests that sections III, IV, and V of Hg had already been completed by the time the scribe copied section II (Group D), that, in other words, this was the last section to be copied. MR observe (1.268) that the ink of section II, folios 58–87, is a lighter shade than the remainder of the manuscript. Doyle and Parkes (1979:xxvii–xxviii) reason from this fact that this section was written "at a somewhat different time and in one closely consecutive series of sessions. If its exemplar or exemplars, making up the whole of block D, had been available in the course of the copying of section III or IV, the material could have been as well fitted in either before block H or before B[2a], as what is accommodated there; or if it had already been copied separately, one of those sections could have been divided to allow for its insertion. If the original name of the previous narrator in the first line of *ParsT*, at the beginning of section V, subsequently erased and rewritten as 'Maunciple,' were 'Somnour' (rather than 'Frankeleyn,' as surmised by Manly and Rickert 1940:1.276–77), section II, where *SumT* comes last, might have been completed later than V and at first intended to precede it; but after the alteration, whereby sections IV, III, and V are linked in that order, II could be placed only as it is today" (cf. MR 1.273).

Blake, arguing that Hg is not only the earliest extant manuscript but also that the El tale order derives from it (and is therefore like all other orders non-Chaucerian) disagrees with Doyle and Parkes, holding that the Hg editor had all his materials, including block D, from the beginning of work, that the scribe copied block A first, and then block I, and had intended to place D immediately before I (1979:5), but later decided to move D forward because the Wife of Bath is referred to in earlier tales (*MerT*, *ClT*): "He therefore decided to put D before MLPT because that was the only place it could be fitted in before MeT and ClT without considerable rewriting" (1979:14, 1980:8–9). Blake's reasoning has in turn been vigorously disputed by Benson, who holds that the El order is authorial, and writes that "it seems clear that the Hg scribe did get his work in bits and pieces, did not know what the overall plan of *The Canterbury Tales* should be, and did have to decide on his own where some of the tales (those of Block D) should go," but that he "was not faced with the task of creating an order for an unorganized pile of tales and links" (1981:104). As suggestive as the evidence of block D and *SumT* in Hg is, its implications cannot be accurately assessed in this limited context, and the wider argument clearly lies beyond the scope of this volume.

Table of Correspondences

The Table of Correspondences provides the following information about the base-group manuscripts and CX[1]:

1. The number of total variants for each manuscript, i. e., the number of instances in which each manuscript varies substantively from the present edition.
2. The number of variants unique to each manuscript.
3. The number of variants which each manuscript shares only with non-base-group manuscripts.
4. The number of variants which each manuscript shares with each of the other base-group manuscripts.

These figures are somewhat affected by passages missing from some manuscripts: Ad[3], line 1914; Cp, lines 1731, 1873; Gg, lines 1665–1746 (loss of leaves), 1907–12, 2285–94 (loss of leaves); He, lines 1718–89, 2229; La, lines 1731, 1873; Pw, lines 1731, 2159–end; CX[1], line 2229. Where He is Out it is replaced in the collations by Ne, a closely related *b* manuscript, and the figures in the table for He include the variants of Ne where Ne is so used. Similarly, the figure 38 for CX[1] readings shared only with non-base-group manuscripts does not include those readings, 32 in number, in which CX[1] agrees with Ne, whether He is Out or not. The losses of Gg (15 percent) and Pw (22 percent) cannot be made good from another manuscript, and, if one assumes a constant

Table 1. Table of Correspondences

Manuscript	Total no. of Recorded Variants	Unique Variants	Variants Shared Only With Non-Base-Group Manuscripts
Hg	5	0	3
El	101	21	23
Ad[3]	145	26	33
Cp	265	11	22
Dd	168	12	26
Gg	171	51	31
Ha[4]	276	104	58
He	458	65	198
La	380	70	56
Pw	310	35	130
CX[1]	403	1	38

Agreements with Other Base-Group Manuscripts										
	Hg	El	Ad[3]	Cp	Dd	Gg	Ha[4]	He/Ne	La	Pw	CX[1]
---	---	---	---	---	---	---	---	---	---	---	---
Hg	. .	3	2	2	2	0	1	2	1	0	1
El	3	. .	22	22	9	30	17	19	18	13	18
Ad[3]	2	22	. .	23	31	34	31	32	26	48	31
Cp	2	22	23	. .	35	29	46	63	216	62	56
Dd	2	9	31	35	. .	21	46	99	41	42	101
Gg	0	30	34	29	21	. .	22	43	31	36	36
Ha[4]	1	17	31	46	46	22	. .	53	49	47	56
He/Ne	2	19	32	63	99	43	53	. .	74	62	299
La	1	18	26	216	41	31	49	74	. .	71	69
Pw	0	13	48	62	42	36	47	62	71	. .	61
CX[1]	1	18	31	56	101	36	56	299	69	61	. .

rate of variation, their figures in the Table should be adjusted appropriately for accurate comparison: Gg would thus show 197 variants, 59 unique and 33 shared only with non-base-group manuscripts; Pw would have 380 variants, 42 unique, and 150 shared only with non-base-group manuscripts.

Descriptions of the Manuscripts

Hengwrt (Hg)

Hg is described in MR (1.266–83), who date it 1400–10, and further by Doyle and Parkes (1979:xix–xlix), whose analysis of handwritings in the manuscript lends broad support to MR's dating. Recently there has been some debate over whether the same scribe wrote both Hg and El: Doyle and Parkes (1978:

170) and Samuels (1983) argue for that hypothesis; Ramsey (1982; 1986) argues against it (see further the discussion of Cp, below).

MR explain how rats have gnawed away the "upper outer corner of every leaf, the right-angled triangle of loss measuring c. $3\frac{1}{2}$" at the top by 4" on the side." They err in saying that "no letter of the text is gone until f. 96b" (1.269–70), for the text of *SumT* is damaged beginning at folio 82*v* and continuing on the verso of folios 83, 84, and 86. The missing letters are supplied in the present edition from El, and marked with half-closed brackets. In lines 1676, 1788, 2048 and 2052 (see the notes to these lines) the Hg text has been corrected by later fifteenth-century hands. These corrections are accepted in the present edition and reported in the collations as Hg_2 corrections, but do not figure in the Table of Correspondences. At line 2064 a later hand has indicated a transposition of word order; the transposition is rejected by this edition.

The reasoning for the choice of Hg as the Variorum base text for *The Canterbury Tales* has been addressed at some length by earlier editors of the series and need not be repeated here. The essence of the decision to choose Hg over El, however, is that the former shows markedly less evidence of editing. As Doyle and Parkes put it (1978:186), "in Hengwrt, and in the Trinity Gower, [the scribe] appears to be an accurate as well as a proficient copyist, and the differences between the texts of Hengwrt and Ellesmere can only be explained by the fact that [he] was copying from different exemplars, and that Ellesmere's exemplar had been prepared by an editor." The Hengwrt manuscript's early date, "its great freedom from accidental errors and its entire freedom from editorial variants" (MR 1.276), and the fact that its "spelling reveals no fundamental incompatibility with what can be recovered for Chaucer's and Gower's original orthographies (differing as they do)" (Doyle and Parkes 1979:xxi) combine to make it a uniquely valuable witness of what Chaucer wrote. On the other hand, evidence for editing in El is not indisputable (I will return to it under the description of El itself), and the point should be made that the goal of this edition is not to argue the value of Hg at the expense of El, but to present with as much clarity as possible the evidence of the textual history of *SumPT*. I have judged that this goal is best served by consistent adherence to Hg as the chosen base text, emending only in clear cases of simple scribal error or conclusive evidence from the manuscript tradition of faulty text in Hg. I make no claim that what Chaucer wrote will thereby necessarily have emerged, however reliable Hg may be, but in following this course I do hope to have presented the reader with the most easily seized picture of the relations among the MSS while at the same time presenting a text of considerable historical plausibility.

The reading of Hg has been emended for this edition in five instances. The emendation is drawn from the text standing at the head of the standard order with the chosen reading: El (2271), Ad[3] (1870, 2287), Ha[4] (2289), and CX[1]

(2289). The lemma shown is the reading of the present edition; the variant is Hg.

1870   **more]** wel m.
2271   **up]** on
2287   **and ech]** ech
2289   **or elles]** or
2289   **Ptholome]** Protholomee

The reasoning behind these emendations is given in the notes accompanying the lines, but a few remarks are perhaps in order here. Three of these variants are matters of fairly obvious scribal error. The remaining two corrections (at lines 2271, 2287) are based on overwhelming manuscript evidence against the Hg reading, which is not, however, deficient in sense or meter. One notes the curious anomaly of an emendation technically supplied by CX[1] and the perhaps surprising lack of participation of El in the emendations. In lines 1870 and 2289, El shares the rejected Hg reading; in line 2287 El has a unique variant of its own.

The enormously influential editions of Skeat and Robinson have been based largely upon El, and the differences between those and the present edition will be of particular interest. These (along with differences from MR and PR) are gathered here below for convenience of discussion. The affiliations of El will be taken up in some detail under the description of that manuscript, but it may be worth repeating here two salient facts about the relationship between Hg and El for *SumPT*: 1) Hg and El appear to share an exemplar from the beginning of *SumP* through about line 1991 of *SumT*; 2) after about line 1991 El separates from that exemplar to join with one, or perhaps more than one, of considerably less reliability.

In the following 52 instances this edition has accepted Hg readings not chosen by some other modern editions. The lemma shown is Hg; the first manuscript of the standard order with the variant is shown, followed by those modern editions (beginning with Skeat) which print the variant. For full information on the manuscripts and the reasoning behind the decision to retain the Hg reading, consult the Collations and Textual Note for the appropriate line.

1665   **he]** *om.* El SK–RI
1693   **from]** of Ad[3] MR PR
1694   **ther gonne dryve]** they g. d. Dd MR PR
1696   **swarmeden aboute]** swarmed al a. Ha[4] RB[1] RB[2] RI; swarmeden al a. MR PR
1721   **nat to]** n. for to El SK–RI
1744   **yaf hem]** y. hym El SK RB[1] RB[2] RI
1754   **wente ay hem]** w. h. ay Ad[3] MR
1757   **at dore]** at þe d. Cp MR
1768   **whos]** w. þat Ha[4] SK RB[1] RB[2] RI
1784   **laboured I have]** l. h I Cp SK RB[1] RB[2]
1828   **on]** ouer Cp RB[1] RB[2] RI

1855	**Seith**} Seyde Ad³ RB¹–RI
1864	**triklyng**} trillyng Ad³ MR–RI
1868	**his**} my Ad³ MR PR
1872	**althogh that they were**} a. they w. El SK–RI
1887	**mountayne**} mount El MR
1983	**the**} is Cp SK MR
1988	**man**} *om.* El SK RB¹ RB² RI
1991	**thyne aqueyntances nat**} t. acqueintance n. Cp MR PR
1991	**for to**} to Ad³ SK RB¹ RB² RI
1999	**holy meke a**} h. and m. a Ha⁴ SK RB¹ RB²
2015	**certes**} eke El RB¹
2035	**This**} That El SK RB¹ RB² RI
2052	**he noot nat**} and he noot El SK–RI
2108	**Or**} For El SK RB¹ RB² RI
2108	**mote we**} moste we El SK RB¹ RB² RI
2111	**fro this world wolde us**} wolde vs f. t. w. El SK RB¹ RB² RI
2113	**the**} this El SK–RI
2125	**and**} ȝow a. Dd RB¹ RB²
2134	**as muche**} also m. El SK RB¹ RB² RI
2137	**upon**} by El RB¹ RB² RI
2140	**thanne put**} t. p. In El RB¹ RB² RI
2150	**is**} nys El SK–RI
2160	**he**} it El SK–RI
2176	**today**} this day El SK RB¹ RB² RI
2178	**ther nys**} is noon El SK RB¹ RB² RI
2204	**yow**} ye El RB¹ RB² RI
2204	**therby**} her by El SK RB¹ RB² RI
2212	**diffame**} disclaundre El RB¹ RB² RI
2212	**wher I speke**} ther I s. El SK RB¹ RB² RI
2213	**The**} This El SK RB¹ RB² RI
2220	**swich**} of s. El SK–RI
2226	**a soun**} the s. El SK RB¹ RB² RI
2235	**ther**} euere El SK RB¹ RB² RI
2235	**lite and lite**} litel a. litel El RB¹ RB² RI
2236	**nys**} is El SK RB¹ RB² RI
2240	**certeynly**} certeyn a El SK–RI
2245	**thyng**} thynges El SK RB¹ RB² RI
2245	**of which I have**} w. I h. Gg RB¹ RB² RI
2261	**this**} his El SK RB¹ RB² RI
2262	**adown**} doun El SK RB¹ RB² RI
2289	**Euclyde**} E. did (Ry¹) RB¹ RB² RI

Again, one notes the striking contrast between El before and after line 1991; in only 6 instances up through line 1988 does El present a reading differing from Hg which other modern editions have preferred; from that point on, there are 27. One notes as well how insubstantial are the differences in most of the competing readings: in only 13 cases (at lines 1744, 1868, 1983, 1999, 2035, 2108 [2], 2113, 2204, 2213, 2226, 2240, and 2261) is anything like a true difference in sense involved, usually a choice of pronouns, and even in these cases the difference in sense is generally inconsequential.

My conservative adherence to Hg dictates against emendation on the basis of meter. Indeed, the regularity of Chaucer's meter in *The Canterbury Tales* has been for some years a matter of dispute, and it would be folly to enter the debate armed with no more evidence than is provided by *SumPT*. The tale does, however, offer some evidence in corroboration of those who see Chaucer's use of the pentameter line as supple and varied. It is particularly worth noting those lines, not necessarily instances of contested readings, where the vigor of natural speech rhythms is heard in the line: 1828, 1832, 2033, 2125, 2220. Instances of well recognized forms of metrical variation found among these disputed lines include the following.

    a.   The headless line: 2140.
    b.   The Lydgate line: 1721, 1768, 1828, 2220.
    c.   Inhibition of elision at the caesura: 2125, 2134.
    d.   Others: 1696, 1991.

In line 1696 there is a question not so much of meter itself as pronunciation (see note to this line). In line 1991, in both Hg and El, the plural *acqueyntances* makes the line one syllable too long.

Ellesmere (El)

MR describe El and date it 1400–10 (1.148–59). It is a beautiful manuscript, the most heavily and elaborately decorated of the manuscripts of *The Canterbury Tales*, and very carefully prepared. El has served as the base of several of the most important of the modern editions of *The Canterbury Tales*, and its importance for *The Canterbury Tales* has recently been reasserted by its influence in RI.

In general, MR consider El to be, like Hg, independent of the genetic groups into which they divide the manuscripts, but in *SumPT* the case is different: "Hg and El are apparently from [a common ancestor] in FrPT (*Bo*^{1} and Bo^2 with them) and SuPT to 1991 (*Bo*^{1} and Bo^2 with them)" (MR 1.150). After line 1991, however, Hg and El diverge radically. As MR put it, "it looks as if the excellent MS used by Hg–El had become inaccessible to the El scribe at some-point between 1991 and 2015 and he had turned to the copy used by *d*^{*1} and Gg–Si *Ad*^{3} Ch Ra^3–Tc^1–Gl, and when this gave out at 2158, used [the common ancestor of] *cd*^{*2}" (2.241). Blake (1983:398) objects, writing that "to posit three different exemplars for El . . . is far beyond the bounds of the available evidence," and he finds the variants MR cite to argue for the exemplar shifts to be insignificant and likely to have arisen by convergent variation. It is of course difficult to be certain of the affiliation of two manuscripts of such quality as Hg and El, since the number of errors is so small. The case is doubly difficult in the present instance, in that Hg is serving as the base text, and only six of its readings are considered errors. Three of these readings are shared by El (at lines 1870, 2289 two readings), and of these the last (**Ptholome]** Protholome) is of no classificatory value. On the basis of their critical text, MR found 15 agreements in error between Hg and El through line 1991, and none after that point (2.239).

The number of agreements of El with other base-group manuscripts is indicated in the Table of Correspondences. On the whole these figures corroborate the assessments of MR about the affiliations of El, but we may examine them one at a time: the evidence that between lines 1991 and 2015 El switched away from Hg has been discussed above under the description of Hg, but one can add these facts: 90 percent of the El agreements with Ad^3, 82-83 percent of the agreements with Cp, Gg, and Ha^4, and 78 percent of the agreements with La fall after line 1991. The numbers are small, of course, and too much weight should not be given to these percentages, but a contrast in affiliation before and after line 1991 does seem clear.

The next question is whether one can determine the nature of the new El exemplar(s), and the answer is unfortunately less clear. As noted in the discussion of Hg, MR hold that El switched first to the copy used by $d*^1$ and Gg–Si Ad^3 Ch Ra^3–Tc^1–Gl. The base-group manuscripts capable of testifying to this claim are Pw (for $d*^1$), Gg, and Ad^3. The evidence for an affiliation with Ad^3 for this stretch of text is strongest, with 11 agreements. Gg is with El in 9 readings, as is Pw, which then goes Out at line 2158. Some of these agreements are no doubt accidental convergence, but my collations reveal a unanimous agreement of El Ad^3 Gg and Pw in lines 2015, 2030, 2035, 2052, 2055, and 2150, the accumulated weight of which is difficult to attribute to coincidence. MR erroneously claim that these manuscripts are found together in line 2108; they overlap in the line, but do not all share any one reading. My inclusion of line 2150 in the group of agreements differs from the MR report because they print the El Ad^3 Gg Pw reading. The shift in affiliaton of El after line 1991 seems clear, and the character of its association with the group defined by MR is in general supported by my findings. It will be noted, however, that the coherence of the Ad^3 Gg Pw group in itself is not terribly impressive; 8 of the 11 readings shared by Ad^3 and Gg from line 1991 through line 2150 are shared by El, but the total shared readings of Ad^3 and Gg through line 2150 ($d*^1$ ends at line 2158) is only 22. The evidence overall suggests that the Ad^3–$d*^1$–Gg group is most coherent in the very section in question, but is otherwise rather amorphous. One may thus accept the MR claim (2.241) that for this section El "turned to the copy used by $d*^1$ and Gg–Si Ad^3" but add that this information is not very revelatory.

Because the $d*^1$ manuscripts lack the concluding episode of the tale, breaking off as has been noted after line 2158, El perhaps switches its affiliation again after line 2158. MR felt that the switch was to the common ancestor of $cd*^2$ (2.241). The base-group manuscripts which can supply information on this question are Cp and La. The 136-line section in question constitutes a little more than a third of the total, and the fact that 14 of the 24 agreements of Cp and El, or 64 percent, and 9 of the 18 agreements of La and El, or 50 percent, fall within this stretch lends some support to the MR hypothesis. The agreements of El, Cp, and La together in this section are found in lines 2160, 2175, 2185, 2220, 2236, 2240, 2261, and 2289. For several reasons the testimony of Cp and La is inconclusive here: first, the variants are markedly trivial, largely explicable as accidental convergence. MR cite line 2175 (**if**} if that) and line 2185 (**sire quod he**} q. h.) They also cite line 2178, but Cp and La present differing variants in that case: (**ther nys**} is noon El Cp; t. is none La). In three instances, at lines 2160, 2220, and 2240, where MR print the El Cp La reading, the evidence gathered here adds further, though frail, corroboration to their interpretation.

Given the evidence of the base-group manuscripts, then, it certainly seems possible that El shifted exemplars at about lines 1991–2015, and that the exemplar was connected with Ad³, Gg, and Pw. Whether there was a second shift in exemplars after line 2158, where Pw breaks off, is less clear. MR state that "after 2158, there are some indications that Gg–Si Ad³ Ch Ra³–Tc¹–Gl continue together, that El (and Ps) are with them, and that all are derived from the same ultimate ancestor as *cd**²" (2.241). All in all, the evidence for two switches of exemplar by El is suggestive but inconclusive.

MR write that "although El has long been regarded by many scholars as the single MS of most authority, its total of unique variants, many of which are demonstrable errors, is approximately twice that of Hg, as is also its total of slips shared by other MSS by [accidental coincidence]. . . . Since it is very clear that an intelligent person, who was certainly not Chaucer, worked over the text when El was copied, the unsupported readings of this MS must be scrutinized with the greatest care" (1.150).

The argument that El is a much-edited manuscript has been accepted by many critics, notably (as mentioned above) by Doyle and Parkes, but, in the introduction to the text of RI, Larry Benson has re-affirmed his confidence in El, writing that the MR theory of an El editor "has now been refuted by George Kane" (RI xl). "Refuted" may be a stronger word than is warranted here, but certainly Kane attacks head-on Manly and Rickert's arguments for and evidence of editing in El. Arguing (Kane 1984:213–22) that most if not all of the variants they take for deliberate changes are in fact easily described in terms of predictable variation arising from the conditions of scribal copying, Kane writes that "Ellesmere's status has still to be assessed, but it is certainly not to be measured in terms of [MR's] evidence for 'editing'" (1984:222). It is of course one thing to claim that the differences between two texts may be accounted for in terms of the unconscious variation of one term for another and quite another to demonstrate that the differences arose only in that way, but Kane's arguments certainly make one wonder about the confidence with which MR sort El variants in *SumT* into "apparently editing, in 1746, 1968" and "not editing, in 1700, 1981" (2.239). On the other hand, unless one dismisses the evidence that the Hg and El scribe are the same person (for which see above under the description of Hg), one must admit that the differences between the two texts are most easily explained by the operations of a second party. The more thoroughly one demonstrates the predictability of a scribe's behavior within a given textual context, the less explicable are the differences between these two fine texts, if they were produced by one scribe. The variables in that case would be the presence or absence of an editor and the difference(s) in exemplar(s). It may be worth while to focus momentarily upon the unique variants in El which occur within the section of the text before line 1991, that is, the section for which MR hypothesize a shared exemplar. Lemmata are Hg and variants El:

1700   **looked hadde]** h. looke (The mismanagement of the verb suggests that this is an unconscious slip.)

1746   **Yif us]** Yif hym (Though MR label this "probably editing," one would expect an editor to have carried through with *yif hym* in line 1750, but El does not, reading *yif us* with Hg. The variant was probably induced by *yaf hem* in line 1744.)

1950   **Have spended]** I h. spent (Here we have what might fairly be considered editorial work: the inclusion of *I* is necessitated by its omission in line 1949. El is not alone in omitting *I* in 1949, nor in reading *in a* for *a* in line 1949 to make up the syllabic loss, and indeed the El uniqueness here consists only in the form of the verb [Gg, another manuscript which omitted *I* in line 1949, also added *a* in line 1949 and wrote *I h. spended* in line 1950]. Other manuscripts coped in other ways. The question remains whether this El variant demonstrates the work of an editor or of a resourceful scribe, but the variant does seem consciously wrought, if only in response to an earlier error.)

1968   **hymselve]** it selue (This qualifies, perhaps, as a pedantic sophistication, the antecedant for the pronoun being the neuter "ech thyng.")

1981   **and]** *om.* (Cannot be deliberate, as both sense and meter are destroyed.)

The conclusions which may be drawn from this small body of evidence are not many, but it must be admitted that the 5 unique variants of El in lines 1665–1981 offer little support for seeing the operations of an editor bent on mending meter or, for that matter, mending anything.

El is variant uniquely in 16 readings after line 1991: at lines 2002, 2088 (two readings), 2172, 2190, 2211, 2212, 2218, 2232, 2245 (two readings), 2249, 2278 (two readings), and 2287 (two readings). Because MR evidently consider the variant in line 2047 (**bitwix]** bitwene) nonsubstantive, one cannot easily determine whether the El reading is unique, but no other base-group manuscript has it. Of these readings, MR (2.240) classify the following as editorial (I print a longer lemma than in the Collations, for clarity):

2088   **I wol no ferther say]** ther is namoore to s. (This does look editorial; it is certainly substantive for an unconscious change.)

2172   **I se wel that som thyng]** I trowe s. maner t. (I have included two lemmata here for clarity; El shares the omission of *that* only with Ps, which MR feel was probably copied from El [2.240], so the entire half-line is in effect unique. This is the strongest evidence so far of editorial work.)

    2190   **Sire quod this frere**} S. q. he (The El version of the line is acephelous, and though it could well be a deliberate change it does not fit the argument of an El editor mending meter.)

    2212   **diffame**} disclaundre (This may have been generated by the El exemplar; Cp, La and others read *sclaundre*.)

    2232   **hym**} thee (It is hard to imagine this as an editorial decision; the resulting "lat thee nevere thee" is so consummately ugly one must believe the variant is accidental, the second "thee" inducing the first.)

An instance (not cited in MR) of apparent editorialism among the El unique readings is in line 2245, where El reads *alle thynges* for the usual *alle thyng*.

In sum, the evidence available from *SumPT* for editorial work in El is not convincing but, after line 1991, neither is it dismissable. In comparison to Hg at least, and where the two manuscripts are working with different exemplars, the evidence of editorial work in El is sufficient to give one pause and, in practical terms, to regard a debatable El reading with somewhat narrower eyes. The confident pronouncements of MR on the edited quality of El are not well served by the evidence of this tale, but the issue which needs to be addressed in another forum than this one is the radical increase in unique variants where Hg and El do not share an exemplar. One wonders why there should be 3 times as many unique readings in the 46 percent of the text in which El and Hg do not share an exemplar as in the 49 percent for which they probably do. It could be that the scribe (or the editor?) recognized, as do we, the reduced quality in the exemplar(s) which entered the El *SumT* at or about line 1991, and began to intervene in ways of which we find little or no evidence before that point.

Additional 35286 (Ad³)

Ad³ is described in MR 1.41–47, and dated 1430–50. It is a manuscript of some value, whose "text was originally near the archetype but in its descendants was much contaminated and altered" (MR 1.43). Ad³ shares more variants with Pw than any other base-group manuscript in *SumT*, with Gg coming second, which may be taken as evidence (noted more fully under the description of El) of an important link between Ad³ and the *d**1 group and Gg. In lines 1870 and 2287 Ad³ supplies emendations for the present edition.

Ad³ is uniquely variant in 26 readings: in lines 1670, 1687, 1763, 1768, 1773, 1779, 1818, 1825, 1900, 1927, 1933, 1947, 1950, 1969, 1988, 2010, 2026, 2139, 2148, 2159, 2162, 2173, 2178, 2181, 2237, and 2294. Most of these are the product of apparent inattention, though a few suggest editing, perhaps in the Ad³ exemplar:

    1687   **seith he a**} shekyn his
    1763   **spare**} spel
    1768   **whos**} the w.

1773	**upon this bench faren**}	f. vpon thi b.
1818	**is**}	ay is
1900	**preye**}	trewly p.
1927	**and**}	a. in
2139	**here my feith**}	by my fey (two lemmata; *fey* is not unique).
2178	**so poure a**}	that p.

Ad³ supports readings adopted by other modern editions but not the present one in lines 1693, 1744, 1754, 1855, 1864, 1868, 1991, 2015, 2035, 2108, 2212, 2213, 2235, 2262, and 2289. Those readings that converge with neither Hg nor El are listed below:

1693	**from**}	of Ad³ Cp Dd Ha⁴ He La+ Pw MR PR
1754	**wente ay hem**}	w. h. ay Ad³ Cp Dd Gg La+ PN¹ TH¹⁻³ MR
1855	**Seith**}	seyde Ad³ Dd Gg Ha⁴ He Pw+ RB¹–RI
1864	**triklyng**}	trillyng Ad³ Cp Dd Ha⁴ He La Pw+ MR–RI
1868	**his**}	my Ad³ Dd Gg Ha⁴ Pw+ MR PR
1991	**forto**}	to Ad³ Dd Gg He+ SK RB¹ RB² RI

Corpus Christi 198 (Cp)

MR describe Cp in 1.92–99, dating it 1410–20. Along with La among the base-group manuscripts, Cp represents the *c* group (Cp, La, Sl²). As shown in the Table of Correspondences, Cp and La share 216 variant readings in *SumPT*, a greater number than for any pair of texts except He and CX¹, and a full 80 percent of the Cp variants. MR state that "as the least altered copy of a very early lost MS of high quality, Cp is of some authority; but as this lost MS ([common ancestor of *c*]) was itself derived from the same source as [the common ancestor of *d*] and [the common ancestor of *b*] and others, it is not a major tradition" (1.96).

The 265 variants of Cp mark it as a manuscript outside the textual mainstream of *SumT* as we consider it today, but the Cp scribe himself seems to have been both careful and resourceful. According to Doyle and Parkes (1978:192–93), this scribe also wrote Ha⁴, but according to Ramsey (1986:126–34) he did not. Smith (1988) in turn contests Ramsey's arguments. Cp has fewer unique variants than any base-group manuscript other than Hg. In contrast, La, Cp's cousin in the *c* line, has 70 unique variants. The evidence overall suggests that Cp is a careful copy in the *c* line, a particularly good witness to the nature of that textual tradition in *SumPT*. The 11 unique readings of Cp are found in lines 1694, 1789, 1849, 1880, 1899, 1918, 2155, 2161, 2180, 2241, and 2264. Of these, two (at lines 1789, 2155) are simply slips; one (at line 2241) is a variant in the imperative not reported by MR and thus not necessarily unique at all; of the remainder the following are of some potential interest:

1694	**ther gonne dryve**}	þey g. to d. (printed by UR)
1849	**so freendly yow my conseil**}	so f. my c. to y.
1880	**body**}	cheekes

1899	**which that}** þe w.
1918	**shal seyn}** s. ʒou sayn
2180	**youre}** þis
2264	**a frere}** þe f.

Cp has not been very influential in the formation of modern editions of *SumPT*; no readings supported by Cp alone, without Hg, El, Ad³, or Dd, are to be found among modern editions.

Cambridge University Dd.4.24 (Dd)

Manuscript Dd is described by MR (1.11, 100–107) and dated 1400–1420. The unique Dd readings are in lines 1752, 1756, 1769, 1840, 1851, 1982, 1984, 2229, 2230, 2250, 2274, and 2291. Only Hg and Cp have fewer unique readings. If one drops those readings corrected by the Dd scribe himself (and MR show that Dd is carefully corrected), the number that remains (seven) is impressively small. Two of the unique Dd readings enter the printed tradition with TH¹:

1756	**what}** that Dd TH¹–UR
1982	**set youre herte}** setteth y. h. Dd TH¹–SP¹

but nothing can be inferred from this evidence. MR do not record the variant verb forms in line 1982, so the Dd reading may not be unique at all, and the *what/that* variant is too easy to make anything of.

Dd has been accorded considerable respect by those involved in the construction of the modern *Canterbury Tales*. It has participated in a number of readings in other modern editions against the authority of El, though never alone, as the following instances show.

1784	**laboured I have}** l. h. I Cp Dd Gg Ha⁴ La Ne Pw+ CX¹–RB¹ RB²
1828	**on}** ouer Cp Dd Ha⁴ He La+ CX¹–WR RB¹ RB² RI
1855	**Seith}** seyde Ad³ Dd Gg Ha⁴ He Pw CX¹–WR RB¹–RI
1991	**thyne aqueyntances nat}** t. acqueintance n. Cp Dd He La CX¹–PN² MR PR
1991	**forto}** to Ad³ Dd Gg He+ CX¹–TR SK RB¹ RB² RI
2125	**and}** ʒow a. Dd Ha⁴ He CX¹ UR–WR RB¹ RB²

Cambridge University Gg.4.27 (Gg)

MR describe Gg in 1.170–82, dating it 1420–40, and it is described further in Parkes and Beadle (1980). In *SumPT* Gg is affiliated with Ad³, as noted earlier under "The Textual Tradition." It is a manuscript of some considerable interest, both because of the authority granted it by several editors and because of the oddity of its many unique variants. To MR, Gg "is a MS of the highest importance. It represents, in the main, the El tradition without the El editing" (1.176). The performance of Gg in *SumPT* does not entirely match the expectations raised by that enthusiastic appraisal. Though as pointed out above in the discussion of El, editing is difficult to define and demonstrate, many of the unique Gg variants in *SumPT* make plausible sense, and cumulatively add up to a text which could be called "edited," and which it would be unwise to trust without independent support. Examples of unique Gg readings include

1763	**thy}**	ȝoure
1840	**nat}**	*eras.*
1869	**me right}**	to me
1920	**a manner}**	a noþer
1938	**up at a sours}**	ryȝt at a s.
1988	**what}**	as
2034	**quod he}**	anoon
2050	**Of}**	In
2099	**thanne}**	*om.*
2116	**sith}**	s. þat (printed by SK)
2131	**han}**	hald
2153	**quod he}**	he seyde
2174	**me}**	vs
2185	**sire quod he}**	q. he s.

The most idiosyncratic of Gg's unique errors have suggested to some writers that the scribe might have been a non-native speaker of English, perhaps a Fleming (MR 1.178, Caldwell 1944), though Parkes and Beadle (1980:3.47–49) have argued recently that the oddities of Gg spelling are explicable in terms of his (native English) dialect. As MR point out (1.179), there is some evidence that the Gg scribe "did not understand well what he was copying"; they note specifically mistaken division and joining of words, and misreadings that destroy the sense of the passage. Examples from *SumT* of the former include,

1877	**diversly}**	dyuers lyf
1914	**youres}**	ȝoure is
2115	**litel tyme}**	lytyme

and of the latter,

1890	**wel ye}**	wolde
1895	**preestes}**	postellis
2033	**alyve}**	a loone (Gg$_2$ *corr.*)

As the last instance suggests, a good many such errors were corrected in the manuscript, and MR point out that "the scribe was unusually careful {as} is shown by the very large number of erasures and rewriting of words and parts of lines" (1.177–78).

Gg has been of some influence in the shaping of modern editions of *SumPT*, as the following instances in which a Gg reading has been preferred to Hg or El demonstrate (printed editions beginning with SK):

1754   **wente ay hem]** w. h. ay Ad³ Cp Dd Gg La+ MR
1757   **at dore]** at þe d. Ad³ Cp Dd Gg Ha⁴ La Ne+ MR
1784   **laboured I have]** l. h I Cp Dd Gg Ha⁴ La Ne Pw+ SK RB¹ RB²
1838   **quod he now]** q. he Cp Gg He La Pw+ SK RB¹
1855   **Seith]** seyde Ad³ Dd Gg Ha⁴ He Pw+ RB¹–RI
1868   **his]** my Ad³ Dd Gg Ha⁴ Pw+ MR PR
1983   **the]** þis Cp Gg La Pw+ SK MR
1991   **forto]** to Ad³ Dd Gg He+ SK RB¹ RB² RI
2245   **of which I have]** w. I h. Gg+ RB¹ RB² RI

Gg has suffered the loss of leaves both at the beginning (lines 1665–1746) and end (lines 2285–94) of the text.

Harley 7334 (Ha⁴)

Ha⁴ is described in MR (1.219–30) and dated about 1410. They write that Ha⁴ in *SumPT* is "with *a–Ln–b**, but much edited" (1.221). The 46 variants which Ha⁴ shares with Dd (representing *a*), the 53 with He/Ne, and the 55 with CX¹ (both representing *b*) lend some support to that analysis, but the number of agreements with Cp, La, and Pw (46, 49, and 47) of the *cd** group, is almost identical. The MR statement that "[Ha⁴] seems, on the whole, to share its least trivial errors with *a–Ln–b**; and may have used [the common ancestor of] *a–Ln–b** as the basis for its editorial activities" (2.237) characterizes the case quite well, for Ha⁴ goes a long way toward defining "editorial activity." As noted above in the description of Cp, Doyle and Parkes have identified the Ha⁴ scribe with the scribe of Cp, while Ramsey (1986:126–34) has disputed the identification. If the two manuscripts were copied by one scribe, then given the apparent fidelity of the scribe to his exemplar in Cp, and the uniqueness of the Ha⁴ text, the reasonable inference is that the Ha⁴ text was prepared by an editor. MR write that Ha⁴ was "picked up from many sources and edited with great freedom by some one other than Chaucer," and conclude that it is interesting, but "never authoritative" (1.222).

Ha⁴ in *SumPT* contains by my count 104 unique variants (MR count "c. 90" [2.237]), which places it in a class by itself for uniqueness, mostly due to editorial activity. The statement in MR 2.237 that "Ha⁴ has more than 130 variants" is inexplicable; I count 276, and even allowing for the cases in which I have counted a variant ignored or missed by MR, one suspects a typographical error in their report. The fact that 38 percent of Ha⁴'s variants are unique makes it the most idiosyncratic of the base-group manuscripts. Though Gg would appear to be competitive in that regard, with some 30 percent, it must be recalled that many of the Gg unique variants are palpably unintentional, whereas the great bulk of the unique readings of Ha⁴ are clearly deliberate. A representative sampling of the Ha⁴ unique variants can illustrate the point:

1709   **Yorkshire]** Engelond
1710   **contree]** lond
1718   **houses]** soules

1758	**awey}** out
1768	**goode}** housbond
1787	**oure}** myn
1871	**Cristes}** goddis
1876	**lust}** delit
1904	**holy writ}** oure lore
1948	**nothyng therof}** þer of nought
1991	**forto flee}** fro þe f.
1996	**herkne}** werk
2005	**is a synne}** is a þing
2038	**And thow also most}** A. quod þe juge also þou most
2040	**knyght}** felaw
2046	**vertuous}** vertues and eek
2139	**here my feith}** h. my hond
2190	**Sire quod this frere}** T. f. sayd s.
2196	**the savour}** sauyour
2210	**by God}** I wis
2250	**it liked me}** I comaunded be
2255	**cartwheel}** large whel
2260	**for his worthyness}** god him blesse
2290	**cherl}** clerk

Ha[4] also contains unique pairs of spurious lines before lines 2005, 2013, 2038, and 2049. Despite the widespread suspicion, almost contempt, with which Ha[4] has come to be regarded, in 12 instances some modern editions have adopted a reading offered by Ha[4] which is not supported by El or Hg. In lines 1696, 1768, and 1999 Ha[4] is the manuscript of greatest authority, and indeed in line 1768 the Ha[4] reading is unique, as it is in line 2289, where it supplies an emendation adopted by this edition. Printed editions are shown beginning with SK:

1693	**from}** of Ad[3] Cp Dd Ha[4] He La Pw+ MR PR
1694	**ther gonne dryve}** they g. d. Dd Ha[4] He La Pw+ MR PR
1696	**swarmeden aboute}** swarmed al a. Ha[4] He RB[1]–RI (see note)
1757	**at dore}** at þe d. Ad[3] Cp Dd Gg Ha[4] La Ne+ MR
1768	**whos}** w. þat Ha[4] SK RB[1] RB[2] RI
1784	**laboured I have}** l. h I Cp Dd Gg Ha[4] La Ne Pw+ SK RB[1] RB[2]
1828	**on}** ouer Cp Dd Ha[4] He La+ RB[1] RB[2] RI
1855	**Seith}** seyde Ad[3] Dd Gg Ha[4] He Pw+ RB[1]–RI
1864	**triklyng}** trillyng Ad[3] Cp Dd Ha[4] He La Pw+ MR–RI
1868	**his}** my Ad[3] Dd Gg Ha[4] Pw+ MR PR
1999	**holy meke a}** h. and m. a Ha[4]+ SK RB[1] RB[2]
2125	**and}** ʒow a. Dd Ha[4] He+ CX[1] RB[1] RB[2]

Helmingham (He)

Manuscript He is described by MR (1.11–12, 256–65). It is made up of a vellum core filled out front and back with paper. MR date the vellum core 1420–30, and the paper addition, which contains *SumPT*, 1450–60. The hand of the paper section is an untidy cursive. "MS He is always the highest member of the *b* group. . . . A careless copy of a very bad and much edited ancestor, He is worth little in the making of the text" (MR 1.258). Clearly, the only reason for the inclusion of He among the base-group manuscripts is that it is the earliest representative of *b*, the textual tradition that produced CX[1]. In fact, CX[1] is closer in *SumPT* to New College D 314 (Ne), the manuscript which stands in for He when it is Out, as it is at lines 1718–89 (the figures for He in the Table of Correspondences include variants here in Ne). Ne is described by MR in 1.381–86, and dated 1450–70. They write that "Ne comes off the *b* line between [the ancestor of] He and [the common ancestor of] *Cx*[1] [CX[1] and Tc[2]]; at times it seems to be from the same exemplar as He. . . . It is chiefly valuable for establishing the [common ancestor of] *b* reading when He and *Cx*[1] disagree" (1.382). The deplorable quality of He and the *b* tradition is easily visible in the number of He variants from the text printed here: 457. The *b* text entered the printed tradition with CX[1], with sad and long-lasting results, but neither He nor Ne has had any influence on modern texts. The relations among He, Ne, and CX[1] will be discussed under CX[1].

Lansdowne (La)

La is described by MR at 1.304–308, and dated 1410–20. It is very closely associated with Cp, and with Cp and Sl[2] forms MR's group *c*. La is far less careful than Cp, as its 380 variants suggest, and as its 70 unique variants confirm. There is some evidence that might be adduced to support MR's statement that La is "obviously much edited" (1.306), but in *SumPT* most of La's unique variants are the result of carelessness rather than deliberation. The following are typical:

1673	**And}**	As
1711	**lymytour}**	litour
1755	**hir hostes man}**	he osteman
1768	**the}**	*om.*
1857	**say hym}**	sawhe
1863	**I roos}**	he r.
1906	**mendynantz}**	amende fautes

Even among its unique variants, however, there is some evidence that La and Cp are closely related, for in 14 instances Cp is variant where La has a unique variant, suggestive of a common difficulty. The following are illustrative:

1744	**alle}**	any Cp+; euery La;
1891	**Oreb}**	or elles Cp+; or La
1912	**we mendinantz we freres}**	we mendenaunte f. Cp+; me vendinant f. La
1964	**that covent}**	hem Cp+; *om.* La
1964	**foure and twenty}**	one or tuo Cp La$_1$; on tuo La
2070	**myght and mynde}**	m. a. my witte Cp+; witte a. my witte La
2266	**under}**	vnto Cp+; in to La+ UR

Petworth (Pw)

Pw is described by MR at 1.410–14, and dated 1420–30. It represents the *d* group manuscripts among the base-group (MR 1.412), and, as its 130 variants shared only with non-base-group manuscripts demonstrate, it is very often away from the base-group in *SumPT*. The greatest interest of Pw is its breaking off *SumT* after line 2158, the implications of which are discussed above, in "The Textual Tradition."

Descriptions of the Printed Editions

Caxton 1478 {1476} (CX¹)

CX¹ is described by MR (1.79–81). Recent scholarship would revise the *STC* dating from 1478 to 1476 (see Blake 1985:1). In *SumPT* CX¹ is evidently a careful setting of its exemplar; all but one of its variants is shared by at least one *b*-group manuscript, and even that one reading, a unique variant at line 2079, has a close counterpart in the *b* manuscript Tc² (**thilke**] that He+; that strong ~ CX¹; that stonge Tc²). Admittedly, in 33 readings Tc² is the only *b* manuscript to join CX¹ (readings unique to CX¹ Tc² are marked with *): at lines *1679, *1710, 1737, 1744, 1761, *1790, 1840, *1847, *1851, *1917, *1920, *1938, *1941, 1950, *2011, *2018, 2053, 2068, 2082, *2084 (3 readings, one unique), 2095, *2104, *2109, 2124, *2146, 2215, *2218, *2220, 2238, *2250, and 2289. Still, the rate of convergence with the other *b* manuscripts is impressive.

It has been argued that Tc², described by MR (1.527–31) and dated 1480–1500, was copied from a shattered copy of CX¹ itself (Bevins 1951:44–47; Boyd 1984:22–24). The evidence in *SumPT* tends to support this argument but does not settle the case beyond doubt. Others (Zupitza 1893:3.paras. 8–10; Greg 1924:751; Koch 1902:li–lii; MR 1.530, 2.57–58) have argued that CX¹ and Tc² are copies of the same exemplar. Some of the more interesting of the readings shared by CX¹ and Tc² are these:

1679   **peynes**] preuytes Tc² CX¹; poyntis Ne
1710   **A**] Is a Tc² CX¹
1790   **text**] playn t. Tc² CX¹
1847   **wake**] wakyng He+; make Tc² CX¹
1851   **Now**] But He+; And Tc² CX¹
1917   **was man in Paradys certeyn**] w. out to labour certeyn Tc² CX¹
1941   **sours**] sowne Tc² CX¹
2018   *Spur. l.*: A jug he was a man of hiȝe astate He; Which hasty was in Jugement algate Tc²+ CX¹ *Out*: Ne
2084   **wommen**] men Pw (Pw₁ *corr.*) Tc²+ CX¹
         myghte] m. ride and Tc² CX¹
         wade it] w. Cp La Tc²+ CX¹
2095   **at**] of Ha⁴ Tc²+ CX¹

2104   **ne of oure]** ne of ful He+; ne of o. chirche ful Tc² CX¹
2146   **a yifte]** som good y. Tc² CX¹
2218   **ymaginacioun]** abominacioun He+; dilectacion Tc² CX¹

In line 2018 the *b* ancestor was clearly Out; Ii shares the spurious line with CX¹ and Tc². In line 1917 CX¹ or its exemplar made reason out of a puzzle: *chaast* (chaste) was read as *cast* (thrown) in the *b* line at some point, and the line as rewritten in CX¹ makes good on the line's new logic.

In six instances, Tc² reads as this edition does, while some or all of *b* (He, Ne, CX¹) are variant:

1747   **tryp]** *Thus* Tc²; crip CX¹ Ne   *Out*: He
1967   **in]** *Thus* Tc²; on CX¹ He Ne
2211   **be wreke]** *Thus* Tc²; awreke CX¹ Ne+; a vrech He
2245   **thyng]** *Thus* Tc²; this t. CX¹ He Ne+
2052   **noot nat]** *Thus* Ne Tc² CX¹; woot nat He
2260   **for his worthyness]** *Thus* Tc² He; f. h. wordyness CX¹ Ne

In nine cases, CX¹ and Tc² have the reading of the current edition while He and Ne are variant: at lines 1901, 1919, 1927, 2052, 2105, 2174, 2178, 2215.

In the following 30 cases Tc² departs in variation from the rest of *b*: at lines 1675, 1728, 1742, 1757, 1803, 1830, 1867, 1912, 1924, 1932, 1982, 1984, 2013, 2029, 2068, 2079, 2083, 2100, 2111, 2114, 2117, 2126, 2154, 2169, 2187, 2220, 2226, 2270, 2279, and 2293. In all these cases (except perhaps at line 2154) the Tc² reading is easily explained as a further degradation of the CX¹ reading. Tc² has 4 variants in which it differs from CX¹ but agrees with He and thus may preserve the reading of CX¹'s exemplar:

1842   **no beest for me were]** f. me no b. w. He Tc²+; f. me that no b. w. Ne CX¹
1878   **guerdon]** gwerdons He Tc²+; guerdoms CX¹ Ne
1903   **it]** it ynow CX¹ Ne; þat ynowe He Tc²
2116   **or]** *Thus* Ne CX¹; and He Tc²+

However, in these four readings CX¹ agrees with Ne, a manuscript much more like CX¹ than He is. The salient fact is that Tc² never joins Ne against CX¹, which suggests that the convergences of Tc² and He listed above are more likely to be accidental than genetic.

Caxton 1484 {1482} (CX²)

Six years after issuing CX¹, Caxton published a second edition, which included emendations derived from a manuscript of higher quality than his earlier exemplar. CX² makes 104 changes, correcting CX¹ to the reading of the present edition in 82 instances, substituting 11 new variants for variants in CX¹, and introducing 11 new variants where CX¹ agrees with the present edition. CX² thus has 332 variants from the present edition.

Ten of the new variants in CX² lack manuscript support: at lines 1679, 1781,

1912, 1945, 2049, 2176, 2213, 2214, 2218, and 2285. Of these, only two are not easily dismissed as inadvertent.

1679   **peynes]** preuytes (Tc^2) ~ CX^1; tormentes ~ CX^2–PN^2
2285   **covent]** brethren ~ CX^2–TR

In line 1679, *tormentes* restores the sense of the line destroyed by the CX^1 mistake of *prevytes* for *peynes*, in all likelihood an independent correction. The reading in line 2285, plausible enough to have persisted through TR, represents a rationalizing substitution of a clear term for a marginally more difficult one.

Manuscript support for the other 12 new variants is scattered, and many of these variants offer no testimony on the nature of the manuscript used by Caxton; for example, the following variants can easily be understood as independent slips or corrections:

1680   **say]** ne s. (Ry^1) CX^2–PN^2
1699   **clapte]** clippid (Ii+) CX^2–PN^2
1834   **God defended]** G. offendith (Ne+) CX^1; G. offendyd (Ra^1) CX^2–PN^2
1983   **the]** þis Cp Gg La Pw+ CX^2–TR SK MR
2042   **do sleen hem]** h. s. Gg He Pw+ CX^1 TH^1–SP^1 UR; do h. s. (Tc^1) CX^2–PN^2
2201   **sayde]** had s. (Sl^2) CX^2–PN^2 UR

Offering ambiguous or contradictory testimony are

2079   **thilke]** that strong ~ CX^1; that ilke (Bo^1+) CX^2–PN^2 UR
2235   **ther]** euere El Ad^3 Gg Ha^4+ CX^2–SP^3 TR–RB^1 RB^2 RI

The reading at line 2079 is found only in Bo^1 and Ph^2, which are with $d*^1$ at this point, but the agreement could be accidental. The reading at line 2235 is shared with Gg–Si, Ad^3 and $cd*^1$, and no a manuscripts. It is, however, so widespread otherwise that it might be an easy mistake, and independent with CX^2.

Dunn (1940) and others have concluded that Caxton's new manuscript may have been of or related to the group a manuscripts. The variants supporting an affiliation with an a manuscript are these:

1860   **fifty]** this xl He+ CX^1; this f. (En^1+) CX^2–UR
2226   **or]** or of a Cp Dd Ha^4 La+ CX^1 WN PN^2; or of (En^1+) CX^2

The correction of *xl* to *fifty* in line 1860 could point to an a manuscript; *this f.* is found in En^1 and Ds. But it could easily be a partial correction based on the meaning of *jubilee* in line 1862. The variant reading in line 2226 is shared with three a group manuscripts (En^1 Ds Ma). In sum, the positive evidence is suggestive but in short supply. Ma is the manuscript about which one feels the greatest suspicion, especially given Pearsall's conclusion, based on the text of *NPT*, that Caxton's manuscript for correction was "of the a type, probably one of the survivors closest to Cn" (1984*a*:107). Ma is the closest manuscript to Cn.

Arguing on the other side, in 13 instances Dd (and most of *a*) fail to support CX^2's convergence with the current edition against CX^1. Further, in 9 of these cases Dd (and most of *a*) actually support CX^1 (e.g. in lines 1816, 1820, 1888, 1935, 1957, 2029, 2067, 2125, 2181 [2], 2191, 2225, and 2235). El and Ad^3, also argued by Dunn to be similar to Caxton's correction copy, support all but two of these corrections (see lines 2235, 2278; 1917, 2005). Thus for *SumPT* the correction copy seems to be more like El and Ad^3 than like Dd and the rest of *a*.

Something can perhaps be learned of Caxton's methods of correcting CX^1 from line 1862:

> **allone]** al about He; al aboue (Ne+) CX^1; all a. (Hk) CX^2–PN^2

In line 1861, for *God be thanked of His lone* CX^1 reads (following his *b* manuscript) *G. be t. of H. loue*. CX^2's correction of this reading required correction of line 1862 as well, to preserve the rhyme on *lone*. It is perhaps revelatory of Caxton's habits that he made his correction so partially, correcting only *aboue* to *alone*, and retaining *all*. We can be fairly confident that the manuscript supplying his corrections read simply *alone*, since only Hk reads *all alone*, and whatever manuscript he was using we know it was not Hk, for Hk is defective in 1861, omitting the last phrase entirely. The same sort of partial correction is probably visible as well in line 2042, where CX^1's omission of *do* was corrected, but the transposition was not:

> **do sleen hem]** h. s. Gg He Pw+ CX^1; do h. s. (Tc^1) CX^2–PN^2

So interpreted, line 2042 could be counted among those new CX^2 readings influenced by an *a* manuscript.

For a general treatment of both of Caxton's editions, see Boyd (1984).

Pynson 1492 (PN¹)

PN^1, which has 361 variants from the present edition, appears to have been set from CX^2. In line 1781 and only there, PN^1 is with CX^1 against CX^2:

> **quod]** saide Ne+ CX^1 PN^1; sayd he ~ CX^2 WN PN^2

The PN^1 reading is probably either an error on top of an error or a commonsensical correction; WN and PN^2 follow CX^2, so the PN^1 correction is not inevitable. PN^1 restores the reading of the current edition in only 6 instances (at lines 1739, 1744, 1929, 1984, 2104, 2176), which does not, especially given the nature of the corrections, suggest a conscious intent to improve the text of CX^2. Three of these changes are likely to have been inadvertent, though the change in line 1984 suggests a sensitivity to meter, while in line 2176 an obvious tense error is corrected. In 45 readings PN^1 departs from CX^2 to create a new variant. For 23 of these there is manuscript support: at lines 1674, 1675,

1682, 1754, 1765, 1835, 1897, 1912, 1934, 1938, 1939, 1968, 2022, 2024, 2052, 2074, 2167, 2175, 2234, 2256, 2271, 2289, 2294. For the remaining 22 there is no manuscript support: at lines 1688, 1692, 1693, 1747, 1755, 1778, 1783, 1837, 1845, 1849, 1894, 2010 (2), 2012, 2084, 2086, 2188, 2194, 2202, 2231, 2244, 2274. The unprecedented readings are quite uniformly simple errors, mostly misreadings. Only the variant at line 1755 (see Textual Note) and perhaps at line 2231 (**It**} This) have interest, showing potential editorial involvement.

From the 23 new PN^1 variants with manuscript precedent it is impossible to draw any conclusion, except that the influence of manuscripts on PN^1 is largely illusory. The manuscripts which share these readings are distributed with almost perfect randomness, and the readings themselves are easily understood as accidental, shared with manuscripts because they were wide-spread and easy to make in the first place.

Wynkyn de Worde (WN)

WN, which has 346 variants from the present edition, appears to have been set from CX^2, not from PN^1. Of the 52 divergences that separate PN^1 from CX^2 (for which see the description above of PN^1), only 4 appear in WN:

1688	**of**} *om.* ~ PN^1 WN	
1934	**buf**} but El+ PN^1 WN	
1939	**into**} in Gg+ PN^1 WN UR	
2176	**had a**} haue a ~ CX^2	

In all, WN diverges from PN^1 70 times. By contrast WN is apart from CX^2 only 26 times. WN's divergences from CX^2 include 5 agreements with the present edition; in addition to the convergence with PN^1 in line 2176, WN restores the text as printed here, either by independent thought (likely in lines 1844 and 1913) or happenstance, in the following places:

1757	**at dore**} at þe d. Ad^3 Cp Dd Gg Ha^4 La Ne+ CX^1–PN^1 TH^1–UR WR MR	
1864	**triklyng**} trillyng Ad^3 Cp Dd Ha^4 He La Pw+ CX^1–PN^1 PN^2–WR MR–RI	
1884	**accepteth**} exceptith (Ne+) CX^1–PN^1 PN^2	
1913	**acceptable**} exceptabil He+ CX^1–PN^1	

In one reading (at line 2226) WN reads with CX^1 against both PN^1 and CX^2, but this convergence seems accidental, as do the 4 agreements with PN^1 listed above.

WN introduces 17 new variants into the printed tradition, of which 12 are unique (mostly careless slips): at lines 1670, 1728, 1747, 1760, 1807, 1809, 1939, 1979, 1987, 2100, 2165, and 2267. None of the 5 readings with manuscript support (at lines 1827, 2052, 2077, 2169, 2205) is significant or informative. Three are quite easy slips, and none of the 17 manuscripts involved is supportive of more than one reading, nor are there any groupings discernible.

One may reasonably conclude that WN is CX^2 reset, with no important changes, perhaps some editorial tinkering, several typographical errors, and a marginal further degradation of the text.

Pynson 1526 (PN²)

PN^2, which has 341 variants from the present edition, evidently was set from CX^2, from which it differs in only 20 readings. These divergences include only 3 agreements with CX^1 (at lines 1935, 2176, 2226) and only 2 with PN^1 (at lines 2176, 2244). PN^2 shares 6 of WN's 26 divergences from CX^2 (at lines 1757, 1913, 1987, 2169, 2176, and 2226), but none of these 6 shared readings is striking, and it is unlikely that PN^2 derived any of them through consultation of WN. The fact that PN^2 has 12 readings never before printed likewise indicates that its convergences with WN against CX^2 are coincidental. Four of these new variants lack manuscript support (at lines 1739, 2161, 2163, and 2192), and manuscript support for 7 of the remaining new readings (at lines 1772, 1994, 2005, 2145, 2146, 2182, and 2209) is so scattered that the readings, like the unsupported variants, must be regarded as independent creations of PN^2. So too must be a reading (at line 2161) shared with the present edition and printed for the first time in PN^2.

Thynne 1532 (TH¹)

According to Pearsall (1984*a*:110–11), agreeing with Greg (1924:757), the TH^1 text of *NPT* was set up from WN. It was not, apparently, collated with a manuscript: "The changes introduced are of a familiar kind and can be readily explained in terms of independent editing by TH^1" (Pearsall 1984*a*:111). By contrast, Ross (1983:100) finds that in *MilT* "TH^1 is never with WN except coincidentally." Also in contrast is the evidence for *MilT* that TH^1 used a manuscript of the *c* or *d* family: "The relative frequency of their occurrence as possible sources for the TH^1 variants suggests that a manuscript close to *c*/*d* may have been his source, but the inconsistency of the sources also indicates that his manuscript source was not actually Cp La or Pw" (Ross 1983:101). Baker (1984:67) concludes that TH^1 was probably set from WN in *ManT*, perhaps with consultation of CX^2, but the paucity of the evidence precludes his hypothesizing about TH^1's possible use of manuscripts. For *SqT* Baker (1986) concludes that TH^1 was set from PN^2 "with consultation with both CX^2 and WN" (p. 132), and that Thynne used manuscripts very close to Dl, Mc, and Ra^1, and for the latter part of *SqT*, either Ra^2 or Ht, or one of their "close relatives" (p. 127). We do know that William Thynne gathered and used manuscripts in the preparation of his first edition (see Blodgett 1984), but the evidence gathered by the Variorum editors suggests that his procedures varied from tale to tale. Furthermore, other investigators have likewise proposed different copytexts for TH[1]: CX[1] (Skeat 1905:xxvi), WN (Greg), and "one or the other of Pynson's two editions" (Blodgett 1984:46–47).

It is difficult to identify sources for Thynne's text of *SumPT* because the evidence to be sifted is voluminous. TH[1] is the first to print the base text in 159 readings: at lines 1665, 1668, 1669, 1679 (2 readings), 1680, 1682, 1685, 1692, 1698, 1699 (2 readings), 1706, 1710, 1720, 1726, 1729, 1730, 1735, 1739 (2 readings), 1741, 1744 (2 readings), 1747, 1755 (2 readings), 1756, 1770, 1773 (2 readings), 1781, 1789 (2 readings), 1790 (2 readings), 1793, 1794, 1797, 1807, 1808, 1810, 1814, 1816, 1825 (3d lemma), 1827, 1828, 1847, 1849, 1851, 1856, 1862, 1865, 1867 (3 readings), 1872 (2 readings), 1875, 1876, 1877, 1879, 1884, 1887, 1889, 1891, 1900, 1903 (2 readings), 1907, 1909, 1910, 1920, 1925, 1929 (2 readings), 1930 (2 readings), 1931, 1935, 1937, 1941, 1943, 1946 (2 readings), 1947, 1949, 1950 (2 readings), 1955, 1959, 1960, 1961, 1963 (2 readings), 1967, 1974, 1976, 1977, 1979, 1984 (2 readings), 1987, 2002, 2006 (3 readings), 2010, 2011, 2028, 2047, 2049, 2058, 2064, 2065, 2074 (2d lemma), 2079, 2082, 2090, 2097, 2098, 2099, 2100, 2102, 2103, 2104 (2 readings), 2106, 2108, 2109, 2140, 2153, 2156 (2 readings), 2158, 2161, 2163, 2169, 2172, 2180, 2182, 2184, 2192 (2 readings), 2201, 2209, 2213, 2215 (2 readings), 2243, 2244, 2245, 2247, 2255, 2256, 2262, 2274, and 2286.

TH[1] also introduces 133 new variants with manuscript support: at lines 1693, 1697, 1704, 1721, 1722, 1724, 1726, 1728, 1743, 1745, 1756, 1766, 1780, 1783, 1792, 1796, 1798, 1804, 1810, 1814, 1820, 1823, 1829 (2 readings), 1842, 1848, 1851, 1856, 1858, 1863, 1868, 1875, 1876, 1878, 1886, 1892 (2 readings), 1899, 1914, 1919, 1927, 1931, 1938, 1944, 1946, 1951, 1953 (2 readings), 1959, 1960, 1969, 1971, 1982 (see note), 1985 (2 readings), 1986, 1987, 1989, 1991, 1992 (2 readings), 1994 (2 readings), 1999, 2002 (2 readings), 2006, 2013, 2015, 2020 (2 readings), 2030, 2035, 2038 (2 readings), 2049, 2055, 2059, 2061, 2063, 2075, 2082, 2086, 2096, 2105, 2108, 2110, 2119, 2122, 2127 (2 readings), 2129, 2133, 2137, 2142, 2144, 2145, 2150, 2153, 2155, 2156 (2 readings), 2161 (2 readings), 2172, 2178, 2181, 2187, 2189, 2191 (2 readings), 2198, 2202, 2203, 2209, 2212, 2214, 2220 (2 readings), 2222 (2 readings), 2226, 2227, 2241, 2250 (2 readings), 2251, 2256 (2 readings), 2272, 2277, 2289, and 2290.

TH[1] also prints 19 new variants without manuscript support: at lines 1686, 1690, 1795, 1800, 1819, 1834 (2 readings), 1842, 1843, 1920, 1925, 1928, 2014, 2062, 2077, 2145, 2211 (2 readings), and 2279. TH[1] thus makes over 300 changes in the text, a rate of almost 1 in every other line.

As for its copytext, *SumPT* offers little decisive evidence. TH[1] shares 137 variants with CX[1], 135 with CX[2], 138 with PN[1], 135 with WN, and 137 with PN[2]. Most of these variants appear in all the previous printed editions. One can assemble those cases where a printed edition deviates, with TH[1], from the sequence CX^1–PN^2, but no clear picture emerges. CX^1 and TH^1 are together against the rest of the group at lines 1939, 1964, 2042, 2096, 2218, 2235, 2246, and 2248; but CX^1 diverges from CX^2–TH^1 at lines 1860, 1864, 1983, 2235, and in 3 other instances that effectively eliminate CX^1 as copytext: at lines 1945, 2214, and 2285 CX^2–TH^1 add significant words not present in CX^1 or any extant manuscript. PN^1 and TH^1 are together against the rest of the group at lines 1682, 1745, 1912, 2074, and 2175, but PN^1 abandons the group at lines 2010 and 2084. WN and TH^1 are together against the rest of the group at lines 2052 and 2055, but WN leaves the group at lines 1757 (as does PN^2) and 1864. PN^2 and TH^1 are together against the rest of the group at lines 1772, 2005, and 2146; but PN^2 abandons the group at lines 1739 and 1757 (with WN). CX^1 and PN^2 are with TH^1 against the rest in a reading at line 1935. CX^2 never leaves the group but also has no exclusive convergences with TH^1.

Facts emerge more clearly in considering Thynne's use of manuscripts in constructing his text of *SumPT*. Of the 133 new variants with manuscript support, 102 fall before Pw breaks off at line 2158, and of these 102, Pw shares 64. In this same stretch of text Cp shares 14, while La shares 21. In lines 2159–2294 (after Pw has broken off), Cp shares 15 of the 31 variants, while La shares 16. The hypothesis that Thynne had access to and used a manuscript of the *cd* group is given support by these figures. TH^1 is variant with Pw and without Cp in 78 readings, and in only 15 readings with Cp and not Pw (through line 2140), which would suggest that the manuscript he used was closer to the *d* than to the *c* group. Since Pw and other *d* manuscripts break off after line 2158, we know that if Thynne was using a *d* manuscript he either turned to another manuscript to compare against his copytext of the *Tale* or was using a manuscript which (or whose exemplar) picked up the rest of the tale from another source. It seems most reasonable to assume that Thynne's manuscript contained the whole of *SumPT*, or he would presumably have chosen another to work with initially for this tale. Since the affiliation between TH^1 and Cp and La continues strongly (indeed intensifies) after line 2158, we can assume that his manuscript was one that switched to $cd*^2$ as opposed to one that picked up the end of *SumT* from other traditions (e.g., Nl from $b*$, En^3 and Ad^1 from *a*).

The extant manuscripts which fit these requirements are En^2 and Ha^2, and it is noteworthy that En^2 supports 72 of the variants first printed in TH^1 (19 after line 2158), and that Ha^2 supports 75 of those variants (16 after line 2158). These two manuscripts, moreover, support 4 of the variants shared by CX^1 and TH^1 against the other editions (at lines 1939, 2042, 2235, and 2246); 2 of the exclusive convergences of PN^1 and TH^1 (at lines 2074 and 2175); and one such convergence of WN and TH^1 (at line 2052). En^2 supports 10 new variants where Ha^2 does not; Ha^2 supports 13 new variants where En^2 does not. Substantial examples of the new TH^1 variants supported by these manuscripts include the following:

1722	**mowen}** m. elles Cp La Pw En^2 Ha^2+ TH^1–UR
1726	**Ye whan that}** If t. Cp La Pw En^2 Ha^2+ TH^1–SP^2
1745	**that}** as Pw En^2 Ha^2+ TH^1–SP^1
1783	**or}** and Cp La Pw En^2 Ha^2+ TH^1–TR
1810	**defautes}** all fautes Pw Ha^2+ TH^1–UR; al defautes En^2
1823	**sire}** maister Ad^3 Gg Pw En^2 Ha^2+ TH^1–SP^3
1829	**lyth}** þat l. Ha^4 He Pw En^2 Ha^2+ TH^1–UR WR
1829	**oure sty}** þe s. Pw Ha^2+ TH^1–SP^3
1892	**lyves}** saules Pw Ha^2+ TH^1–UR
1919	**no text of it}** no t. þer of Pw En^2 Ha^2+ TH^1–SP^3
1953	**gold}** good Ad^3 Gg Pw En^2 Ha^2+ TH^1–SP^3 TR
1999	**holy meke a}** h. and m. a Ha^4 $Ha3_1$+ TH^1–SP^3 TR–RB^1 RB^2
2015	**certes}** eek El Ad^3 Gg Pw En^2 Ha^2+ TH^1–SP^3 RB^1
2119	**help}** *om.* Pw En^2 Ha^2 (Ha^2_1 *corr.*)+ TH^1–SP^1
2153	**quod he}** q. þe frere Pw Ha^2+ TH^1–UR
2161	**with}** *om.* Cp La En^2 Ha^2+ TH^1–SP^3
2178	**ther nys}** is noon El Cp Ha^4 En^2 Ha^2+ TH^1–SP^3 WR–RB^1 RB^2 RI
2181	**ne greveth me}** me g. Cp La En^2 Ha^2+ TH^1–SP^3
2203	**aught}** nouȝt Cp Gg La Ha^2+ TH^1–UR
2209	**manere}** m. of Gg Ha^2+ TH^1–UR
2212	**diffame}** sclaundre Cp La En^2 Ha^2+ TH^1–SP^3
2227	**his}** thi Ad^3 Ha^2+ TH^1–UR
2251	**Tel}** T. on Cp La En^2 Ha^2+ TH^1–SP^3
2256	**that}** *om.* La En^2 Ha^2+ TH^1–SP^1
	it} he Cp La En^2 Ha^2+ TH^1–SP^3
2289	**Euclyde}** Ouyde did (Ii) TH^1–SP^1; Ouyde Ha^2+

Ha^2 was probably owned by Edward Fox (1496?–1538), Bishop of Hereford (1535), "one of the King's most trusted and powerful agents" (MR 1.205), secretary to Wolsey, and frequenter of the court from at least as early as 1528 (*DNB* 7.553–55). Thynne, as another habitué of the court, could easily have had access to the manuscript through Fox. This last suggestion is speculative, of course, but its plausibility suggests that the relationship between Ha^2 and TH^1 be examined carefully in our continuing work on the text of *The Canterbury Tales*.

A high percentage of the 19 variants introduced in TH^1 without manuscript support are rationalizations (at lines 1819, 1834, 1843 [2 readings], 1920, 1925, 1928, 2014, 2062) and modernizations (at lines 2077, 2145, 2211 [2 readings]). There are what appear to be slips in lines 1690, 1842, and 2279, and transpositions (of which Thynne seems to have been particularly fond, judging by the variants he chose from manuscript) in lines 1686, 1795 and 1800.

All in all, the text of *SumPT* was improved by Thynne's editorial work, and it was, for the first time, work that could be called editorial. His choice of manuscript was not what one might have wished, but the text that resulted is appreciably better than anything in print before. TH^1 has 306 variants from the present edition.

Thynne 1542 (TH²)

TH² is a reprint of TH¹, following TH¹ in all but 2 of its 306 variants (restoring the text of the present edition in line 1825 and introducing a new variant in line 1918) and introducing 6 further new variants (at lines 1744, 1901, 1932, 2027, 2028, and 2171), 3 of which are clearly compositor's errors. That two changes come together in lines 2027 and 2028 suggests that those are deliberate modernizations, but at line 1932 *prayers* for *preyere* is probably unconscious.

Thynne 1545 [1550] (TH³)

TH³ was published probably circa 1550, not 1545, the traditional *STC* date. This third edition, which has none of the variants first introduced by TH², is a careful reprint of TH¹, from which it differs in only 3 readings. At line 1724 TH³ replaces a variant in TH¹ with a new variant; at lines 1807 and 1916 it introduces variants, both accidental, where TH¹ agrees with the present edition.

Stow 1561 (ST)

ST is a reprint of TH³, as is indicated by the fact that ST follows TH³ in all 3 of that text's newly introduced variants; see also the arguments of Hudson (1984:59–60), which are based on evidence from other texts. ST differs from TH³ in only 4 readings. In line 1754, ST replaces a TH variant to reiterate an error from earlier editions:

> **wente ay hem]** w. him ay Ne+ CX¹,² WN PN² ST–SP³

but the variant is not suggestive of collation against manuscripts or editions earlier than TH³. ST also adds 3 variants never printed before:

> 1742   **And]** *om.* (Ps) ST SP²–UR
> 2071   **byreved]** bireuen ~ ST–UR
> 2232   **hym]** hem ~ ST–SP³

None of these indicates anything other than casual error. On balance, ST reproduces TH³ with great care, changing the text neither for better nor worse.

Speght 1598 (SP¹)

SP¹ was apparently set from ST, diverging from it only twice. At line 1714 SP¹ introduces a new variant where ST agrees with the present edition, and at line 1742 SP¹ agrees with the present edition (and CX¹–TH³) against ST. Thus SP¹, like ST, has 311 variants from the present edition.

Speght 1602 (SP²)

In 1599 Francis Thynne, son of the editor, sent to Speght his "Animadversions" (ed. Furnivall 1875) on the 1598 edition, and his criticisms led Speght to make a large number of changes in the 1602 text, though for *SumT* at least the result was not on balance a better text. SP^2 has 333 variants from the present edition, 22 more than either ST or SP^1. Because ST and SP^1 are nearly identical, one cannot demonstrate beyond doubt which of the two served as copytext for SP^2. However, evidence in other tales (see Baker 1990:106) indicates that ST was the copytext for SP^2, and in *SumT* SP^2 twice joins ST against SP^1 and has no agreements with SP^1 against ST. The following discussion assumes that ST is the copytext.

SP^2 diverges from ST 52 times. In 11 of these instances SP^2 agrees with the present edition (an asterisk marks readings printed first in SP^2): at lines 1690, 1721, 1745, 1804, 1982, 1994, *2007, *2042, 2119, 2220, and 2256. In 8 other divergences SP^2 introduces a different variant never before printed: with manuscript support at lines 1928, 2096, 2289; without manuscript support at lines 1772, 1912, 2082, 2121, and 2246. SP^2 adds 33 variants where ST is with the present edition. Two are variants printed previously only in CX^1, at lines 1839 and 2238; the others are printed for the first time in SP^2. Among the latter, 23 lack manuscript support: at lines 1691, 1695, 1805, 1809, 1829, 1890, 1941, 1949, 1977, 1984, 2016, 2030, 2053, 2063, 2067, 2108, 2122, 2140, 2168, 2201, 2243, 2256, and 2272.

There is little evidence that Speght made use of manuscripts in emending his text of *SumPT*. Fully 28 of the 41 readings printed for the first time in SP^2 have no manuscript support, and support for the remainder is too scattered and too thin to permit inferences about possible sources. The new readings with manuscript support are listed below:

1771	**curteisly}** al c. Ha^4 SP^2–WR	
1928	**for}** on Ad^3 Ha^4 Pw+ SP^{2,3} TR WR	
1955	**seche}** to s. Ad^3 Cp He La+ SP^2–TR	
2007	**is}** *thus* SP^2; is a He+ CX^1–SP^1	
2028	**ther}** t. as Cp La+ SP^{2,3} TR	
2042	**he did}** he let Ha^4 SP^{2,3} WR	
	do sleen hem} *thus* SP^2; h. s. Gg he Pw+ CX^1 TH^1–SP^1; do h. s. (Tc^1) CX^2–PN^2	
2096	**hooly al}** h. (Ha^3+) SP^{2,3}	
2134	**oother}** another (Fi+) SP^{2,3}	
2163	**ther}** *om.* El+ SP^2	
2227	**shrewe}** beshrew (Py) SP^{2,3}	
2253	**that}** *om.* La+ SP^2–UR	
2289	**Euclyde}** E. did (Ry^1) SP^{2,3} RB^1 RB^2 RI	

In all, 48 manuscripts may be adduced to support one or more of these readings, and no manuscript agrees with more than 6 of them. Ha^4 does show up 5 times, twice uniquely (at lines 1771, 2042), but the convergence could easily be accidental. Indeed, the fact that 5 of these 13 readings are supported by only one manuscript suggests coincidence throughout. For example, the reading in line 2289 is a reasonable (and perhaps correct) solution to the problems posed by a particularly vexing line (see Textual Note to line 2289) which might occur to any editor wrestling with it.

The 28 SP[2] variant readings which have no manuscript support point to a pattern of uniformly distributed tinkering with the text, modernizing, ill-considered rationalizing, and regularizing the meter, sometimes all at once. Particularly striking is the persistent adding of syllables to lines already regular, betokening an incomprehension of the syllabic value of final *e* in Chaucer's verse, e.g.,

1695	**on}** all on	~ SP[2]–UR
1772	**God yelde yow ful ofte}** g. y. it you for f. o.	~ SP[2,3]
1805	**right wel}** I fare r. w.	~ SP[2]–UR
1809	**the chirche}** t. whole c.	~ SP[2]–UR
1941	**to}** up to	~ SP[2,3]
1977	**And}** A. holy	~ SP[2,3]
2030	**they}** t. that	~ SP[2,3]
2108	**oure bookes}** needs al o. b.	~ SP[2,3]
2122	**afire}** on a fire	~ SP[2,3]
2168	**speke}** to s.	~ SP[2,3]
2201	**hadde herd}** hadde h. fully	~ SP[2,3]
2256	**looke}** l. well	~ SP[2,3]
2272	**By}** By good	~ SP[2,3]

There are 3 certain compositor's errors and 1 likely one:

1890	**wel ye}** w.	~ SP[2,3]
1949	**as}** *om.*	~ SP[2,3]
2243	**stood the}** s. t. t.	~ SP[2]
2246	**be ye nat}** be not not	~ SP[2]

Results unfortunately do not match Speght's visible efforts in this edition; as Pearsall puts it, "the tradition of the printed texts was by now so degenerate that no attempt to improve a text set up from a printed copy could do more than tinker with its defects" (1984*b*:87).

An interesting editorial innovation in SP[2] is the identification of sententious phrases, signaled by a pointing hand that appears next to lines 1793, 1879, 1973, 1989, 2001, 2009, 2015, 2049, 2051, 2054, 2074, 2085, 2173, and 2242. The only other change in the apparatus for this text is the placement of the "argument of the tale," in SP[1] at the front of the volume, in SP[2] between *SumP* and *SumT*.

Speght 1687 (SP[3])

Alderson points out that the circumstances of the publication of SP[3] "combine to suggest that one of the primary objectives of this edition was to establish a *de facto* copyright in Chaucer's works" (1970:48). There is little evidence of editorial activity in *SumPT*. The apparatus differs from that in SP[2] only in the marking of sententious passages; SP[3] uses stars instead of pointing hands, and fails to mark line 1793. SP[3]'s text of *SumPT* diverges from that of SP[2] only twice, correcting its compositor's errors in lines 2243 and 2246 to join the present edition. The title-page claim to the use of manuscripts in preparing SP[3] is, as Pearsall says, "false, though it is an interesting sign of the times, and of the interest in antiquity" (1984*b*:91).

Urry 1721 (UR)

It is difficult to assess the performance of UR in *SumPT*. UR is the most vilified of the printed editions, and the most idiosyncratic. But it is also one of the most purposive editions; Urry used manuscripts, common sense, and a clear idea of Chaucer as a poet to make slightly over 250 changes in the text as it was received, and he improved the text—by modern standards—about as often as he worsened it.

UR's text, which resulted from a great deal of editorial activity, has 339 variants from the present edition and thus represents no improvement over Urry's base text, which must have been one of the previous published editions. UR shares between 179–83 variants with members of TH[1]–ST and 182–86 variants with the members of SP[1-3]; with the members of CX[1]–PN[2] only 123–35 variants. Alderson (1970:93; 1984:97) reports that Urry had access to a copy of TH[2], but it seems to have had no effect on his choices of readings. In instances where there is disagreement among members of TH[1]–ST, UR joins TH[2] only three times, never exclusively, but converges 10 times with each of the other editions. Only with ST does UR have convergences not shared by any of the other members of the group, and Alderson notes (1970:98, 1984:99; cf. MR 1.115) that "a 1561 Stow is extant in which Urry's collation of that text with several manuscripts is identifiable." However, there are only 2 convergences of ST and UR against TH[1-3], and these are shared with members of SP[1-3].

When members of ST–SP[3] are divergent, UR is more often with ST than with any other member of the group (27 times with ST, 25 with SP[1], 15 with SP[2], 17 with SP[3]). Such data seem to favor ST or SP[1] as copytext, but most of the convergences involve agreements with the present edition (i.e., common readings with ample manuscript support), and UR's agreements with SP[2,3] (see lines 1695, 1771, 1805, 1809, 2063) tend to be more impressive than UR's agreements with ST SP[1] (see lines 1721, 1772, 1804, 2042). Moreover, as Alderson reports (1970:98; 1984:99), UR reproduces Speght's "argument" and, like SP[2] (also SP[3]), places it between the prologue and tale (see the collations below). On the other hand, in *SumPT* UR fails to highlight any of the passages marked as sententious in SP[2] (also SP[3]), though UR elsewhere follows some of these indications (see Alderson 1970:262n27; 1984:270–71).

Whatever base text Urry used, the influence of Speght's revised edition is evident. More evident still is Urry's exercise of editorial prerogative, which for convenience may be measured by comparing UR with SP². UR diverges from SP² in more than 250 readings, 100 times to agree with the present edition. Thirty-eight other divergences, likewise with manuscript support, are new variants printed for the first time in UR. These appear in lines 1666, 1687, 1694, 1696, 1701, 1716, 1724, 1742, 1746, 1778, 1783, 1814, 1818, 1823, 1829, 1850, 1873, 1883, 1912, 1939, 1949, 1981, 2002, 2014, 2033, 2097, 2111, 2123, 2145, 2168, 2191, 2211 (2 readings), 2226, 2231, 2266, 2278, 2290. Among manuscripts listed in UR or possibly consulted by Urry (see Alderson 1970:106–12, 263n75; 1984:104, 271n35), none supports more than 7 of the new variants. And none of the variants is particularly striking, certainly no more striking than some of UR's 66 variants that are without precedent either in manuscripts or in printed editions. Many could be the result of accidental convergence; it is noteworthy that Ha⁴, a manuscript not associated with UR, supports 10 of UR's new variants. One may observe further that UR, as Alderson notes (1970:93–94; 1984:97–98), was not printed from a corrected copy of an earlier edition but from a transcription of such a text made by Urry—"I transcribe every line, so that I, that am not a swift penman, find I have set myself a tedious task" (quoted from Alderson). By the time of his death in 1715 Urry had completed a fair copy to the end of *FranT*, which in the UR order is past *SumT*. UR's text, then, probably includes transcription errors as well as typesetting errors, which combine to obscure further Urry's use of his sources.

Nevertheless, one cannot discount the influence of manuscripts on UR. In 26 instances UR converges with the present edition against all previous editions: at lines 1665, 1673 (2 readings), 1699, 1726, 1728, 1811, 1840, 1846, 1847, 1887, 1908, 1936, 1988, 1995, 2003, 2048, 2051, 2060, 2068, 2080, 2156, 2174, 2202, 2220, 2290. At least 2 of these convergences involve substitutions that seem to require consultation of manuscripts: at lines 1840 and 1947. It is difficult to determine which manuscripts assisted most in such corrections, since many of Urry's manuscripts support them. And where evidence is scant (see line 1887, where Urry was doubtless counting syllables) accidental convergence still seems the most likely hypothesis.

The independent changes that Urry makes in *SumPT* (all unique readings) may be classified as either metrical adjustment or modernization/rationalization. Urry believed Chaucer's meter to be perfectly iambic, and sought in his edition to excavate or reconstruct a Chaucer of Augustan regularity. As the Preface of Timothy Thomas says, "whenever he could by no other way help a Verse to a Foot, which he was perswaded it had when it came from the Maker's hands, but lost by the Ignorance of Transcribers, or Negligence of Printers, he made no scruple to supply it with some Word or Syllable that serv'd for an Expletive" (as cited in Alderson 1970:122–23; 1984:110). The syllables thus added were quite often ungrammatical or unhistorical:

1670	**lye]** ylye
1671	**my tale telle]** m. t. ytell
1672	**bosteth]** ybostith
1922	**seyde]** saidin
2121	**weex wel neigh wood]** woxin n. w.
2122	**wolde]** woldin

Sometimes an inflectional ending would be spelled *id, in, ith* for *ed, en, eth* to indicate that it should be sounded for the rhythm. Very often a line was smoothed with the addition (1684 **to]** unto) or subtraction (1703 **Unto]** To) of syllables, or addition of entire words or phrases:

1680	**say]** yet s.
1704	**he quook]** still he q.
1813	**by]** and by
1824	**for Seinte]** now f. S.
1825	**He]** For he
1900	**preye]** did p.
1903	**for it]** ynow f. it
1977	**buylden]** b. up
2011	**I koude of ire seye]** Of i. right k. I s.
2028	**ther]** t. where
2032	**lord]** l. lo
2039	**art cause]** the c. a.
2108	**oure bookes]** alle o. b.
2172	**se wel]** se right w.
2208	**ful]** alle f.
2256	**looke]** l. to
2272	**By]** And by

and subtraction of words:

1685	**a]** *om.*
1786	**a]** *om.*
2068	**he]** *om.*
2078	**But]** *om.*

It is clear from a number of readings that though Urry professed to believe in the metrical value of unstressed -e and inflections in Chaucer's lines he very often overlooked opportunities to use them. A particularly striking example is line 1899, "No drynke which that myghte hem dronke make," which appears in UR as "No kind of drink, that dronkin might hem make." To be fair, Urry inherited a version of this line that lacked *which* and contained the transposition in the last phrase; only a good manuscript could have provided him lines both metrical and grammatically correct. Therein lies, of course, the fatal weakness of Urry's aspirations. With neither the knowledge of Middle English required to recognize bona fide metrically significant unstressed syllables nor a consistent use of a better manuscript to serve as a base for his adjustments, he could hope only to create a metrical Chaucer, not to rediscover one.

Modernizations and/or rationalizations account for over a dozen of the unique UR readings. Syntax as well as lexis is subjected to modernization, and everywhere there is visible an effort to excavate a clean, rational Chaucer.

1666	**frere his}**	f. he star'd h.
1669	**I}**	And
1734	**his way}**	away
1745	**that}**	as if
1872	**althogh that they were}**	albeit they w.
1903	**War that I seye}**	W. what I s.
2041	**nat doon that I comanded}**	n. d. what I c.
2194	**ye}**	we ~ PN^1 UR
2205	**How that me thynketh}**	H. me t.
2247	**gowne clooth}**	g. of c.
2252	**gowne clooth}**	g. of c.

Tyrwhitt 1775 (TR)

Tyrwhitt collated his manuscripts against SP^3, recording variants from his manuscripts on fresh interleaved pages, and ultimately into a copy of SP^2, which, annotated in Tyrwhitt's hand with his changes, and identical to TR, has come down to us (Windeatt 1984:123; see also Hench 1950). Two of the SP^2 unique readings remain

1829	**lyk}**	as ~ SP^{2,3} TR
1984	**meke}**	good ~ SP^{2,3} TR

but overall TR represents a massive improvement in the text of *SumPT*. Though some 15 readings suggest at least the possibility that Tyrwhitt consulted UR upon occasion, he seems to have taken some pains to avoid that edition, regarding it as "the worst that was ever published" (TR 1.xx). Of the 104 variants introduced into the print tradition by UR, TR follows in only 5 (at lines 1696, 1746, 1823, and 2211 [2 readings]), and each of these readings is supported by at least one of the manuscripts Tyrwhitt used. TR also agrees with UR against SP^2 in 10 variants present in earlier editions: at lines 1754, 1772, 1848, 1867, 2004, 2064, 2096, 2125, 2140, 2245. Each of these readings likewise is supported by manuscripts that Tyrwhitt is known to have consulted. To measure the considerable achievement represented by TR, then, one must compare it to SP^2 rather than UR.

TR follows only 84 of the 333 SP^2 variants and agrees with the present edition in 226 readings where SP^2 has variants. Seventy-seven of the readings shared with the present edition are printed for the first time in TR: at lines 1686, 1687, 1693, 1694, 1698, 1714, 1748, 1757, 1761, 1764, 1778, 1780, 1782, 1792, 1794, 1810, 1817, 1818, 1819, 1822 (2 readings), 1823, 1843,

1858, 1860, 1899, 1906, 1912, 1920 (2 readings), 1932, 1937, 1944, 1946, 1949, 1950, 1955, 1973, 1985, 1990, 1993, 2010, 2012, 2014 (2 readings), 2020, 2032, 2035, 2046, 2053 (2 readings), 2054, 2062, 2084 (2 readings), 2088, 2097, 2105, 2111, 2120, 2121, 2124, 2127, 2146, 2148 (2 readings), 2161, 2173, 2177, 2204, 2209, 2218, 2236, 2250, 2279, 2289 (2 readings).

TR introduces 32 new variants, 28 with manuscript support. The readings not supported by manuscript are these:

1695	**Twenty]** A t.	
1798	**in the yerd I trowe that]** I trow that in the y.	
1812	**Graunt]** Grand	
1821	**Jesu Crist]** our Lord I. C.	

The reading in line 1821 was quite possibly suggested by En^3, which reads *our Lord Iesu*. The variant in line 1695 represents a metrical adjustment to a headless line, which adjustment Tyrwhitt explicitly acknowledges (4.273; see Textual Note to line 1695). The other two readings may well have been unconscious changes.

The 28 new variants supported by manuscript are in lines 1673, 1692, 1698, 1703, 1768 (2 readings), 1777, 1792, 1816, 1828, 1834, 1856, 1872, 1886, 1938, 1991, 1993, 2084, 2091, 2109, 2116, 2128 (2 readings), 2160, 2212, 2213, and 2272 (2 readings). Tyrwhitt lists the manuscripts he collated or consulted (TR 1. xx–xxiii). These are, with the number of agreements with TR indicated:

Ad^1	7	En^3	7	Ha^5	8	Ld^2	6	Sl^1	3
Bo^2	1	Ha^1	0	Ht	1	Ne	0	Sl^2	3
Bw	1	Ha^2	6	Ii	1	Ry^1	5	Tc^1	5
Dd	9	Ha^3	2	La	3	Ry^2	6	Tc^2	1
En^1	9	Ha^4	11	Ld^1	1	Se	1		

Additionally, he had access to collations of Dl (0) and En^2 (9) done by Thomas in the preparation of UR (Windeatt 1984:123). According to Tyrwhitt himself, the manuscripts to which "the most credit is certainly due" (1.xxiii) are Ha^5, Dd, En^3, Ad^1, and En^1. "The manuscript to which Tyrwhitt's collation practice reveals that he gave most authority was A [Ha^5]. . . . In the absence of A, Tyrwhitt makes most use of C.1 [Dd], and failing both of these he tends to use C [Ha^4]" (Windeatt 1984:124). As the figures above suggest, these new variants support the assessment of Tyrwhitt himself and Windeatt, though the high number of agreements with Ha^4 is perhaps somewhat unexpected. TR is with Ha^4 5 times exclusively:

1768	**goode]** housbond Ha^4 TR WR	
1768	**whos]** w. þat Ha^4 TR–RB^1 RB^2 RI	

1792 **al}** ay Ha[4] TR WR
2272 **By}** By verray Ha[4] TR WR
2272 **which}** *om.* Ha[4]+ TR WR

There is 1 variant shared exclusively with Ha[5],

2091 **ay at}** ay to (Ha[5]) TR

and 1 with Dd (also shared with Ps, but that manuscript was already in the Royal Library of France):

1673 **that it is}** t. is but Dd+ TR

Because Ha[4] and Dd are members of the base-group, somewhat more information is available on the relationship between TR and those manuscripts, but it tends only to confirm in general terms the findings of Windeatt. TR is variant overall in 146 readings. Of these, 57 are shared with Dd and 48 with Ha[4]. A significant proportion of these, 21 readings, are shared by both Dd and Ha[4], in part because Ha[4] and Dd are not unrelated in *SumPT* (see above, "The Textual Tradition") and probably also in part because Tyrwhitt would consider such agreement between his two highly regarded texts as weighty. The Ha[4] Dd TR agreements are clustered heavily in the first half of the text; there are only 4 after line 1983. Though Ha[4] continues to share variants beyond that point with TR at about the same rate as earlier, the incidence of Dd shared variants becomes rather spotty: there are 4 in the 120-line section 1995–2114, 7 in the following 30 lines, and only 5 in the remaining 150 lines. A similar on-again-off-again relationship between TR and Dd seems to hold throughout, whereas the variants shared with Ha[4], though fewer, are very evenly distributed, as if Tyrwhitt trusted Dd thoroughly some of the time, and trusted Ha[4] less, without support, but always considered its testimony worth consideration.

Wright 1847–51 (WR)

The edition of Thomas Wright, which "represented Chaucer's most famous work for almost a half century" (Ross 1984*b*:156, which see *passim* on WR), contains in its introduction the promise of the first clean break from the previous printed editions and the return to manuscript authority: ". . . it is clear that, to form a satisfactory text of Chaucer, we must give up the printed editions, and fall back upon the manuscripts; and that, instead of bundling them all together, we must pick out one best manuscript which at the same time is one of those nearest to Chaucer's time" (WR 1.xxxv). Unfortunately, the potential of the new editorial method was undone by Wright's choice of manuscript: Ha[4]. WR is the first of the printed editions to be constructed on "best-text" principles, being essentially a printing of Ha[4]. The choice of Ha[4] as the base manuscript, though understandable, even predictable, given the reputation of superiority enjoyed by that manuscript among those of Wright's generation, was nonetheless unfortunate, since Ha^4 is a highly idiosyncratic text (see above under "Description of Manuscripts"). Also unfortunate was the lack of consistency of the edition. Though it is difficult to imagine what the proper treatment of Ha^4 would have been, WR often emended without notice, and few remarks are forthcoming on the principles of emendation. TR was of course the immediate predecessor of WR, and there is no question that WR used it. Wright also claimed to have collated La, but felt he had "reaped little benefit from collating a number of manuscripts" (WR 1.xxxvii). The use of La is sporadic, and the resulting text is neither an improvement on TR nor a faithful transcription of Ha^4.

WR follows 231 of the 276 Ha^4 variants, including several spurious lines. In 7 readings WR is variant without Ha^4, agreeing 3 times with TR and not La (at lines 1793, 1846, 1993), once with La and not TR (at line 1739), twice with both (at lines 1838, 1935), and once with neither (unique reading at line 1973).

1739	mele and cheese} m. or c. Cp La Ne Pw+ CX^{1,2} WN PN^2 WR; m. c. Ha^4+
1793	a glorious} a ful g. Dd He+ CX^1–PN^2 TR WR
1838	quod he now} q. he Cp Gg He La Pw+ CX^1–RB^1
1846	and} a. so Dd He Pw+ CX^1–SP^3 TR WR
1935	His foore} h. lore Cp He La Pw+ CX^1 PN^2–WR
1973	worthy is} is w. Cp Ha^4 He La Pw+ CX^1–UR; is w. of ~ WR
1993	hire} Ire Ad^3 Pw+ TR WR PR

Wright promised to correct errors in his base text, dividing errors into those cases of scribal error "which it requires very little knowledge to perceive and correct" (1.xxxvi) and those in which an Ha^4 reading, "although affording a tolerable meaning, has appeared to me a decided bad one" (1.xxvii). In the former cases, he wrote, "I have not thought it necessary to load the book with notes pointing out the alterations," while in the latter case he promised "always (when there is room for the least doubt) [to give] the original reading of the manuscript in a foot-note" (1.xxxvii). While the promise not to load the book with notes was kept (unfortunately), the second promise was not. Of the 39 instances in which WR emends Ha^4 to match the present edition, he signals only 7 (at lines 1718, 1729, 1734, 1860, 1876, 1879, 2059) with a note, and in lines 1718 and 1876 he acknowledges only one of the two emendations he makes. No consistent reasoning is discernible in the choice of which changes are signalled and which are not.

In line 1904 WR notes a La and TR reading, while printing the reading of Ha^4 (and this edition). WR notes that the four pairs of (spurious) Ha^4 lines following lines 2004, 2012, 2037, and 2048 are not found in TR, but his note for the pair of lines following line 2037 mistakenly identifies the lines "not in Tyrwhitt" as 7612–13 (D 2030–31), whereas they are in fact WR 7620–21. The two pairs of lines are almost identical, so the mistake is understandable. It is less understandable why, though the other pairs of lines not found in TR are excluded from the WR line numbering, so that the WR and TR line numbers remain parallel, this pair of lines is counted in the numbering, throwing off the alignment with TR. At line 2220 WR, following Ha[4] in reading *eft* for *erst* notes that "some of the MSS read *erst*." In fact, according to MR, all do except Ad[1].

Modern Editions: Skeat 1900 (SK), Robinson 1933 (RB[1]), Manly-Rickert 1940 (MR), Robinson 1957 (RB[2]), Pratt 1974 (PR), Riverside 1987 (RI)

SK is based upon El, which Skeat called "the best [manuscript of *CT*] in nearly every respect" (SK 4.xvii), more specifically upon the Chaucer Society printing of that and other manuscripts: "[M]y work," wrote Skeat of the edition, "is entirely founded upon the splendid 'Six-text' Edition published by [the Chaucer] Society, supplemented by the very valuable reprint of the celebrated 'Harleian' manuscript [Ha[4]] in the same series" (SK 4.vii).

SK follows El in 36 of its 101 variants from the current edition (at lines 1665, 1695, 1721, 1744, 1872, 1988 [2 readings], 2035, 2052 [2 readings], 2088 [2 readings], 2108 [2 readings], 2109, 2111, 2113, 2134, 2144, 2150, 2160, 2176, 2178, 2186, 2204, 2212, 2213, 2220, 2226, 2235, 2236, 2240, 2245, 2260, 2261, 2262), corrects to the reading of the present edition in 65 readings (at lines 1676, 1700 [2 readings], 1720, 1746, 1794, 1870, 1887, 1934, 1949 [2 readings], 1950, 1952, 1968, 1981, 1994, 2002, 2015, 2030, 2047, 2055, 2062, 2116, 2126, 2128, 2133, 2137, 2140, 2162, 2163, 2170, 2172 [3 readings], 2175, 2181, 2185, 2190, 2192, 2200, 2204, 2211, 2212, 2218 [2 readings], 2219, 2224, 2227, 2229, 2232, 2235, 2245 [2 readings], 2246, 2249, 2255, 2259, 2268, 2278 [2 readings], 2285, 2287, 2289 [2 readings], and 2290), and departs from El in 15 variant readings (at lines 1768, 1784, 1804, 1838, 1895, 1918, 1927, 1983, 1991, 1999, 2096, 2116, 2201, 2211, and 2289). The reasons for these last departures from El are generally metrical, and in this preference and these readings SK is usually in the company of both earlier and later editors. In 4 readings (at lines 2116, 2201, 2211, 2289) SK introduces a variant not seen in print before. Two of these lack manuscript support:

2211   **on oother wise may**] on him o. weyes El; in o. w. m. Ha[4]+ UR–WR; on o. weyes m. ~ SK
2289   **or elles**] or as ~ SK PR

The reading in line 2211 suggests that, dissatisfied with the unique El reading (Skeat's note shows he that recognized the insertion of *him* as an error), Skeat nevertheless preferred the Hg–El *on* to the Ha[4] *in*, and preferred the El *weyes* to the Hg–Ha[4] *wise*. In the note to line 2289, Skeat writes that "MS [Ha[4]] supplies *elles*, but I believe *as* to be right" (SK 5.341). The SK reading in line 2201 (**hadde herd**] had h. al) is supported only by En[3] and Ad[1]. Skeat cites

Ad[1] as his source; it replaces Pw in the Six-Text transcription (Furnivall 1868–77) because Pw lacks the final portion of the tale.

Ha[4] alone supports the reading in line 1768 (whos} w. þat Ha[4] TR–RB[1] RB[2] RI) and alone among the Chaucer Society texts supports that in line 1999 (holy meke a} h. and m. a Ha[4]+ TH[1]–SP[3] TR–RB[1] RB[2]). Gg alone shares the reading in line 2116 (sith} s. at Gg SK). On the whole, however, SK prints readings with widespread support. Six of his departures from El are shared with Cp, 10 with Gg, 6 with Ha[4], 6 with La, and 8 with Pw.

The textual notes which accompany SK at the bottom of the page are thorough, though of course dealing almost exclusively with variants found in the "Six-Text" manuscripts; the notes are attached only to lines in which SK differs from El, but, as claimed, "every instance of this character is invariably recorded in the footnotes" (SK 4.xviii). I noticed only one small error: the note for 1696 is misnumbered as 1693. For a discussion of SK, see Edwards (1984).

RB[1] is based on El; manuscripts figuring in its construction were chiefly the seven others transcribed for the Chaucer Society (Hg Gg Cp La Pw Ha[4] Dd; see Furnivall 1868–77; 1885; 1902) and also Cn and Mg, which were available to Robinson. The RB[1] textual introduction makes clear that, conservative and scrupulous in dealing with the textual evidence as Robinson was, metrical considerations were clearly important to him, and he often chose readings from manuscripts other than El when they offered greater metrical regularity. Indeed, RB[1] rejects El and prints 61 readings that agree with the present edition: at lines 1676, 1695, 1700 (2 readings), 1720, 1746, 1794, 1870, 1887, 1934, 1952, 1968, 1981, 1988, 1994, 2002, 2030, 2047, 2055, 2062, 2088 (2 readings), 2109, 2116, 2126, 2128, 2133, 2144, 2162, 2163, 2170, 2172 (3 readings), 2175, 2181, 2185, 2190, 2192, 2200, 2211, 2218 (2 readings), 2219, 2224, 2227, 2229, 2232, 2245, 2246, 2249, 2255, 2259, 2260, 2268, 2278 (2 readings), 2285, 2287, 2289, 2290.

RB[1] departs from El and the present edition in 15 readings: at lines 1696, 1768, 1784, 1804, 1828, 1838, 1855, 1895, 1918, 1927, 1991, 1999, 2125, 2245, 2289. In 9 of these instances RB[1] agrees with SK; Ha[4] supports 4 of the remaining 6 instances. One reading (at line 2245) is supported only by Gg of the base-group manuscripts, and Cn; and in the vexing line 2289 the RB[1] reading is supported only by Ry[1]. RB[1] differs from the present edition in 39 other readings: at lines 1665, 1721, 1744, 1872, 1949 (2 readings), 1950, 1988, 2015, 2035, 2052 (2 readings), 2108 (2 readings), 2111, 2113, 2134, 2137, 2140, 2150, 2160, 2176, 2178, 2186, 2204 (2 readings), 2212 (2 readings), 2213, 2220, 2226, 2235 (2 readings), 2236, 2240, 2245, 2261, 2262, 2289. For a general treatment of RB[1], see Reinecke (1984).

MR's text, which reconstructs on the basis of all known manuscripts of *The Canterbury Tales* a putative first scribal copy (O[1]), differs from the present edition in 27 readings: at lines 1665, 1693, 1694, 1696, 1721, 1754, 1757, 1804,

1855, 1864, 1868, 1872, 1887, 1895, 1918, 1927, 1983, 1991, 2052 (2 readings), 2113, 2150, 2160, 2220, 2240, and 2289 (2 readings). Two of these readings Manly and Rickert regarded as errors introduced into O[1]: *mount* for *mountayne* in line 1887 (but see the Textual Note to line 1887 for evidence that their decision was never completely settled), and *Protholomee* for *Ptholome* in line 2289. At line 1993 MR and the present edition share a reading that Manly and Rickert likewise regarded as a scribal error in O[1] (see the Textual Note, below). In general, the differences between MR's text and the present one (listed in the description of Hg, above) arise from a greater adherence on the part of this edition to Hg. Each of these differences is discussed in the appropriate Textual Note below.

There are a number of differences between the reporting of variants in MR and in this edition. These differences are gathered together below and categorized roughly for the convenience of interested readers. There is room for doubt in how exactly to categorize some of the differences. An item noted under "Lines for which variants are not reported" might have been more properly listed under "Differences of opinion on substantiveness," or vice versa. In other words, MR may have not reported a variant either because they did not see it or because they considered it non-substantive or, as is several times demonstrable—and entirely understandable—because of simple clerical error. I have tried to sort these out reasonably, but interested readers should consult both categories. As is several times noted herein (see especially the Textual Note to line 1671), the Variorum guidelines call for a more thorough reporting of variant forms in imperative verbs than was practiced by MR. Such differences are found listed below.

1. Lines for which variants are not reported or are mis-reported in MR: 1683, 1725, 1729, 1742, 1743, 1744, 1745, 1756 (2 variants), 1769, 1777, 1788, 1789, 1793, 1794, 1797, 1802, 1824, 1829, 1847, 1850, 1851, 1858, 1863, 1872, 1883, 1886, 1887, 1891, 1892, 1893, 1895, 1915, 1917, 1940, 1964, 1983, 1991, 1995, 1998, 2034, 2073, 2096, 2168, 2212 (variant reported correctly in Corpus of Variants, incorrectly in analysis [2.241]), 2220, 2250, 2291.

2. Differences of opinion on substantiveness.
    A) Lines for which readings are reported as variants in MR and not in these Collations: 1701, 1926, 2081, 2122, 2281.
    B) Lines for which readings are reported as variants in these Collations and not in MR:
        i.   Variants in imperative forms: 1671, 1824, 2053, 2074, 2075, 2189, 2198, 2203, 2230, 2241, 2246.
        ii. Others: 1696, 1720, 1774, 1847, 1908, 1982, 2003, 2008, 2018, 2047, 2067, 2070, 2099, 2104, 2120, 2222, 2238, 2252.

3. Other: 1671 (ambiguous scribal correction), 1748 (spelling difference), 1857 (difficult reading; interpretation of scribal practice), 1968 (spelling difference), 2161 (spelling difference).

The particulars of each of these differences are reported in the Textual Notes accompanying the relevant lines.

MR's record of variants on their collation cards differs from that in their Corpus of Variants on 11 occasions. For lines 1940, 1964, 1983, 1991, 2073, and 2096 an omitted variant is correctly noted on the MR collation card; typographical error in moving from the card to their Corpus of Variants apparently accounts for the omission. On the other hand, for lines 2003, 2018, 2120, 2222, and 2252 the changes seem to be deliberate: all 5 involve readings that are corrected in their respective manuscripts. For a general critique of MR, see Kane (1984).

RB^2, which shares 48 of RB^1's 54 variants from the present edition, shows the influence of MR in the 7 changes that distinguish RB^2 from RB^1: 6 of these (at lines 1838, 1949 [2 readings], 1950, 2015, 2186) agree with the present edition, and one (at line 1864) does not. On RB^2 generally, see Reinecke (1984).

PR, presented as a revision of RB^2, is significantly influenced by MR. Pratt himself notes that he was "less conservative than [Robinson] in admitting readings from Manly and Rickert; in fact the present text [PR] represents as accurately as possible Manly's 'latest common original of all extant manuscripts' (O^1)" (PR 561). PR varies, consequently, from the present edition in only 23 readings. Seventeen of these variants are shared by RB^2: at lines 1665, 1696 (but see the collation and Textual Note, *infra*), 1721, 1804, 1855, 1864, 1872, 1895, 1918, 1927, 2052 (2 readings), 2113, 2150, 2160, 2220, and 2240. The remaining 6 readings are at lines 1693, 1694, 1868, 1991, 1993, 2289. PR rejects 4 MR readings also rejected by this edition (at lines 1754, 1757, 1887, 1983), is variant without MR in line 1993 (**hire**] Ire Ad^3 Pw+ TR WR PR), and follows SK in the emendation of line 2289. Each of these differences from the present edition is discussed above in the description of Hg or below in the appropriate Textual Note.

RI, which for *The Canterbury Tales* is "a revision of Robinson's work, with errors corrected and relatively few new readings introduced" (RI xlv), makes 4 changes from RB^2: aligning with the present edition in lines 1784, 1999, and 2125; and variant in line 1993.

The Present Edition

This edition is based on Hg, and follows that manuscript's spelling, modernizing as follows: *u* and *v*, *i* and *j* are adjusted according to modern usage, *th* is used for þ, capitalization is modernized. Also, Hg's one roman numeral (in line 1964) is spelled out as a word (because El also has a numeral, the spelling of the word is taken from Dd, the next manuscript in the standard order). The words or letters lost from Hg because of the activity of rats are supplied from El and signalled by half-closed brackets. Punctuation is modern, but deliberately quite light. Word division is generally adjusted to conform to modern usage, though there are certain problems; often enough the joining of such pairs of words as "no thyng" into "nothyng" works counter to the rhythm of the line, and suggests, artificially, a metrical roughness. Generally, "thyng" preceded by such adjectives as "no," "some," or "swich" receives stress (in lines 1715, 1948, 1966, 1988, 2124, 2143, 2181, 2229, 2245, and perhaps 2172); in lines 1668, 1753, and 1866 it does not. In those cases where "thyng" is the stressed syllable, it seems more accurate to leave the words divided as they are found in Hg. Since in only one instance (at line 1866) does "thyng" occur in an unstressed position while preceded by a word with which it might be joined according to modern conventions, for the sake of consistency all "thyngs" are left unattached.

As Blake (1977:57–60) has pointed out, there is a certain arbitrariness about italicizing non-English words in editions of Middle English texts. Because the status of French words in English texts, in particular, is difficult to assess (were they already domesticated when they appeared, or were they still "French"?), Blake argues against marking such words or phrases with the conventional modern italics which imply that the word or phrase would have been perceived as "foreign" to the original audience. Friar John uses several French and Latin phrases in the course of *SumT*. The status of the Latin phrases is clear enough: not only are these not English, they are snatches of the language of the Church. The status of the French is more difficult to assess. On the one hand, one is tempted to italicize the words precisely to call attention to the Friar's pretentiousness, his parading of his learning and verbal sophistication, of which his French phrases are but one instance. On the other hand, critical interpretation should not conceal itself within typographical decisions, and Blake is surely correct in arguing that in a similarly non-cosmopolitan setting, *Piers Plowman* B Prologue 223–24, it is inconsistent to imply (by italicizing) that "Dieu vous save Dame Emme!" is foreign or exotic while the text presents us with the image of the (English) fair field full of folk singing it. Similarly, Friar John clearly expects Thomas, later identified—perhaps more pejoratively than technically—as a churl, to understand him when he exclaims "je vous dy Thomas, Thomas" (1832), as he must expect Thomas's wife to understand his remark "Now dame, . . . je vous dy sanz doute" (line 1838). The French phrases are thus not italicized. This decision is given some support by the scribe's habit in Hg and El of writing Latin, but not French, in a somewhat heavier and larger hand than the surrounding English text.

The Collations record substantive variants from the text as printed here, following generally the principles underlying MR (but see the description of MR, above); there are sometimes differences in the forms of the lemmata owing to the greater number of manuscripts collated by MR and the collation of printed editions here. Variants are recorded in a standard order in the Collations, Hg first, followed by El, and then the remaining base-group manuscripts in alphabetical order. Variants in the printed editions are recorded in chronological order, CX[1] being considered for these purposes a printed edition rather than a manuscript. When a variant found in base-group manuscripts is reported or implied by the MR Corpus of Variants to be in other manuscripts, a + sign signals this fact; the reader interested in the distribution of such a variant can turn to MR for fuller particulars. The absence of the + sign thus usually means that the variant is not found among non-base-group manuscripts, but in a few cases it means only that MR do not report the variant at all. When a printed edition shows a variant not supported by any of the base-group manuscripts, the distribution of the variant is signalled in one of two ways: if MR report no manuscript with the variant, a ~ sign precedes the sigil of the printed edition; if MR report one or more manuscripts with the variant, the sigil of the first (understood alphabetically) manuscript from their report is given in parentheses before the printed edition sigil. If more than one manuscript is reported by MR to have that variant, a + sign is added.

The Collations are followed by Textual and Explanatory Notes, separated by a § sign where both occur together for a line. The Textual Notes seek to present and in some instances analyze the textual history of a given locus (e.g., manuscript evidence, editorial decisions and the textual comments of earlier editors) as a supplement to the Collations. The Explanatory Notes gather the commentary which has accrued on specific passages. Citations of the major editions in these notes are abbreviated to their Variorum sigils. Thus in this context TR refers to Tyrwhitt's line notes (found in TR 4.273–77; Tyrwhitt's line number is also given), WR refers to Wright's note to the textual locus in question, for *SumPT* found in WR 2.16–40; SK refers to Skeat's notes found in 5.330–41. RB with no superscript refers to the explanatory note to the relevant line in both RB[1] (pp. 810–13) and RB[2] (pp. 706–08); where there is any difference between the notes of the two Robinson editions, the particular sigil will be given. Similarly, the notations Richardson (RI) and PR refer to the appropriate explanatory note in those editions (RI, pp. 876–79) unless further specifications are given. MR without further specification refers in all cases to the relevant textual note (styled "Critical Notes") in MR 3.465–68.

Part Seven
The Summoner's Tale

Ther as that Somnours han hir heritage
And god that made after his ymage
Mankynde saue and gyde vs alle and somme
And leue thise Somnours goode men to bicomme
Lordynges I koude han told yow quod this frere
Hadde I had leyser for this Somnour heere
After the text of Crist Poul and John
And of ful many othere Scriptures mony oon
Swiche peynes that youre hertes myghte agryse
Al be it so no tonge may deuyse
Thogh that I myghte a thousand wynter telle
The peynes of thilke cursed hous of helle
But for to kepe vs fro that cursed place
Waketh and preyeth Jhu for his grace
So kepe vs fro the temptour Sathanas
Herketh this word beth war as in this cas
The leoun sit in his awayt alway
To sle the Innocent if that he may
Disposeth ay youre hertes to withstonde
The feend that yow wolde maken thral and bonde
He may nat tempte yow ouer youre myght
For Crist wol be youre champion and knyght
And prayeth that this Somnours hem repente
Of hir mysdedes er that the feend hem hente

Here endeth the freres tale

The prologe of the Somnours tale

This Somnour in his Styropes hye he stood
Vp on this frere his herte was so wood
That lyk an aspen leef he quook for Ire
Lordynges quod he but o thyng I desire
I yow biseke that of youre curteisye
Syn ye han herd this false frere lye
As suffreth me I may my tale telle
This frere bosteth that he knoweth helle
And god it woot that it is litel wonder
Freres and feendes been but lyte a sonder

The Prologe of the Somnours tale

This somnour in his stiropes hye he stood;   1665
Upon this frere his herte was so wood
That lyk an aspen lief he quook for ire.

Out: Gg (*lines* 1665–1746, 2285–94); He (*lines* 1718–89); Pw (*lines* 2163–2294)
Rubric: **The Prologe of the Somnours tale**] Here endeth the freres tale   Here
bygynneth t. p. o. t. S. t. Ad³; Her endeþ þe Frere his tale Cp; Hic desinit fabula fra*tris* Et
incipit p*ro*logus So*m*monitoris Dd; Here endith þe frere his tale and here bygynneth t.
sompnour his p. Ha⁴; Here endith the Frere his tale Begynnyng o. t. S. p. He; Explicit
fabula. Incipit p*ro*log*us* ap*a*ritoris La; Thus endeþ þe frere his tale and here bygynneþ t. p. o.
t. somnour Pw; Here endyth the Freris tale. And begynnyth t. S. p. CX¹–WN TH¹–SP¹;
Here endeth the Freres tale and here begynneth t. S. p. PN²; T. S. P. SP²,³ TR WR; Here
beginneth t. S. P. UR   *Out:* Gg
    1665 **stiropes**] styrop Cp Ha⁴ La Pw+ CX¹–PN² WR   **hye**] vp Ha⁴+ WR
he] *om.* El Cp Dd He La Pw+ CX¹–SP³ SK–RI
    1666 **this**] þe Ha⁴+ WR   **frere his**] f. he star'd h. ~ UR   **so**] *om.* (Gl+) UR

1665 **he:** Though all modern editions omit *he*, the Hg reading is retained here be-
cause the MS evidence is inconclusive (15 MSS share the Hg reading); and because the Hg
and El+ readings yield equal sense. Kerkhof (1982:235–36) documents Chaucer's use of the
"resumptive pronoun," and one might argue that it would be easier for a scribe to drop *he*,
especially since *hye* could be pronounced as two syllables, than to add *he* to a line that did not
need it. On the other hand, *hye he* could result from misreading such spellings of *high* as occur
in Cp and La, *heyhe* and *hihe*, respectively. Most importantly, however, this edition will follow
the principle of presenting a "best text," and will retain Hg readings except in cases of clear
error or unambiguous MS evidence against Hg.
    1667 Root (1906:250) is the earliest to see a dramatic appropriateness in the Sum-
moner's wrath and its connection to *SumP:* "he is quaking like an aspen leaf for wrath, and,
unable to wait for the slower revenge of his tale, serves an *hors d'oeuvre* in the shape of a not
very savory anecdote, which describes the particular place in hell reserved for these cursed
friars." Tupper (1914:112) likewise sees the image as significant, arguing that "Wrath in its
general aspect is represented by the Friar-Summoner's Tales"; and he finds it appropriate that
"he whose tale and 'morality' expose the evils of Wrath 'quakes for ire like an aspen leaf'"
(1914:113). Benson (1980:71), examining the role of gesture in *CT*, sees the standing and
quaking as the first of several important gestures in *SumT*. For Beichner (1961:376) the
Summoner's anger is provoked by his sense that the Friar in *FrT* 1663–64 has hedged him
about logically, giving him the choice of silence (repentence) or scurrilous response (confirma-
tion of his sinfulness), but Zietlow (1966:7) argues that on the contrary the Summoner is
angry because of the falseness of the Friar's attack. The pilgrims "could hardly miss the
disparity between the summoner who could not recognize the devil and the Summoner who
diabolically attacks the Friar where he is most vulnerable." Merrill (1962:346) suggests that
the "irous" opening of *SumT* deliberately echoes the opening lines of *FrP* (1265–66): "This
worthy lymytour, this noble frere, / He made alwey a manere louryng cheere." Giaccherini

"Lordynges," quod he, "but o thyng I desire.
I yow biseke that of youre curteisye,
Syn ye han herd this false frere lye,   1670
As suffreth me I may my tale telle.
This frere bosteth that he knoweth helle,

1668   **but}** *om.* (Ne+) CX^1–PN^2
1669   **I}** And ~ UR   **that}** *om.* He+ CX^1–PN^2
1670   **frere}** *om.* Ad^3; freres ~ WN   **lye}** ylye ~ UR
1671   **suffreth}** suffre Pw   **my tale telle}** a tale t. Cp He La Pw$_1$+ CX^1; telle a t.
Pw; m. t. ytell ~ UR
1672   **bosteth}** ybostith ~ UR

(1980:155) feels, however, that Merrill overstates the importance of wrath in the Summoner's understanding of Huberd. Craik (1964:116) finds a parallelism between this passage and the quarrel between Cook and Manciple, H 46–49, while Richardson (RI) notes the parallel simile involving the fearful, trembling Criseyde in *TC* 3.1200; RI's note to that passage adds that the simile is not found before Chaucer.

    1668 **Lordynges:** Brewer (1984c:211) notes that this address demonstrates that *SumT* was meant for *CT*, "and for its present place and speaker," but adds that "the poem soon becomes told in the general Chaucerian narrative tone."

    1671 **suffreth:** MR do not record variants in imperative forms (*suffreth / suffre*) on the grounds that the erosion of the distinctions between plural and singular forms was well under way during the 15th century, a position supported by Visser (1970:1.15) and Mustanoja (1960:474). The Variorum editors, however, consider the distinction—though not maintained by many scribes—to be of historic and metrical interest, and such variants are reported in these collations. All instances are listed in the description of MR in the Textual Commentary, above.

         my tale telle: The present collation of Pw's reading assumes that the scribe wrote "telle a tale," then corrected the error by introducing transposition marks. MR's collation supposes that the scribe initially omitted the phrase "a tale," then corrected by adding it to the end of the line with transposition marks to signal its proper placement.

    1672–74 As Havely (1975:135) observes, the Summoner here alludes to the Friar's avowed knowledge of hell in *FrT* 1645–52. Zietlow (1966:6) argues that in seizing upon the Friar's "overblown pretensions to knowledge of moral geography" the Summoner demonstrates that he is not, as the Friar apparently believed, obtuse. Lawlor (1968:119–20) adds that the Summoner ". . . is shrewd enough to pick up the point the Friar has last made, and hurl it back. . . . If the summoner of [*FrT*] was a surrogate-figure for the real Summoner, his fellow-pilgrim, can we resist asking how the other person of the story, the devil, is related to the Friar himself?"

    1672 **bosteth:** UR frequently uses a y- prefix, found in no MS and indeed quite unhistorical, to smooth a line to conform to his sense of Chaucer's metrical regularity. See Alderson (1970:122 *et passim*).

And God it woot that it is litel wonder;
Freres and feendes been but lyte asonder.
For pardee ye han ofte tyme herd telle   79r   1675
How that a frere ravysshed was to helle
In spirit ones by avisioun,
And as an aungel ladde hym up and down
To shewen hym the peynes that ther were,
In al the place say he nat a frere.   1680
Of oother folk he say ynowe in wo.
Unto this aungel spak the frere tho,
    'Now sire,' quod he, 'han freres swich a grace

1673   **And]** As La   **God it woot]** g. w. Cp He La Pw+ CX¹–SP³   **that it is]**
t. is Ad³ Ha⁴ He La+ CX¹–SP³ WR; t. is but Dd+ TR; it is Pw+
1674   **but]** ful (Gl) PN¹   **asonder]** in sunder La+
1675   **ofte tyme herd]** h. o. t. Ad³+ PN¹; o. t. here ~ UR
1676   **ravysshed]** vanysshed Hg (Hg₂ *corr.*) El Ad³+   **to]** in Cp La Pw+
1678   **as]** *om.* He   **an]** *om.* La
1679   **peynes]** preuytes (Tc²) CX¹; tormentes ~ CX²–PN²   **ther were]** w. t.
He+ CX¹–PN² UR
1680   **the]** that Dd+   **say]** ne s. (Ry¹) CX²–PN²; yet s. ~ UR
1682   **this]** þe (Gl+) PN¹ TH¹–UR   **the]** this Dd Ha⁴+ CX¹–PN² WR
1683   **a]** *om.* La Pw+

1675–99   A great variety of sources or inspirations have been suggested for this "vision," for information on which see "Sources and Analogues" above. Most recent commentary accepts the suspicion of Tatlock (1914:143) and the argument of Fleming (1967) that the vision of *SumP* is an inversion of a tale (now known as the Maria Misericordia) told by Caesarius of Heisterbach in the 13th century, according to which a Cistercian monk sees a vast number of his fellows beneath the mantle of the Virgin (ed. Strange 1851:2.79–80; trans. Scott and Bland 1929:1.546). Fleming (1976) argues that the story was appropriated during the 13th and 14th centuries by the Dominicans and Franciscans, and put to use especially in the service of their lay confraternities. See further in the Introduction under "Sources and Analogues: The Summoner's Prologue."

In terms of the road-side drama, Baird (1969:105–06) suggests that the Summoner has picked up the notion for his vision of Satan's posterior from *FrT* 1637–38, where the fiend promises that the summoner will learn more of hell's *privetee* than a master of divinity.

1676   **ravysshed:** Doyle and Parkes (1979:xliii; read 79r for their 79v) describe the Hg correction as being of an early hand over an erasure.

1683–84   Levy (1966:47) writes that "this seemingly innocent question is of more significance than is apparent on the surface, since the *Summoner's Tale* is centrally concerned with the very question of just what kind of special grace the friars do have."

1683   MR do not report that La omits *a*.

That noon of hem shal come to this place?'
'Yis,' quod this aungel, 'many a milioun.'   1685
And unto Sathanas he ladde hym doun.
'And now hath Sathanas,' seith he, 'a tayl
Brodder than of a carryk is the sayl.
Hold up thy tayl, thow Sathanas,' quod he,
'Shewe forth thyn ers and lat the frere se   1690
Where is the nest of freres in this place.'
And er that half a furlong wey of space,

1684　　to] in Dd Ha⁴+ CX¹–SP³ TR WR; in to He La+; unto ~ UR
1685　　this] the He+ CX¹–PN²　　a] *om.* ~ UR
1686　　he ladde] he hadde Cp He La+; l. he ~ TH¹–UR　　doun] adown He La+
CX¹–UR
1687　　seith he a] shekyn his Ad³; such a He+ CX¹–SP³; s. he La+; said he a (Bo¹+)
UR
1688　　of] *om.* ~ PN¹ WN　　a] þe Cp La Pw+　　the] a Pw
1690　　and] *om.* ~ TH¹–SP¹
1691　　Where] Wheras ~ SP²,³
1692　　that] *om.* Ad³+; þan Ha⁴ Pw+ TR WR　　half] *om.* He+ CX¹–PN²
wey] were ~ PN¹　　space] pase He

1685　　**Yis:** RB takes the word as an "emphatic form of assent, used here in response to
the negative implication of the question, that no friars go to hell. 'Yes, on the contrary, many
million,' is the answer"; while Richardson (RI) suggests that it is "used sarcastically, to negate
the proposal."

1687　　TR (n. 7269) explicitly adopts the reading of Dd *En³* to emend earlier editions,
and explains that lines 1687–88 are printed in parentheses because "*he* refers to the Narrator,
the Sompnour." But *he* in fact is the angel.

1688　　**carryk:** According to Thomas (UR), "A large Ship of burden . . . from the
[Italian] *Carica*, Burden, etc.," an understanding echoed by Pollard (1894:2.68) and SK; SK
adds that this is the earliest known example of the word in English. The TR glossary offers
simply "a large ship," and assigns the word a French etymology. *MED* s.v. *carik(e* n. (1) has
"A type of large ship [orig. Spanish or Italian]."

　　sayl: SK, followed by RB and Richardson (RI), suggests that in this simile
"possibly Chaucer was thinking of the wings of Lucifer, greater than any sails, as described in
Dante's *Inferno* [34.48]." This idea Spencer (1927:197) finds "very doubtful," but Schless
(1984:194–95) supports SK by noting Curry's (1923:253) association of the passage from
Dante with the Summoner's joke about Satan's anus.

1690–91　　SK, Brusendorff (1925:411), RB and Richardson (RI) note a parallel idea in
Rom 7575–76, where Dame Abstinence says to Wikked-Tonge, "For thou shalt for this sinne
dwelle / Right in the devils ers of helle." Fansler (1914:164–65) admits the possibility of an
influence from *RR* but argues that the notion seems to have been proverbial. As RB notes, in
Rom the punishment is not restricted to friars. RI observes that the *Rom* passage may render
RR 12249 ("cul [variant 'puis'] d'enfer") or "it may derive from Chaucer's usage here."

1692　　**that:** RB (textual note) suggests that þan (Ha⁴ Pw) may be the right reading,
but cites line 1856 for contrary evidence.

Right so as bees out swarmen from an hyve,
Out of the develes ers ther gonne dryve

1693 **Right**] And r. ~ PN¹ **so**] *om.* Pw+ TH¹–UR **out swarmen**] s. o. Cp
Ha⁴ He La Pw+ CX¹–UR WR **from**] of Ad³ Cp Dd Ha⁴ He La Pw+ CX¹–WR MR
PR
1694 **ther gonne**] t. g. thei Ad³+; þey g. to Cp UR; they g. Dd Ha⁴ He La Pw+
CX¹–SP³ WR MR PR

---

half a furlong wey: A furlong is one-eighth of a mile, or 220 yards, but
Chaucer here intends a measure of time, the length of time required to walk one-sixteenth of
a mile. RB takes "a furlong wey" in *MLT* 557 to be similarly a temporal expression, and
Richardson (RI) cites *MilT* A 3637. RB and Richardson (RI) take a temporal *furlong wey* to
be two and one-half minutes, based on Chaucer's *Astrolabe* 1.16 ("3 milewei maken an
houre"), and *half a furlong way* thus to amount to about one and a quarter minutes. RI
points, however, to Isaacs (1961:328–29), who argues that Chaucer's use of the phrase is
casual and inexact, sometimes suggestive of a longer and sometimes a shorter interval. Of
this instance, Isaacs feels Chaucer intended "the shortest interval of all." Havely (1975:135)
agrees that the duration of half a furlong cannot be defined exactly, and adds that "we're
probably not expected to work out the 'muzzle velocity' of 20,000 friars in . . . precise detail;
this kind of arithmetical problem isn't considered until the end of the Tale."

1693–98 Whittock (1968:138) notes of this image of swarming friars a parallel in the
Wife of Bath's depiction of friars: "As thikke as motes in the sonne beem" (*WBT* D 868),
which motes "have now been transformed into a hellish swarm." RB and Richardson (RI)
point to Chaucer's use of the swarming bees image in *TC* 2.193 and 4.1356, and the RI note
to *TC* 2.193 cites the parallel in *RR* 8721–22, noted also by Koeppel (1892:243) and
Whiting (1968:B167). Knight (1973:70) calls this passage the "first fluent paragraph in
what has been a terse prologue so far. The grotesque little scene has the impact of a short
cartoon, offering us brisk action and broad comedy."

1693 The SK textual note numbered 1693 (4.371) is in fact the note for line 1696,
misnumbered.

from: MR (3.465) say of this line that "the evidence is decidedly in favor of 'out
swarmen of'"; indeed, only Bo² El *En¹* Hg and Ln read *from*. But there is no reason on its face
to question the line as it is found in Hg and El stylistically, and one might argue that *out
swarmen of an hyve* has an inelegant surfeit of initial vowel sounds, and further, that *of* is likely
to have been induced by *wey of space* in line 1692. Kane (1984:217) suggests consulting the
OED articles on the prepositions *from* and *of*; the *MED* article on the parallel *outcasten*
suggests that during Chaucer's lifetime either *from* or *of* was possible in such constructions.

1694 **ther:** Though, as in line 1693, Hg is supported by El (and two unauthoritative
MSS) in reading *ther gonne dryve*, MR evidently regard the numeric weight of MS support for
they gonne dryve as definitive here. The evidence of Chaucer's use of *ginnen* in other contexts is
inconclusive: there are no other instances of the impersonal *ther gonne* construction listed in
Tatlock and Kennedy (1927:381), while Chaucer does use *they gonne* (in, e.g., *ClT* 1103 and
TC 5.28). On the other hand, he apparently used *they gonne* only after the subject had been
named, never as here, in the construction "they gonne [verb] [subject]." For Chaucer's use of
ginnen, as in this instance, to force the verb into rhyme position, see Smyser (1967) and
Homann (1954).

Twenty thousand freres on a route   1695
And thurghout helle swarmeden aboute
And comen again as faste as they may gon
And in his ers they crepten everychon.
He clapte his tayl agayn and lay ful stille.
This frere, whan he looked hadde his fille   1700
Upon the tormentz of this sory place,
His spirit God restored of his grace
Unto his body agayn and he awook.

1695   Twenty} A t. ~ TR   on} in El+ SK; all on ~ SP²–UR
1696   thurghout} þoght Cp La Pw+   swarmeden aboute} they swarmed al a.
Dd+ UR TR; swarme al a. Cp La Pw+; swarmed al a. Ha⁴ He+ CX¹–SP³ WR RB¹–RI
1697   again} *om.* Ha⁴   may} mighte Cp+ TH¹–UR
1698   in his} into h. He+ CX¹–UR   crepten} crepen Ha⁴ La+ TR WR; crepe in
He; c. in (Ne+) CX¹–PN²
1699   He} And He+   clapte} clippid (Ii+) CX¹–PN²   his tayl agayn} a. h. t.
He+ CX¹–PN²   ful} *om.* Cp He La Pw+ CX¹–SP³
1700   looked hadde} h. looke El   his} al h. El+   fille} wyl He+ CX¹
1701   the} þis Cp La Pw+   tormentz} torment Ha⁴+ UR WR   of this sory}
vpon t. sor La
1703   Unto} To ~ UR; Into (En³+) TR

1695   **Twenty:** This is a headless line, and TR (n. 7277), adducing *SqT* 383, com-
ments: "I have added A for the sake of the verse. Chaucer frequently prefixes it to Nouns of
number." SK (5.xviii, 330–31) criticizes TR for concealing Chaucer's use of headless lines.

      on: MR write that "the uses of prepositions are so different in early and modern
English that one is often surprised. In this line 'on' was clearly the reading of O¹" (3.465–
66). Skeat (SK) explains his decision to print El's *in* by noting that the words are equivalent
and by pointing out the similar line in *HF* 2119, "Twenty thousand in a route."

1696   **swarmeden:** The spelling variation *swarmed* (found in Dd Ha⁴ He) may have
led MR to regard *swarmeden* as dissyllabic. This interpretation would account for their deci-
sion, followed by PR, to print *swarmeden al*, though Hg and El have only *swarmeden*. Kane
(1984:215) objects to MR's printing of *al* and their handling of this line: "There is no note to
this line and no sign of awareness that *aboute] al aboute* is in this context a predictable
variation to a more emphatic reading by an enthusiastically participating scribe." The issue
may not be quite that straightforward, for among the base-group MSS only those with
swarmed have *s. al*, so *al* may also have been generated by a need felt by some scribes to
supply a syllable required by the meter. When all is said and done, the reading of Hg and El
is perfectly acceptable metrically as it stands if *swarmeden* is allowed three syllables.

1701   **Upon:** PN¹ prints *Uopn.*

      the: MR report the Cp La *þis* and the Pw *þise* as separate variants in their
collations, but both are variant spellings of *these* (*OED*, s.v. *these*: A. γ, ε) and are accordingly
combined into one variant here.

But nathelees for fere yet he quook
So was the develes ers ay in his mynde   1705
That is his heritage of verray kynde.
God save yow alle save this cursed frere.
My prologe wol I ende in this manere."

Here endeth the prologe of the Somnours tale
Here bygynneth the Somnours tale   79v

1704   **for fere yet]** y. for f. (Bo¹+) TH¹–UR   **he quook]** still he q. ~ UR
1705   **the]** *om.* La   **develes ers]** devil He+ CX¹   **ay]** ʒit Ha⁴ WR
1706   **That is]** Than is it He+ CX¹–PN²; Which is Pw
1707   **cursed]** accursid ~ UR
Rubrics: **Here endeth the prologe of the Somnours tale   Here bygynneth the Somnours tale]** H. b. t. Somonour his t. El RB¹–RI; H. e. t. p. H. b. t. S. t. Ad³; H. b. t. S. t. Cp; Hic desinit *prologus* Et incipit fabula Dd; Narrat Ha⁴; H. e. t. S. his p. And h. b. he his t. He; Explicit *prologus*. Incipit fabula ap*ari*toris La; Thus e. t. p. o. t. Somnour And h. b. t. S. t. Pw; H. e. t. p. And b. t. S. t. CX¹; H. e. t. S. P. H. b. t. S. t. CX²–PN¹; H. e. t. S. p. WN; H. e. t. S. p. & h. foloweth his t. PN²; H. e. t. S. p. and foloweth his t. TH¹–SP¹; The S. Tale. SP²–WR

1707   Zietlow and Havely note the parallelism and contrast between this and the Friar's "pious hopes that the summoners may become good men [*FrT* 1644] and that this particular Summoner may repent before the Devil takes him [*FrT* 1663–64]" (Havely 1975: 135). Zietlow, followed by Giaccherini (1980:36), emphasizes the differences: "The malice behind the two prayers is equally intense, but unlike the Friar, the Summoner makes no attempt to veil his. The Summoner is an evil man . . . but he is no hypocrite" (Zietlow 1966:15). Taking a different approach, Andreas (1990:144) says that the benediction "reveals the ambivalence and affectionate abuse characteristic of carnivalesque humor. . . . Is the second 'save' a verb or a preposition—or is it both?"
          save . . . save: Baum (1956:243) includes this play on the double sense of *save* in his list of Chaucer's puns, and Huppé (1964:202) sees this pun as part of a larger pattern of mimicry in *SumT* whereby the Summoner mocks friar Huberd: "The Summoner mimics the Friar's prayer that summoners may repent."
1708   **My prologe:** The meta-textual effect here Muscatine (1966:90) considers one of Chaucer's "occasional inconsistencies of perspective," but Baum (1956:241–42) takes it as deliberate: "the Summoner himself can hardly be speaking, for Prologues are part of the machinery of the whole *Canterbury Tales*, and none of the pilgrims could think of himself as having one. It is a small jest shared by Chaucer and his Summoner."
          Rubrics: After the rubric introducing *SumT*, SP²–UR print the "argument" of the tale that appears in the prefatory matter of SP¹ under "Arguments to euery Tale and Booke": "A begging Fryer comming to a Farmars house, who lay sicke, obtaineth of him [of the sick Man UR] a certaine legacie, which must bee equally deuided among his Couent. A requitall to the Frier, shewing their cousenage, loytering, impudent begging, and hypocriticall praying."

Lordynges, ther is in Yorkshire, as I gesse,
A merssh contree called Holdernesse,   1710

1709 **ther is]** quod he He+ CX[1]   **Yorkshire]** Engelond Ha[4] WR   **as]** is as
He; *om.* Ha[4]+ WR
1710 **A]** Is a (Tc[2]) CX[1]   **merssh]** mersschly Ha[4] WR   **contree]** lond Ha[4]
WR   **called]** that c. is He+ CX[1]–PN[2]

1710 **merssh:** All editors since SK spell *mersshy*, though Hg and El spell as printed
here. *MED* lists *merssh* as a noun (s.v. *mersh* n., b) and *mersshy* as an adjective (s.v. *mershi* adj.),
but also lists *merssh* as a variant of *mersshy*. MR reasonably consider these as non-substantive
variations in spelling, and this edition follows their example in omitting them from the
collations. The Hg–El version of the line is, however, worth preserving as perhaps indicative
of authentic Chaucerian metrical practice, featuring the suppression of an unstressed syllable
at the caesura. Among the base-group MSS, He spells *merssh*, while Ad[3], Cp, Dd, La, and Pw
spell *mersshi*. ST–UR spell *marishe*. The Ha[4] reading *mersschly* is not reported in the MR
collations, but is noted in their errata (MR 6.672).
   Holdernesse: "This district lies on the coast of Yorkshire," WR. SK particular-
izes somewhat further: "Holderness is an extremely flat district; it lies at the S.E. angle of
Yorkshire, between Hull, Driffield, Bridlington and Spurn Point." Root (1906:250) appears
to see a significance in the specificity of the setting: "Quite possibly Chaucer knew some
variant of [the *Tale of the Priest's Bladder*], now lost to us. The definite localization of the
incident at Holderness in Yorkshire makes this probable." He does not explain further.
   In two essays (1923 and 1925) Kuhl makes a case for topical significance in the
choice of setting. He argues that Chaucer was very familiar with a number of people from
Holderness, notably Peter de Bukton, and that it was no coincidence that *SumT* "should have
for its setting a place where lived a person known to have been in the poet's London circle"
(1923:123). Further, Holderness had something of a name at the time for clerical abuses, was
"notorious for the benefices farmed out to members of the exchequer and the chancery"
(1923:123). Another connection was Walter Skirlawe, archdeacon of Holderness, "closely
associated with his native community, at the very time that Bukton was steward of that
region" (1923:124). Skirlawe was an enormously powerful man, Bishop of Coventry, Lich-
field, Bath, Wells, and eventually Durham, in addition to holding a truly astonishing num-
ber of other lucrative posts while living in London. The connection is perhaps given further
significance, Kuhl feels, by "the fact that *every* archdeacon of Holderness in the poet's day was
a prominent royal official at chancery or the exchequer—including Chaucer's successor as
Comptroller of Customs—it is [therefore] difficult to believe that the setting for the tales
dealing with the corruption of the church is accidental" (1923:125). Holderness had political
significance in the late 1380's as well, Kuhl argues, noting that "Queen Anne upon coming
to England in 1381 was given Holderness in her own right. In 1388, however, the lordship
was seized by Gloucester. Now church (Skirlawe and other arch-supporters of the pope) and
state (Gloucester and his faction) were solidly united in making 'mersshy Holdernesse' their
spoils" (Kuhl 1925:336). He concludes that "in the sumner's mention of Holderness . . .
lurks a satiric allusion, a reference to contemporary events that must have moved [Chaucer's]
hearers—now safely seated in power—to uproarious laughter" (1925:338).
   Manly suggests a different topical value for the setting, noting the prominence

In which ther wente a lymytour aboute,
To preche and eek to begge, it is no doute.
And so bifel that on a day this frere
Hadde preched at a chirche in his manere,
And specially aboven every thyng   1715

1711   **lymytour**] lymour He; litour La
1713   **that**] it Ha⁴ WR
1714   **Hadde preched**] He p. He   **at a**] atte Cp La Pw+; in a He+ CX¹–UR
his] þis Cp La Pw+ SP¹

---

of another Holderness event, the quarrel, begun in 1381, "between the canons of Beverley Minster and Alexander Neville, archbishop of York, whose jurisdiction they denied" (1926*b*: 106–07). One of these canons was Richard de Ravenser, king's clerk, whom the evidence suggests Chaucer must have known, along with Walter Skirlawe (pp. 108–11). For Manly the significance of Holderness begins with the archdeacon "of heigh degree" in *FrT* (1302), the master of *FrT*'s summoner, perhaps an allusion to Ravenser himself, archdeacon of Lincoln, who, if not actually "such a greedy prelate as Chaucer describes, at least . . . made out of his various offices, which he could not possibly have discharged with proper attention to each, a large amount of money, which he did not redistribute in his lifetime" (p. 111). Ravenser was a sometimes associate of Michael de la Pole (pp. 117–18), and the lord of the court (line 2162) could be an allusion to de la Pole himself, with "four houses in Hull and many manors in Yorkshire as well as in other counties" (p. 119). Though Manly states that "Professor Kuhl has argued that this lord was Sir Peter de Bukton" (p. 119), Kuhl does not appear to have made such a claim in print. Fleming (1966:689) criticizes Manly's approach, and disputes his claim (Manly 1926*b*:104) that Chaucer had a specific Franciscan house, in Beverley, in mind. Although Olson (1986:215 n. 2) suggests consulting the *Victoria History of the County of York* (ed. Page 1913.3:264–65) for information on "the Franciscan building program in the Holderness area," the information there concerns Beverley, and Fleming notes that "neither during the fourteenth century nor at any other time was Beverley in geographical or ecclesiastical Holderness. Indeed, there were no friaries at all in Holderness in any case, and the nearest ones were not in Beverley but in Hull" (p. 689). See further under note 2116. Giaccherini (1980:140) responds skeptically to the notion that the setting in Holderness is a key to the tale, and Havely (1975:135–36) feels that "such theories have little to do with the work as we have it," adding that "there does not seem to be anything especially Northern in the rest of the story." On the question of Northern speech in *SumT* see the note to *lixt* in line 1761.

    1711   **lymytour:** Richardson (RI) refers to her note to *GP* 209, where she glosses this term as follows: "Each convent had its own assigned limits (for begging) and these districts were sometimes subdivided into smaller 'limitations.'" See further Andrew (1993:222).

    1714   Richardson (RI), citing Williams (1960:39–41), notes that friars were allowed to preach in parish churches only with the permission of the local priest or license of the bishop of the diocese.

    1715–23   In this passage Knight (1973:71) notes a shift in style from *SumP*, featuring

Excyted he the peple in his prechyng
To trentals, and to yeve for Goddes sake
Wherwith men myghte holy houses make,
Ther as dyvyne service is honoured,
Nat ther as it is wasted and devoured,   1720
Ne ther it nedeth nat to be yeve,

1716   **Excyted he the**] He e. t. He La+; E. t. Ad³+ UR
1717   **to yeve**] *om.* Cp La Pw+
1718   **Wherwith**] Ther with Cp La Pw+; Wher þat Ha⁴+   **houses**] soules Ha⁴
Out: He 1718–89
1720   **as**] *om.* El (El₁ *corr.*) Ne+ CX¹–PN²   **it**] *om.* La+   **is**] *om.* Pw+ (Pw₁
corr.)   **devoured**] hono (*del.*) d. Ne
1721   **Ne ther**] Neither Ha⁴ WR   **nat to**] n. for to El Cp Dd₁ Ha⁴ La Pw+
TH¹–SP¹ UR–RI

---

extended syntax and long learned words to "imply the smooth-tongued friar of the story. . . .
The pace is less hectic, expressive of a silver tongue, not violent action."

1717   **trentals:** SP² is first to gloss this term, correctly, as "thirty masses." Thomas
(UR) cites Skinner (1671, s.v. *trentall*) in offering the sense "a Service performed for the dead
the Thirtieth day after their decease," but immediately adds, citing Lobineau (1707 s.v.
Tricenarium), "or rather, a service of Thirty Masses performed for the dead, which sometimes
began the next day after the person's decease, and was repeated on the Anniversary: It also
signifies the Obventions, or Allowances to the Priests for performing those Services." "*Un
trentel*, Fr. was a service of thirty Masses, which were usually celebrated, upon as many
different days, for the dead," says TR (n. 7299), citing Du Cange (1710, s.v. *Trentale*). WR
adds, "for which of course the friars required a much greater sum than for a single mass."
Hertzberg (1866:624) notes that the friars, highly advanced in ecclesiastical efficiency, appar-
ently said the masses one after another on the same day. SK adds that the term "also meant, as
here, the sum paid for the same to the priest or friar." Most modern commentary makes
points similar to these, and SK and Richardson (RI) suggest the interest of the "Trentale
Sancti Gregorii" (ed. Furnivall 1903:114–22) for a version of the origin of trentals. See
further in note 1728.

1718   Owing to the loss of a leaf, He lacks lines 1718–89; the *b* group is represented
in this section by Ne.

1720   **devoured:** The Ne scribe appears to have caught the first part of *honoured* from
the line directly above. MR ignore this error and its correction.

1721   **nat to:** The MS evidence is heavily on the side of suppressing *for*, but one could
reason that as the only dispensable word in a nine-word line, *for* fell victim to scribal econ-
omy. According to Mustanoja (1960:514) the use of *for to* with the infinitive was losing
ground to *to* in the 14th century, and in the period 1384–1425 in London the proportion of
to to *for to* is 5:1, but "individual authors and scribes show . . . considerable variance in this
respect." Metrically, the line as found in Hg and as printed here lacks an unstressed syllable,
and all editors since UR have preferred to print *for to*. The Hg scribe wrote a virgule, his
common mark for caesura, after *nat*, possibly indicating he read it as a Lydgate line (see
Killough [1982]). The Hg line does not charm, but it is entirely plausible.

As to possessioners that mowen lyve—
Thanked be God—in wele and habundaunce.
"Trentals," seyde he, "delivereth from penaunce
Hir freendes soules as wel olde as yonge,   1725
Ye whan that they been hastily ysonge,

1722   **possessioners**] possessours Pw+   **mowen**] m. elles Cp La Pw+ TH[1]–UR
1724   **seyde he delivereth**] s. he delyuered Ad[3]+; quod he d. Dd+ UR; d. s. he (Ps) TH[1,2]; d. quod he ~ TH[3]–SP[3]
1725   **soules**] soule La+   **olde as yonge**] o. and y. La+
1726   **Ye whan that**] If t. Cp La Pw+ TH[1]–SP[3]; Ye w. Ne+ CX[1]–PN[2]   **been hastily**] h. b. Ha[4]+ WR; b. so h. Ne+ CX[1]–PN[2]

1722   **possessioners:** "The regular orders of monks, who possessed landed property, and enjoyed rich revenues," according to WR, an identification implicitly accepted by Hertzberg (1866:624); but to Jephson (Bell 1855:2.104) the term also includes parochial clergy, "who of course possessed [property] as laymen did." Manly (1928:589) seems to accept this view. SK and RB incline toward the belief that the reference is particularly to the seculars, SK noting "the occurrence of *preest* in l. 1727, *curat* in 1816, and *viker* and *persone* in l. 2008." Hartung (1967:179) argues for monks, on the grounds that "friars had their battles with the monks as well as with the seculars and in these battles the word 'possessioner' became an opprobrious term directed against the monks." He notes that the passage from Jerome's *Epistola adversus Jovinianum* which furnished Chaucer with his description of Jovinian (see note 1929) includes the "contemptuous reference to Jovinian as 'formosus monachus' ['fair monk']." Jerome's attack on worldly monks shares details with the portrait of Chaucer's *GP* monk, including his *fair* skin and the fact that "A fat swan loved he best of any roost." In the operative passage, Jerome twice refers to the fairness of worldly monks, and compares Jovinian to a swan. Giaccherini (1980:141) feels that monks are intended here, though the seculars are separately reviled in lines 1816–18 and 2008–09, while Richardson (RI) takes both seculars and monastics to fit the description, and then adds that "Friar John's later use of the term designates chantry priests specifically." The term *possessioners* does not, however, occur a second time in *SumT*.

1723   **Thanked be God:** SK (note to line 1722) takes *Thanked be God* to be "a parenthetical remark made by the Somnour who tells the story, as it is hardly consistent with the views of the friars," though he does not set the phrase off in quotation marks. On the other hand, RB and Giaccherini (1980:141) hold that the phrase belongs to the friar, and is part of his portrait as hypocrite. The placement of quotation marks can be a problem where Chaucer, as in the opening lines of *SumT* proper, moves into indirect discourse, beginning with "for Goddes sake" in line 1717. In line 1724 comes the shift to direct quotation, clearly signalled by *seyde he*.

1724–34   Chapman (1929:182) takes these lines as the formal recapitulation of the friar's sermon on giving, focusing on the appeal to the welfare of loved ones: "Who would fail to be moved by this harrowing picture of friends in torment, and not give all possible for their prompt delivery?"

1725   **soules:** Though MR report the singular *soule* in Bw, they apparently fail to notice it in La.

Nat for to holde a preest joly and gay;
He syngeth nat but o masse in a day.
Delivereth out," quod he, "anon the soules;
Ful hard it is with flessh hook or with oules   1730
To been yclawed or to brenne or bake;

1728   **nat]** *om.* Ne+ CX¹   **in]** on Ad³ Dd La Ne Pw+ CX¹–PN² TR; *om.* (En³+)
TH¹–SP³   **a]** *om.* ~ WN
    1729   **Delivereth]** Deliuerd La   **quod he anon]** a. q. he Dd Ne+ CX¹–PN²; q.
he Ha⁴; a. La+
    1730   **flessh hook]** fleschehokes La+   **or with]** and Ne+ CX¹–PN²; eiþer w. Pw
    1731   **to brenne or bake]** brend or I bake Ha⁴ WR   *Out:* Cp La Pw+

    1727   RB paraphrases, "A secular priest, without incurring condemnation for being
jolly or gay, will sing only one mass in a day," but the sense seems as likely to be a continua-
tion of the argument begun in line 1717 against donations to secular priests which would
"hold them jolly and gay." See note 1728.
        gay: Ross (1972:93) argues that the word often has sexual connotations in
Chaucer, but finds the use of the word here "complex and perplexing."
    1728   **o masse in a day:** SK notes that "it would appear that the friars used occasion-
ally to sing all the thirty masses in one day, and so save a soul from twenty-nine days of
purgatory." Relying on Smith (1870:8), SK provides an illustration: "The wardens are there
directed to summon the Minorite Friars to say the dirge, 'and *on the morwe* to seie a *trent* of
masses atte same freres.'" Birney (1960:206) suggests that John implies that thirty friars will
say mass at once, completing the thirty masses in the time of one. Adams (1962:128) feels
that the friar's argument over the efficacy of the concentration of thirty masses on a day opens
the theme of "the problem of distribution" in *SumT*, which is raised again as John urges
Thomas (lines 1967–99) to concentrate his gifts to a single house of friars, and culminates in
Jankyn's ultimate division of the gift Thomas actually gives. Craik (1964:119–20) feels that
the friar "reduces trental masses to a mere magic charm," while Havely (1975:136) suggests
that "the friar seems to be trying to outbid possible competition for trentals-business."
    1729   **Delivereth:** MR do not record *Deliuerd* in La.
    1730–31   WR and others note that the iconography of "the infernal regions" sug-
gested by the friar's sermon was traditional in "the old paintings and illuminations," but it is
important to recognize that the Friar's sermon deals with purgatory, not hell. Jephson writes
that "the popular preachers and painters of the middle ages used to represent the punish-
ments of sin as consisting of a literal tearing, burning, and freezing of the flesh, intending
them to be understood metaphorically; but the unlearned of course applied these representa-
tions in a literal sense" (Bell 1855:2.104). SK cites instances of saints tortured with awls, RB
notes that torture with fleshhooks and awls is more commonly found in descriptions of hell
than of purgatory, and Stanford (1920) uses the detail to argue that Chaucer's image of
purgatory was influenced by "the popular, as opposed to the theologian's, idea of purgatory,"
possibly the version of *Saint Patrick's Purgatory* found in the *South English Legendary* (ed.
Horstmann 1887:204–220, especially lines 168–70, 203, 207–8, 211–12, 233–34, and
285) which "is nearest to the friar's account. It contains all his details, including the burning

Now spede yow hastily for Cristes sake."
And whan this frere hadde seyd al his entente
With *qui cum patre* forth his wey he wente.
Whan folk in chirche hadde yeve hym what hem leste   1735
He wente his wey no lenger wolde he reste.
With scryppe and typped staf ytukked hye

1732   *Spur. line after* 1732 To kepe ȝou fro (f. þe La) peynes of (of þe La) feendes blake
Cp La Pw+
    1733   this] þe Cp La Pw+   al] *om.* Ne+ CX¹
    1734   his wey] *om.* Cp Ha⁴ La Pw+; away ~ UR   he] is Ne+
    1735   in chirche hadde yeve hym] in the c. hadde y. Ne+ CX¹–PN²
    1737   scryppe] skippe (Tc²+) CX¹   typped] piked Ha⁴+ WR   ytukked
hye] tukked ful h. Cp La Pw+

---

and baking, reiterates the awls and hooks, and is the one account of purgatory in any
language, so far as observed, that mentions awls" (Stanford 1920:380–81). Spencer (1927:
196), endorsing Stanford's argument, suggests that, based on their use (e.g., drawing, rend-
ing) in medieval visions of hell, the awls were probably more like hooks than the shoemaker's
tool. Manly (1928:589) points to a manuscript illumination that is "most distressing" in its
depiction of such tortures. See Kolve (1984:261–64) for the coincidence of imagery of cooks
and cooking and the imagery of hell, which may account for the culinary language of these
lines.
    1733–34   Pearsall (1985:223), arguing against those who read *SumT* as angry and
vituperative, fitting the angry Summoner, notes that these lines "have an airy freedom, the
friar giving a cheery wave, perhaps, as he hastens to his next engagement. The narrator makes
little comment." Rogers (1986:59) feels that "the *entente/wente* rhyme is suggestive once one
notices the emphasis in the early lines of the tale on how the friar is always *going* somewhere
to get money or other offerings—lines 1736, 1738, 1754, 1765. When he has what he
wants, he moves on." Craik (1964:120) finds the couplet suggestive of the friar's "mechanical
recitation of the formula as he briskly steps down from the pulpit to collect money," while
Benson (1980:72) adds that "the lines imply a haste which reflects the friar's purely acquisi-
tive motives."
    1734   **qui cum patre:** As noted in WR and in subsequent commentary, this formula
was a common conclusion to prayers and sermons. Hertzberg (1866:624) notes its use at the
end of Chaucer's *Retraction*. SK and RB offer its full form: "*qui cum Patre et Spiritu Sancto vivit
et regnat per omnia secula seculorum*" ("who with the Father and the Holy Spirit lives and reigns
forever and ever"). Manly (1928:589) adds that here "as often, it is used as a formula of leave-
taking."
    his wey: WR emends Ha⁴ because these words "seem necessary for the metre."
    1737   **scryppe and typped staf:** Fleming (1966:692), followed by Havely (1975:
137), points out that the scrip and staff, traditional icons of the pilgrim, "were the subject of
much indelicate satire" in *RR*, and that Christ (Luke 9.3) forbade his disciples and Franciscan
rules forbade friars to carry either, the latter point also noted by Kaske (1972:122), Szittya
(1974: 40), Giaccherini (1980:145), and Richardson (RI). "It seems," Fleming adds, "that the

In every hous he gan to poure and prye
And beggeth mele and chese or ellis corn.
His felawe hadde a staf typped with horn,   1740

1738   **hous**} mannys h. Ne+ CX¹   **he gan to**} and g. to Ha⁴
1739   **beggeth**} begged Dd Ha⁴ Ne+ CX¹–WN TH¹–WR; begge ~ PN²   **mele**
and chese} m. or c. Cp La Ne Pw+ CX¹,² WN PN² WR; m. c. Ha⁴+
1740   **horn**} an h. Ad³+

---

scrip and staff imply a condemnation of the friar. So, I think, do his poking and prying [line 1738]."

    ytukked hye: Chute (1946:279) feels that the friar tucks his gown up in order to move with greater speed.

    1738   Williams (1953:512) notes that in *De periculis novissimorum temporum*, William of St. Amour's attack upon the mendicants, William develops a reading of Paul's description in 2 Timothy 3.6 of those who in the perilous times of the last days will creep into houses and lead silly women captive; these *penetrantes domos* are the friars, "men who will make their way into house after house, captivating weak women whose consciences are burdened by sin." William adds, however, that the image of seduction was to be understood figuratively as the corruption of the weak soul. The imagery of Friar John's activities in Thomas's house suggests to Williams (1953:511–12) that Chaucer was also influenced by vernacular antifraternal texts which imputed actual sexual activities to the friars. Fleming (1966:693), in a remark cited approvingly by Szittya (1974:44), adds that "it is obvious that our friar measures up to both the text and the gloss" of 2 Timothy 3. Szittya (1974:44) adds that "the *penetrans domos* forms part of the apostolic pattern in the tale, since he was seen both by Paul, in his letter to Timothy, and by the antifraternal commentators, as a *pseudoapostolus*." Havely (1975:137) concurs, noting that in Luke 10.7 Christ tells his disciples "Go not from house to house," and Giaccherini (1980:145) adds that the imagery of Friar John's intrusiveness "throws a decidedly oblique light" on his real intentions. Fleming later notes the repetition of *hous* in the description of the friar's activity, beginning with "holy houses" in line 1718 and begging "hous by hous" in line 1765. "Chaucer is here using privileged language," he argues, for "the word 'house' is charged with the special meaning William of Saint-Amour gave it to mean 'conscientia': 'creepers into houses,' those who go from 'house to house,' are the friars, who insinuate themselves into the parochial confessional" (Fleming 1983:9).

    1740–45   On this scene Jephson (Bell 1855:2.105) notes, "Thus Jacke Upland asks the supposed friar, 'Why writest thou her names in thy tables that yeveth thee mony? sith God knoweth al thing: for it semeth by thy writing, that God would not reward hem; but thou writest in thy tables, God would els forgotten it' [ed. Heyworth 1968:66; ed. SK 7.195 § 34]. The meaning of recording the names, however, was that they might be remembered in the prayers of the brotherhood." SK also cites *Jacke Upland* and makes a similar point.

    1740–42   The *tables* are the friar's "folding set of writing tablets" (Richardson, RI), while the *poyntel*, his stylus, is glossed in SP¹⁻³ as "a writing pin," and by Thomas (UR) as "a Pencil, a writing pen." SK notes that "in Horman's Vulgaria, leaf 81, we read:—'Tables be made of leues of yuery, boxe, cyprus, and other stouffe, daubed with waxe to writte on.' And again, in the same:—'Poyntellis of yron, and poyntyllis of syluer, bras, boon, or stoone.'"

A peyre of tables al of yvory,
And a poyntel polysshed fetisly,
And wroot the names alwey as he stood

1741   **al of yvory]** of y. Cp La Pw+; of clene y. Ne+ CX¹–PN²
1742   **And]** *om.* (Ps) ST SP²–UR   **polysshed]** y ponysshed Ne; p. ful (Bo¹+) UR
1743   **wroot]** wote Pw   **the names alwey]** alway t. n. Pw+ TH¹–TR   **as]** þer Pw+

Richardson (RI) adds that "such writing materials date back to classical antiquity." In arguing for a parodic pattern involving the figures of Moses, Elijah, and Aaron (see lines 1885–1903), Lancashire (1981:23) notes that "John, like Moses, comes pleading with two tablets," and that Moses records God's gift of the Law on his tablets, while the friar has his brother record (and erase) the names of their benefactors on his.

        horn . . . yvory: Ewald (1911:79) considers that Chaucer intends us to see irony in a "begging" friar who owns a horn-tipped staff, ivory tablet, and beautiful stylus. Kaske (1972:123–24) suggests "a striking though belated parallel in an obviously priapic reference by Benedick near the end of Shakespeare's *Much Ado*: 'There is no staff more reverent than one tipp'd with horn,'" adding that the *peyre of tables* would take on the "inevitable complementary significance." He argues further that Chaucer may be alluding to the image, commonplace in Classical literature, of the twin gates of dreams, horn and ivory, from which come respectively true and false dreams, noting (pp. 124–26) that the substances horn and ivory themselves came to stand for truth and falsity in medieval commentary, so that the "rather obtrusive juxtaposition of *horn* and *yvory*" suggests that the friar's *tables al of yvory* "are thus subtly identified from the beginning as a pair of 'false tables'" (Kaske p. 126). Giaccherini (1980:145) feels the context excludes the possibility of the sexual reading, but agrees fully with the second argument.

        1740   **felawe:** SK writes that "the friars often begged in pairs; in this way, each was a check upon the other as regarded the things thus obtained." Rules of the order, according to Manly (1928:589), required that friars beg in pairs; Richardson (RI) adds that they did so in accordance with Christ's directions to his disciples in Luke 10.1. Fleming (1967:99) detects "peculiarly Dominican satire" in the image of John's companion, for the Dominican Constitutions specifically provided for a *socius* for travelling Preachers, and stipulated that the two were to be inseparable during their journey outside the convent. Szittya (1974:40) notes that in contravention of the Franciscan order and Christ's instructions in Luke 10.1, the friar goes not two by two but three by three.

        1742   **polysshed:** MR do not report *y ponysshed* in Ne. Perhaps because the line is acephelous, Ha⁴ (among the base ten MSS) and CX¹–WN read *y-policht*, apparently the reading of the *b* ancestor.

        1743–45   In his study of gesture in *SumT*, Benson (1980:72) remarks that "writing is not a gesture under normal circumstances, but here, because it is done only for effect . . . it becomes a bit of stage business which not only helps us to visualize the friar at work, but which also functions to reveal his hypocrisy."

        1743   **wroot:** MR do not record *wote* in Pw.

Of alle folk that yaf hem any good,
Ascaunces that he wolde for hem preye.   80r   1745
"Yif us a busshel whete, malt, or reye,

1744   **Of**} And Pw   **alle**} any Cp+; euery La; a. the (Cn+) CX¹–PN²   **yaf**
hem} y. hym El Ad³ Ha⁴ Ne Pw+ CX¹,² WN PN² TH² WR–RB¹ RB² RI
1745   **that**} as Pw+ TH¹–SP¹; as if ~ UR   **hem**} him Ad³+
1746   **us**} hym El   **whete malt**} w. or m. Ha⁴+ UR–WR; w. mele Ne+ CX¹

1744   **Of**: MR do not record the Pw reading *And*.
        hem: One could logically reason either way on the reading *hem* vs. *hym*. Arguably, *hem* is preferable here because it is logical to see that people offer their gifts to the friars as a pair, while *hym* would refer only to the friar's "felawe," who records in his ivory tablet the names of people who offer gifts. If Chaucer had intended the gifts to be given to one friar, it would surely be John, the main character, he would have in mind, and not his nameless companion. The MSS provide little help: "The groups split so badly on 'hem' and 'him' that it is clear that there was much editing, but the upper MSS in the Hg *a cd*² Ra³ groups have 'hem'" (MR 3.466).
1745   **Ascaunces**: SP¹⁻³ gloss "as who should say, as though," while Thomas (UR) glosses "Askew, aside, sideways; in a side view." Tyrwhitt (TR, n. 7327) notes the Thomas gloss but remains unsatisfied. "It will be better," he writes, "to examine the other passages in which the same word occurs, before we determine the sense of it. See [*CYT* 838], *Ascaunce* that craft is so light to lere. [*TC* 1.205]. *Ascaunce*, lo! is this not wisely spoken? Ibid. 292. *Ascaunce*, what, may I not stonden here? Lydg. Trag. [Lydgate's *Fall of Princes*] fol. 136. b. *Ascaunce* I am of maners most chaungeable. In the first and last instance, as well as in the text, *ascaunce* seems to signify simply *as if*; *quasi*. In the two others it signifies a little more; *as if to say*. This latter signification may be clearly established from the third line, which in the Italian original [Filostrato di Boccaccio, 1.i.] stands thus: *Quasi dicesse*, e no ci si puo stare? So that *Ascaunce* is there equivalent to *quasi dicesse* in Italian. As to the Etymology of this word I must confess myself more at a loss. I observe however that one of a similar form in the Teutonic has a similar signification. Als-kacks; *Quasi, quasi vero*. Kilian [Kilian 1599]. Our *as* is the same with *als*. Teut. and Sax. It is only a further corruption of *al so*. Perhaps therefore *ascaunce* may have been originally *als-kansse*. *Kansse* in Teut. is *Chance* Fr. and Eng. I will just add that this very rare phrase was also used, as I suspect, by the Author of the *Continuation of the Canterbury Tales*, first printed by Mr. Urry. *Prol.* ver. 361. And al *ascaunce* she loved him wel, she toke him by the swere. It is printed *a staunce*." SK takes over part of this information, adding more ME citations, and concludes that the word is "a hybrid compound. The first part of it is E. *as*, used superfluously and tautologically; the latter part of it is the O. F. *quanses*, 'as if.'" Livingston (1925:71–72) argues that the first syllable is not English *as* but rather an intensifying prefix from Latin *ex-*, which "may have originally lent an intensive force (*just* as if)," but Spitzer (1945:21–22) accepts the SK explanation as "quite plausible," suggesting however that the *as-* might be the English form "*a-* [= *on*] which is found in *ahead*, *a-skew*, etc." *MED*, s.v. *ascaunce* 1 (b) *Conj.*, offers the meaning "as if, pretending that," and concurs with the SK etymology.
        hem: MR do not record *him* in Ad³.
1746–53 Raizis (1969:144) argues that these lines influenced Nikos Kazantzakis,

A Goddes kechyl, or a trype of cheese,

1747   **kechyl}** kyrtel ~ PN¹   **trype}** crip Ne CX¹–PN¹ PN²; cup ~ WN

---

who commented upon them in his travel journal *England* (Kazantzakis 1941:124–28) and echoed them in his novel *The Fratricides* in a scene featuring an unscrupulous itinerent monk begging in a mountain village: "My blessings upon you, my children. . . . My blessings and those of the Virgin Mother. Bring whatever you have as an offering to the Virgin: money, bread, wine, eggs, cheese, wool—whatever you have—bring it and come to pray" (Kazantzakis 1954:11). Speaking of Chaucer's ear for individual speech mannerisms, Everett (1955:145) comments that "the wheedling tone of the begging Friar . . . is conveyed by the grammatical construction of his speech, which, after the opening 'Yif us' (repeated in 1750), consists almost entirely of a string of nouns or noun clauses . . . broken by parentheses intended to suggest disparagement of himself or his kind, or flattery of his victim." She notes further that "the Friar's assumed respect is conveyed, not only by the parenthetic 'leeve dame, Our suster deere' but also by the exclusive use of the plural pronouns. Contrast the Friar's speeches to Thomas in which he sometimes uses the plural pronouns and sometimes the singular, the latter indicating familiarity or (in 2154–5) rage."

Lancashire (1981:23–24), arguing for a parodic parallel between Friar John and Elijah (of 3 Kings [AV 1 Kings] 17), notes that "what Elijah begs, a little grain-meal cake, is exactly what John usually wheedles from housewives."

1747   **Goddes kechyl:** A *kechyl* is a little cake, according to *MED* deriving from OE *coecel*. The meaning of *Goddes kechyl* has elicited considerable discussion. In SP¹'s "Annotations, with some Corrections," one finds "A *kichell*) A cake which Horace [*Epistles* 1.10.10, ed. Morris 1911:71] calleth *Libum*: Vtque sacerdotis fugitivus liba recuso ["like a priest's runaway slave, I spurn cakes"]: and with vs it is called a Gods kichell, because godfathers and godmothers vsed commonly to giue one of them to their godchildren, when they asked blessing." This information is reprinted in the glossaries of SP²,³, s.v. *kichell*. The cakes in Horace are offerings given to the priest, and plentiful in his household. Thomas (UR) glosses "a little cake," and is the first to note the OE ancestry of the word. TR (n. 7329) rejects Speght's hypothesis, which is inferred by Tyrwhitt to apply as well to *Goddes half peny* in line 1749: "This is all *gratis dictum*, I believe. The phrase is French, and the true meaning of it is explained by M. [Bernard] de la Monnoye in a note upon the *Contes de B{onaventure} D{es} Periers*, t. ii. [1735] p. 107. *Belle serrure de Dieu}* Expression du petit peuple, qui raporte pieusement tout à Dieu.—Rien n'est plus commun dans la bouche des bonnes vieilles, que ces especes d'Hebraïsmes: *Il m'en coute un bel ecu de Dieu*; *Il ne me reste que ce pauvre enfant de Dieu*; *Donez moi une benite aumône de Dieu* [*Fair lock of God*) Expression of the common people, who piously attribute eveything to God. —Nothing is more common in the mouth of old matrons than these sorts of Hebraisms: 'It cost me a pretty penny of God'; 'I have only this poor child of God'; 'Give me a blessed alms of God'}." WR, Düring (1883–86:3.373–74), SK, Manly (1928:590) and RB repeat TR, Düring adding that "it appears to mean also a gift given with good will and bringing God's reward to the giver." Manly remarks that the idiom, "usually applied to something of small value, is still current." *MED* s.v. *God* 4b.(c) offers for *goddes hal-peni* (*kechel*) the meaning "a halfpenny (a little cake) given in charity." See also note 1749.

trype: Noting that Cotgrave (1611) defines "Les *tripes* d'un fagot" as the small-

119

Or ellis what yow lyst, we may nat chese.
A Goddes half peny or a masse peny,
Or yif us of youre brawn if ye have eny.   1750
A dagon of youre blanket leeve dame,

1748   **we]** I Ne+ CX¹–UR   *Spur. line* A bosshel malt or ellis of peese Pw
1750   **brawn]** *om.* Pw
1751   **dagon]** dagget Ne+ CX¹

---

est sticks in a faggot, the TR glossary suggests the word "evidently means *a small piece* of cheese"; SK also cites Cotgrave, and glosses "a morsel." *OED* gives "Trip, *sb.³ Obs.* Derivation uncertain. a. ?A piece of rind of cheese," citing this line. The next instance recorded is dated 1823.

1748   MR read *busshel* and *elles* in Pw; the Chaucer Society edition of Pw agrees with the reading given here.

we may nat chese: Szittya (1974:40) remarks that although the friar pays lip service here to Christ's instructions to his disciples in Luke 10.7 to accept what is offered them, "he encourages the most lavish bequests."

1749   **Goddes half peny:** Hertzberg (1866:624), rejecting the explanations of SP and TR for *Goddes kechyl* (see note to line 1747) and *Goddes half peny*, argues that the "compounding with God appears to me to indicate only a gift which the poor intended as an offering to the church."

masse peny: Jephson (Bell 1855:2.105), followed by SK, writes "probably a penny for saying a mass. Thus, Jacke Upland [ed. Heyworth 1968:65–66; SK 7.195 § 33]: 'Freer, when thou receivest a penie for to say a masse, whether sellest thou God's bodie? &c.'" Havely (1975:137) notes that "the taking of 'A Goddes halfpenny or a masse-peny' was strictly forbidden by section 4 of the Rule [of St. Francis]—though this article must often have been ignored in between St. Francis's time and Chaucer's."

1751–53   Knight (1973:71) remarks on the "real bite and force" given to this passage by Chaucer's use of initial stresses and internal pauses.

1751   **dagon:** The earliest, and subsequently most usual, gloss on this word is in SP¹, "(*fractura*) a pece," to which SP²,³ add "or remnaunt"; these glosses are echoed in John Minsheu's *Ductor in Linguas* of 1617: "a *Dagon* is an old word vsed by *Chaucer* in the *Sompners* tale. . . . a peece or remnant" (cited in Alderson 1970:194). Thomas (UR) accepts this understanding and adds "from *Dagge*," by which word he understands "Lachets (or Slips) cut out of leather." "It seems," he continues, "to have an affinity with the [Welsh] *Dogn*, A certain quantity, or proportion." The TR glossary offers "slip or piece," while Pollard (1894:2.70) suggests simply "fragment." *MED* offers "a remnant or scrap (of cloth)," citing only this line, and suggests, as does Baugh (1963:411), a possible connection with *dagge* (1.2), "A shred, tag, or strip."

blanket: Southworth (1953, item 29) argues that since *blanket* falls between *brawn* and *bacon* in the friar's litany of acceptable gifts, it probably means a piece of stewing meat rather than bedding, as in "blanket of veal." Though a request for a kind of meat might seem more rational in this context than a blanket, especially part of one, *MED* shows no instances of *blanket* used in ME in that sense, and *dagoun* is, as RB² reasons, associated at least

Oure suster deere, lo, heere I write youre name.
Bacoun or boef or swich thyng as ye fynde."
A sturdy harlot wente ay hem bihynde
That was hir hostes man and baar a sak,   1755

1752   **Oure suster deere lo]** O. s. d. Cp+; Loo d. s. Dd; Lo s. d. lo La   **heere I
write]** h. w. I Dd+
    1753   **boef]** chese Ne+ CX[1]   **ye]** we Ha[4] WR
    1754   **wente ay hem]** w. h. ay Ad[3] Cp Dd Gg La+ PN[1] TH[1-3] UR TR MR; ay w. h.
Ha[4] WR; w. him ay Ne+ CX[1,2] WN PN[2] ST–SP[3]; w. alway Pw+
    1755   **hir hostes man]** he osteman La; hir hoste Ne+ CX[1,2] WN PN[2]; theire hors ~
PN[1]   **and baar]** a. evir he b. Ne+ CX[1]–PN[2]

---

tenuously with cloth. Baugh (1963:411) adds that Southworth's suggestion gets no support
from French usage.
    1754   **sturdy harlot:** A harlot, says Thomas (UR glossary), is a "loose person"; TR
(note to *GP* 647, with reference to the present line) says that "it seems always to have been a
disgraceful appellation." Pollard (1894:2.70), Manly (1928:677), and RB (glossary) offer
"rascal"; Baugh (1963:411) and Ross (1972:102), "rogue." But SK and *MED* (s.v. *harlot* n. 4.
[a]) cite this line to illustrate respectively the meanings "a person of low birth, servant lad";
"a male servant, menial." Havely (1975:127) accepts the neutral definitions (as do Fisher
1977:135 and RI) but considers that the term is used here "in a rather contemptuous sense."
He adds that "[friars] were not supposed to take a third person with them—especially not for
the purpose mentioned here" (p. 137). Birney (1960:207) detects in *sturdy* a suggestion of the
friar's "confidence in his powers to wheedle a heavy sackful that morning," and Craik (1964:
120) concurs: "evidently it needed a strong man to carry off these poor trifles."
        wente ay hem: The variations on *wente ay hem* are, like those in line 1744,
widespread and random: "The position of 'ay' and the choice between 'ay' and 'alway' was
here, as usual, determined less by MS tradition than by scribal habit" (MR 3.466). MR do
not explain why they consider *wente hem ay* the correct reading; presumably the number of
MSS with that reading carried more weight for them than the agreement of El and Hg.
    1755   **hostes man:** SK, following Jephson (Bell 1855:2.106), understands *hostes man*
to be the "servant to the guests at the convent. *Hoste* seems here to mean 'guest,' which is one
of the meanings of O.F. *hoste*," though he adds that this sense is rare in ME. Manly (1928:
590), RB, and PR concur in this understanding, Manly reiterating SK's quotation from
Wyclif "to show that the man who carried the bag for the friars was commonly nicknamed
after Judas Iscariot." Williams (1953:505–07) suggests that the man "is surely a relic of the
bursarius, or spiritual friend, who received goods and especially money, which the Franciscans
were forbidden to touch," adding that the *bursarius* and such devices as handling money with
sticks (to avoid touching it) were fraternal practices roundly condemned by their enemies.
Baugh (1963:411) remarks that the explanation in SK "appears to be a guess." Fisher (1977:
135) queries it. Richardson (RI) notes a different explanation by Hartung (1967:176) that
"the *hostes man* . . . is the servant of the innkeeper at whose inn the two friars are staying," a
view Hartung feels is supported by lines 1778–80, which show the friar's fellow and his
knave approaching the inn. Martin and Wright (1990) review the interpretative history and
endorse Hartung's understanding; they observe that 4 MSS read "*his* hostes man," and sup-

And what men yaf hem leyde it on his bak,
And whan that he was out at dore anon
He planed awey the names everichon
That he biforn hadde writen in his tables.
He served hem with nyfles and with fables.   1760
  "Nay ther thow lixt, thow somnour," quod the frere.

1756   **what}** that Dd TH¹–UR   **yaf}** ȝeue Gg+   **hem}** him Ne Pw+ CX¹–
PN²   **it}** *om.* La+
1757   **whan that}** whan Cp Gg Ne Pw+ CX¹–UR; *om.* La+   **at dore}** at þe d.
Ad³ Cp Dd Gg Ha⁴ La Ne+ CX¹–PN¹ TH¹–UR WR MR; of þe d. Pw+
1758   **awey}** out Ha⁴ WR   **the}** *om.* Pw+
1760   **served hem}** s. Pw+; seruen h. ~ WN
1761   **ther}** t. in Pw+   **thow lixt thow}** thow Ne; thow l. Pw+ CX¹–UR
quod} sayd Ha⁴ WR

---

pose that this reading, while not authoritative, does suggest that "scribes very close to Chaucer's lifetime seemed to interpret 'hostes man' as the servant of the host at the inn where the two friars are lodging" (p. 272). The omission of *man* in the *b* MSS, represented here by Ne, both suggests confusion over the meaning of the phrase and introduces further confusion, leading eventually to the PN¹ *hir hors*. *Hostes man* is sufficiently confusing, and once *man* drops out of the line nothing in the context of this passage accounts for a *host*. PN¹'s stab at sense, "he carries the bag, so he is their horse," is intelligent enough.

1756   MR do not report *that* for *what* in Dd or *ȝeue* for *yaf* in Gg.

1757   **at dore:** Among manuscripts only Bo¹ Ph² Tc² support the Hg El reading, but scribes frequently substituted *atte* (= *at the*) for *at*; and here the latter form provides a smoother meter.

1760   RB notes the analogous "sert de fable" in *RR* 11332.

nyfles: Glosses begin with that of Thomas (UR; echoed by most subsequent glossators): "Trifles; Trifling news." Manly (1928:686) offers "silly stories," which RB (glossary) and RI repeat. Baugh (1963:411) and PR suggest "fictitious tales"; Donaldson (1975: 247) "tricks." The most elaborate gloss is in SK (6.178): "'mockeries, pretences,' from OF *nifler* 'to sniff or mock at' (Godefroy); cf. OF *nifle* 'nose.' *NED* [*OED*] says 'perhaps' connected with Lat. *nichil* 'a nothing, a trifle.' There may be also a connection with sniff, sniffle; cf. *nese* and *sneeze*, etc.; and so a suggestion of the 'sniveling priest.'" Baum (1956:241) writes that "there is possibly a play here," while Adams (1962:130) suggests that the word associates the friar's sermons with "windy expulsions," which clarifies "why Friar Huberd chose this point to interrupt the Summoner." *MED* lists "a small or flimsy article of dress, ?a kerchief of fine material" as the most frequent meaning, but offers "a trick, a jest" for the meaning here (s.v. *nifle*).

1761   Jephson (Bell 1855:2.106) writes: "The friar's vehement denial is admirably managed. The general resemblance of the sompnour's picture is so perfect, that even he is carried away by its spirit, and believes it real; but he thinks he can at least dispute the trifling circumstance of the blotting out of the names." Lumiansky takes the interruption as a confirmation of the "pertinency of this attack" (1955:140); Craik (1964:99) adds that "the

"Pees," quod oure hoost, "for Cristes moder deere;
Tel forth thy tale and spare it nat at al."
"So thryve I," quod this somnour, "so I shal."

1763 **thy]** ʒoure Gg **and]** *om.* Cp La+ **spare]** spel Ad³ *Out:* He
1764 **quod this somnour]** q. the s. Gg Ha⁴ La Ne+ CX¹–SP³ WR; Host, quoth he,
and ~ UR *Spur. line* Ffor hym ne for noon oþere what so fall Pw

---

thrust has really gone home; the Friar displays his guilt." Zietlow (1966:19) adds that "the implication, unintended, of course, is that the Summoner has been accurate up to this point. The Friar's haste to correct the record on this point suggests that he perceives the resemblance in the others." Craik (1964:98) and Havely (1975:127) note the parallelism of this interruption to that in *FrT* 1332–37, Havely writing that the particular pattern "(interruption by the 'victim' of the tale and restoration of order by the Host) . . . doesn't occur elsewhere in the *Canterbury Tales*; the angry exchanges between Miller and Reeve, Pardoner and Host, for example, are confined to the prologues or endings of the tales concerned. The effect of the Summoner's and Friar's interruptions is therefore to reinforce the dramatic framework of their two tales." Giaccherini (1980:146) comments that the outburst demonstrates that the friar has recognized himself and his methods in the Summoner's narration. Kazantzakis (1941:125) remarks that "thus [the friar] collected charity, loaded up, saddled his mule, and the moment he had left the village behind him, he erased all the names he had promised to commemorate." The erroneous attribution of a mule to the friar is interesting because, in the scene in *The Fratricides* which is modeled on *SumT*, Kazantzakis's monk is riding a mule; see note 1746–53.

  lixt: SK says "Chaucer makes no attempt here, as in the Reeve's Tale, to imitate the Yorkshire dialect," but Manly (1926*b*:105–06) argues that in both *FrT* and *SumT* Chaucer makes "a definite attempt to use dialect for the production of a sense of reality. . . . not by writing the tales in dialect throughout, but by introducing into the dialogue words which distinctly belong to the dialect and subtly create an atmosphere and a background." Several examples are offered for *FrT*, but only the form *lixt* for *SumT*. Muscatine (1957:199) argues against "any local peculiarity of dialect" in *SumT*, noting (p. 269) that "the words 'tholed,' 'caples,' and 'lixt' (for 'liest') are commonly found in Midland and Southern texts."

  1762 **for Cristes moder deere:** In an observation repeated by Giaccherini (1980: 137), Fleming (1967:106) argues for the importance of the image of Maria Misericordia in *SumT* (see notes to lines 1675–99 and 2116); he sees a deep irony in the Host's invocation of the Virgin to quell the Summoner's and Friar's wrath: "Slaves of the letter and vessels of wrath like their own fictional creatures, brothers only in the confraternity of the Old Law, these two fulminating officers of the Church must be pacified by the rough ministrations of a layman."

  1764 The line has a vexed textual history. Not only is there a spurious line in Pw, Ra² is *Out* and includes the spurious line *what sir frere pees for he shal* ahead of line 1763, while Fi, Ha², and Sl¹ read *allredy oste* for *quod this Somnour*. Nl reads *All redy sir hoost* for the same phrase. UR's *Host, quoth he and* might thus have been inspired by some MS reading.

So longe he wente hous by hous til he   1765
Cam til an hous ther he was wont to be
Refresshed moore than in an hundred placis.
Syk lay the goode man whos the place is,

1765   **he wente hous by hous]** he w. fro h. to h. Dd Ne+ CX¹–TR   til] quoþ
Cp La+; that (Bo¹+) PN¹
1766   **Cam til an hous]** T. he c. to an h. Cp La+; C. to an h. Dd Gg Ne Pw+ CX¹–
TR   ther he] t. as he (Ii+) TH¹–SP³
1767   **than]** þat La   **placis]** place La
1768   **the]** *om.* La   **goode]** bond Ad³ Cp Dd La+; housbond Ha⁴ TR WR
whos] the w. Ad³; w. þat Ha⁴ TR–RB¹ RB² RI; þat of Pw+   **is]** *del.* La

---

1765–69   Knight (1973:71–72) remarks upon the "driving character" of this passage:
"There is a strongly monosyllabic tone here, and also the poetry occasionally uses a rare word
like 'Refresshed' to keep in key with the 'learned' aspect of the poem's action."
1767   **Refresshed:** Huppé (1964:203) writes that "the Wife of Bath's spectacular
word-play on 'refresshed' tends to remain on one's mind, and the way the friar greets
Thomas' wife seems to suggest not only his accord with the wife, but the presence of hanky-
panky."
1768   MR explain the roughness of the line thus: "The earlier draft seems to have read
'that of the place is', which is metrically satisfactory. In changing 'that of' to 'whose' Chaucer
apparently did not observe the effect on the rhythm, or else O¹ carelessly omitted Chaucer's
'that', which was restored only by Ha⁴ (3.466). SK, RB and RI borrow *that* from Ha⁴ to
make a line which has the virtue of being better metrically than that of Hg–El, but once
Chaucer had committed himself to rhyme *placis* (which he tried nowhere else in *CT*), a line
no better than this one was probably inevitable.
   Syk: According to Whittock (1968:137), the fact that Thomas's illness "does
not deter the friar from begging, indeed becomes even an excuse for it, emphasises further his
ubiquitous imposition."
   goode man: SK takes the phrase to mean simply "the goodman, or master of
the house." He continues by noting that "[Ha⁴] has *housbond-man*, and [Cp and Ln] *bonde
man*; all with the same sense." But "master of the house" has connotations very different from
"bond man." According to *MED, housbond* can mean, in addition to married man, "2. (a) The
master of a house, paterfamilias; the male head of a household, householder," or "3. (a) A
bondman, villein; also, a customary tenant who has a holding of land in addition to the croft
land attached to his homestead"; but *god man* is either "1. (a) A good man, righteous man" or
"2. (a) The male head of a household, a householder, master; (b) a citizen of a town, a master
in a craft or guild; a burgess." Of these possibilities, reading 2. (a) of *god man* seems most
appropriate; though both lord and lady repeatedly refer to Thomas as "a churl" (at lines 2206,
2218, 2232, 2238, 2241; as does the narrator, echoing their words in indirect discourse at
line 2290), the term need not imply bondage. *MED*, s.v. *cerl*, in fact cites line 2206 as an
instance of the meaning "2. A person lacking in refinement, learning, or morals; boor,
ignoramus." Birney (1960:207) points out that Thomas is not penniless: "That Thomas lives
in a house of his own in the suburbs of a town may be inferred from lines 1765–8, 1778–80,
1853, 2180; that he is a man of means is clear from 1949–53, 2099"; Birney also observes

Bedrede upon a couche lowe he lay.
"*Deus hic*," quod he, "O Thomas, freend, good day," 1770
Seyde this frere curteisly and softe.

1769   **Bedrede**} And Cp La+   **couche**} bench Ne+ CX¹   **lowe**} seke Dd
(Dd₁ *corr.*)
1770   **freend**} *om.* Ne+ CX¹–PN²
1771   **curteisly**} al c. Ha⁴ SP²–WR   **softe**} fre Ne+ CX¹

(p. 208) that "he is no 'lewed' serf but a townsman who has, or had, money, still keeps good fare, and can summon servants to his aid when he needs them (2156)." Ruggiers (1965:102) refers to Thomas as "a well-to-do householder." In the RI note on *ShT* B² 29, the phrase is said to be "quite frequently used in contexts of cuckoldry," as in *Mankind* (ed. Eccles 1969:176–77), lines 703–04. See also the note on *my churl* in line 2238.

1769   **lowe:** MR report *seke* in Dd, but do not report its correction.

1770   **Deus hic:** "God be here! the ordinary formula of benediction on entering a house," according to WR, Jephson (Bell 1855:2.106), Hertzberg (1866:624), SK, Manly (1928:590), RB and Richardson (RI). Huppé (1964:202) remarks that *SumT* "requires an actor's gift to give its full dimension . . . The friar's speech must be read aloud to catch the unctuousness of his saffroning his speech with Latin and French." Fleming (1966:693), Szittya (1974:39), and Havely (1975:137) underline the specifically fraternal nature of the greeting. Havely, following Szittya (1974:38–39), writes that "The Rule of St Francis . . . says of travelling friars that 'Whenever they enter a house, their first words shall be: "Peace upon this house," and, as it is written in the Holy Gospel (Luke, x, 5–8), they may then eat of any dish that is set before them.' Friar John's behaviour on entering Thomas's house is a characteristic distortion of this. His blessing and good wishes are followed up by a heavy hint that another 'mery meel' would not come amiss." Fleming notes (1966:693) that Saint Francis appears with the motto "Pax huic Domui" in some medieval pictorial representations, and Szittya (1974:40) remarks that the friar abbreviates the greeting, "with emphasis no doubt on *hic*, in view of [his] love of fine food and drink." Fleming adds later (1983:8) that the friar's greeting "most easily means 'God is here'—a perhaps inflated claim with which to announce his arrival," while Olson (1986:217) agrees, characterizing the greeting as "ostentatiously belched."

Thomas: Levitan (1971:241) suggests that Thomas may have this name in memory of Saint Thomas Aquinas, a Dominican, who in Dante's *Paradiso* 11 praises Saint Francis (present with him on the rim of a wheel; see note 2255) and then castigates the present Dominicans for their degeneracy. Clark (1976a:164) suggests rather that Thomas's name is meant to remind us of Doubting Thomas and (the same person) Thomas of India. Andreas (1990:145) notes that the name fits this skeptical anti-hero well. See further in note 1980. Noting the importance of puns in *SumT*, Aers (1986a:43) suggests "Thom-arse" as one reading of the name.

1771   **softe:** Bishop (1987:111–13) notes a patterned association of this word with the friar in different senses (*traductio*) to establish his character. The other instances are in lines 1777 and 1840.

"Thomas," quod he, "God yelde yow. Ful ofte
Have I upon this bench faren ful wel;
Heere have I eten many a murye mel."
And fro the bench he droof awey the cat,   1775

1772   **Thomas]** O T. Ha⁴ WR   **quod he]** sayde he Cp La+; *om.* Ha⁴ Ne Pw+
WR   **yow ful ofte]** it y. f. o. Ha⁴+ PN²–SP¹ UR–WR; y. f. o. tyme quod he Ne+ CX¹;
y. wel o. Pw+; it y. for f. o. ~ SP²,³
   1773   **Have I]** I h. Ne+ CX¹–PN²   **upon this bench faren]** f. vpon thi b. Ad³;
on t. b. f. Ne+ CX¹–PN²   **ful]** *om.* Cp La+
   1774   **many]** ful m. Dd Gg+; mery many Ne (Ne₁ *corr.*)

1774   MR ignore the error and correction in Ne.
1775   **he droof awey the cat:** This line has received a steady stream of critical
approval, beginning as early as Godwin (1804:4.188), who writes that "the entrance of the
friar into the house of the sick man, his driving away the sleeping cat from the bench he
thought proper to occupy . . . are all in the most exquisite style of comic delineation," while
Jephson (Bell 1855:2.106) says that "it is by this sort of by-play that Chaucer gives such a
marvellous reality to his scenes. He does not say that the friar made himself quite at home,
but he makes you *see* it with your eyes." Lowell (1870:193; 1904:259) notes that "sometimes
[Chaucer] describes amply by the merest hint, as when the Friar, before setting himself softly
down, drives away the cat. We know without need of more words that he has chosen the
snuggest corner." This comment is echoed approvingly by Root (1906:251)—who takes the
scene as contributing to the "masterful portrait of the dissembling friar"—and later by Chute
(1946:280) and Speirs (1951:150). SK notes simply that "the friar made himself quite at
home." Even Cowling (1927:170), who judges that "in construction this is Chaucer's weakest
tale," notes this passage among "the additions which Chaucer made to the central incident"
whereby "it became a tale." Shelly (1940:252) singles out the line as "one of the homeliest
and most effective bits of realism in all Chaucer," while Bennett (1947:74) writes that "men's
actions are ever betraying their character in Chaucer, and the comfort-loving nature of the
Friar is revealed in [these] few lines." Birney (1960:207–08) denies that the friar chooses the
cat's bench because it is the snuggest, arguing rather that it is the most strategic spot, "so
close he can dominate the helpless ear of his victim," though Giaccherini (1980:147) argues
that the point is not whether John regards this spot as the warmest, softest, or most strategic,
but rather that "it is *his* spot, where he has always sat and therefore considers his property."
Craik (1964:122) feels that "the friar's unfeeling treatment of the cat (for there seems to be
plenty of room on the bench for his things as well as for himself) and his deliberate settling
into the warm place it has just left, speak his whole character," but Benson (1980:73) asserts
that "sentimentality about animals is a vice peculiar to the post-Romantic mind," and Chau-
cer would hardly have objected to the friar's treatment of the cat as "unfeeling." Corsa
(1964:188) sees the gesture as revealing "his arrogant presumption to ownership of all he
sees," and Kean (1972:2.89) takes it as one of "unconscious self-betrayal." Others see the
action as revealing John's "supremely grasping nature" (Hanning 1985:13–14) and his "easy
and insinuating assumption of privilege, the unhurried deliberateness, the gentleness, of a

And leyde adoun his potente and his hat
And eek his scrippe, and sette hym softe adown.
His felawe was go walked into town,
Forth with his knave into that hostelrye
Wher as he shoope hym thilke nyght to lye.   1780
   "O deere maister," quod this syke man,

1776   **adoun}** doun Cp+
1777   **scrippe}** scripte Pw   **hym softe}** himself (Ha⁵+) TR
1778   **go}** *om.* Ne+ CX¹ TR   **walked}** walken ~ PN¹   **into}** in þe Cp Gg
Ha⁴ La+ UR WR; into þe Ne Pw+ CX¹–SP³
1779   **his}** *om.* Ad³   **into}** vnto Gg+; to Ha⁴   **that}** þe Ha⁴+ WR
1780   **thilke}** that Ne+ CX¹–PN²; that ilke (Mm+) TH¹–UR   **lye}** by ly Ne
(Ne₁ *corr.*)
1781   **O}** O my ~ UR   **quod}** saide Ne+ CX¹ PN¹; sayd he ~ CX² WN
PN²   **this}** the Ha⁴+ WR

---

cat's, and withal the ruthlessness, and obliviousness of all but physical advantage" (Pearsall 1985:224). Gray (1990:202) sees in the gesture a "moral emblem" of "a thoughtless, self-obsessed and self-important man," one with the force of "what Joyce would call an 'epiphany'—'a sudden spiritual manifestation, whether in the vulgarity of speech or of gesture.'"
   Rowland (1971:18 and 70) feels that John's action indicates his enthusiasm for food. She also argues (pp. 70–72) that cats were commonly associated with Satan, and that heretics and worshipers of Satan were often accused of copulating with Satan or kissing his fundament while he was in the form of a cat, and thus that "by taking the cat's place, the Friar not only shows his greed and cunning but may suggest that he is a substitute for the demonic powers with which the cat, by long tradition, is invested" (p. 73). The scene has even found its way into a discussion of medieval attitudes toward animals (White 1965:40).
   1777   **scrippe:** MR do not report the variant in Pw. *MED* lists *script(e* as an error for *scrip(pe*, and cites the Pw reading of this line as a variant.
   1778   "It is . . . somewhat alarming," writes Fleming (1967: 99), "to learn that while John is becoming engaged in a patently scandalous situation at Thomas' house," his fellow, who is provided to help protect against scandal, walks into town.
   was go walked: The expression is equivalent to "gone a-walking." SK is critical of TR for suppressing "this characteristic idiom," and in an extensive note to *PardP* C 406, explains the origin of such constructions: "the verb *go* could be combined with what was *apparently* a past participle, in such a manner as to give the participle the force of a verbal substantive. In other words, instead of saying 'he goes a-hunting,' our forefathers sometimes said 'he goes a-hunted.'" Manly (1928:590) and RB repeat this information. The RI note on *BD* 387 ("I was go walked") is cross-referenced to the present line and refers to Mustanoja (1960:558, 582), who argues (p. 558) rather that the construction exemplifies "a semantic weakening of *go* . . . and [is] roughly equivalent to *was walked.*" See also Higuchi (1990).
   1780   **lye:** MR ignore the Ne error and correction.
   1781–83   Shelly (1940:252) feels that "Thomas greets the friar with feigned affection and respect," and "with an irony that is lost upon the friar" notes that he has not seen him in

"How han ye fare sith that March bigan?
I say yow noght this fourtnyght or moore."
"God woot," quod he, "laboured I have ful soore,
And specially for thy savacioun   80v   1785
Have I seyd many a precious orisoun,
And for oure othere freendes, God hem blesse.
I have today been at youre chirche at messe,

1782   ye] *om.* Ad³+   that] *om.* Ha⁴ La Ne+ CX¹–UR WR
1783   yow noght] n. y. ~ PN¹   fourtnyght] f. day Pw+ UR   or] and Cp La Pw+ TH¹–TR; ne Ne+ CX¹–PN²
1784   I have] h. I Cp Dd Gg Ha⁴ La Ne Pw+ CX¹–RB¹ RB²   ful] *om.* Dd+
1786   a] *om.* ~ UR
1787   oure] your Ad³+; myn Ha⁴ WR   othere] *om.* Ad³ Dd (Dd₁ *corr.*)+
1788   today been] this day b. Ne Pw+ CX¹–TR; to day done Cp La+   at messe] a m. Cp La+; *om.* Hg (Hg₂ *corr.*)

---

two weeks, but Benson (1980:72) feels it would be a mistake to take Thomas's words as ironic. Speirs (1951:151) agrees with Shelly, arguing that Thomas "is not taken in," as does Giaccherini (1980:147), while Birney (1960:208) goes further, suggesting that Thomas's greeting is only "apparently artless" and that the remark that he has not seen him in two weeks sets a trap. The friar claims to have labored in praying for Thomas and their friends, but does not mention the child who died within the period of his absence and who presumably lies buried in the yard of the church where the friar preached that morning (Birney 1960:209); Zietlow (1966:7–8) agrees with this understanding, seeing Friar John's falling into this trap as the first sign of his characteristic insensitivity and imperceptiveness.

1782   **March:** Havely (1975:137–38) feels that "the reason or reasons for Chaucer's choice of March as the time for the story don't seem to be much clearer than those for his choice of Holderness as the place. . . . It could be that he wanted to suggest a time when 'madness' (in the sense of practical jokes, etc.) might be expected—or that he was used to making spring a time for action in his tales. . . . But there is no further mention of March or suggestion of spring in the rest of the Tale," an understanding echoed by Giaccherini (1980: 140). Lancashire (1981:20) argues that the significance of the date is that it points to Lent, a time of fasting, and thus anticipates ironically the friar's claims to superior abstemiousness and his claims of spiritual affinity to Moses and Elijah.

1783   **fourtnyght:** Spelling variations are not recorded in these collations, but it is interesting to note that RB and RI spell *fourtenyght* (though both Hg and El spell as printed here), consistent with Robinson's conviction that Lydgate lines "are almost unknown in those works of Chaucer of which a good text is preserved" (RB² xli).

1784   **I have:** Most MSS read *haue I*, but there seems no compelling reason to choose that reading—as all printed editions except MR, PR, and RI do—over the Hg El reading.

1788   **at messe:** The phrase is added to Hg in a hand Doyle and Parkes (1979:xlvi) describe as "a large slanting Secretary, probably of the second quarter of the fifteenth century." MR do not report that Hg has been corrected here.

And seyd a sermon after my symple wit,
Nat al after the text of holy writ,   1790
For it is hard to yow as I suppose,
And therfore wol I teche yow al the glose.
Glosyng is a glorious thyng certeyn,

1789   **And**} A Cp   **after**} to Dd Ne+ CX¹–PN² TR   **symple**} lewd Ne+
CX¹–PN²
1790   **al**} *om.* He+ CX¹–PN²   **text**} playn t. (Tc²) CX¹–PN²   **holy**} al h. He
1791   **to**} for Ha⁴+ WR
1792   **And**} *om.* Cp La+   **wol I teche**} w. I telle Dd Gg La+; tel I He+ CX¹–
PN²; I w. t. Pw+ TH¹–UR   **yow**} to y. Cp+; *om.* La   **al**} ay Ha⁴ TR WR; *om.* Ad³+
1793   **a glorious**} a ful g. Dd He+ CX¹–PN² TR WR; g. Pw+

1789   **And**: MR do not record the variant in Cp.

1792   **glose**: SK states: "gloss, interpretation, as distinguished from the text." Manly (1928:590) quotes from an unidentified source: "Ancient Bibles gave the text with voluminous paraphrase and comment called Glossa Ordinaria. Secular texts—Vergil's *Aeneid* and many standard treatises on various subjects—were also provided with glosses." RB compares *MLE* B¹ 1180 and *MkT* B² 3330.

1793   **Glosyng**: The earliest editors gloss "to gloss" with only pejorative meaning: SP¹ has "Flatter: *also*, perswade," which SP²,³ repeat, adding however the sense "the exposition of a darke speech." Thomas (UR) offers the sense "To interpret," while noting that "it is generally used in an ill sense for To put a fair interpretation with an intention to deceive." Shain (1953:242–43) and Carruthers (1972:208–09) note especially that Chaucer frequently uses this term in a purely pejorative sense, e.g. *MerT* E 2351; *SqT* 166; *ManP* 34; *Rom* 5097; and *TC* 4.1471, and Shain writes that "Chaucer's interest in his portrait of the *glosynge* Friar may not, in the absence of other evidence, substantiate the opinion that Chaucer had taken a Wyclifian stand on Bible literalism, but we are aware of an attitude toward the pulpit art of *glosynge*." Birney, arguing that Chaucer intends us to sense Thomas's mounting anger with John, agrees, adding that "the irony here is deepened, since the friar would not be such a fool as to be unaware of the *double entendre*, but he would presume that Thomas was too simple to perceive it" (1960:209). Richardson (RI, note to line 1792) feels that "for Chaucer *glose* is usually pejorative," and quotes RB (note to *MkT* B² 2140): "From the original sense of 'gloss,' 'interpret,' the word passes to the idea of an irrelevant or misleading comment, and so to outright deception." Hanning (1985:10) also documents the pejoration of the term, adding that it bore by Chaucer's day "the additional signification of flattery or cajolery." Robertson (1962:331–32) insists that it is the friar's abuse of exegesis, not the exegesis itself, that is satirized "humorously but with some bitterness" here, and Fleming (1966:694 and 1983:18) agrees, writing that "it is the quality of the friar's exegesis—not the fact of it—which is ridiculed." But Besserman (1984:65–66) argues that in view of the portrait of the glosing friar in *SumT* Chaucer's "allegiance to the orthodox view of biblical interpretation . . . needs to be proved, not merely assumed." Huppé (1964: 203) suggests that "perhaps it was from the friars that the Wife [of Bath] learned her way with the difficulties of the biblical text." Levy (1966:48–49) feels that the friar glosses "to display what he considers his superior talents because of his special grace."

For lettre sleeth so as we clerkes seyn.
Ther have I taught hem to be charitable   1795
And spende hir good ther it is resonable,
And ther I say oure dame; a, where is she?"

1794   **lettre]** letters Pw+   **so]** *om.* Gg He+ CX¹–UR   **we]** thise El+; *om.* Cp La+
1795   **taught hem]** h. t. ~ TH¹–UR
1796   **ther it]** t. as it Ad³+ TH¹–SP³   **is]** *om.* La
1797   **And]** *om.* Cp La+   **a]** *om.* Ha⁴ He La (La₁ *corr.*)+ CX¹–PN² WR

---

a glorious: MR do not report the omission in Pw. WR appears to have taken *ful* from TR, as it is not in Ha⁴ or La. Since the Chaucer Society text of Ha⁴ (Furnivall 1885) also prints *ful*, one suspects that the transcriber was consulting WR here rather than looking directly at the MS.

1794   *Marginal gloss:* Litera occidit et cetera El.

Commentators since Jephson (Bell 1855) note the influence here of 2 Corinthians 3.6: "For the letter kills, but the spirit gives life." Haeckel (1890:68) lists this among Chaucer's proverbs. Arguing that in addition to gleaning biblical allusions from such sources as Jerome's *Epistola adversus Jovinianum*, Chaucer often used the Vulgate at first hand, Landrum (1924:96) counts "twenty-three scriptural references or allusions" in *SumT*, of which Chaucer "may claim fifteen," of which fifteen this is the first. Fleming comments that "the ironic point is, of course, that there never was a more hidebound literalist than the friar, as his preposterous dilemma over the division and distribution of Thomas' gift demonstrates" (1966:694, and similarly in Fleming 1983:17–18). Carruthers (1972:212) makes the same point about the friar's "extraordinary respect for the letter," which is "the real source of his defeat" when confronted by the "problem" of dividing the fart. Richardson (1970:156) points out that Thomas's gift "sleeth" the friar's pride, while Havely (1975:138) notes that exegesis "could provide charlatans like Friar John with glib excuses for their own sins of omission or commission." Alford (1984:199) remarks that the friar's citation of 2 Corinthians is "full of self-incriminating irony. Paul is in the very midst of condemning those who, like the friar, exploit the gospel for private gain." Alford adds that there is perhaps also irony in Paul's description of truthful preachers who are in "the good odour of Christ" (2 Corinthians 2.15), "a suggestive metaphor to say the least," an idea voiced also by Burlin (1977:272, n. 19). Both Alford and Cooper point to the ironies awaiting the friar: the fart is an insult, "unmistakably, defiantly, unredeemably literal" (Alford 1984:200), and since the fart as text "has no semantic [content], there can be no gloss, only the bare fact" (Cooper 1983:132).

lettre: MR incorrectly report *lettres* in La.

1797–1815   Bennett (1947:94–95) takes this passage to "illustrate the way in which [Chaucer's verse form] was made to reproduce conversation and to suggest character. . . . The light, conversational tone is admirably suggested by the wealth of monosyllables which carry each line rapidly forward, and may well be compared with the slower moving lines which describe the Friar's first movements on the wife's entry. In the dialogue speed, however, is all-important, and to this the diction makes a notable contribution. Otherwise the run-on lines, the break of the couplet so that each character has one line of it, the numerous inversions at the beginning of the lines, the varying position of the pause, the interplay of speech rhythm

"Yond in the yerd I trowe that she be,"
Seyde this man, "and she wol come anon."
"Ey maister, welcome be ye by Seint John,"   1800
Seyde this wyf, "How fare ye hertely?"
The frere ariseth up ful curteisly

1798   **in the yerd I trowe that**] in þe ʒerd I trowe La Pw+ TH¹–SP³; I trow that in the y. ~ TR

1800   **welcome be ye**] w. ye be ~ TH¹–SP³; ye be w. ~ UR

1802   **The**] This Ad³ Gg He Pw+ CX¹–TR   **frere**] ferere La   **ariseth**] riseth La Pw+   **up**] and He   **ful**] wel Pw+   **curteisly**] coryously He+ CX¹

---

and metrical accents seem to give to these lines the actuality of speech, and with this actuality something of the speaker's own character." Knight (1973:72) likewise praises Chaucer's handling of the verse: "The initial stresses express [the friar's] confident manner, and the use of 'I' as two of them states his self-importance—the first person seems to be used more in this speech than anywhere else in Chaucer."

1797   **ther:** MR incorrectly report þe in Gg for *ther*.

1800–02   Giaccherini (1980:148) feels that the wife addresses Friar John in "perfectly normal words and tone, with no hidden intentions, in contrast to her husband."

1802–05   Though Jephson (Bell 1855:2.107), echoed by SK, sees nothing remarkable in the friar's embrace, noting that "kissing was formerly the ordinary mode of salutation, as it still is in some parts of the continent," and though Manly (1928:590) sees "no sinister implications," some early and all later critics have detected a satirical edge in the passage. Meyer (1913:105–06) comments that the friar knows "better than one might have expected of a religious how to flirt," and RB notes that "the tight embrace and the *chirkyng* are not altogether in keeping with the office and character of the priest," while Chute (1946:280) feels John "rather overdoes the holy salutation that is expected of him." Kellogg (1953:274) adduces two texts contemporary with Chaucer which bear on the case: Gower's *Vox clamantis* (ed. Macaulay 1899–1902:4.150–51) complains of the abuse of the kiss of peace, and "the *Regimen Animarum* (1343), an unpublished English handbook for priests, warns in similar fashion that the abuse of the clerical kiss with its attendant familiarities renders the character of the priest vile and contemptible." Williams too (1953:511) finds the kiss "capable, at least, of giving scandal." For Fleming (1966:693) the kiss "is certainly suspicious when judged by the canons of clerical seemliness." Havely (1975) and Richardson (1970:150 and RI) find the behavior "suspicious," and Havely (p. 139) reminds us that "Chaucer also uses the expression 'lecherous as a sparrow' to describe the Summoner," which Giaccherini (1980:149) takes as an instance of inadvertent auto-accusation on the narrator's part. Ross (1972:124, 207), who sees the kiss as devoid of sexual import in itself, likewise sees the sparrow noises as "a little too familiar." Huppé (1964:203) too finds the kiss itself "unexceptional," but adds that "not only the friar's lip-smacking, but also the reference to the sparrow, suggest lechery," while Harrison (1956:43), seconded by Birney (1960:209), notes a parallel in "the lecherous sparrow, 'Venus sone'" of *PF* 351. Andreas (1990:143) adds that this allusive bird "anticipates the blasphemous parody of Pentecost in the tale, where flatulence displaces the Holy Spirit which is iconologically associated with the dove."

1802   **ariseth:** MR do not report riseþ in Pw.

131

And hire embraceth in hise armes narwe,
And kiste hir swete and chirteth as a sparwe
With his lippes. "Dame," quod he, "right wel,   1805
As he that is youre servant every del,
Thanked be God that yow yaf soule and lyf.
Yet say I nat this day so fair a wyf
In al the chirche, God so save me."
   "Ye, God amende defautes sire," quod she.   1810
"Algates welcome be ye by my fey."
   "Graunt mercy dame, this have I founde alwey.
But of youre grete goodnesse, by youre leve,

1803   **And**] *om.* He   **embraceth**] embrased Cp+
1804   **kiste**] kysseth Ad³ Cp Gg He La Pw+ CX¹–TR   **swete**] swetely Pw+
TH¹–SP¹ UR   **chirteth**] chircheth Ad³+; chirkeþ Cp Dd Gg Ha⁴ He La Pw+ CX¹–RI
1805   **right wel**] I fare r. w. ~ SP²–UR
1807   **Thanked**] Thankyth ~ WN   **yow yaf**] ȝaue me He; yaf you (Ne+) CX¹–
PN²; you haue (Si) TH³–UR
1808   **this**] to Cp He La+ CX¹–PN²
1809   **the chirche**] t. whole c. ~ SP²–UR   **God so**] so g. He La+ CX¹   save
me] m. s. ~ WN UR
1810   **defautes**] þe fautis Gg+ CX¹–PN²; all fautes Pw+ TH¹–UR
1811   **be ye**] ye Gg+; ye be He+ CX¹–SP³
1812   **Graunt**] Grand ~ TR   **this**] that He+ CX¹–TR
1813   **by**] and by ~ UR

1804   **chirteth as a sparwe**: The reading *chirteth*, shared by Hg, El, Ch, Ha³, and Mc, is little more than a spelling variant of *chirketh*, but MR report both forms in their collations, and both *OED* and *MED* accord the forms separate entries: *OED*, s.v. *Chirt*, cites Trevisa's *De Proprietatibus Rerum* ix.v. (Tollemache MS), "Exciteþ briddes and foulis to chirtynge" (Edition of 1495, "chyrterynge"). Similarly, *MED*, s.v. *Chirtinge*.

1807–09   Kazantzakis (1941:125) remarks on the friar's "psalming voice" in this passage.

1809   **God so save me**: The phrase is perhaps more difficult than *God so me save*, and it is certainly less characteristic; *God me (thee, him, my soul) save* is a frequent Chaucerian rhyme phrase (13 in *CT* alone, 3 in *TC*), and in the two instances of WN and UR the familiarity of the phrase overcame the power of the rhyme to retain the correct reading. UR's reading is corrected on the *errata* sheet appended to the volume.

1810   **God amende defautes**: "A sort of modest *disqualifying* of herself, as much as to say, 'I know I have many faults, but may God amend them," Jephson (Bell 1855:2.107). SK adds "it was usual, I believe, to use a form of deprecation of this sort in reply to praise. The sense is—'but I am aware that I have defects, and may God amend them.'" RB and RI (footnote) echo this idea.

1812   **Graunt mercy**: Manly (1928:590) explains, "'much thanks,' a French expression colloquially pronounced 'grammercy.'"

I wolde pray yow that ye nat yow greve.
I wol with Thomas speke a litel throwe.   1815
Thise curatz been ful necligent and slowe
To grope tendrely a conscience.
In shrift, in prechyng is my diligence,
And studie in Petres wordes and in Poules.
I walke and fisshe Cristen mennes soules,   1820

1814   **wolde]** wol (Ht+) TH¹–SP³   **pray yow]** y. prayin (En³+) UR   **nat
yow]** y. n. Ha⁴ He+ CX¹–PN² WR; nold n. Pw; n'old ~ UR   **greve]** agreue Ad³+
1815   **throwe]** word He+ CX¹
1816   **curatz]** curatours Dd He Pw+ CX¹–PN²   **ful necligent and slowe]** so n.
a. s. Dd+ TR; nat worth a tord He+ CX¹
1817   **a conscience]** a mannys c. He+ CX¹–UR
1818   **shrift in prechyng]** s. and in p. Cp La+ CX¹–SP³; s. and p. Ha⁴ He+ UR
WR   **is]** ay is Ad³
1819   **And]** A. to ~ TH¹–UR; *om.* Ha⁴   **in]** on He+ CX¹–UR   **in Poules]** P.
He Pw+ CX¹
1820   **I]** And Ad³ Ha⁴+   **walke]** w. about He+ CX¹   **and]** to Gg+ TH¹–
UR   **fisshe]** clens He+ CX¹   **Cristen]** *om.* Cp Dd He La+ CX¹

1816   **curatz:** "The secular or parochial clergy, who had *cure* (cura) of souls, which the
religious orders could not properly be said to have, because their jurisdiction was not con-
fined to the ordinary limits, but extended, like that of a missionary, to whomsoever they
could persuade," Jephson (Bell 1855:2.108); SK takes the word as evidence that *possessioners*
in line 1722 denotes the secular clergy. Williams notes that the friar's disparagement of the
confessional powers of secular clergy is emblematic of one of the chief points of friction
between friars and the seculars (1953:510), and Fleming (1966:693) adds that this friction
was aggravated "by the promulgation of the bull *Ad fructus uberes* in 1281." This bull of Pope
Martin IV gave the friars extensive rights to preach and hear confessions; it was modified by
Boniface VIII in 1300 (Kelly 1986:203). Giaccherini (1980:142) notes that the passage
seems to fit the character of Huberd revealed in *GP* 218–19.
1817   **grope:** According to Manly (1928:590), "the usual technical term for 'examina-
tion at confession.'" Baum (1956:238), Birney (1960:216), Adams (1962:130), Huppé
(1964:204), Richardson (1970:156–57), and Ross (1972:99) feel that in this context a dou-
ble meaning is intended, and Havely (1975:139) notes that "the modern (physical) meaning
was also current in Chaucer's time—and it may be part of the joke against the friar that the
word is used in *this* sense to describe his activities later on [2141 and 2148]. The use of
the vivid verb to express *both* the professed spiritual methods and the real material aims of the
friar thus helps to highlight his hypocrisy."
1818–21   Shain (1955:241) suggests that the metaphors in this passage show the
influence of pulpit rhetoric on Chaucer.
1820   All editors since Jephson (Bell 1855) draw our attention to Luke 5.10 and
Matthew 4.19. SK and Richardson (RI) also point to *Rom* 7490. Levy (1966:72) sees in the
allusion an attempt on the friar's part "to suggest his direct relationship to the Apostles," and

To yelden Jesu Crist His propre rente;
To sprede His word is set al myn entente."
    "Now by youre leeve, O deere sire," quod she,
"Chideth hym wel for Seinte Trinitee.

1821   **Jesu Crist**] J. Pw+; our Lord J. C. ~ TR
1822   **sprede**] speke Pw+   **word**] wordes Cp He La Pw+ CX^1–UR   **is**] I
La+   **set**] *om.* Ad^3 Ha^4 Pw+ CX^1–UR WR
1823   **Now**] N. sir He   **leeve**] feiþ Pw+ UR TR   **O**] *om.* Dd He Pw+ CX^1–
UR   **sire**] maister Ad^3 Gg Pw+ TH^1–SP^3; maister mine ~ UR
1824   **Chideth**] Chyd Ha^4 WR   **hym**] h. right Ha^4 WR   **for Seinte**] f. god
in Cp La+; now f. S. ~ UR   **Trinitee**] charite Dd He+ CX^1–TR

Richardson (1970:150) feels that the allusion has an ironic implication, for Friar John fishes
not for men's souls but for food. Knight (1973:72) remarks that "the wonderfully self-
confident 'I walke' is just the statement of a man who would, as here, regard Christ as more
or less his equal," and later (1986:106) notes that the friar places himself "right in the New
Testament." According to Szittya (1974:30–31), *SumT* contains five biblical allusions asso-
ciating the fraternal with the apostolic life, of which this is the first; these are "spaced so
evenly throughout the tale, at structurally significant points . . . that some sort of pattern
seems intended." These particular biblical verses, he argues, were central in the polemics
from both sides of the mendicant-secular controversies. The other allusions are in lines 1973,
1980, 2184–88, and 2195–96. Havely (1983:251) writes that Matthew 4.19 had been used
ironically in earlier vernacular anti-fraternal texts: "as early as 1247 . . . Matthew Paris had
described [friars] as 'no longer fishers of men, but fishers for coins' (*Chronica Majora*, IV,
635)," while Rutebeuf "referred to the Dominicans in similar terms (*Des Jacobins*, 33–6),"
and in Boccaccio's *Decameron* 3.7 "Tedaldo degli Elisei warns his mistress of how friars like
fishermen casting nets gather up numbers of 'devout ladies, widows and other foolish women
and men.'"
    1821–22   Havely (1975:139) suggests that the metaphor here "could be a distorted
echo" of Matthew 22.21: "Render, therefore, to Caesar the things that are Caesar's, and to
God the things that are God's." Rogers (1986:59) remarks that with the *rente / entente* rhyme
". . . the hypocritical friar attempts subliminally to identify the money he gets with the *rent*
due to Christ."
    1821   **Jesu Crist:** Though the collation does not reveal it, the TR reading may have
been inspired by En^3, one of the MSS he used, which reads *our lord Ihū*.
    1824–31   Chute (1946:280) feels of this passage that "the wife is excellently done,
harassed by the irritability of a sick man and very sorry for herself," and Giaccherini (1980:
150) sees in her allusions to Thomas's sexual coldness in front of the friar a certain "insensitiv-
ity if not absolute obtuseness," while Merrill (1962:341) suggests that the wife's request that
John chastise Thomas "originates not from a sincere concern over her husband's irritability,
but from her sexual frustration." Allen (1987:1) finds the wife sluttish, not concerned about
the death of her son: "Disgusted with her husband's unmanly malaise, she seems eager
enough to forget the dead child and go on about making another one." She is, according to
Ruggiers (1965:102), "a self-pitying woman," and Huppé (1964:204), who also sees satire
directed at her, suggests that she "agrees vigorously that her husband needs some words of

He is as angry as a pissemyre,   81r   1825
Thogh that he have al that he kan desire;
Thogh I hym wrye anyght and make hym warm,

1825   He] For he ~ UR   as angry] an angry man Ad³; ay angry (Ne+) CX¹–TH¹
TH³–TR   as a] as is a He+ CX¹–PN² TR
1827   I] that I (Bw+) WN   hym wrye] w. h. Pw+   anyght] *om.* He+ CX¹–
PN²   hym warm] so w. He

---

advice from a man like the friar, who knows that women have certain natural desires which must be satisfied." Fleming (1983:12) comments that the wife's "real complaint would seem to be [Thomas's] phlegmatic disposition in bed rather than his choleric excesses out of it."

Merrill argues (1962:342) that Thomas's sin is not ire, as the wife claims and John assumes, but spiritual sloth, as described in *ParsT* 722–23. Wenzel (1970:450–51) cites a penitential treatise by Grosseteste to explain the relation between Thomas's irascibility and his sexual disinterest. Grosseteste presents the sins as excesses or deficiencies of specific virtues, and accordingly considers lechery as a deficiency in continence, and *insensibilitas* (Thomas's apparent problem) as an excess of continence, which "sometimes occurs because of anger." Wenzel thus sees in Thomas "a typically incontinent man, who sins against continence not only by having too much of it . . . but eventually also by lacking it altogether." Malone (1989) agrees, but adds that with the death of his (only?) child and the pain of disease, Thomas has ample reason to be uninterested in sex. The wife shows "insensitivity" in the modern sense with her remark that Thomas has "al that he kan desire" (line 1826).

1824   **Chideth:** As is their practice, MR do not report the variations in the imperative; see note to line 1671, above.   §   Underlining the disorderliness of the confession scene, "with the penitent's wife giving technical instructions to the confessor," Fleming (1983:12) points out that Chaucer's Parson contrasts "chyding" with charitable chastisement, and includes it among the sins of wrath.

for Seinte Trinitee: MR incorrectly indicate that Cp La omit *for.*   §   "*Saint* means properly *holy*, and so is applied to the Trinity, the Saviour, charity, &c., as well as to Christian men and women. Seinte is the feminine form of the adjective, to agree with Trinite, a feminine noun in Latin and French," Jephson (Bell 1855:2.108). SK adds the gloss, "for (the sake of the) holy Trinity."

1825   **pissemyre:** An ant, so called because of the urinous smell of an ant hill (*OED*). Ross (1972:157) notes that "there is no evidence" that the comparison here was common or proverbial. Chaucer's use is the earliest recorded. Richardson (1970:151 and similarly in 1975:230) remarks that this simile and the *boor* image of line 1829 mark Thomas's initial irascibility as petty, "but the friar mistakenly assesses it as the ferocity of a lion [see line 1989] and delivers a completely unjustified sermon." The friar then betrays the very ire he inveighs against "by behaving both like a lion [line 2152] and like a wild, rather than a tame boar [line 2160]" (pp. 151–52). Haskell (1976:58–59) makes a similar argument and, arguing that ants were proverbially seen as emblems of patient providence and honest labor, suggests that Thomas's ant-like anger is thus justified, the "righteous wrath" of *ParsT* 535, in contrast to the sinful wild-boar-wrath of the friar in line 2160. See further in note 2160.

And on hym leye my leg outher myn arm,
He groneth lyk oure boor lyth in oure sty.
Oother disport right noon of hym have I;   1830
I may nat plese hym in no maner cas."
    "O Thomas, je vous dy, Thomas, Thomas.

1828   on} ouer Cp Dd Ha⁴ He La+ CX¹–WR RB¹ RB² RI   outher myn} o. Cp
He; and eke m. Dd+ TR; and m. (Cn+) CX¹–PN²
    1829   lyk} as ~ SP²,³ TR   lyth} gronyng Cp La+; þat l. Ha⁴ He Pw+ TH¹–UR
WR; *om.* Ad³+   oure sty} s. Cp Ha⁴+ UR WR; his s. La; þe s. Pw+ TH¹–SP³
    1830   right noon of hym} of h. r. n. Ad³ Cp Dd Ha⁴ He La+ CX¹–WR; of h. n.
Pw+
    1831   nat} *om.* Ha⁴ WR
    1832   *Spur. line* Ieo vous dy trescher et bien amy o Thomas Cp La+

1828   **on:** The bulk of the MSS, including all of *a*, *b*, and *c*, appear to read *ouer*, though
as MR point out (3.466) "it is often difficult to distinguish between 'on' and the abbreviated
form of 'ouer' in the MSS."
    1829   **boor:** On the use of the image see note 1825.
        oure sty: MR do not report the *oure* / *þe* variant in Pw.
    1830   **disport:** Ross (1972:75) argues that though the word is generally used to mean
simply pleasure, in this context the wife's meaning is clearly sexual.
    1832   The repetition of Thomas's name has received considerable comment, Huppé
(1964:202) finding it "monotonously condescending," Coghill (1967:123) believing it
"maddening to poor Thomas," and Brewer (1984*b*:115) calling it "obviously patronising . . .
contemptuous cajolery." Corsa (1964:189) writes that the name, "sweet and 'softe' on his
unctuous tongue, iterates and reiterates throughout the scene, the Latin and French affecta-
tions coating in honey the pious cant they preface." Clark (1976*a*:169) wonders whether
"Chaucer has the friar address Thomas by name 18 times during his homily (about once
every 20 lines)" to establish and recall a parallel between the main characters and the double
figure of Thomas of India and Doubting Thomas.
        je vous dy: Manly (1928:590) writes that the phrase "does not imply any
special knowledge of French on the part of the friar. Such expressions were common enough
in fourteenth century England. But he seems fond of them." RB feels that the friar's French
phrases "were in familiar use" and do not suggest a French source for *SumT*. Richardson (RI)
argues that "ability to speak French generally indicated social or educational superiority, and
cites John Trevisa's translation of Ranulph Higden's *Polychronicon*: "Oplondysch men wol
lykne hamsylf to gentil-men and fondeth with gret bysynes for to speke Freynsh, for to be
more ytold of." Ruggiers (1965:101) feels that "Chaucer may have wished to suggest a
certain continental affectation in his friar-preacher," while Levy (1966:60 n. 19), arguing for
the operation of Pentecostal parody in *SumT*, suggests that "one of the effects of the descent
of the Holy Ghost upon the Apostles was to confer upon them the gift of tongues. . . . Both
Friar John in his casual dropping of French phrases and Friar Huberd with his affected lisp
seem to be desirous of creating the impression that they have been specially inspired with the
gift of eloquence"; Giaccherini (1980:165) cites Levy and agrees, noting that one might add
Latin phrases as well. Havely (1975:139) suggests that "the friar's use of French phrases when

This maketh the feend; this moste been amended.
Ire is a thyng that hye God defended,
And therof wol I speke a word or two."   1835
    "Now maister," quod the wyf, "Er that I go,
What wol ye dyne? I wol go ther aboute."
    "Now dame," quod he, "now je vous dy sanz doute,

1833   **feend**] feen Gg (*corr.*)   **this**] it La+; thus ~ UR   **moste**] wil Pw+
1834   **hye**] holy He+ CX¹; *om.* ~ TH¹–UR   **God defended**] G. haþ d. Pw+ TR;
G. offendith (Ne+) CX¹; G. offendyd (Ra¹) CX²–PN²; G. hyghly d. ~ TH¹–UR
1835   **therof**] therfore (Ha³) PN¹   **wol**] wold Ha⁴+ WR
1836   **that**] þan Gg   **I**] yee He+ CX¹
1837   **dyne**] dame ~ PN¹
1838   **quod he now**] q. he Cp Gg He La Pw+ CX¹–RB¹

---

speaking to Thomas and his wife [see also line 1838] shows that he has social pretensions as well as commercial aims, and that he likes to appear 'genteel' in front of the churls." He suggests further a connection between this affectation and the Friar's lisp in his portrait (A 264–65) designed to "make his Englissh sweete upon his tonge" and "thus presumably to make a better impression on his 'clients,' especially the female ones." The decision not to italicize the friar's French phrases here and in line 1838 is explained above (see "The Present Edition" in the Textual Commentary, pp. 98–99).

    1833   **feend:** MR ignore *feen* and its correction in Gg.
        this: UR's *thus* is corrected to *this* in the *errata*.
    1834   **hye God defended:** Any number of MSS (probably an *a* type, according to Dunn [1939]) could have given CX² the reading *hye* (correcting CX¹'s *holy*), but since only one extant MS (Ra¹) has the CX² *offendyd*, Caxton's mending of the faulty rhyme in CX¹ was probably an independent correction. The line provides rather striking evidence of Caxton's unsystematic method of working with his "very trewe book" in making CX². § Manly (1928:590) glosses *defended*: "forbade."
    1838–50   Lounsbury (1892:2.520–21) takes this passage as an example of "the conventional attacks on the clerical orders . . . rather peculiar to the time than to the poet himself. . . . [Chaucer's] attack, to be sure, is almost invariably made in the way of suggestion or of ironical insinuation rather than after a direct and aggressive fashion. . . . [The friar] professes that he will be contented with homely fare, and is particular to request that nothing more be prepared for him than the liver of a capon, a piece of soft bread, and the head of a roasted pig. Then he proceeds to deliver a discourse upon gluttony." Meyer (1913:104) notes that the friar seeks to attenuate the shamelessness of his dinner order through the diffidence of his words. Williams (1953:507–08) connects the passage to the anti-fraternal writings of William of St. Amour and his followers, citing in particular *RR* 11740–756 and *Rom* 8738–748 (incorrectly for 7038–048). Noting the way Chaucer uses the wife to reveal the friar's character (and then dismisses her from the story), Craik (1964:123) refers to the passage as a "rich compound of affectation, epicurism, hypocrisy and flattery," while Huppé (1964:204) remarks that "the friar's description of his gluttony as a form of abstinence indicates how much he shares with the wife her ability to make words be obedient." Lawlor (1968:120)

Have I nat of a capoun but the lyvere,
And of youre softe breed nat but a shyvere,　　　　　　　　　　1840
And after that a rosted pigges heed
(But that I nolde no beest for me were deed),

　　1839　**Have I nat}** H. I He Pw+ CX¹ SP²,³; H. n. La+　　　**but}** nouȝt b. Pw
　　1840　**softe}** white Dd He+ CX¹–TR　　　**nat}** no Dd; *om.* Ad³ Cp Ha⁴ La Pw+
CX¹–SP³ WR; *eras.* Gg
　　1842　**that}** *om.* He+ CX¹–TR　　　**nolde}** wolde Cp Ha⁴ He La+ WR; n. not ~
TH¹–SP³　　　**no beest for me were}** f. me no b. w. Cp Dd Ha⁴ He La Pw+ TH¹–SP³ TR
WR; f. me that no b. w. (Ne) CX¹–PN² UR

---

remarks that Friar Huberd's tale has nothing better than these "mock-hesitations of delicate greed" and this "unctuous *bonhomie*," while Levitan (1971:240) sees the friar's "divers tongues" as inversions of the Pentecostal eloquence of the Apostles, and Kaske (1972:122) notes that the friar's proposed menu is in vivid contrast to Christ's instructions in Luke 10.7–8. On the style of the passage, Brewer (1984*b*) remarks "how intensely, yet apparently 'objectively' are the hypocrisy, greed and complacency of the Friar . . . realised in, for example, the negatives in the speech where he builds up the exquisite finickiness of his gluttony to the richly contradictory positive of a roasted pig's head." Similarly, Knight (1973:72) praises the way in which the friar's "little French tag, the rather stylish rhyme on 'lyvere' / 'shyvere' and the learned words in [lines 1843–45] all play their part in creating this superbly comic and sharply edged piece of poetry."

　　1838　**now:** WR either misses the second *now*, found in Ha⁴, or edits it out silently by following La or (more likely) TR. The Chaucer Society transcription (Furnivall 1885) seems, as in line 1793, to have followed WR rather than Ha⁴ itself, for it also omits the second *now*. According to MR (3.466), "although few MSS repeat 'now' in this line, all of them are MSS near the top of their groups. It seems therefore possible that this was the reading of O¹ and that most MSS dropped the second 'now' as being a repetition. It is, however, necessary for the metre if 'dame' is monosyllabic, as usual." Apparently on the force of this argument, RB² restores the *now* omitted in RB¹. For the tendency to omit *now*, RI (textual note) compares line 1918.

　　　　je vous dy sanz doute: On Friar John's French see note 1832.

　　1842　Jephson (Bell 1855:2.109) suggests that the friar's humanitarian sentiment "is perhaps in imitation of his founder, St. Francis, whose charity overflowed even upon the lower animals, whom he called his brothers and sisters, insomuch that he could not be prevailed upon to remove certain of them which found shelter in the folds of his ample hood." SK, with greater cynicism, takes the disclaimer as "a strong hint that [Friar John] always expected some special provision to be made for him." Irony was detected in the disclaimer early on; Spurgeon (1925: section 4.70) cites an anonymous Puritan pamphlet of 1643: "This is like old *Chaucers* tale of a Fryar, whose belly was his god, he would feed upon the sweetest, Mutton, Goose, and Pig, but a pitiful man! he would have no creature killed for him, not he."

Thanne hadde I with yow homly suffisaunce.
I am a man of litel sustenaunce;
My spirit hath his fostryng in the Bible.   1845
The body is ay so redy and penyble
To wake that my stomak is destroyed.
I pray yow dame ye be nat anoyed,

1843   **with yow homly**] w. y. holly Cp He La+ CX^1–PN^2; ynowe for my ~ TH^1–UR

1845   **hath his fostryng**] is fostred Cp He La+; haþ f. Pw+; h. his offryng ~ PN^1
in] on Ha^4 WR

1846   **The**] My Dd He+ CX^1–TR   **ay**] euer He; *om.* ~ UR   **so**] *om.* He+
and] a. so Dd He Pw+ CX^1–SP^3 TR WR   **penyble**] pensibil He+

1847   **To**] Tha to He   **wake**] wakyng He+; make (Tc^2) CX^1 **that my sto-
mak**] t. I He; t. m. body (Ne+) CX^1–SP^3 **is**] am nyȝe He; is ful (Ha^3+) CX^1–PN^2

1848   **ye be**] be ye Ad^3 Pw+ TH^1–SP^3; þat ye be Cp Dd Ha^4 He La+ CX^1–PN^2
UR–WR

1843   **homly suffisaunce**: Brewer (1984c:214) notes that *suffisaunce* is one of Chaucer's favorite words, "meaning 'satisfaction' or 'sufficiency,' first recorded in English in the *The Book of the Duchess* (ll. 702 and 1037) and recurring throughout Chaucer's works." He continues that the phrase "homly suffisaunce" is a paradox that satirizes the friar and his meal order; it offers "an amusing set of inverted meanings and implicit criticism" (p. 214).

1845   SK, RB and Richardson (RI) suggest John 4.34 or Job 23.12 as sources, but Landrum (1924:97) suggests rather Matthew 4.4: "Non in solo pane vivit homo, sed in omni verbo quod procedit de ore Dei" ("Not in bread alone does man live, but by every word that comes forth from the mouth of God"), "especially since the speaker is discoursing delightfully upon the *contrast* between his easy satisfaction in such food as capons and roasted pig and his zest for spiritual nourishment." Wood (1984:43–44) agrees emphatically with Landrum on the importance of Matthew 4.4 here, though taking a somewhat more solemn view of the ironies. Matthew 4.4 is also cited in Jerome's *Epistola adversus Jovinianum*, which Chaucer appears to have used intensively in writing *SumT*. See note 1877.

1847   **that my stomak**: MR incorrectly report *I* for *that I* in He.

my stomak is destroyed: In discussing the irony of the friar's discourse on his abstemiousness, Whitmore (1937:107) notes that "the destroyed stomach permits him to indulge only in light meals—capon liver, bread, and roast pork." Fleming (1966:694) comments that "those of Chaucer's readers who also had their 'fostryng in the Bible' would have been more awake than the friar to the implications of I Corinthians 6:13: 'Food for the belly and the belly for food, but God will destroy both the one and the other.'"

1848–50   Though Birney (1960:210) takes line 1848 as evidence that the wife "is not looking happy" about the friar's dinner order, and is "already disillusioned with the friar," Giaccherini (1980:150) disagrees, taking the friar's expression as merely a common courtesy. One might add that the friar's wish that she "be not annoyed" is in reference to the two following lines, meaning that he hopes she will not be annoyed that he has been so forthcoming in speaking of his "abstemiousness." Giaccherini (1980:150) finds the fact that the wife

Thogh I so freendly yow my conseil shewe;
By God I wolde nat telle it but a fewe."   1850
  "Now sire," quod she, "but o word er I go,
My child is deed withinne thise wykes two,
Soone after that ye wente out of this town."

1849 **Thogh**] ffor Ha[4] WR   **so freendly yow my conseil**] so f. my c. to y. Cp;
y. my c. so frely He; so f. my c. La+; f. to y. my c. Pw+; y. my c. so f. (Ne+) CX[1,2] WN PN[2];
y. my c. f. ~ PN[1]
  1850 **God**] *om.* Ha[4]   **wolde nat telle**] nold han told Dd He+ CX[1]–TR; nolde n.
t. Gg Ha[4] Pw+ WR   **a**] to (Ii+) UR
  1851 **Now**] But He+; And (Tc[2]) CX[1]–PN[2]   **but**] nowe He+   **o**] a Dd
I] ye Ad[3] Pw+ TH[1]–SP[3]
  1853 **Soone after**] Siþþen Cp La+

---

disappears from the story at this point insufficient to support Birney's argument (1960:211)
that she was "in connivance with her husband to stay away until Thomas had somehow
contrived to get rid of [the friar], if possible, permanently." For Fleming (1983:13) the friar's
"confidential insinuation that to listen to this outrageous hypocrisy is itself a remarkable
privilege" is "the bloom on the branch," the punch line of the scene.
  1850 **God**: MR do not report the omission of *God* in Ha[4].
  1851–53 Birney (1960:210) argues that the wife's revelation "recalls for us her hus-
band's opening words and charges them with searching irony. If the death of her child were
not in any case uppermost in her mind, the memory would be bitterly reawakened by the
tardy appearance of this neglectful friend and self-appointed spiritual brother whose prayers
were wanting when most needed." Levy too (1966:49) sees her words as a complaint, ques-
tioning the friar's claims to special grace. Whittock (1968:139) refers to the wife's grief.
Huppé (1964:204), by contrast, finds that "she remembers [her son's death] with extraordi-
nary casualness," an interpretation shared by Giaccherini (1980:150), Benson (1980:72), and
Fleming (1983:13). Fleming feels that her remarks suggest a vulnerability to the "false
wonders of a pseudoapostle." Benson (1980:72) wonders, given the friar's embrace of the
wife, "whether or not the comment is made principally for Thomas' benefit, assuring him . . .
that she too has not seen the friar in two weeks." Malone (1989:5) regards her speech as
"strictly informative."
  1851 Fleming (1983:13) notes that the wife here repeats her intention to go (voiced
first in line 1836), but "we never hear the door slam," and she still seems to be in the room at
line 1983.
    o: Because MR do not report the *o word* / *a word* variant, it cannot be deter-
mined whether the Dd reading *a word* is found among non-base-group MSS.
  1853 **town**: SK takes *town* to mean either village or "precincts of this farm-house."
See note 2177–80.
  1853–54 Havely (1975:19–20) remarks that "Chaucer here emphasizes the slickness
of the friar's pat response by rhyming the first line of his speech . . . with the last of the
wife's."

"His deeth say I by revelacioun,"
Seith this frere, "at hom in oure dortour.   1855
I dar wel seyn that er that half an hour
After his deeth I say hym born to blisse

1854   **say I}** I s. Pw
1855   **Seith}** Seyde Ad³ Dd Gg Ha⁴ He Pw+ CX¹–WR RB¹–RI
1856   **that}** *om.* Ad³ Ha⁴ La Pw+ TH¹–WR   **er that}** er Dd+; with in He+
CX¹–PN² UR; er þan La+ TR
1857   **say hym}** sawhe La

1854–1944   RB and Richardson (RI) note that Curry (1926:201–17) connects belief
in such visions with writers like Augustine, Gregory, Vincent of Beauvais, and Aquinas. The
friar's claim of fraternal visionary experiences and praise of the efficacy of fraternal prayer have
their roots, according to Williams (1953:511), in charges leveled at the friars by William of
St. Amour: "True apostles, he writes, do not commend themselves, or say their usages are
better than those of others. Nor do they glory in the miracles the Lord performs through
them. Only false apostles glory in the special favors God shows them." Haskell (1971:223)
believes that the friar's claim is meant to remind us of Simon Magus's magical restoration to
life of a child in the apocryphal *Acts of Peter* (ed. James 1924:325–29). See further note 2094..

1854–68   Whittock (1968:139–40) takes this scene to be "the best illustration of the
friar's evil," as "with practised ease the friar shifts into exploiting [the wife's] grief. . . . Here
his hypocrisy and inhumanity are inseparable from the blasphemy." Whittock adds that "the
passage invites the reader to suspect that the friar's 'convent' would support him in his lie,
and so merit their position on the circumference of the wheel when the time for distribution
comes." Pearsall (1985:225) sees the friar's recovery from potential embarrassment as "Fal-
staff-like," turning the awkwardness into "another triumph for himself and his order." Lan-
cashire (1981:24), arguing for a set of parodic parallels between Friar John and Elijah (see
note 1746–53), sees in this claimed vision a parallel to Elijah's miraculous resurrection of the
son of the widow who had nourished him in 3 Kings (AV 1 Kings) 17.

1855   **Seith:** The MS evidence is weighted heavily in favor of *seyde* here, and all
printed editions save SK so print. The scribes have less tendency than one might expect to
vary according to preference on *seyde* / *seyeth* (one exception is in line 2097), so the evidence is
not easily dismissed as coincidental convergence. The justification for retaining the Hg read-
ing is primarily that it is supported by El, Cp, and La among the early MSS. The line is
adduced by MR (2.239) as suggestive of a common exemplar for Hg–El. Though the prefer-
ence throughout the text seems to be strongly in favor of *seyde* to introduce direct and
indirect discourse, there are other instances of such a tense shift as one finds here, e.g. in lines
1685–87 (quod . . . seith) and 2040 (quod . . . spak . . . seith), where the MS testimony is
virtually unanimous, so it does appear that Chaucer found such shifts acceptable. Given that
neither stylistic nor semantic issues are at stake here, and given the stated principles of
emendation for this edition, the Hg reading is unenthusiastically retained.

1857   SK notes that "visions of saints being carried to heaven are not uncommon.
Bede relates one, of Saint Earcongota." The reference is to *Ecclesiastical History* 3.8 (ed. King
1930:1.363–65).

In myn avisioun, so God me wisse.
So dide oure sexteyn and oure fermerer,
That han been trewe freres fifty yeer.   1860
They may now, God be thanked of His lone,

1858   **avisioun**} visioun (Ne+) CX¹–PN² UR   **so God me**} G. so me Ad³ Gg+;
so G. my soule He+ CX¹–PN² UR; G. me so Pw+ TH¹–SP³
    1860   **fifty**} many a Ha⁴+; this xl He+ CX¹; this f. (En¹+) CX²–UR
    1861   **be thanked**} byþanke Cp Pw+   **of His lone**} o. h. loue (Ne+) CX¹; alout
He

---

say hym: MR report the La variant as *hym*} *he*, but the La scribe regularly spells
sawhe for the preterite of "to see," which MR apparently read as *saw he*. The variant is best
understood as the omission of *hym*.
    1858   **avisioun**: MR report the variant *visioun* for their entire *b* group (He Ne CX¹
Tc²), but the reading of He is *avisioun*.
    1859   **fermerer**: Thomas (UR) understands this to be the curator or overseer of an
infirmary, and TR follows suit, deriving the word from the Latin *Infirmarius*. Jephson (Bell
1855:2.109) takes this to be "the officer who had charge of the farms or granges," but SK and
RB take the *fermerer* to be "the friar who had charge of the infirmary. Put for *enfermerer*, from
O. Fr. *enfermerier*," notes SK, who also cites *fermorie*, meaning *infirmary*, in *Piers Plowman* B
13.108.
    1860–62   TR explains (n. 7442) that "peculiar honours and immunities were granted
by the Rule of St. Benedict to those Monks" who completed fifty years, or the jubilee, in the
order. "It is probable," TR adds, "that some similar regulation obtained in the other Orders."
This note is reprinted by WR and echoed by Hertzberg (1866:624) and SK. Jephson (Bell
1855:2.109) adds that "one of these privileges was that of walking alone, which, for obvious
reasons, was forbidden to the other religious." Havely (1975:139–40) suggests that "to 'walk
alone' seems to be a very attractive prospect for the friar; he refers to it in a pious awestruck
tone, similar to that in which he describes the child being 'born to blisse.' The advantage
from his point of view is probably that it would allow him greater scope for salesmanship of
the kind he practises here."
    1860   **fifty**: CX² may have followed a manuscript here (according to Dunn [1939] an
a type), or simply have used the sense of *Jubilee* to correct from CX¹ *xl* to *fyfty*. WR expressly
emends Ha⁴ by way of La, whose reading "would seem by the context to be the correct one."
    1861   **lone**: Thomas (UR) glosses, "A lone, a thing lent; Lending," and is therefore
dissatisfied with the sense of the line: "There seems to be a corruption both in this verse and
the next, of *love* into *lone*, and *above* into *alone*, which might easily happen, *u* and *n*, *b* and *l*
being very alike in the old MSS. Those two Verses may be easily understood if thus read;
Thei may now (God be thankid of his love) Makin ther Jubile, and walke above, ... In
[CX¹] they are so read with a very little variation . . . but all the subsequent Editions read
lone and *above*." Pollard's note (1894:2.74) and the RB glossaries also give "loan," but SK's
glossary offers "gift, grace," and RI "grace," which seems more appropriate for a visionary
experience. *MED*, s.v. *lon(e*, offers several instances of the word with a spiritual meaning,
though it does not cite this line.

Maken hir jubilee and walke allone.
And up I roos and al oure covent eke,
With many a teere triklyng on my cheke;
Withouten noyse or clateryng of belles,   81v   1865
Te deum was oure song and no thyng elles,
Save that to Crist I seyde an orisoun,
Thankynge Hym of His revelacioun;

1862   **allone]** al about He; ailone La; al aboue (Ne+) CX^1; all a. (Hk) CX^2–PN^2
1863   **And]** But Ha^4 **I roos]** he r. La; I aroos Pw+ TH^1–SP^3 TR
1864   **triklyng]** trillyng Ad^3 Cp Dd Ha^4 He La Pw+ CX^1–PN^1 PN^2–WR MR–RI; trynkelynge Gg   **on]** vpon Pw+   **my]** our Ad^3 Pw+ CX^2–TR
1865   **or]** and Dd He+ CX^1–PN^2; of Pw+   *Lines 1865–66 trans.* Ha^4 WR
1867   **Save that]** Sone aftir He+ CX^1–PN^2 **seyde]** bad Dd He+ CX^1–PN^2 UR TR   **an orisoun]** a holy o. He+ CX^1–PN^2
1868   **His]** my Ad^3 Dd Gg Ha^4 Pw+ TH^1–WR MR PR; my good He+ CX^1–PN^2

1863   MR do not report the variants in either La or Ha^4.
1864   **triklyng:** MR argue (3.466) that "in many MSS *ll* and *kl* are very hard to distinguish. 'Tryllyng' is here the predominant form; 'tryklyng' appears only in the Hg–El group and is suggested by Gg, though the closely related Si has 'tryllyng.' 'Tryllyng' is the less familiar term, and therefore probably correct." One notes that in *PrT* B^2 1864 the evidence for *trikled / trilled* is numerically reversed. In any case, as in line 1838, the MR argument may have persuaded Robinson to abandon the Hg–El reading in RB^2. As in line 1855 the Hg–El reading is taken by MR as possible evidence of the use of a common exemplar, and as in line 1855 the Hg reading is retained here because of the Hg–El agreement and for want of any compelling reason to emend it.
1866   **Te deum:** "A song of praise," notes Richardson (RI), "that regularly concluded matins." Jephson (Bell 1855:2.109–10), echoed by SK, writes that "nothing but a thanksgiving would have been appropriate for a child dying in infancy, of whose translation to paradise the friar also pretends he had had a vision." Rejecting this "unmedieval suggestion," Tatlock (1914:144) argues instead that *Te Deum* would be sung "in honor of the miraculous vision." "It was quite usual," he continues, "to [sing *te Deum* and ring bells] after a miracle, in its honor and to call people together." Further, "Thomas and his family had taken out letters of fraternity in the friar's convent (2126–8), and it was customary to toll a bell at the death of a member. The reason why the friar says scornfully that in his case they did not make all this noise might be that anybody living within earshot would know the convent-bells had not rung that night." Birney and Richardson (1970:149) similarly feel that the friar's claim not to have rung bells is an attempt "to transform the sin of omission into a seeming virtue" (Birney 1960:211), while Pearsall calls the detail "shrewd" (1985:225) and the product of "quick thinking" (1986:140).
1868   **His:** The MS evidence, like the modern editions, is divided on *His* versus *my*. More than 30 MSS read *my* (*a*, the Gg–Si group, and *d**^{1}), and *b* reads *my good*; but Hg–El are joined here by most of *cd**^{2}, suggesting a second exemplar's reading, and *His* is at least as good sense.

For, sire and dame, trusteth me right wel,
Oure orisons been moore effectuel,   1870
And moore we seen of Cristes secree thynges
Than burrel folk, althogh that they were kynges.

1869   **me right**} to me Gg; ye me r. ~ UR
1870   **moore**} wel m. Hg El+   **effectuel**} spirituel Cp La+
1871   **Cristes**} goddis Ha⁴ WR; *om.* Gg+
1872   **folk**} pepil He+ CX¹–PN²   **althogh that they were**} a. they w. El Gg+
SK–RI; a. that they ben Dd Ha⁴+ TR WR; al be they He+ CX¹–PN²; or þouȝe they w.
Pw+; albeit they w. ~ UR   *Lines* 1872 *and* 1874 *comb.* (1873 *out*) Than burel folk in
richesse and wynnynges Cp La+

1869–76   The friar's claim that an abstemious life was necessary for those who would
seek heavenly visions is a commonplace. Curry (1926:216–17) demonstrates that his pre-
scription for abstinence is based on writers like Cornelius Agrippa, but comments, "in this
particular case one cannot forget the pig's head and the capon's liver." Lawlor (1968:120)
admires the passage for its "searing irony of hypocrisy given its smoothly practised run," and
its "wickedly exact ear for speech."
    1870   **moore:** As in a number of lines earlier (1693, 1694, 1696, 1710, 1754, 1757,
1855, 1864, 1868), Hg and El are in nearly solitary agreement here, in this case on the
inclusion of *wel*, supported only by Bo¹ and Bo². Though the resulting line is metrically
inelegant, the agreement of these MSS, even against the numeric weight of the contradictory
testimony, might make a reasonable case for printing *wel*, were it not that it was probably
caught from the previous line by their exemplar. See MR (2.239).
    1871   **Cristes secree thynges:** Whittock (1968:141) notes an echo here of *MilT*:
"Nicholas there, like the friar here, used his claim to know 'Goddes pryvetee' as a means for
gulling another for his own ends." He adds that this line leads up to Thomas's "gift," the
"thyng . . . hyd in pryvetee" of line 2143. Fleming (1983:13) detects in this claim "a typical
mendicant interest in what is rather loosely called Joachism." For a brief description of
Joachism and the dispute between the seculars and mendicants (on the one hand) and the
Spiritual Franciscans (who sought to follow Francis's rule strictly) versus the Conventuals
(who argued for an accomodation of the Rule to economic realities) on the other hand, see
above in the Critical Commentary under "*The Summoner's Tale* and Anti-fraternalism"; see
also Williams (1953 and 1960).
    1872   Cp, La and some other MSS combine the first part of this line and the last part
of line 1874, skipping line 1873. The MR report of this line is somewhat confusing owing to
typographical error and inconsistency: they use *a.* to mean *al* in He+ and to mean *although* in
Ad³+; they do not report that Hg includes *that*; and they omit *were* from their report of
Pw+. It is interesting to note, finally, that the reading adopted in MR has support from only
6 MSS: El Gg Gl Ht Ps Si.
    burell folk: *burell* is a coarse wool fabric. SP²–UR gloss *borell* as "plaine, rude";
Thomas (UR) adds that the word "signifies a sort of course cloth [citing 'Gros drap' in the
glossary to Lobineau (1707:2, col. 1781)]. It seems to be a diminutive of Boor [citing Kilian
1642]. *Boer*, Agricola, ruricola; from *Bouwen*, To plow." TR, WR, SK, RB, and RI, following
a hint from Thomas (UR), take the phrase as whole to mean "laymen." WR says that "the

We lyve in poverte and in abstinence,
And burrel folk in richesse and dispence
Of mete and drynke and in hir foul delit.   1875
We han this worldes lust al in despit.
Lazar and Dives lyveden diversly,

    1873   **We}** To Pw+   **poverte}** pensifnes He+ CX[1]   **and in}** a. (En[1]+) UR
Out: Cp La+
    1874   **dispence}** in d. Ad[3] Dd Pw+
    1875   **Of}** In Ad[3] Gg La Pw+ TH[1]–UR   **in}** *om.* Pw+   **hir}** *om.* He+ CX[1]–
PN[2]   **foul}** ful Ha[4] WR
    1876   **this}** al t. Ad[3] Ha[4]+ WR; the He+ CX[1]–PN[2]   **worldes}** worldly Pw+
TH[1]–SP[3]   **lust}** delit Ha[4]   **al}** *om.* Ha[4]+
    1877   **Dives}** dyuers Gg+   **diversly}** dyuers lyf Gg; ful d. He+ CX[1]–PN[2]

---

term appears to have arisen from the material of their clothing which was not used by the clergy." More flamboyantly, White Kennett's *Parochial Antiquities* of 1695 derives *burell* from "*Bordel*, Hence in *Chaucer* a *Borel-Man* a loose idle fellow, and *Borel-folk* Drunkards and Epicures" (cited in Alderson 1970:200). John Cowell's *Law Dictionary: or the Interpreter of Words*, published in 1727, cites this line in glossing "*Borel-Folk*, *i.e.*, Country People, from the Fr. *Boure*, *i.e. Floccus*: Because they covered their Heads with such Stuff" (cited in Alderson 1970:211).

    1873–1941   Lowes (1915:278–79), arguing against Tupper's thesis (Tupper 1914, 1915*b*) that *SumT* is directed only against Wrath, points out the "68 line sermon directed against Gluttony" which begins here. "Its purport is unmistakable," he continues; "it is a panegyric on the abstinence of friars as contrasted with the ways of 'burel folk.'" Tupper (1916:76) responds that "the speech is only an episode that does not influence the story's current, and has, moreover, no ironical association (and this is decisive) with the narrator of the tale, the Summoner, the Man of Wrath revealed in the short prologues."

    1873   **and in:** UR's omission of *in* suggests that Urry pronounced *poverte* with three syllables; in line 1907, where the line requires a disyllable, UR spells *Povert*.

    1874   See note to line 1872 for Cp and La.

    1876   WR expressly adopts the reading of La since Ha[4]'s *delit* "seems to have been an error of the scribe, who had in his ears the last word of the preceding line."

    1877   **Lazar and Dives:** Editors since SK cite Luke 16.19–31. Düring (1883–86: 3.374) notes that "Dives, the rich man in the parable of Lazarus . . . is taken by Chaucer here, as in later English Bibles, as a proper name." The mention of Dives and Lazarus begins a series of biblical allusions which has been demonstrated to have been available to Chaucer in Jerome's *Epistola adversus Jovinianum*. Koeppel (1891*a*:176–78) is the first to document Chaucer's use of Jerome for the allusions to Moses, Elijah, Aaron, and Adam which follow, though he does not specifically mention the Dives passage. Tupper (1915*b*:8) cites the *Epistola adversus Jovinianum* 2.17 (*PL* 23.311): "Qui divitem purpuratum propter epulas narrat in tartaro et Lazarum pauperem ob inediam dicit esse in sinu Abrahae" ("Who tells of purple-clad Dives in hell for his feasting, and says that poor Lazarus for his abstinence was in Abraham's bosom"). Birney notes the jingle on *Dives . . . diversly . . . diverse* in lines 1877–78, adding that Friar John "seems to pun out of sheer rhetorical habit" (1960:212).

And diverse gerdoun hadde they therby.
Who so wol praye, he moot faste and be clene,
And fatte his soule and make his body lene.   1880
We fare as seith th'apostle; clooth and foode
Suffiseth us thogh they be nat ful goode.
The clennesse and the fastyng of us freres
Maketh that Crist accepteth oure prayeres.
Lo, Moyses fourty dayes and fourty nyght   1885

1878   **gerdoun**} guerdons He+ TH¹–UR; guerdoms (Ne) CX¹   **they**} *om.* Dd+
1879   **he**} hym Gg+; *om.* Ha⁴ Pw+ CX¹–PN²   **moot**} *om.* Ha⁴
1880   **body**} cheekes Cp
1882   **they**} wee He   **ful**} right He+; *om.* Cp Ha⁴ La+ WR
1883   **and**} of (Bo²+) UR   **fastyng**} fasteinges La
1884   **accepteth**} exceptith (Ne+) CX¹–PN¹ PN²

1879   **he moot:** WR prints *he must* because "these words, omitted in the Harl. MS., seem necessary to the sense."

1880   *Marginal gloss:* Melius est animam saginare quam corpus El Ad³. Richardson (RI) translates: "It is better to fatten the soul than the body." Koeppel (1892:266) is the first to note a similar line in the *Testament* of Jean de Meun, l. 345: "Amegrient leurs ames plus que leurs cors n'engressent" ("They starve their souls even more than they fatten their bodies") (ed. Méon 1814:4.18); it is duly reported in SK, RB, and RI. MR (3.504) identify the source of the Latin gloss as Jerome's *Epistola adversus Jovinianum* 2.6 (*PL* 23.293), next noted in RI.

1881–82   Düring (1883–86:3.374) suggests an allusion here to 2 Corinthians 14.14 (intending 10.14), but 1 Timothy 6.8, as suggested by editors as early as Jephson (Bell 1855:2.110), seems more relevant. Koeppel (1891*a*:176–77) signals the likelihood that Chaucer's proximate source was in fact the *Epistola adversus Jovinianum* 2.11 (*PL* 23.301): "Unde et Apostolus: 'Habentes,' inquit, 'victum et vestitum, in his contenti simus'" ("Hence the Apostle says: 'Having food and clothing let us therewith be content'"). The evidence is also marshalled in Tupper (1915*b*:8). Szittya (1974:44) adds that "one suspects the apostles found sustenance from somewhat less than capon livers and roast pigs' heads."

1882   *Marginal gloss:* Victum et vestitum hiis contenti sumus El Ad³.

1883–84   As Owen points out (1966:561–62 and 1977:164–65), the rhyme *freres-prayeres* occurs four times in *SumT*, "always with the same 'sentence,' the claim for special efficacy" (Owen 1966:561). The other three pairs are at lines 1905–06, 1911–12, and 1939–40.

1883   **fastyng:** MR do not report the variant of La.

1884   *Marginal gloss:* de oracionibus et Ieiunijs El.

1885–93   Editors since Jephson (Bell 1855:110) have seen an allusion here to Exodus 34.28, though Düring (1883–86:3.374) suggests Exodus 24.18. As in lines 1877 and 1881–82 (see notes above), Chaucer's source was probably Jerome's *Epistola adversus Jovinianum*, in this case 2.15 (*PL* 23.306), as documented by Koeppel (1891*a*:177) and Tupper (1915*b*:8): "Moyses quadraginta diebus et noctibus jejunus in monte Sina, etiam tunc probans non in

In to the temple whan they sholde gon
To preye for the peple and do servyse,
They nolden drynken in no maner wyse
No drynke which that myghte hem dronke make;
But there in abstinence preye and wake   1900
Lest that they deyden. Tak hede what I seye;
But they be sobre that for the peple preye,
War that I seye; namoore, for it suffiseth.
Oure Lord Jesu, as holy writ devyseth,
Yaf us ensample of fastyng and prayeres;   82r   1905
Therfore we mendynantz, we sely freres,

1896   whan] w. that Ad³+
1897   and] a. to Pw+ PN¹
1898   nolden] wold nouȝ La+
1899   No] N. kind of ~ UR   which that] þe w. Cp; t. He+ CX¹–UR
myghte hem dronke] h. m. d. Cp+; h. d. m. Gg (Gg₁ *corr.*) Pw+; d. m. h. Ha⁴+ TH¹–UR
WR
1900   there] euere Cp La+   preye] trewly p. Ad³; to p. Cp He La+ CX¹–PN²;
did p. ~ UR   wake] to w. He
1901   deyden] dedyn Dd Gg (Gg₁ *corr.*) Ha⁴ He Pw+ TH² WR
1902   But they be sobre] S. ben t. ~ UR
1903   that] what ~ UR   namoore] *om.* He+ CX¹–PN² UR   for it] f. þat I
nowe He+; f. it ynow (Ne+) CX¹–PN²; ynow f. it ~ UR
1904   holy writ] h. god Cp La+; oure lore Ha⁴ WR
1905   Yaf] ȝiueþ Cp La+   and] a. of La+
1906   mendynantz] mendicantis He+ CX¹–UR; amende fautes La   sely] pouere
Cp He La+ CX¹; *om.* Gg+

---

and La, all of which read *that othere p.*, *the* might appear at first as necessarily the better
reading, but Wright (1928:167) notes that "the neuter *þat* . . . remained with the meaning
the for some time longer [than 1300] before words beginning with a vowel," and Mustanoja
(1960:169) adds that "*that* frequently occurs for the definite article before *one* and *other*."
Rennhard (1962:109–10) attests to 33 ME examples. The construction is also found in
Chaucer's *Bo* 4, pr. 6, line 120 in RB²: "that othere cerklis"; and (see MR 8.236) *ParsT* 234:
"that othere good werkes."
    1902–07   Jephson (Bell 1855:2.111) takes the passage to be "an insinuation that the
parochial clergy did not lead very sober lives." Koeppel (1891a:177) feels that "Chaucer
shows the friar losing the thread here to show how mechanically and absentmindedly he
intones his homily." Szittya (1974:33) sees in this passage an instance of the friar's "general
comparison between his own way of life and that of Christ and the apostles."
    1904   **holy writ:** WR notes the readings of La and TR.
    1906–10   Knight (1973:73) finds here an example of *frequentatio*, "where information
is gathered together into a dense and rich pattern."

Been wedded to poverte and continence,
To charitee, humblesse and abstinence,
To persecucioun for rightwisnesse,
To wepyng, misericorde and clennesse;   1910
And therfore may ye se that oure prayeres,
I speke of us, we mendinantz, we freres,
Be to the hye God moore acceptable
Than youres, with youre festes at the table.

1907 and] a. to Ad³ Cp Dd Ha⁴ He La+ CX¹–PN² WR   *Out:* Gg+
1908 humblesse] humbilnes He La Pw CX¹–SP³   and] a. also Cp La+   abstinence] patience Cp He La+ CX¹   *Out:* Gg+
1909 To] *om.* La   for] f. every He+ CX¹–PN²   *Out:* Gg+
1910 clennesse] to c. (Ha³+) CX¹–PN² TR   *Out:* Gg+
1911 *Out:* Gg+
1912 we mendinantz we freres] we mendenaunte f. Cp+; we mendeaunts we f. Ha⁴ WR; we mendecant f. He+ CX¹; me vendinant f. La; mendyuaunt we f. ~ CX² WN PN²; mendicaunt we f. (Nl) PN¹ TH¹–SP¹; mendicants we f. ~ SP²,³; we Mendicants we f. (Bo¹) UR   *Out:* Gg+
1913 acceptable] exceptabil He+ CX¹–PN¹
1914 youres] ȝoure is Gg   youre festes] y. feste Cp La+ TH¹–SP³; þe fest Pw+   the] ȝour Ha⁴ He+ CX¹–WR   *Out:* Ad³

1906 Lines 1906 and 1912 are very nearly identical in their second half, and both rhyme *freres* with *preyeres* in the lines which precede them. The omission of *sely* in the exemplar of Gg (giving a reading of *we freres*) caused the Gg scribe to eye-skip to the identical phrase in line 1912; Gg thus lacks lines 1907–1912, as does the related Si (which also omits *sely*), and Tc¹.

   mendynantz: Though TR prints *mendiants*, in "Additional Notes" (3.319–20) Tyrwhitt writes, "In Ms. A. [Ha⁵] it is *mendinants*, both here and below [line 1912] which reading, though not agreeable to analogy, is perhaps the true one, as I find the word constantly so spelled in the Stat. 12 R. II. c. 7, 8, 9, 10.'" SK repeats the information.

1908 humblesse: MR do not record these variants on *humblesse*, though they do report "over eras. of humblenesse? Ln." The difference in the forms is a syllable more or less.

1911–13 That similar claims might indeed have been made by some friars is suggested by Wyclif's claim, cited in SK, that "the thridde deceyt of thise ordris is that thei passen othere in preyeris, both for tyme thei preyen and for multitude of hem" (ed. Matthew 1880:317). Friar John's claim, that his order's prayers are actually "more acceptable" than laymen's, differs somewhat from the particular "deceyt" cited by Wyclif.

1912 Chaucer's vivid evocation of colloquial speech rhythms seems to have been beyond the reach of some scribes and most early editors. The possibilities for variation included the number and spelling of *mendinantz*, the doubling of the apposition *us*, *mendinantz*, *freres*, and the possibility of reading *mendinant* (singular) as an adjective.

Fro Paradys first, if I shal nat lye,   1915
Was man out chaced for his glotonye,
And chaast was man in Paradys certeyn.
  But herkne, Thomas, what I shal seyn;

1915 Fro] ffor Ad³ La Pw+
1916 out chaced] c. o. ~ TH³–SP³
1917 chaast] chased Ad³+; cast He+ CX¹   was man in Paradys certeyn] m.
w. in p. c. Pw+; w. out to labour certeyn (Tc²) CX¹
1918 herkne Thomas] h. now T. Ad³ Dd Gg He Pw+ CX¹–TH¹ TH³–TR SK–
RI; h. þere Cp La+; now h. T. Ha⁴ WR; h. yow T. ~ TH²   what] that Dd+; wha
Pw   shal seyn] s. ȝou sayn Cp; s. þe seyn Ha⁴ WR; wil seyn Pw

---

1915–17 Another use of the *Epistola adversus Jovinianum* (2.15; *PL* 23.305), as Skeat
is apparently first to recognize. He directs the reader to his note (SK 5.278) to *PardT* C 505,
which points out that MSS Hg, El, Cp, Ha⁴ and Pw quote "Quamdiu ieiunauit Adam, in
Paradiso fuit; comedit et eiectus est; eiectus, statim duxit uxorem" ("So long as Adam fasted
he remained in Paradise; he ate and was cast out; cast out he immediately took a wife").
Though Reiss (1984:51) feels that the friar's wit cannot conceal the impoverishment of his
"simplistic and dubious assertions" of biblical interpretation, Richardson (RI) notes the par-
allel idea of gluttony as the original sin in *PardT* 504–11 and *ParsT* 819.
    Tupper (1915*b*:9) writes that "it is significant that this very passage from
Jerome is used by the Pardoner in his attack upon Gluttony. . . . This use of a common source
in these two tales on the Sins is suggestive," and argues that the "generous use by the
Summoner of the Jovinian treatise furnishes another strong link between Chaucer's Friar-
Summoner tales and their immediate precursor, the contribution of the Wife, the largest
borrower from Jerome's tract." Arguing against Tupper's theory that each of several Canter-
bury Pilgrims stands for a particular one of the Seven Deadly Sins, and that the Summoner
specifically stands for Wrath, Lowes (1915:279) notes this passage on gluttony: "It *is* signifi-
cant, and it *is* suggestive, for it proves irrefragably (if proof were needed) that the *friar's* first
homily is directed against *Gluttony*, and . . . Mr. Tupper failed to see the implications of his
own very sound observation."
    1915 Fro: MR do not report *ffor* in Ad³ or Pw.
    1917 chaast: MR do not report *chased* in Ad³, though they do report it a variant in
other MSS. They record the CX¹ reading as a spurious line. It is easy to see what happened:
the *b* MSS spell *cast* for *chaast*, and CX¹ made a shift to cope by "casting" Adam out to labor
rather than in(to) Paradise. § Tatlock (1916:232) considers *chaced . . . chaast* "the most
delightful and the most natural pun in Chaucer. . . . Chased out, and chaste in, what a
beautiful thought! Of course the friar does not know he is punning, it is merely the way his
mind works." Though RB considers word play "by no means certain" here, the turn is also
accepted as a pun in Baum's survey (1956:233). Huppé (1964:205), emphasizing the friar's
predilection for word-play, calls the pun "atrocious," while Ruggiers (1965:104) sees it as an
instance of the tale's habit of "playing on words both advertently and inadvertently." Ross
(1972:55), referring to the pun as "probably a tired old pulpit joke," argues that the two
words were homophones in ME.
    1918–34 Whittock (1968:137) takes this passage to illustrate that "the imitation of

I ne have no text of it as I suppose,
But I shal fynde it in a maner glose,   1920
That specially oure swete Lord Jesus
Spak this by freres whan he seyde thus,
'Blessed be they that poure in spirit been,'
And so forth al the Gospel may ye seen

1919   **I ne]** I Cp Dd He La Pw+ CX¹–TR   **no text of it]** no t. of þat Cp La+; of
it no t. Gg+; no t. þer of Pw+ TH¹–SP³   **I suppose]** I can s. He+
1920   **shal]** *om.* He+ CX¹–UR   **it in]** in Dd+; *om.* He+ CX¹–PN²   **a maner]**
a noþer Gg; a m. thyng of He+; a m. thing of a (Tc²) CX¹–PN²; m. of a ~ TH¹–UR
1921   **swete Lord]** l. s. Pw+
1922   **this]** thus Cp La+; *om.* Pw+   **by freres]** by vers Cp La+   **seyde]** saidin
~ UR
1924   **al]** in Ha⁴ WR   **may ye]** y. m. Ha⁴+ WR

[the friar's] manner could become boring were it not for our rising amazement at each
additional stroke of impudence."
    1918   **herkne Thomas:** MR remark (3.466), that "'Now' seems to have been in the
earlier draft and to have dropped out, but was replaced in Ha⁴, Ra³–Gl, though not in the
Hg–El line." Compare line 1838 and note, above. It might also be argued that the Hg–El
reading, as printed here, is authentic though metrically difficult, and that early scribes added
the *now* as a straightforward solution. The line is one of several in which Chaucer seems to
have privileged realistic speech rhythms above regularity, e.g., lines 1828, 2033, 2125, 2220.
    1919–23   Williams (1953:511) suggests that in this passage Chaucer "illustrates a
remark of [Richard Fitzralph, Archbishop of Armagh] that when he challenged the friars to
produce one scriptural text commanding poverty or proving that Christ ever begged volunta-
rily or spontaneously, they complained that he respected only the text of Scripture, not the
gloss." Robertson points out that "'Poverty of spirit' or humility is a virtue in which our friar
is obviously lacking; he has, in fact, just been boasting about how acceptable to God are the
prayers of the abstinent, vigilant, continent, and otherwise virtuous friars like himself"
(1962:332). Fleming (1966:694) comments that the friar's "quite deranged hermeneutics can
yield only comical results," adding that the explication of Matthew 5.3 "smacks of the
Joachism of Gerard of Borgo San Donnino's 'Introduction' to the *Evangelium Aeternum*,"
while Huppé (1964:205) remarks that "if the Wife of Bath could find in the miracle of the
loaves and fishes the justification of her sexual activity, the friar is certainly entitled to see
himself and his order in the Beatitudes." Clark (1976b:54–55) sees in the passage a dramati-
zation of fraternal financial interest in opposing the translation of scripture during Chaucer's
lifetime: the friar "knows that an understanding of the letter of the Gospel, which might
come from an English translation of the Scripture, would reveal the hypocrisy of his own
distortion of sacred text."
    1922   **by:** RB glosses "concerning."
    1923   As Jephson (Bell 1855:2.111), followed by all modern editors, points out,
Chaucer here alludes to Matthew 5.3.

Wher it be likker oure professioun   1925
Or hire that swymmen in possessioun.
Fy on hir pompe, and hir glotonye,
And for hir lewednesse I hem diffye.
Me thynketh they been lyk Jovynyan,

1925　**likker**] like Cp La Pw+; l. to He+ CX^1–PN^2　　**professioun**] perfection ~ TH^1–SP^3

1926　**hire**] hem Cp+

1927　**Fy**] ffor He+　　**and**] a. in Ad^3; a. on Cp Dd Gg Ha^4 La Pw+ TH^1–RI

1928　**for**] on Ad^3 Ha^4 Pw+ SP^{2,3} TR WR; of Dd He+ CX^1–PN^2; in ~ TH^1–SP^1; eke on ~ UR　　**hem**] am Pw (Pw$_1$ *corr.*)

1929　**lyk**] l. to Dd Gg He+ CX^{1,2} WN PN^2　　**Jovynyan**] Iomman (Ne+) CX^1–PN^2

1926　**hire**: MR print *hirs*, following El. They distinguish among *hirs* (El), *heres* (Dd, Ha^4, He, CX^1), *hem* (Cp), and *hire* (Hg, Gg, Ad^3, La, Pw and many others). The distinction *hirs / heres* is a spelling difference only (see *MED*, s.v. *heres* pron.); *hire* is the same word without the genitive -s (as *MED*, s.v. *her(e* pron. poss. pl. 2, offering early and late examples, including the Hg reading of this line, and Mustanoja [1960:164] attest). Accordingly, only the variant of Cp is reported here.　§　The reference, says Hertzberg (1866:624), is to the Benedictines; Williams (1953:510) believes that it is to monks in general. Koeppel (1891a: 177) suggests that here, as the friar begins to scorn other clerics, his discourse regains the animation it had lost in lines 1902–03.

1927　Knight (1973:73) identifies the line as an example of *apostrophe*.

and: A second *on* after *and*, the inclusion of which yields a more regular iambic line, is found in *a*, most of *cd*2*, and much of *d*1*, while *b*, a scattering of *cd*2* and *d*1* MSS, Bo^1 and Bo^2 support Hg and El in reading as printed here. The unanimity of Hg and El carries considerable weight with this edition (see notes to lines 1693, 1754, 1870, and 1887). On the metrical question, see note 1918 for other irregular lines which mimic the effects of natural speech rhythms. Both Hg and El punctuate to indicate a caesura after *pompe*. So read, the line begins with a trochee and suppresses the unstressed syllable at the caesura to yield a (quite effective) Lydgate line.

1928　**diffye**: RB understands *diffye* to mean "distrust," while PR and *MED* suggest the stronger "scorn," and RI "repudiate."

1929–31　"The learning, the arresting simile is meant to impress Thomas further, as is the rare word 'vinolent' (though the terms of comparison, 'swan' and 'botel', show how the friar cannot get his mind away from food and drink)" (Knight 1973:73–74).

1929　**Jovynyan**: TR (n. 7511) suggests that this is the (4th-cent. heretic) Jovinian "against whom St. Jerome wrote; or, perhaps, the supposed Emperour of that name in the *Gesta Romanorum*, c. lix" (ed. Oesterly 1872:360–66). Jephson (Bell 1855:2.111) supposes the reference is to the emperor, as do Pollard (1894:77) and WR, who echoes the TR note. Hertzberg (1866:624) also sees either figure as possible, but Düring (1883–86:3.374) identifies him as Jerome's enemy, and is seconded by Koeppel (1891a:177–78), who, followed by SK, RB, and Richardson (RI), cites Jerome's reference in the *Epistola adversus Jovinianum* 1.40

Fat as a whale and walkyng as a swan,   1930
Al vynolent as botel in the spence;

1930   a] *om.* La (La₁ *corr.*)+   and] *om.* He+   walkyng] walken Dd Ha⁴ He+
CX¹–PN² WR   as] and as La; like He+ CX¹–PN²
1931   Al] As Cp La+ TH¹–SP³   as] as a Dd La+ CX¹–PN²; as þe Pw+

---

to "iste formosus monachus, crassus, nitidus, dealbatus, et quasi sponsus semper incedens" ("that beautiful monk, fat, sleek, whitewashed, and always parading like a bridegroom") (*PL* 23.268). Tupper (1915*b*:9) independently makes the same argument, adding that Chaucer might also have had in mind the *Epistola adversus Jovinianum* 2.21 (*PL* 23.315–16). Lowes (1915:280), again disputing Tupper's argument that *SumT* is a tale programmatically concerned with the sin of Wrath (see above, notes to lines 1873–1941 and 1915–17), also notes this use of Jerome as an explicit condemnation of gluttony: "He is preaching, then, a sermon against Gluttony. And, as in the case of the *Friar's Tale* Chaucer 'doubles the story's aptness' [quoting Tupper] by the exquisite irony of the contrast between the homily and the friar's own hypocritical *Delicacie* [lines 1838–45]." See further under "Thematic Issues" in Critical Commentary, pp. 37–38, above. Lowes returns to this passage later, in writing of Chaucer's ability to incorporate allusions to his reading into apparently highly mimetic scenes. He remarks (1934:235) that "as the passage proceeds it outdoes even Saint Jerome in robustness."

1930   **walkyng as a swan:** SK glosses "with slow and stately gait," but Silvia (1964: 249) argues that swans walk awkwardly, and suggests that Chaucer did not have in mind the large white bird in his simile, but rather a bridegroom (ME "swain," the unique reading of Bo², which Silvia notes and dismisses), translating Jerome's *sponsus* (see note to 1929). Chaucer used the variant spelling "swan," Silvia continues, "to make sure that the rime *Iouynyan/swan* would not be lost. . . . [T]he rendering of *swan* by MnE *swain* brings to the passage a logical comparison and consistency of image not present if *swan* refers to the bird." Hartung disagrees: beginning with a paleographical argument, he writes that Chaucer may have seen in his source manuscript not *sponsus* but *cygnus*, because "both words have the same beginning configuration (*sp-cy*) which could easily be subject to scribal confusion. The *o* of *sponsus* and the *g* of *cygnus* could also be confused if due to a variety of causes the *o* might seem to have a tail. In both words these letters are immediately followed by *n*. And both words would have had the same terminal abbreviation" (1967:178). Furthermore, "the passage has a decidedly aquatic bent. The friar . . . criticizes those 'that *swymmen* in possessioun.' As a result of their high living they are . . . 'fat as a *whale*'" (1967:178). As for the awkward gait, "in the gait of swans, as in other things, one must admit that beauty is in the eye of the beholder," but Hartung reckons that the "grotesque clumsiness" of the possessioners is precisely the point of Chaucer's comparing them to swans (1967:178). Rowland (1971: 89–90) offers some evidence that the swan was proverbially associated with sloth and inebriation.

1931   **vynolent:** SP²,³ gloss "drunke, smelling of wine," and Thomas (UR) "full of wine." Jephson (Bell 1855:2.111) and SK take the whole phrase to mean "as full of wine as a bottle in the cellar or buttery."

Hir preyere is of ful greet reverence;
Whan they for soules seye the psalm of Davit,
Lo, 'buf,' they seye, *'cor meum eructavit.'*

1932   **preyere**] prayers (Ps+) TH[2]   **of ful greet**] f. of g. Cp La+; f. g. Dd+; of f.
litil He+ CX[1]–SP[3]; of little ~ UR
1933   **seye the psalm**] t. p. s. Ad[3]
1934   **buf**] but El+ PN[1] WN; boþ Pw+   **meum eructavit**] mundum creavit
He+

1932   **of ful greet reverence:** "The Eddit. have changed this to *ful litel*; but the
reading of the Mss. may stand, if it be understood ironically," states TR (note 7314; properly
7514); the reading in the *b* MSS, Ha[3] and Ii was *full little*, so the editions did not "change" it
as much as inherit it.
   1933–34   Thomas (UR glossary, p. 76) identifies the quotation as being from Psalm
44.2 (AV 45.2) and translates the Latin thus: "My heart hath belched out, or, . . . *boileth, or
bubleth up.*" Jephson (Bell 1855:2.112), Düring (1883–86:3.374), and all modern editors
note the biblical source. The Douay translation (1609) renders *eructavit* as "hath uttered." SK
suggests that "the interjectional 'buf!' is probably intended to represent the sound of eructa-
tion." Or as Thomas (UR glossary, s.v. *Bouffe*) glosses the word, "A Note of Belching." SK
holds that "the Somnour here takes *eructauit* in the most literal sense," while Reiss (1984:51)
takes the literalism to be the friar's. Jephson (Bell 1855:2.112) notes that "The priests are
said to say 'for soules' because it is one of the psalms in the *Officium defunctorum.*" Hamilton
(1942:655–57) argues that commentators have been too concerned with the pun and failed
to recognize that the real center of Chaucer's satire here is the inappropriateness of Psalm 44
being said for the dead. The Ellesmere reading of *but* for *buf*, then, would be acceptable,
contrasting "what might be expected in a reverent prayer for the dead with what actually
takes place" (Hamilton 1942:657). Beichner (1956:136) by contrast argues that "any at-
tempt to minimize the importance of the double meaning of *cor meum eructavit* in order to
emphasize the inappropriateness of *Psalm* xliv as a prayer for the dead is an effort to shift
attention from what is primary to what is secondary or accidental," and he connects the friar's
pun with both a rich Latin tradition of such puns in satirical contexts and exegetical com-
mentary on Psalm 44 in which "the handling of the literal meaning of *eructavit* is often such
that it must have brought a gleam of humor to the eye of the reader or a smile to the lips of
an audience who heard the Psalm explained" (1956:137). Giaccherini (1980:143) similarly
rejects Hamilton's argument, noting that the alimentary joke accords perfectly with Friar
John's personality as the Summoner reveals it. McPeek (in RB[1]) adduces a parallel in the
Goliardic *Magister Golias de quodam abbate* and reiterates it (1951:334) despite RB's demur-
ral: RB notes that the Latin poem does not pun on the psalm, and suggests that Chaucer has
"used or adapted a current joke." Adams (1962:129) hears "a definite ironic reference to the
friar's own preaching." Ross (1972:49) feels that "belches are never very funny, but Chaucer
does about as well as anyone," while Whittock (1968:138) and Levitan (1971:240) see
dramatic irony in the line, the belching here anticipating the fart.
   1933   **Davit:** SK suggests that "*Davit* is put for *David*, for the rime," in Hg El La;
except for Gg (which has *-th* and rhymes it with *erouctauyth*), all other collated texts up to SK
spell *David* with a final *d* and rhyme it with a final *t*, a rhyme that Kittredge (1892:5)
assumed to be Chaucer's and "intentionally humorous."

Who folweth Cristes Gospel and His foore   1935
But we that humble been and chaast and poore?
Werkers of Goddes word, nat auditours.
Therfore, right as an hauk up at a sours
Up spryngeth into th'eyr, right so prayeres
Of charitable and chaste bisy freres   1940

1935   **His foore]** h. lore Cp He La Pw+ CX¹ PN²–WR; here f. Dd+
1936   **that humble been]** be h. He+   **and chaast]** c. He La+ CX¹–SP³
1937   **Werkers]** Werkes La+   **Goddes]** good He+   **word]** wordes Ad³+
CX¹–PN²; workis He+   **nat]** and eke Cp La+; and Ha⁴+; and n. He+ CX¹–UR; *om.*
Pw+
1938   **Therfore]** For He   **up at a sours]** rype at a s. Cp La+; up on a s. Dd Ha⁴+
TR WR; ryȝt at a s. Gg; up on his cours He+ PN¹; up on his s. (Tc²) CX¹,² WN PN² UR;
at a s. (Gl+) TH¹–SP³
1939   **spryngeth]** pryngyth ~ WN   **into]** vnto Cp+; in Gg+ PN¹ WN UR
right] *om.* He Pw+ CX¹ TH¹–SP³   **so]** so the (Ha³+) UR; *om.* La+
1940   **Of]** And Pw   **and chaste bisy]** a. c. He+ CX¹; chastite of b. Pw; c. and b.
~ UR

1935   **His foore:** Properly glossed first in SK, *foore* is a track or trail, and *folwen fore* is
to follow in someone's footsteps. The word was apparently sufficiently rare (in El it is glossed
steppes at *WBP* 110) to cause a great many scribes to substitute the plausible *lore*. See *MED*,
s.v. *fore* n. 2 (b).
    1937   All modern editions cite James 1.22, "Estote autem factores verbi, et non au-
ditores tantum" ("But be doers of the word, and not hearers only"). This passage is also found
in the *Epistola adversus Jovinianum* 2.3, "in the third sentence after the sentence containing
the lion image" that Chaucer uses in *FrT* 1657, as Correale (1965:173–74) points out.
    1938   **up at a sours:** This "thoroughly masculine metaphor" (Ruggiers 1965:104) is
glossed "like a falcon soaring, which she always does before swooping down upon her prey"
by Jephson (Bell 1855:2.112). SK provides a citation of "the Book of St. Alban's, fol. dI,
back . . . . 'Iff your hawke nym the fowle a-lofte, ye shall say, she toke it *at the mount* or *at the
souce*'; where the *r* is dropped." Thomas (UR) credits Holme (1688, Bk. 2, ch. 11, p. 240) for
providing the information that "*Soar* is a Term in Falconry, when the Hawk *soars* or lies aloft,
termed also Towering; and *Source* is when he takes the Game in flight." See also the eagle in
HF (544), which "with hys *sours* ayen up wente." Richardson (1970:150) remarks that the
friar's choice of image "is an ironic revelation of his true nature, for the hawk is a notorious
bird of prey." Haskell (1971:222) argues that the friar's simile is meant to suggest the flight
and fall of Simon Magus as told in the apocryphal *Acts of Peter* (ed. James 1924:331–32).
Lancashire (1981:24–25) suggests that the image is meant to remind us of Moses's "mysteri-
ous ascent on eagles' wings to God on Sinai" (Exodus 19.4). For further comment on the
metaphor see note 1941, and for Simon Magus, note 2094.
    1940   **and:** MR fail to report the omission of *and* in Pw.

Maken hir sours to Goddes erys two.
Thomas, Thomas, so mote I ryde or go,
And by that lord that clepid is Seint Yve,
Nere thow oure brother sholdestow nat thryve.

1941   **Maken]** Makyng Ad³ Pw+   **hir]** hem (Ne+) CX¹–PN²   **sours]** sowne
(Tc²) CX¹   **to]** up to ~ SP²,³   **two]** and who Cp La+
1942   **Thomas Thomas]** T. þerfore Cp La+; T. riȝt Pw+   **so]** so as Pw
1943   **that]** þe Gg+   **lord]** god Cp La+   **clepid is]** c. was Pw+ CX¹–PN²
1944   **Nere thow oure brother]** Ne t. o. b. wer He+ CX¹–UR   **sholdestow]**
þou shuldest Pw+ TH¹–UR   **nat]** neuer Ad³ Dd Ha⁴ He+ CX¹ WR

1941   **Goddes erys two:** Lowes (1934:239) notes the "graphic immediacy of concep-
tion" in the phrase. "The *ear* of God is little more than an abstraction. . . . 'God's *two ears*'
startlingly visualizes, humanizes God. And the daring familiarity which the friar allows
himself is not only an apt touch in a masterpiece of satirical portraiture but also, once more,
an instance of Chaucer's imaginative coalescence with his subject." Huppé (1964:205–06),
reminding us of lines 1695–98 with their image of friars flying through hell like bees, writes
that "the friars may say that their 'sours' (leap) carries them to the 'sours' (source), God's
'eres,' but the audience knows enough to supply the right reading, devil's 'ers.' The meta-
phor, however, even read without its double meaning has a somewhat unfortunate implica-
tion: God's ears become the victims of birds of prey; and the Summoner would agree that this
is precisely what the friars are—birds of prey." Owen (1966:561–62) takes the metaphor as
giving "the authenticity of self-delusion to the Friar's hypocrisy." See further note 1938.
    1943   **Seint Yve:** The identity of this saint is not clear. Jephson (Bell 1855:2.112)
suggests the "exemplary priest of Lantriguier, in Bretagne." Hertzberg (1866:624) offers two
possibilities: "Ivo Presbyter (d. 1303) and Bishop Ivo (fl. 7th C.)." Düring (1883–86:3.374)
cites his note to *ShT* B² 1417 (line 5387 in Düring), where he adduces an archbishop of
Chartres who died in 1115 and was canonized, but Düring allows that there are two other
saints named Ivo. SK observes that the present line is reproduced exactly in *ShT* B² 1417;
SK's note to that line reads "'St. Ivia, or Ivo,' says Alban Butler [1833], 'was a Persian
bishop, who preached in England in the seventh century' [see Butler 1956:2.157–58]. He
died at St. Ive's in Huntingdonshire. A church was also built in his honour at St. Ive's in
Cornwall. His day is April 25." RB and Havely (1975:142) take him to be the parish priest
of Brittany, Havely adding that he was trained as a lawyer before his ordination and made his
legal training available to his parishioners, and "thus seems to be a fairly appropriate saint for
a subtle and legalistic persuader like Friar John to swear by, when claiming to be concerned
about an ordinary 'churl.'" Cline (1945:482) argues for the appropriateness of bishop Ivo of
Chartres, and RI (in a note to *ShT* B² 1417 [VII 227]) agrees, but Gerould (1952:17) argues
that the bishop was beatified but never canonized, and feels that the reference is more likely
to be to the Benedictine priory in Huntingdonshire named for Yve than to the seventh-
century saint, "the vaguest of figures" or the Breton saint who "never became famous outside
the province. . . . and could not appropriately be referred to as 'that lord.'"
    1944   Again suggesting a specifically anti-Dominican slant to the satire (see note
1740), Fleming (1967:98–99) observes that both John and Thomas are satirized in Thomas's

[In o]ure chapitre praye we day and nyght   82v   1945
To Crist, that He thee sende heele and myght
Thy body for to welden hastily."
   "God woot," quod he, "no thyng ther of feele I.
As help me Crist, as I in fewe yeres
Have spended upon diverse manere freres   1950
Ful many a pound, yet fare I nevere the bet.
Certeyn my good have I almoost biset;

1945   **In oure]** ure Hg (*eaten away*); For in o. ~ CX²–UR   **chapitre]** chapitle
Pw+   **day]** both d. He+ CX¹
    1946   **that He]** to He+ CX¹–PN² UR   **thee sende]** s. t. Cp Dd He La+ CX¹–
PN² UR   **heele]** both helth He+ CX¹–PN² UR; helth (Ra²+) TH¹–SP³
    1947   **to welden]** w. Ad³; to wendyn Gg He+   **hastily]** ful h. He+ CX¹–PN²
    1948   **quod he]** þer of Gg+   **no thyng ther of]** þer of nought Ha⁴ WR
feele] wot Cp La+
    1949   **As]** So Gg+   **me]** *om.* Pw+   **Crist]** god Dd He+ CX¹–PN²   **as]** *om.*
~ SP²˒³   **I]** *om.* El Cp Gg He La+ CX¹–UR RB¹   **in]** in a El Gg+ UR RB¹; haue in
Ad³ Pw+; in ryght He
    1950   **Have spended]** I h. spent El RB¹; Dispended Ad³; H. I s. Cp La+ CX¹–UR; I
h. s. Gg He+; S. Pw   **upon]** of He La; on (Ad²+) CX¹–PN² UR   **diverse manere]**
d. m. of Ad³+; many d. Dd Ha⁴ He Pw+ CX¹–PN² WR
    1951   **Ful]** Wel Pw+ TH¹–SP³   **nevere]** ne Pw
    1952   **have I almoost]** I. h. a. El+; a. h. I. La+; is a. Pw

---

regarding his "investment in the friars and fraternity as an investment in his physical rather
than his spiritual health, a kind of medical expense." See also below, note 2128.
   1945   Hg is eaten away on the upper left corner; the text is supplied from El.
   1948–52   Zietlow (1966:8), arguing that Chaucer makes the friar consistently obtuse
to parallel him with the summoner of *FrT*, remarks that "instead of perceiving Thomas'
feelings—made almost as clear in these words as is the fiend's true identity when he says 'I
am a feend; my dwellyng is in helle' [*FrT*] 1448—the friar continues to go about his
business as if the relationship with Thomas had not changed. The Summoner's friar and the
Friar's summoner both treat their interlocutors as 'brothers' even after the bond of brother-
hood has proven to be specious." Richardson (1975:234) takes Thomas's complaint here as
"the first indication of Thomas' animosity," and links it to the friar's belittling of professional
rivals, a character fault more in line with the Summoner himself, she feels, than an accurate
jab at his enemy Huberd.
   1948   **no thyng:** This spelling of Hg El+ is better than *nothyng*, since the meter
obviously works better with the stress on *thyng*. See "The Present Edition," p. 98, above.
   1949   **I:** Brusendorff (1925:107) feels that Hg and the MSS that share its reading are
"evidently wrong," but MR note of this line that "obviously 'I' belongs in 1949. It seems to
have been transferred to line 1950 by El, the Gg group, and some members of *cd**. The
insertion of 'a' in 1949 was made in only a few of the MSS that moved 'I.'"

Farwel my gold, for it is al ago."
   The frere answerde, "O Thomas, doostow so?
What nedeth yow diverse freres seche?   1955
What nedeth hym that hath a parfit leche
To sechen othere leches in the town?
Youre inconstance is youre confusioun.
Holde ye thanne me or ellis oure covent
To preye for yow been insufficient?   1960
Thomas, that jape nys nat worth a myte;

    1953   **gold**] good Ad³ Gg Pw+ TH¹–SP³ TR; g. fold (f. *del.*) La   **al**] almost Ha⁴
Pw+ TH¹–SP³ WR
    1954   **doostow**] why d. Cp La+
    1955   **yow**] the Dd He+ CX¹–UR   **seche**] to s. Ad³ Cp He La+ SP²–TR; forto s.
(Ne+) CX¹–PN²
    1956   **hym**] hem La
    1957   **the**] ony He+ CX¹; *om.* Dd+   **town**] tyme He+
    1959   **thanne me**] me t. La Pw+ TH¹–UR   **or ellis**] and eke al Dd He+ CX¹–
PN² UR; or Ha⁴+
    1960   **been**] *om.* Ha⁴+ TH¹–UR WR   **insufficient**] nat sufficient He+ CX¹–
PN²
    1961   **nys**] is Ad³ Cp Dd Ha⁴ He La Pw+ CX¹–PN² WR

    1954–69   Crowther (1980:12–13) feels that Friar John's argument against division is misappropriated from manuals of religious instruction which emphatically required the penitent to confess all his sins to one confessor and not partition them among several (e.g., *ParsT* 1006). Thus when Friar John urges Thomas to confess to him, he discovers that he has unwittingly argued against himself: "Thomas not only remains true to the letter and spirit of confession, but he also delivers a devastating rebuke to the Friar's misappropriation of a point of doctrine." Pearsall (1985:226) remarks of the style and humor of the passage that "there is much to take delight in here, in the spectacle of a skilled rhetorician in full spate (the scornful mock-imperatives of 1963–5 are particularly effective). . . . The artistic and dramatic power of the lines almost overwhelms our moral consciousness as Chaucer . . . draws us to a delighted assent in the vitality of his creations, in the teeth of our objections to their vicious greed and hypocrisy."
    1955   See the discussion of letters of confraternity in note 2128.
    1956   **parfit leche:** Richardson (1970:154) suggests that though *leech* meaning a parasitic human is not attested before the 18th century, "it is at least possible that Chaucer might here be punning on the blood-sucker, giving it the metaphoric humanization which later became standard usage."
    1961   **jape . . . myte:** Haeckel (1890:60) lists this phrase among possible proverbs.
          jape: Citing the glossary of SP² or SP³, Thomas (UR) glosses *jape* anecdotally: "A jest. A word (says [Speght]) by abuse grown odious, and therefore by a certain curious Gentlewoman scraped out in her *Chaucer*, whereupon her serving man writeth thus; *My Mistress cannot be content / To take a Jest as* Chaucer *ment; / But using still a Woman's fashion, /*

Youre maladye is for we han to lyte.
'A, yif that covent half a quarter otes;
A, yif that covent [foure and twenty] grotes;
A, yif that frere a peny and lat hym go.'   1965
Nay nay, Thomas, it may no thyng be so.
What is a ferthyng worth parted in twelve?

1962   **we}** ʒe Cp Gg La+; þat we He+   **han}** h. ʒiuen us Cp La+   **to}** so Cp La+

1963   **A}** And He+ CX¹–PN²   *Lines 1963–64 trans.* Dd He+ CX¹–PN² UR
1964   **A}** And Gg He+ CX¹ TH¹–SP³ TR   **that covent}** hem Cp+; *om.* La **foure and twenty}** one or tuo Cp La₁; on tuo La
1965   **A}** And Gg He+ CX¹–TR   **that}** þe Cp La+
1966   **it}** I Gg (Gg₁ *corr.*)   **no thyng be}** nought b. Ha⁴+ WR; b. nothing ~ UR
1967   **worth}** *om.* Pw+   **parted}** depart Ha⁴+ WR   **in}** on Dd Gg He+ CX¹–PN² TR

Allows it in the last Translation: / She cannot with a Word dispense, / Although I know she loves the sense; / For such an use the World hath got, / That Words are Sins, but Deeds are not." See further Ransom (1993:195).

1963–67   Whittock (1968:139) feels that "the eloquence here calls such attention to itself that amusement robs it of any power to convince." Knight (1973:74) notes that the tropes of the passage are "intended to bowl Thomas over and loosen his purse strings, not save his soul."

1964   **A:** MR erroneously report *And* for *A* in Ha⁴; their collation card shows that Ha³ reads *And*.

      foure and twenty: The spelling is taken from Dd; Hg El Ad³ He Pw read *.xxiiij.*

1967   **What is a ferthyng worth:** Noting of the Friar of *GP* 264 that "somewhat he lipsed, for his wantownesse," Whitesell (1956:161) suggests that "perhaps it is his pronunciation of the word *ferthyng* which leads to Friar John's undoing." Baum (1958:167) lists this as a pun, but notes that "it presents a phonetic problem." Though *th-t* is not a recognized assimillatory change, he concludes that "probably the approximation of sound justifies the pun." Compare Gg's spellings at lines 1933–34, reported in note 1933 above. As Birney (1960:213) puts it, "whether or not a pun lurks in 'ferthyng,' the whole passage is plainly anticipatory," and all commentators since agree. Levy (1966:59) reminds us that we are told of Friar Huberd in *GP* A 253–55 that "For thogh a wydwe hadde noght a sho, / So plesaunt was his 'In principio,' / Yet wolde he have a ferthyng, er he wente," concluding that "it is indeed a *ferthyng* that Thomas offers Friar John before the Friar leaves." Or, to use Knight's phrase, the friar receives "a smelly homonym" of the farthing (1986:107). Howard (1976: 257) alone finds the pun ugly: "If puns are 'the lowest form of humor,' if they go back to an infantile or primitive response to experience and language, this unsophisticated pun blends perfectly with the Summoner's unsophisticated aggression."

      Proposing that such riddles as "Comment partiroit on une vesse en douze parties" ("How can one divide a fart into twelve parts") or "Comment pourroit on partir une

Lo, ech thyng that is oned in hymselve
Is moore strong than whan it is toscatered.
Thomas, of me thow shalt nat been yflatered; 1970
Thow woldest han oure labour al for noght.
The hye God that al this world hath wroght
Seith that the werkman worthy is his hire.

1968   **ech}** e. a La   **that}** *om.* Pw+   **oned}** houed La; counted Pw+   **in}** by
Cp La+   **hymselve}** it selue El; them selue (Bo²) PN¹
1969   **strong}** straunge Cp La+   **than}** *om.* Pw+   **to scatered}** to sclatered
Ad³; skatered Cp Dd La+ CX¹–PN² TR; so sclatered Pw+; so skatered (Ha⁵+) TH¹–UR
Lines 1969–70 trans. Pw (Pw *corr.*)+
1970   **nat}** *om.* Gg (Gg₂ *corr.*)
1971   **Thow}** Tho La   **han oure labour al}** o. l. h. Cp La+; h. o. l. half Dd+; h. al
o. l. (Ph³+) TH¹–SP³
1972   **world}** weld La
1973   **the}** a Ha⁴   **worthy is}** is w. Cp Ha⁴ He La Pw+ CX¹–UR; is worth Dd+;
is w. of ~ WR   **his}** *om.* Ad³+

---

vesse en deux?" ("How can one divide a fart in two?"), found in the 15th-century Chantilly
MS, underlie *SumT*, Green (1987:27) suggests that in asking this question the friar becomes
the "butt of a riddle he is quite unaware of having set." See further under "Sources and
Analogues."
    1968–69   RB, following SK, notes parallel ideas in Aesop's fable of the bundle of
sticks and Boethius's discussion of unity in *The Consolation of Philosophy* Book 3, Prose 11.
Emphasizing the Pentecostal nature of *SumT*'s parody, Levitan (1971:240) remarks that
"while this may be true of Aesop's bundle of sticks . . . it is not true of things spiritual. The
gift of the Holy Ghost, like *caritas*, is not diminished in strength when it is shared."
    1968   *Marginal gloss:* Omnis virtus vnita forcior est seipsa dispersa El Ad³. "Every
strength is more powerful when united than when dispersed." RB notes that the quotation
remains unidentified.
        oned: MR do not report *houed* in La (so transcribed by Furnival, ed. 1868–79).
They may well have read it as *honed*, an aspirated form of *oned*.
    1969–70   Pw corrects the transposition marginally with letters *a* and *b*; MR report
the transposition in Pw but not its correction. Though the transposition also occurs in En¹
and Ds (and in no other MSS), MR fail to adduce it with their evidence for an En¹–Ds
subgroup (2.54).
    1969   Adams (1962:128) suggests a connection here to the "concentrated" trentals of
the friar's sermon (see note 1728). Richardson (1970:154) points out that the pun on *ferthyng*
in line 1967 anticipates the "equitable scattering of something 'strong'."
    1973   *Marginal gloss:* Dignus est operarius mercede et cetera El Ad³. Jephson (Bell
1855:2.113) and subsequent editors cite Luke 10.7, and Haeckel (1890:13) lists this as
proverbial. Adams (1962:129) suggests that "the gift [the friar] gets is just what he is
worth," as Jankyn seems to imply in lines 2280–84. Richardson (1970:156) adds that since
the friar as workman produces nothing but hot air it is fitting that he is paid "in like token."

Thomas, noght of youre tresor I desire
As for myself, but that al oure covent   1975
To praye for yow is ay so diligent,
And for to buylden Cristes owene chirche.
Thomas, if ye wol lernen for to wirche,
Of buyldyng up of chirches may ye fynde
If it be good in Thomas lyf of Inde.   1980

1974   **noght of youre tresor I**] of y. t. n. wol I He+ CX^1–PN^2; n. for y. t. I Pw; of y.
t. I n. ~ UR
    1975   **As**] *om.* Ha^4+ WR   **that**] for t. Ha^4; for La+   **al**] *om.* Ha^4 He+ CX^1
WR
    1976   **is**] ben Dd He+ CX^1–PN^2 **ay**] al Pw+; *om.* He+   **so**] our Pw+; *om.*
Ad^3+
    1977   **And**] A. holy ~ SP^{2,3} **buylden**] holden Dd+; huld up He+ CX^1–PN^2; b.
up ~ UR   **owene**] holy Ha^4+ WR
    1979   **up**] *om.* He+   **of**] on Dd Ha^4+ CX^1–PN^2 WR   **may**] now ~ WN

Szittya (1974:39–40) remarks that Luke 10.7 "was the theological cornerstone of the Francis-can justification of mendicancy as a religious way of life," and thus central to the anti-mendicant pattern of satire in *SumT*, adding that the friar takes the scriptural passage "in precisely the opposite fashion that Francis would have wished." See note to line 1820, above.
    1974–77   Anticipating the Pentecostal parody that concludes the tale, Levy (1966:53) writes that the friar "presents himself as a true descendant of the Apostles by insisting that he does not want money for himself but only for his convent, so that the friars can build Christ's church on earth."
    1976   **ay so:** *al our* was caught from the preceding line by Ha^2 and the ancestor of the *Pw* manuscripts.
    1980   **Thomas lyf of Inde:** On the word order, a genitive construction common in ME, SK refers to his note on *SqT* 209, where he offers multiple parallel Chaucerian examples, and RB refers to his note on *ClT* 1170, where he does likewise.   §   Richardson (RI) notes that Thomas of India is the "Doubting Apostle" of John 20.26–30. Much of the commentary on this line concerns whether literal or figurative churches are intended. WR, quoted by Hertzberg (1866:624), can find "nothing of the sort in the life of St. Thomas," and wonders if "perhaps the friar is made to quote at random, reckoning upon the ignorance of his auditor." Jephson (Bell 1855:2.113) notes that "the Apostle Thomas was the evangelist of the Indies, and recommended himself to a sovereign of that country by his skill in building." Düring (1883–86:3.374–75) writes that "the book which told of St. Thomas (who at the command of Christ went from Caesaria to India as architect to King Gundoforus) was possibly a legend about the stay of this Apostle in India and his heavenly palace built for the king. On the other hand it could be the travel diary of Sir John Mandeville, who sought the grave of St. Thomas in Calamia, and related a variety of wonders" (see Mandeville 1919–1923:1.114). Lounsbury (1892:2.328) says that "the poet's statements in regard to the saints are, at times, marked by that haziness and confusion which occasionally characterizes his knowledge in matters of more importance. . . . If Chaucer found any hints upon the subject [of church

Ye lye heere ful of anger and of ire,

1981   heere] *om.* He   anger] anguyssch Gg+   and] *om.* El   of] *om.* Ad³
He+ UR

---

building] in any account of the saint's career, he did so in sources that do not appear to have come down to us." Pollard (1894:77) says that "St. Thomas professed to be an architect, but the palace he built for the Indian king was in heaven." SK suggests that the reference is "to a well-known legend" and cites many instances of it. Szittya (1974:34) notes that the friar ignores the fact that according to the account in the *Legenda Aurea* of Jacobus Voragine (ed. Graesse 1850:32–39 and trans. Ryan and Ripperger 1941:1.39–46), Saint Thomas gave King Gundofernus's building fund to the poor and was therefore imprisoned; Boyd feels that some written account must have been in the friar's mind, but that it could not have been the *Legenda Aurea*, "for the detail in question is not mentioned by Jacobus" (1967:35). Richardson (RI) writes that "the usual story of the death and restoration of the king's brother suggests that the churches accredited to Thomas were congregations, not buildings," and refers to the *Golden Legend* account, but adds that the version in the *South English Legendary* (ed. D'Evelyn and Mill 1956:2.577) tells of literal construction. Clark (1976a:165) writes that the legend of Saint Thomas as church builder grew out of the apocryphal *Acts of Thomas* (ed. James 1924:364–438). On the development of the legend he quotes Emile Mâle (1913:304): "The Apostles built the edifice of the faith, a temple made of living stones, which is the Church, and even today the word 'edify' has a spiritual meaning. Starting from that point some writer of lively imagination made St. Thomas an architect." Ruggiers (1965:104) detects a subtle flattery here, and Havely (1975:143) elaborates: "Friar John seems here to be cunningly trying to arouse Thomas the churl's interest by referring to the legend of a saint who is his namesake." Szittya (1974:32) notes that the name Thomas, as interpreted by the *Golden Legend* account of his life, means "divisio" or "sectio" ("division" or "partition"), and adds that "such an etymology has an obvious ironic relevance to the Thomas of our tale."

1981–82   Richardson (1970:150–51) notes the repetition of fire imagery in line 2122: "It is precisely with this repetition of the fire image that Thomas decides to give the friar a gift of the physical reality which he HAS been lying there full of." O'Brien (1990:4) reads this moment as a parodic alchemical project: "His anger mounting, Thomas is essentially the cooking machine, the furnace, that lies there steaming."

1981   One may consider that Friar John's sermon on ire begins here, though SK argues that it does not begin until line 2005. Birney (1960:214) notes the tension which builds throughout the extended sermon: "If he had been less in love with himself as a sermonist, the friar would have realized that there are surer ways of soothing a wrathful man than by berating him for his wrathfullness." Craik (1964:125) notes that "Chaucer manages the harangue with great success. He makes it tedious, pompous and shapeless; wearisome to Thomas but not to the reader." Huppé (1964:206) remarks upon the "curiously twisting, turning course" of the speech, noting in particular that the friar's admonition that Thomas not strive against his wife "seems a little irrelevant, not only because 'stryvyng,' like 'strugle' in the *Merchant's Tale*, (2376) seems to have both its literal and a sexual connotation, but also because the admonition seems to echo the Wife of Bath's warning that a husband should not contend with his wife. . . . It appears suddenly that it is not Thomas' anger which is at issue, but rather the anger of the 'sely innocent,' his wife." Fleming, remarking on the vacuity of

With which the devel set youre herte afire,
And chiden heere the sely innocent,
Youre wyf that is so meke and pacient;
And therfore Thomas, trowe me if thee leste,   83r   1985
Ne stryve nat with thy wyf, as for thy beste;
And bere this word awey now, by thy feith;

1982   **With]** w. þe Cp He+   **set youre herte]** s. y. ers Cp La+; setteth y. h. Dd TH[1]–SP[1]   **afire]** of fire La+

1983   **the]** þis Cp Gg He La Pw+ CX[2]–TR SK MR   **sely]** holy Ad[3] Dd (Dd[1] corr.) Ha[4] He Pw+ CX[1]–WR

1984   **wyf]** om. Dd (Dd[1] corr.)   **so]** here so (Ne+) CX[1]–PN[2]   **meke]** good ~ SP[2,3] TR   **and]** a. so (Ne+) CX[1,2] WN PN[2]

1985   **Thomas trowe me]** t. me T. Ha[4] TH[1]–WR; t. me Pw+   **thee]** ȝou Cp La Pw+ TH[1]–UR; þu Dd Ha[4] He+ CX[1]–PN[2] WR

1986   **stryve]** chyde (Si) TH[1]–UR   **nat]** om. La   **as for]** al f. Cp La+; f. He+ **thy]** the Ad[3] Cp Dd Gg He La Pw+ CX[1]–TR

1987   **this word awey]** a. t. w. He+; thise wordes a. ~ WN PN[2]   **now]** om. La+ TH[1]–SP[3]

John's advice, notes that the warning against wrath amounts to an "appeal to carnal prudence" (1983:15). Shaw (1984:9) argues that John's sermon on ire is principally a projection of his own anger on discovering that Thomas has been giving money to other friars.

1982   **set:** MR do not report *setteth* in Dd. *Set* can be either past or present singular, while *setteth* is only present; whether the Dd reading is a true variant is thus uncertain. Cf. notes to *Fasted* at line 1886 and *grynt* at line 2161.

1983   **heere the:** Kane (1984:214) argues for the "good possibility that the original read *hir the*, *heere* having been caught up from line 1981, and *this* being a more explicit substitution." *Hir* does seem a better reading, but if it had been original one would have expected it to have survived in more than one (Ad[1]) MS. MR incorrectly report *this* in CX[1]; it is first printed in CX[2], as is noted on their collation card. They do not explain their decision to print *this*, which is supported by more, but not the better, MSS.

   sely: MR note (3.467) that "'Holy' may be the reading of the early draft. It was retained by a part of *d** and the Ha[4]–*a* line after the substitution of 'sely.'" But Kane (1984:214) argues that *holy* could not have been original, was "induced by the common collocation 'holy innocents,' and impossible in the context."

1986   Havely (1975:143) considers that "it's a bit difficult to see why Friar John is so concerned to warn Thomas against the possible wrath of his wife as well as his own anger. . . . The friar's aim in warning Thomas against his own anger is probably to get him to feel guilty about it, so that he will be prepared to make a formal confession. . . . There may be a more subtle purpose behind the warning about women's anger—namely to make Thomas less willing to oppose his wife when she sides with the friar, as she seems to have done in [lines 1823–31]." It is not clear, in fact, how much of the following argument has to do with the wife; see note 1993.

Touchynge swich thyng, lo, what the wise man seith,
  'Withinne thyn hous ne be thow no leoun;
To thy subgitz do noon oppressioun,   1990
Ne make thyne aqueyntances nat for to flee.'
And Thomas, yet eftsoones I charge thee,

1988   **swich**} this El+ SK   **thyng**} thinges Ad³   **what**} as Gg; *om.* Ha⁴+
WR   **man**} *om.* El Gg He+ CX¹–SP³ TR SK RB¹ RB² RI
1989   **ne**} *om.* Ha⁴+ TH¹–SP³ WR
1990   **do noon**} do thou n. Ad³ He Pw+ CX¹–UR
1991   **thyne aqueyntances nat**} t. acqueintance n. Cp Dd He La+ CX¹–PN² MR
PR; t. acqueyntis Ha⁴ WR; þou n. t. aqueyntaunce Pw+ TR; n. t. aquayntaunce (Ds+)
TH¹–UR   **for to**} to Ad³ Dd Gg He+ CX¹–TR SK RB¹ RB² RI; fro þe Ha⁴ WR
1992   **Thomas yet**} y. T. Ha⁴ Pw+ TH¹–SP³ TR WR   **I charge**} say I Cp La+; c.
I Dd Pw+ TH¹–SP³ TR; warn I He+ CX¹–PN² UR

1988   RB and RI print Hg's *swich* for El's *this*, but accept El's omission of *man*, producing a line not available in any one MS. Chaucer uses both *the wise man* and *the wise* elsewhere (e.g., *MLH* B¹ 113, 117), but the bulk and quality of MS support here is for *wise man*.

1989–91   *Marginal gloss:* Noli esse sicut leo in domo tua euertens domesticos tuos opprimens subiectos tibi El Ad³. "Be not as a lion in thy house, terrifying them of thy household, and oppressing them that are under thee" (Douay). As first noted by Jephson (Bell 1855:2.113), this gloss simply quotes Ecclesiasticus (4.35 in the Vulgate-Douay version; in other versions the passage is numbered 4.30).

1991   Zietlow (1966:10–11) views this advice as characteristic of "the comic incoherence and inconsistency of the sermon," because "the friar's chosen theme is the effect of anger on marriage, not on friendship."

    thyne aqueyntances nat: MR argue (3.467) that "the evidence favors 'acqueyntance' as the reading of O¹. Chaucer seems never to have used the plural as a concrete noun." In fact the present instance is Chaucer's only use of the word as a concrete noun, and manuscript evidence, though heavily favoring the singular form, is inconclusive, showing much editing and casual variation in number and word order; one may suspect that the authoritative reading was troublesome, probably metrically so, given the number of different readings which manage to be metrically smoother than Hg–El by writing the singular *aqueyntance* or by omitting *nat* or *for*. MR erroneously report that Hg, El, Ad³, and Gg read *aqueyntances to flee*, though their collation card correctly shows that Hg and El read *aqueyntances nat for to flee*, while Ad³ and Gg read *aqueyntances nat to flee*, as printed by SK, RB and RI.

1992–2003   Koeppel (1892:256) is the first to identify Chaucer's use of *RR* in this passage, comparing *SumT* 2001–03 with *RR* 9800–04 (ed. Langlois; trans. Dahlberg): "Ne nus serpenz si disleiaus, / Quant l'en li marche seur la queue, / Qui dou marchier pas ne se jeue, / Come est fame quant ele treuve / O son ami s'amie neuve" ("nor is there any serpent as malicious, when one steps on its tail [the serpent does not enjoy being stepped on], as a woman when she finds his new mistress with her lover"). SK notes that this passage of *RR*

Bewar from hire that in thy bosom slepeth;
War fro the serpent that so sleighly crepeth

1993 *Variant form of line* 1996 *bef. line* 1993: Be war her of and herkyn patiently He+
from] of He Pw+ CX¹–UR; for Cp Ha⁴ La+ WR   hire] Ire Ad³ Pw+ TR WR PR
RI   that] t. so He+   bosom] body He+
   1994   War] Be w. El Cp Gg La+; W. þe Pw+ TH¹–SP¹   fro] of Cp La+ TH¹–
UR; for Ha⁴ Pw+ PN² WR   so] *om.* Ad³+   sleighly] prively Ha⁴

---

derives from Ovid, *Ars amatoria* 2.376–78; SK also adduces *RR* 16595–604, which alludes
to Virgil's *Eclogues* (3.95: "latet anguis in herba" ["the snake lies hidden in the grass"]) and,
like *SumT* 1994–95, uses the figure as a warning to men to beware women. Finally, SK
compares *SumT* 2003 with Virgil, *Aeneid* 5.6 ("furens quid foemina possit" ["how furious a
woman can be"]) and with Seneca, *Medea* 579–82 (ed. Costa 1973:45). RB and Richardson
(RI) repeat this information; Richardson, like SK, compares *SqT* 512, and she adds, with
reference to Whiting (1968:S153), that *SumT* 1994–95 are "proverbial after Chaucer."
   1992–95   Zietlow (1966:11) notes that "this traditional view of women confuses the
point. . . . Certainly some clear transition could be made between the injustice of unprovoked
anger and the dangers of provoking anger in others; but the friar does not make it."
   1993   **hire:** All of *d**¹ and all of the Gg–Si group except Gg itself read *ire* for *hire*, and
modern editors have argued vigorously for both readings. SK, arguing for *hire*, calls the
decision of WR to follow TR in printing *ire* an "insidious and uncalled-for alteration." "It is
easily seen how the error crept in," he continues, "from confusion with the friar's sermon
against *ire*; but that does not really begin till we come to l. 2005." SK supports the argument
by adducing source texts from *RR* and the *Aeneid* (see above, note 1992–2003). But as
compelling as these parallels are, it must be admitted that there seems no motive for the friar
to refer to Thomas's wife in such terms, and MR reason that "the evidence seems to indicate
that the early draft had 'ire', which appeared in the fair copy as 'hire', either because the scribe
was careless about initial *h* or because he did not understand the figurative nature of Chau-
cer's language. When Chaucer added the final episode (2159–2294), he may have failed to
note the change made by the scribe. The whole course of the argument from 1981 indicates
that 'ire' was in Chaucer's mind. The scribes and some of the editors were misled by the last
half of 1993. It is unlikely that the Friar intends to call the wife a serpent" (3.467). PR was
apparently persuaded by the MR argument to print *ire*, but of course MR themselves print
hire because they believe it to be the fair copy reading. Though MR's reading of the drift of
the passage seems more reasonable than SK's, the argument from sense is inconclusive for the
very reason that, whatever was in Chaucer's mind, the friar's discourse flows always along
tendentious paths of least resistance and free association, arguing in the short span of lines
1996–2004, for example, against the sin of ire on the contradictory grounds that wives kill
their husbands during arguments, that Thomas's wife is meek, and that no serpent is crueler
than an irate woman. Ruggiers (1965:105) sees in lines 1996 ff. "a bitter commentary upon
marriage" designed to remind Thomas of "all of those men who stirred up the sleeping evil
in the bosom of women and consequently lost their lives." Kane notes that "the words were
as good as identical phonetically, [and] Chaucer had made a pun and probably intended it"
(1984:216). Baum (1956:244) also suggests a pun here. See also note 1994.
   1994   **serpent:** Baum (1956:243–44) suggests the possibility of a sexual innuendo

Under the gras and styngeth subtilly.   1995
Bewar my sone and herkne paciently,
That twenty thousand men han lost hir lyves,
For stryvyng with hir lemmans and hir wyves.
Now sith ye han so holy meke a wyf,
What nedeth yow, Thomas, to maken stryf?   2000
Ther nys, ywis, no serpent so cruel

    1995   **and**] þat Cp La+   **subtilly**] priuely Ha[4] WR; ful s. He+ CX[1]–SP[3]; spit-
ously s. Pw (Pw *corr.*)
    1996   **my sone**] her of He+; of her (Ne+) CX[1]   **herkne**] werk Ha[4] WR
    1997   **That**] ffor t. Ha[4] WR
    1998   **stryvyng with hir lemmans and**] þat þei han ben spitous to Cp La+
    1999   **ye**] þus ye La   **holy meke a**] h. and so m. a Cp La+; h. and m. a Ha[4]+
TH[1]–SP[3] TR–RB[1] RB[2]; h. a m. He+ CX[1]–PN[2] UR
    2001   **nys**] is Cp Gg La+

---

here, writing that "Tatlock [1916:230] noted, without giving details, a coarse pun in the
middle of *Sum T*, 'containing a striking piece of dramatic irony.'" Baum, with reticence
almost as great as Tatlock's, remarks that the passage contained in lines 1986–97 "is both
transparent and complex; and innocent if the point is overlooked." Ross (1972:199) adds that
"the friar is attacking Thomas' wife and cautioning him about the attractiveness of inter-
course," and Huppé (1964:207) too sees the serpent as the wife, who "appears 'meke and
pacient,' but is in fact fearfully dangerous. . . . That anger which the devil slyly implanted in
his bosom turns out really to be his wife's anger. The fact is, his anger is simply a mistake;
only in submission to her demands can Thomas secure himself from her deadly sting. The
argument is, of course, the Wife of Bath's, as is the logic." Owen (1977:165) feels that this
image of the serpent ready to sting that turns out to be not sin but woman is evidence of the
Summoner's faltering as a narrator. See note 1993 for other opinions.
    1995   **subtilly:** *spitously* in Pw is marked for deletion, and *sotilly* added. MR report the
variant as uncorrected, though the correction is noted on their collation card.
    1998   MR mistakenly report that Gg omits *and*. The word is blurred, but both
Furnivall (1868–77) and I see an ampersand.
    1999   *Marginal gloss:* Nota bene Gg.
        holy meke a: Exceptionally, RB[1,2] here follow Ha[4], supported by only a few
MSS of little authority. RI prints the line as given here; Hanna notes (RI, p. 1127) that "the
scribal 'and' produces the easier sense 'holy and meek,' rather than Chaucer's 'completely
meek'; although elsewhere in Chaucer, *hooly* only occurs with an adjectival possessive pro-
noun, cf. the Lydgate, *Life of Our Lady*, and Chauliac readings cited by *MED hooli* adv., sense
3b." § Ross (1972:106) wonders whether the friar's words were "accompanied by a sly
wink."

Whan man tret on his tayl, ne half so fel
As womman is whan she hath caught an ire;
Vengeance is thanne al that they desire.
Ire is a synne, oon of the grete of sevene,   2005
Abhomynable unto the God of hevene,
And to hymself it is destruccioun.
This every lewed viker or persoun

2002 **Whan]** What El   man] a m. Dd He+ CX¹–PN²; men Cp Ha⁴ La Pw+
TH¹–WR   tret] trede Cp Ha⁴ La+ UR WR; trat Gg; tredith He+ CX¹–PN² TR;
treden Pw+ TH¹–SP³   on] vp on Dd+ CX¹–PN²   his tayl] hym He   ne] nouȝt
La+

2003 **womman is]** w. is w. is Gg (Gg₁ *corr.*); a w. is He Pw+ CX¹–SP³   an] *om.*
He+ CX¹

2004 **Vengeance]** Verry v. He+ CX¹–PN² UR TR   that they] her He+ CX¹–
TR

2005 *Spur. lines bef.* 2005: Schortly may no man by rym and vers / Tellen her
thoughtes þay ben so dyuers Ha⁴ WR   **is a synne]** is a þing Ha⁴; a s. is He   oon]
om. Dd (Dd₂ *corr.*) He+ CX¹   of] *om.* Ha⁴ Pw+ WR   grete] gretteste Gg La+ PN²–
UR   of] *om.* Ad³ Dd (Dd₂ *corr.*) He+ CX¹ TR   sevene] synnys Gg

2006 **Abhomynable]** And ful a. He+ CX¹–PN²   unto] to Dd Ha⁴ He+ CX¹–
PN² UR WR   the] t. hygh (Ln+) TH¹–SP³; *om.* La Pw+   God] kyng He+ CX¹–
PN² UR   of] in Pw+

2007 **is]** is a He+ CX¹–SP¹

2008 **This]** Thus Pw+   viker] vicory Ha⁴ La WR

2002 **man:** MR (3.467) note that "'Man' and 'men' are, of course, equivalent forms of
the indefinite pronoun, but some scribes mistook 'men' for the plural noun. The confusion
may have been aided by the contracted form of the *3 sing. pres. ind.* verb, which was unfamil-
iar to some of the scribes."

2003 **womman is:** MR ignore the dittography and correction in Gg.

2005 The spurious lines which precede line 2005 in Ha⁴ are, as Koeppel (1892:256)
and SK note, highly reminiscent of *RR* 16334–36. Koeppel suggests the possibility that
they may be genuine, especially considering that they follow immediately a passage Chaucer
echoed earlier (see note 1993); SK feels they are probably "reminiscences of two *genuine*
lines." WR notes their absence from TR but not their absence from La. Hertzberg (1866:
625) says that they are entirely *mal à propos*.

Ire is a synne: According to SK, the friar's sermon on ire begins with this line.
Tupper (1915c:260), Merrill (1962:346), and RB note parallels between the sermon on ire
which extends from this point (and could be said to begin at line 1981) for nearly 100 lines
and *ParsT* 533ff. Chapman (1929:178), endeavoring to demonstrate Chaucer's knowledge of
artes praedicandi, notes that "the prying limiter . . . does not begin, in the approved manner,
with a text from Scripture, but with a definition of the subject."

2007 **hymself:** The sinner himself, as SK notes.

2008–09 Zietlow (1966:11) points to the ambiguity of "this" which is not resolved

Kan seye, how ire engendreth homicide;
Ire is in sooth executour of pryde.   2010
I koude of ire seye so muche sorwe
My tale sholde laste til tomorwe,
And therfore praye I God bothe day and nyght,
An irous man, God sende hym litel myght.
It is greet harm and certes greet pitee   2015

2009 **homicide**} homice Pw
2010 **is in sooth**} is of s. Ad³; in s. is Cp He La+ CX¹,² WN PN²; in s. ~ PN¹
executour} the e. He+ CX¹,² WN PN²–UR; the e. is ~ PN¹
2011 **I koude of ire seye**} Of i. right k. I s. ~ UR   **so**} right (Tc²) CX¹–PN²
2012 **My**} That my He+ CX¹–UR   **til**} vnto Pw+   **tomorwe**} the morowe ~
PN¹ UR
2013 *Spur. lines bef.* 2013: Ire is þe grate of synne as saith þe wise / To fle þer fro ech
man schuld him deuyse Ha⁴ WR   **praye I**} I p. Cp La Pw+ TH¹–SP³   **bothe**} *om.*
La+
2014 **An**} That to an He+ CX¹–SP³; To an (Se) UR   **God**} he ~ TH¹–SP³; that
he ~ UR; *om.* Cp La+   **sende**} sent Pw+   **hym**} *om.* (Ne+) CX¹–UR
2015 **certes**} eek El Ad³ Gg Pw+ TH¹–SP³ RB¹; also Ha⁴ WR

---

until the end of line 2009 as characterisic of the friar's rhetorical ineptitude or inattention:
"his argument is exasperatingly incoherent and it is no wonder that Thomas becomes so
angry with it." Merrill (1962:348), echoed by Giaccherini (1980:156), notes that the inter-
dependence of backbiting (in which the Summoner and Friar Huberd are engaged) and wrath
is articulated in *ParsT* 564–65, and that ironically "the 'homicide' each commits in anger can
only end in ironic suicide. So blinded by anger is each to his own vulnerability that he finds
himself in the impossible situation of a Siamese twin poisoning his brother."

   2008 **viker or persoun:** MR ignore the Ha⁴ La variant on *viker*, perhaps rightly, but
OED lists *vicary* as a separate word. § Jephson (Bell 1855:2.114) notes that "the friar
characteristically calls the parson and vicar *lewd*, that is, unlearned. The parson is properly the
parish priest, or rector; the *vicar* a substitute appointed by the religious house to which the
great tithes were sometimes granted, on condition that they provided for the cure of souls in
the parish."

   2010 Koeppel (1891*b*:44) and SK note the parallelism to *ParsT* 534: "And as wel
comth Ire of Pride as of envy"; Koeppel notes as well a parallelism to *ParsT* 564: "Of this
cursed synne of Ire cometh eek man-slaughtre."

   2011–12 Craik (1964:126) comments that "the dreadful prospect of twenty thousand
examples [line 1997] is matched by the style of this complacent couplet, with its unspeak-
ably monotonous second line."

   2013 WR observes that Ha⁴'s couplet before this line does not appear in TR, but
WR neglects to point out that the couplet is also absent in La. Hertzberg (1866:625)
remarks that it (as well as Ha⁴'s couplet before line 2049) merely amplifies the point of the
passage and offers nothing new. He regards all of Ha⁴'s spurious lines in *SumT* as scribal
inventions. See also note 2005, above.

To sette an irous man in heigh degree.
   Whilom ther was an irous potestat,
As seith Senek, that durynge his estat
Upon a day out ryden knyghtes two,

2016   **sette**] see ~ SP[2,3]
2018   **that**] *om.* Cp La+   **his**] es h. Pw (Pw[1] *corr.*)   *Spur. line*: A jug he was a man of hiȝe astate He; Whiche (That Ii) hasty was in Jugement algate (Ii+) CX[1]
2019   **out ryden**] ther r. o. He

2016   **heigh degree:** Merrill (1962:347) suggests that "the fact that all three illustrations are concerned with the effects of anger on men of high degree is certainly a satiric jab" at both Friar Huberd and the Summoner, the friars because of their high opinions of themselves and the Summoner because he "holds a position of some authority."

2017   *Glosses:* De quodam potestate iracundo El (*marginal*) Ad[3] (*in text*); Of an Irous potestat Gg.

     As Birney (1960:214) points out, the morals Friar John draws from these exempla put the emphasis "not upon the spiritual harm of anger but on its physical dangerousness"; Owen (1955:230) argues that the Summoner's personal anger distorts his story: "the lecture is now about the sinfulness of anger, now about the dangers of angering." Adams (1962:127), speaking of the moral irrelevance of John's conclusions, feels that John uses the anti-ire parables "to warn Thomas away from 'lords' (covertly meaning the regular clergy) and to recommend the 'poor,' i.e., the friars." Zietlow (1966:12) feels that the anecdote "more appropriately illustrates the evil of following the letter of the law than the friar's ostensible thesis" and notes that "Seneca defines the judge's mistake as the confusion of firmness with inflexibility." Richardson (1970:152) feels that the inversion of justice illustrated by the anecdote of the judge foreshadows the later scene when Friar John complains to the lord and rather than receiving amends receives only more humiliation. Diekstra (1974:6) comments that the exempla "convey a sense of absurdity, of pure chaos lurking round the corner" and "reveal Chaucer's sense of the precariousness of moral balance."

     irous potestat: The story of the irascible judge is told of Gnaeus Piso in Seneca's *de Ira* 1.18.3–6 (ed. Bryan and Dempster 1941:286–87), as TR (n. 7600) is the first to note. But though Lounsbury (1892:2.270) takes this and the anecdotes of Cambyses and Cyrus which follow as "the clearest evidence of Chaucer's actual perusal of the philosopher's work," a more likely source for this and the other two stories is, as Pratt (1966:627–31) shows, the *Communiloquium Sive summa Collationum* of John of Wales: "Comparison reveals that Chaucer's retelling of each anecdote is closer to John of Wales' redaction than to the original story as told by Seneca" (Pratt 1966:627). The same story, as TR, WR, SK and others have noted, is told of emperor Heraclius in the *Gesta Romanorum* ch. 140 (ed. Oesterley 1872:494–95).

2018   The Pw scribe began to write *estate* before *his*, caught himself, and marked the *es* for deletion. MR ignore this activity. Ne lacks this line, as the *b* ancestor must have done, for CX[1], Tc[2], Ii have one spurious line while He has another.

And as Fortune wolde that it were so,   2020
That oon of hem cam hom, that oother noght.
Anon the knyght bifore the juge is broght,
That seyde thus, 'Thow hast thy felawe slayn,
For which I deme thee to the deeth certayn,'
[An]d to another knyght comanded he,   83v   2025
'Go leed hym to the deeth, I charge thee.'
And happed as they wente by the weye
Toward the place ther he sholde deye,
The knyght cam which men wenden had be deed.
Thanne thoghten they it were the beste reed   2030
To lede hem bothe to the juge agayn.
They seyden, 'Lord, the knyght ne hath nat slayn
His felawe; heere he stant hool alyve.'

2020   **that**] right as Ha[4] WR; *om.* Cp La Pw+ TH[1]–UR   **were**] was Dd He+ CX[1]–PN[2]; shuld be Pw+ TH[1]–UR

2021   **noght**] did n. He+ CX[1]

2022   **bifore**] to for La+; afore (Ds+) PN[1]   **is**] was Pw+

2023   **That**] And Cp La+

2024   **the**] *om.* Cp Ha[4] La Pw+ PN[1] WR

2025   **And**] d Hg (*eaten away*)

2026   **Go**] To Ha[4]+   **leed**] lede l. Ad[3]   **the**] *om.* Pw+

2027   **And**] A. it (Ln+) TH[2]   **happed**] happe La

2028   **ther**] t. as Cp La+ SP[2,3] TR; t. þat He; where (Ne+) CX[1]–PN[2] TH[2]; t. where ~ UR

2029   **cam**] þey met He   **which**] w. þat Dd+ CX[1]   **men**] þey Cp La+ had] he h. Gg+

2030   **they**] t. that ~ SP[2,3]   **were**] was El Ad[3] Gg Pw+ TH[1]–TR   **reed**] rerede La

2032   **Lord**] L. lo ~ UR   **ne hath**] h. Ha[4] He+ CX[1]–UR WR; nys Pw+

2033   **felawe**] f. lo Ha[4] WR   **he**] *om.* La+   **hool**] *om.* Cp La+   **alyve**] on lyue Cp Ha[4] La+ WR; a loone Gg (Gg[2] *corr.*); and a. (To) UR

2020   Bowden (1964:89–90) remarks that "the Summoner, unlettered as he is, is aware of the part Fortune plays in life."

2030   MR write of the *was / were* variant that "the early draft had 'was,' which, though apparently changed into 'were' in the expanded copy, is found also in El, which has been with *d**[1] since 1991."

2033   **stant:** Editions since SK print *standeth*, the reading of El and others, perhaps for the sake of a smoother line. The line is a fine example of emphatic speech rhythm.

'Ye shul be deed,' quod he, 'so moot I thryve.
This is to seyn, bothe oon and two and thre.' 2035
And to the firste knyght right thus spak he,
 'I dampned thee, thou most algate be deed,
And thow also most nedes lese thyn heed,
For thou art cause why thy felawe deyth.'
And to the thridde knyght right thus he seith, 2040
'Thou hast nat doon that I comanded thee,'
And thus he dide do sleen hem alle thre.

2034 **Ye]** He Pw+ **quod he]** anoon Gg **thryve]** gone Gg (Gg₂ *corr.*)
2035 **This]** That El Ad³ Gg Ha⁴ Pw+ TH¹–SP³ TR–RB¹ RB² RI **is]** *om.*
La **and two]** t. Dd Ha⁴ La Pw+ CX¹–UR WR
2036 **to]** þoo to Pw+ **right]** *om.* Gg+
2037 **dampned]** deme Ha⁴+ WR; dampne Pw+ **thou most algate]** þe m. a.
Pw+
2038 *Spur. lines bef.* 2038: Than þoughte þay it were þe beste rede / To lede him forþ
in to a fair mede Ha⁴ WR **And thow also most]** A. quod þe juge a. t. m. Ha⁴ WR; A.
t. m. a. (Mc+) TH¹–SP³ **nedes lese]** l. Dd (Dd₁ *corr.*) Ha⁴+ WR; l. n. (Ph³) TH¹–SP³
2039 **art cause]** the c. a. ~ UR **why]** w. that Ad³+; of Pw+ **felawe deyth]**
felawes deth Pw+
2040 **knyght]** felaw Ha⁴ WR **right]** *om.* Ha⁴ Pw+ WR
2041 **that]** what ~ UR **comanded]** comaunde La+
2042 **he dide]** he let Ha⁴ SP²,³ WR **do sleen hem]** h. s. Gg He Pw+ CX¹
TH¹–SP¹ UR; s. h. La+; do h. s. (Tc¹) CX²–PN²

2034 **Ye:** MR do not record *He* in Pw.
2035 **This:** The MSS split almost evenly over the reading *This* or *That*. The line
illustrates exactly MR's argument (2.241) that "[after 1991] all the El readings to 2158,
except unique and those involving other MSS by patent *acco . . .* are with Gg–Si, Ad³ Ch
Ra³–Tc¹–Gl, Ps, and *d*∗¹."
2037 **most:** Gg has *wmuste*, with the *w* expuncuated.
2038 The spurious lines that precede this line in Ha⁴ were caused by an eye-skip back
to *be deed* in line 2029 and a subsequent recopying of line 2030 here. The note in WR on
these spurious lines, misnumbered 7612–13 (D 2030–31; the note actually applies to WR's
lines 7620–21), states: "I retain this and the following line, because they form part of the
Harl. MS., although they seem to be an unnecessary interruption of the sense. They are not in
Tyrwhitt." Having missed the numbering error in WR's note, Hertzberg (1866:625) dis-
putes the claim regarding TR and fails to take notice of the spurious lines. See also note
2013, above.
2040 **knyght:** The Ha⁴ scribe caught *felaw* from line 2039.
2042 **dide do sleen:** RB, followed by Richardson (RI), notes that "the repetition of
the causative *do* is unusual," though Mustanoja (1960:605) apparently does not find it un-
common, writing that "the causative *do* and *let* are occasionally followed by two infinitives, of
do and the principal verb; he cites this line among others.

Irous Cambyses was eek dronkelewe
And ay delited hym to been a shrewe,
And so bifel a lord of his meynee,   2045
That lovede vertuous moralitee,
Seyde on a day bitwix hem two right thus,
'A lord is lost if he be vicius,
And dronkenesse is eek a foul record
Of any man, and namely in a lord.   2050
Ther is ful many an eighe and many an ere

2043   **Cambyses]** Cambustus He+ CX^1 eek] thus e. Dd+
2044   **delited]** delite La+
2045   **of]** as of He; and Pw
2046   **lovede]** l. wele He+ CX^1–UR   **vertuous]** vertues and eek Ha^4 WR
2047   **on]** vpon Pw+   **betwix]** bitwene El; vnto Cp La+   **hem two]** himself
Cp La; h. Gg+; h. self He+ CX^1–PN^2
2048   **lost]** *om.* Hg (Hg$_2$ *corr.*)   **if he be]** if þat he be La+; if he be aught (Ha^3+)
CX^1–SP^3; *om.* Hg (Hg$_2$ *corr.*)   **vicius]** *om.* Hg (Hg$_2$ *corr.*)
2049   *Spur. lines bef.* 2049: An Irous man is lik a frentik best / In which þer is of
wisdom noon arrest Ha^4 WR   **And]** A La+   **is eek]** e. is Dd La Pw+ TH^1–UR
Lines 2049–50 : 2051–52 *trans.* ~ CX^2–PN^2
2050   **Of]** In Gg   **in]** of Ha^4 He+ CX^1–WR
2051   **ful]** wel Pw+; *om.* Ad^3 He+ CX^1–SP^3 **an eighe]** e. Ha^4 La+; an yre Pw+

2043   The story is told in Seneca, *de Ira*, 3.14.1–6 (ed. Bryan and Dempster 1941:
287), and Herodotus 3.34–35 (ed. Godley 1920–30:2.45–47), as first noted in TR (n. 7625),
but as Pratt (1966:630–31) shows, Chaucer's immediate source was probably the *Communilo-
quium* of John of Wales. Lowes (1915:281), arguing against Tupper (1914, 1915*b*, 1915*c*) on
the moral subject of *SumT*, points out that even here in the homily against Wrath the
Summoner includes a warning against Gluttony: "For the story of Cambyses . . . is an
exemplum against Drunkenness as well as Wrath." Zietlow (1966:12) argues that the friar
characteristically distorts the Senecan point of the exemplum, for "the main vice seems to be
Cambises' drunkenness rather than his anger," and in any case for Seneca Cambises is not the
important figure of the anecdote.
      eek: Dd's *thus,* seemingly drawing a conclusion from the preceding action,
suggests that the *a* exemplar perhaps equated *irous Cambyses* with the *irous potestat.*
2047   **betwix:** MR do not report the variant *bitwix / bitwene,* perhaps considering it
insignificant, but *MED* lists the two separately, as descending from different OE words.
2048   **lost if he be vicius:** The phrase is supplied in Hg in a hand described by Doyle
and Parkes (1979:xlvi) as "a large set Secretary of the first or second quarter of the fifteenth
century." See further note 2052.
2049–52   CX^2 through PN^2 transpose the couplet 2049–50 with 2051–52, giving
the line order 2051 2052 2049 2050. The transposition is not attested in any MS.
2049   The spurious lines that precede line 2049 in Ha^4 are, WR notes, peculiar to
Ha^4; see note 2038, above.

Awaityng on a lord, he noot nat where.
For Goddes love, drynk moore attemprely.
Wyn maketh man to lesen wrecchedly
His mynde, and eek his lymes everychon.'   2055
    'The revers shaltow se,' quod he, 'anon,
And preve it by thyn owene experience,
That wyn ne dooth to folk no swich offence.

    2052   **Awaityng]** Awaytand Ha⁴ WR; In waytinge Pw+   **on a lord]** on a man Dd He+; *om.* Pw+   **he]** and he Hg (and *eras.* Hg₂) El Ad³ Cp Gg Ha⁴ La Pw+ WR– RI   **noot nat]** noot El Ad³ Cp Gg Ha⁴ La Pw+ WN TH¹–RI; wot nat Dd He+ PN¹

    2053   **love]** *om.* Pw+   **drynk]** dringeþ Cp Dd He La Pw CX¹–UR   **moore]** *om.* ~ SP²,³   **attemprely]** temperatly (Ne+) CX¹–UR

    2054   **man]** a m. Cp Dd He Pw+ CX¹–UR   **lesen]** lyve He+ CX¹   **wrecchedly]** viciously He

    2055   **eek]** *om.* El Ad³ Gg Pw+ TH¹–SP³

    2056   **quod he]** and þat Gg+

    2057   **owene]** *om.* Pw+

    2058   **ne dooth]** d. Cp La+   **no swich]** s. Dd (Dd₁ *corr.*) He+ CX¹–PN²

    2052 **he noot nat where:** Hg originally read "and he noot nat where"; *and* has been erased and replaced with a dash. MR do not offer an opinion on who corrected the text; according to Doyle and Parkes (1979:xliii), it was the original scribe. Evidence would suggest rather that the correction was made by a later hand (Hg₂). Apart from the added dash, there is no writing here that would permit identification of a scribal hand. But Doyle and Parkes (1979:xlvi) identify two other corrections on the same page (at lines 2048 and 2064) as the work of a later scribe, "Hand F." Why shouldn't all the corrections on folio 83*v* be by the same corrector? We may hypothesize that the long, obvious omission at line 2048 (probably owing to a defective exemplar since the Hg scribe is usually very careful and the omission is so egregious) led a corrector to find a text from which to supply the missing words. It may be that in comparing this text with Hg he noted the discrepancies at lines 2052 and 2064 and introduced the readings of the correction text at these places as well. The correction text must have belonged to MR's Group II (*a*–Ln Ii–Ha³–*b*), since only this group accounts for all the adjustments. Probably the manuscript belonged to the *a*–Ln subgroup since only He of the Ii–Ha³–*b* subgroup matches Hg at line 2048 (the others add *aught* or *caught* after *be*).

        MR choose their reading because it is supported by 32 of the 38 manuscripts in their Group I, by the independent manuscript Ha⁴, by Bo² (now Hg's only cohort in Group IV), and by the unclassified manuscript Py.

    2053 **drynk:** Following their customary practice, MR do not record the variants of the imperative; see note 1671, above.

    2056 This edition follows SK, RB, PR, and RI here in considering *anon* as part of Cambises' speech, but it could be spoken by the narrator, in which case the quotation mark preceding *anon* would be moved to stand before *And* in line 2057.

Ther is no wyn bireveth me my myght
Of hond ne foot, ne of myne eyen sight.'   2060
And for despit he drank ful muchel moore,
An hundred part than he hadde doon bifore,
And right anon this irous cursed wrecche
Leet this knyghtes sone bifore hym fecche,
Comandynge hym he sholde bifore hym stonde,   84r   2065
And sodeynly he took his bowe in honde,
And up the streng he pulled to his ere,
And with an arwe he slow the child right there.
'Now wheither have I a siker hand or noon?'

2059   **is**] nys Pw+ TH¹–UR   **bireveth**] that b. He+ CX¹   **me**] *om.* La (La₁
corr.)   **myght**] wit Ha⁴+
2060   **ne foot**] of f. Ha⁴+ CX¹–SP³ WR; ne of f. Pw+
2061   **ful muchel**] m. þe Gg He+ CX¹–PN² UR; m. Ha⁴ Pw+ TH¹–SP³ TR WR
2062   **part**] tymes ~ TH¹–UR   **hadde doon**] h. El+; did He+ CX¹–UR
bifore] to fore La+
2063   **anon**] ay ~ SP²–TR   **irous cursed**] c. Cp La+; c. i. (Ph³) TH¹–TR
2064   **Leet this knyghtes sone**] T. k. s. l. Hg₂ Dd+ CX¹–PN² UR TR; T. knyght
his s. l. He; L. þise k. sones Pw+   **bifore**] anoon b. Ha⁴ WR; tofore Pw+
2065   **Comandynge hym**] And c. hem Cp La+; C. hem Ha⁴ Pw+ WR; And h.
commaundit He; Comaundid h. (Ha³+) CX¹–PN²   **he**] þey Cp Ha⁴ La Pw+ WR; *om.*
He   **sholde bifore hym**] to forn him for to He; schol b. h. La; s. tofore h. Pw+
2066   **sodeynly**] woodly He+   **in**] on Cp Gg Ha⁴ La Pw+ WR   **honde**] his
h. He+
2067   **streng**] styng Gg (*corr.*)   **pulled**] pulleth Dd He+ CX¹; pulle La; plucked
~ SP²,³
2068   **he**] *om.* ~ UR   **right**] *om.* (Fi+) CX¹–SP³
2069   **wheither have I**] w. h. He; weþe h. I La   **a**] *om.* Gg La+

2061   On the omission of *ful* in Ha⁴ and Pw and some editions, SK writes "[Pw and
Ha⁴] omit it, and actually read *dronk-e*(!), with an impossible final *e*. Tyrwhitt has *dranke*,
omitting *ful*, and even Wright, Bell, and Morris [1866*b*] have *dronk-e*, with the same omis-
sion. Owing to the carelessness of scribes, who often added an idle final *e*, such forms as
dranke, dronke are not very astonishing. But it would be very curious to know *how these editors
scanned this line*" (emphasis SK's).
2064   Hg₂ added *.b.* in the left margin and *.a.* below the line after *sone* to indicate a
transposition. The hand is the same as that described in note 2048. If the transposition were
effected, the Hg line would read as the *a* MSS and CX¹. See also note 2052, above.
2067   **streng:** MR ignore *styng* in Gg.
   pulled: In MR's CV, La's *pulle* is treated as a form of *pulleth*.

175

Quod he. 'Is al my myght and mynde agoon?   2070
Hath wyn byreved me myn eye sight?'
   What sholde I telle th'answere of the knyght?
His sone was slayn, ther is namoore to seye.
Beth war, therfore, with lordes how ye pleye.

2070   **Is}** is is Pw (Pw₁ *corr.*)   **myght and mynde}** m. a. my m. Ad³+; m. a. my witte Cp+; mynde a. might Ha⁴+ WR; witte a. my witte La
   2071   **byreved}** bireuen ~ ST–UR
   2072   **th'answere}** a. Pw+
   2073   **is}** nys Ad³ Dd Pw+   **namoore}** more La+
   2074   **Beth war}** Be war Ad³ Dd Ha⁴ Pw PN¹ TH¹–UR WR   **how ye}** for to Ad³ He+ CX¹–PN² TR; h. to Dd (Dd₁ *corr.*)+

2070   MR ignore the dittography and correction in Pw.

2073   **was:** MR erroneously report *is* for *was* in Ad³, a clerical error; their collation card shows that Ad² reads *is.*

2074–78   "Anything better calculated to make Thomas 'as angry as a pissemyre,' whether he thinks of himself as a 'lord' or 'povre man,' or neither, is hard to imagine," notes Pearsall (1985:227). The "inept use of these examples is not Chaucer's but the friar's," according to Craik (1964:125–26), and the inappropriateness of this moral drawn from these exempla is underlined by both Robertson and Huppé. Robertson (1962:273) writes: "instead of illustrating the disadvantages of wrath to the wrathful man himself, they show the dangers of associating with wrathful persons, especially those with any power. . . . The *exempla* have no relevance to Thomas, who only becomes more wrathful at what he hears, but they do apply to the friar, who is associating with a wrathful man while he is telling them." Huppé (1964:207) observes: "It is a moral which Friar Huberd had taken very much to heart, as we recall from the *General Prologue,* but what it has to do with Thomas' presumed anger is not immediately obvious. However, its relevance derives from the fact that the friar is the wife's spokesman; in his argument he wishes to demonstrate that Thomas' anger is to be defined as his failure to submit . . . to his wife's demands." Owen argues (1955:230–31 and 1977:165–66) that the Summoner's struggle to maintain control of his story and over his own anger ends in defeat with the exempla on wrath leading him off the track in the Cambises exemplum to an attack on the friar's syncophancy, but Pearsall (1985:227) argues that such readings miss the point that the speech "grows out of [the friar's] character and the situation in which he finds himself." Giaccherini (1980:156) also notes the echo of Huberd's *GP* portrait (A 221–32), and adds that the passage ironically anticipates the friar's conversation with the lord of the village. As Richardson (1970:153) puts it, what the friar means is that "one should not tell a lord about the lord's vices, but by an ironic twist of this hypocritical advice, his own final humiliation comes because he has failed to beware of how he 'pleyes' with a lord, has failed to take heed of what he reveals of HIS OWN vices." In exploring the misapplication of proverbs and other monitory elements in *SumT,* MacDonald (1966:462–63) notes that the friar seriously underestimates the intensity of Thomas's wrath, and that while the *sententiae* and *exempla* which pepper his sermon on wrath are legitimate in themselves, "in the actual context of the Friar's misconceptions . . . the monitory elements . . . serve only to emphasize his folly, to provide an ironic background for his own subsequent

Syngeth '*Placebo*,' and 'I shal if I kan,'   2075
But if it be unto a poure man;
To a poure man men sholde his vices telle,
But nat to a lord, thogh he sholde go to helle.
  Lo, irous Syrus, thilke Percien,

2075   **Syngeth**] Syng Ad³ Gg Pw TH¹–UR
2076   **unto**] to Pw+
2077   **a**] *om.* Pw+   **men sholde**] he s. La+; s. he Pw+; s. (En³+) WN; one s. ~
TH¹–SP³
2078   **But**] *om.* ~ UR
2079   **Syrus**] tirrus He; arus Pw+; turrus (Ii+) CX¹   **thilke**] that He+; that
strong ~ CX¹; that ilke (Bo¹+) CX²–PN² UR

---

rage, and thus to prepare for the comic retribution that follows." Merrill (1962:348) and
Zietlow (1966:12–13) compare the friar's handling of the material with Seneca's, Zietlow
writing that one of Seneca's morals is "the baseness of flattery, which, in this case, is worse
than the murder itself. The moral with which the friar concludes his version of the example is
a corruption of this point." See further note 2075.

2074   **Beth**: MR do not report such imperative form differences as *beth / be*; see note
1671, above.

2075   **Syngeth**: MR do not record the different imperative forms here; see note 1671,
above.

Placebo: According to TR (n. 7657), echoed by WR and Hertzberg (1866:
625), "the allusion is to an Anthem in the Romish church, from Psalm cxvi.9, which in the
Vulgate [114.9] stands thus: *Placebo Domino in regione vivorum* ["I shall please the Lord in the
lands of the living"]. Hence the *complacent* brother in the *Merchant's Tale* is called *Placebo*."
Jephson (Bell 1855:2.116), followed by SK, feels that the Psalm "was familiar to everyone in
Chaucer's time, as it formed one of the antiphons in the office for the dead." Düring (1883–
86:3.375), Koeppel (1891*b*:44), RB, Boyd (1967:66–67), and Richardson (RI) also note the
use of the word in *ParsT* 617: "Flatereres been the develes chapelleyns, that syngen evere
Placebo." Though RB adds that *Placebo* "came to be used proverbially for flattering complai-
sance," Fleming (1965:17) argues that the evidence for proverbial status prior to Chaucer is
thin, that of the non-Chaucerian ME instances offered by RB and SK, only the *Ayenbite of
Inwit* (ed. Morris 1866*a*:60) shows ironic use, as in Chaucer, and he suggests that ll. 617–19,
844–58, 1041–42 in the satiric *Roman de Fauvel* (1314) [ed. Långfors 1914–19:26, 34–35,
41] might have been Chaucer's inspiration.

2079   **irous Syrus**: The story of irascible Cyrus is told in Seneca, *de Ira*, 3.21.1–3 (ed.
Bryan and Dempster 1941:287) and in Herodotus 1.189, with further reference in 1.202 and
5.52 (ed. Godley 1920–30:1.235–37; 1.255; 3.59) as first noted in TR (n. 7662), but as in
the stories of the irascible magistrate and Cambyses (see notes 2017 and 2043) Pratt (1966:
629–30) shows that the version in John of Wales's *Communiloquium* is closer to Chaucer than
Seneca's. Birney (1960:212) notes the jingle in this phrase, which he connects with the puns
in lines 1877–78 and 1916–17. Merrill (1962:349) remarks on the parallelism between the
ridiculous over-response of Cyrus and the quarrel between Summoner and Friar: "they, like
Cyrus, allow a minor irritation to crescendo with costly consequences."

How he destroyed the ryver of Gysen   2080
For that an hors of his was dreynt therinne
Whan that he wente Babiloyne to wynne.
He made that the ryver was so smal
That wommen myghte wade it over al.
Lo, what seyde he that so wel teche kan,   2085
'Ne be no felawe to an irous man,

2080   **he destroyed]** d. he Dd He+ CX¹–SP³   **of]** *om.* ~ UR
2082   **that]** as ~ SP²,³; *om.* Pw+ TH¹–SP¹   **to]** forto (Ln+) CX¹–PN² UR
2084   **wommen]** men Pw (Pw₁ *corr.*)+ CX¹–UR   **myghte]** m. ride and (Tc²)
CX¹,² WN–SP³; m. ride or ~ PN¹ UR   **wade it]** w. Cp La+ CX¹–UR; passed Pw; it w.
(En²+) TR
2085   **what seyde]** *om.* Pw+   **he that]** t. he Pw+
2086   **be]** be ye Pw+   **an]** no Ad³ Dd² La Pw+ TH¹–TR; no an ~ PN¹

2080   **Gysen:** As TR first notes (n. 7662), the river is called *Gyndes* in Seneca. Jephson
(Bell 1855:2.117) suggests that the river "is probably that mentioned in Gen. 2:13." TR
(n. 7666) writes that "Sir J. Mandeville [ed. Hamelius 1919–1923:1.25] tells the story of the
Euphrates;—'because that he had sworn, that he sholde putte the ryvere in such poynt, that a
womman myghte wel passe there, withouten castynge off of hire clothes.'" The note is
echoed by WR and SK. Hertzberg (1866:625) says that Chaucer corrupted the name of the
river, but Lange (1938:80) argues that Chaucer gets his version of the name from Mandeville
(ed. Hamelius 1919–1923:1.27), who calls the river *Gyson*. According to Lange, who argues
for close verbal echoes of Mandeville in Friar John's retelling of the story, no one before
Mandeville uses this name. Magoun (1953:119; 1961:80), however, explains that *Gysen* is "a
distortion long antedating Chaucer of Gyndes (Lat. *Gyndes*, acc. *-en*), now Diala or Kerkah(?),
tributary of the Tigris." Magoun notes further that any copy of Seneca Chaucer might have
had would have undoubtedly had the form *Gysen*, as the error was first corrected by Erasmus.
Pratt's establishment (see note 2017) of John of Wales's *Communiloquium* as Chaucer's actual
source seems to settle the issue, and it is interesting to see that his citation of the *Communilo-
quium* (Pratt 1966:630) shows that John also gives the river's name as *gisen*.
      2081   **dreynt:** Though MR report *drenkt* and *drenched* as variants in Gg and La+
respectively, *MED* lists both, along with *dreint*, as past participles of *drenchen*, and they are
excluded from the variants here.
      2084   **wommen:** Leaving aside Pw, only Tc² and Ii read as CX¹ and its successors,
but the error was persistent. TR notes (n. 7666) "That wimmen] So the best Mss. agreably to
the authors just quoted [i.e., Seneca, Herodotus]. The Editt. have—That *men* might *ride* and
wade &c."
      2085   **he:** Commentators since Jephson (Bell 1855:2.117) note the allusion to Prov-
erbs 22.24–25; *he* is thus Solomon. Düring (1883–86:3.375) also adduces Proverbs 14.7, but
its relevancy is not clear.
      2086–88   Landrum (1924:96) takes the close parallelism between "*felawe to an irous
man*" and Proverbs 22.24 "Noli esse *amicus homini iracundo*" as evidence for Chaucer's inde-
pendent use of the Vulgate, but Pratt (1966:631) shows that John of Wales's *Communilo-*

Ne with no wood man walke by the weye,
Lest thee repente'; I wol no ferther seye.
    Now Thomas, leeve brother, lef thyn ire;
Thow shalt me fynde as just as is a squyre.   2090
Hoold nat the develes knyf ay at thyn herte

2087   **walke**} þat walkeþ Pw+
2088   **Lest**} lasse Pw   **thee**} thou (Ne+) CX¹–UR   **I wol**} ther is El SK
no ferther} namoore to El SK; no more Cp La+; no lenger Ha⁴+ WR
2090   **is a**} a He+ CX¹–PN²
2091   **ay at**} alway at Ha⁴; ageyn He; ay þat La; ay yn Pw+ CX¹–UR; ay to (Ha⁵)
TR   *Lines 2091–92 trans.* Ha⁴+ WR

---

quium, the source of Chaucer's anecdotes of irascible men (see note 2017) also provides the passage. Zietlow (1966:13) remarks that the friar's conclusion to the Cambises story is absurd: "the river could hardly have taken such advice."
    2086   Baker (1962:40) calls this "an exquisitely ironic touch in view of the Friar's subsequent behavior."
            to an: Dd had originally written *to an*, but marked out *an* and inserted *non* above it.
    2090   **just as is a squyre:** SP² is the earliest editor to gloss *squyre* as "a carpenter's rule." SK takes the phrase to mean "as exact (i.e. upright) as a square. He means that he will deal out exact justice, and not condone the sick man's anger without appointing him a penance for it. A *squire* is a measuring-square, or T-square." It might also be possible that the friar, urging Thomas to confess (see line 2093) is promising not to be overly strict in assigning penance. Clark (1976*a*:165, 168), arguing that the friar is an ironic parody of St. Thomas of India (see note 1980), notes that the carpenter's square was his iconographic emblem. Whiting (1968:S645) lists this as a proverb. Huppé (1964:208) suggests that the phrase involves "unconscious word-play, involving the squire's suggestion for a just distribution of Thomas' gift." He does not specify whether he means the Summoner's or Chaucer's unconscious; it cannot be the friar who is anticipating the tale's conclusion. Levy (1966:50), Richardson (1970:153–54 and RI), and Giaccherini (1980:157) also suggest that we think about lines 2243–80, where an equally just measurement is made of the fart, and one might add that the measurement is made by another (kind of) squire. Haskell (1976:61) also argues that the square is connected to St. Thomas of India, who is credited "not only with the building of churches, but with his disdain for gold." This image and the following "devil's knife" (see line 2091 and note) form a contrastive pair.
    2091   **develes knyf:** Shain (1955:241) suggests the influence of pulpit rhetoric in the figure of speech (cf. note 1818–21, above). According to Havely (1975:145), "anger is often shown in medieval and Renaissance paintings holding a knife. By claiming that Thomas is pointing the 'knife' at his *own* heart Friar John is reminding him of the suicidal nature of anger which he has already mentioned in [line 2007]." Richardson (1970:153–54) notes that Jankyn the squire will wield the "'develes knyf' provided by the friar's own anger" in the final scene. Haskell (1976:61) also adduces the iconographic association between anger and the knife aimed at the self, and feels that there is perhaps a deliberate contrast intended between this image and the carpenter's square (see note 2090).
            ay: WR notes that Ha⁴'s *alway* "seems to destroy the metre."

(Thyn angre dooth thee al to soore smerte),
But shewe to me al thy confessioun."
"Nay," quod the sike man, "by Seint Symoun,
I have be shryven this day at my curat.   2095

2092   **thee]** me He+ CX^1 **al to soore]** s. for to He
2093   **shewe to]** s. it Pw+
2094   **the]** þis Cp Dd Ha^4+ WR   **Symoun]** Simeon Pw+
2095   **at]** of Ha^4+ CX^1–WR

2093   Richardson (RI) adduces *GP* 218–20 and *Rom* 6364–65 for other statements on the power of friars to hear confessions.

2094–98   SK cites as relevant Wyclif's complaint that the friars "cryen faste that thei haf more power in confessioun then other curatis; for thei may schryve alle that comen to hem, bot curatis may no ferther then her owne parischens (ed. Arnold 1869–1871:3.374)" and *Rom* 6390–98. Fleming (1983:15) indeed takes *Rom* 6390–6440 to be the source of the scene, with the role of friar and curate reversed. Craik (1964:126–27) writes that Thomas's remarks on having been shriven show that he "is not an irreligious man" and constitute an "implied rebuke to the friar for his earlier aspersions on priests [lines 1816–17]." Zietlow (1966:9) argues that Thomas's words are designed to reveal his mounting impatience with the friar's impostures: "The only appropriate course for the friar is to retreat as gracefully as possible; what he does is as obtuse as any of the actions of the Friar's summoner." Koeppel (1891*b*:44), SK, Patterson (1978:366–67), and Richardson (RI) note that the same idea is found in *ParsT* 1008: "I seye nat that if thow be assigned to the penitauncer for certein synne, that thow art bounde to shewen hym al the remenaunt of thy synnes, of which thow hast be shryven of thy curaat, but if it like to thee of thyn humilitee." Arguing that Chaucer incorporated material from his tales, written earlier, into *ParsT*, Patterson notes that the Parson's inclusion of this advice is, given the conventions of such penitential works, eccentric, but "in the context of the *Summoner's Tale*, on the other hand, it is appropriate and subtle: challenged by a grasping penitenciary, Thomas replies with perfect correctness, showing a knowledge of canonistics that makes him more than a match for his ostentatiously learned opponent" (1978:368–69).

2094   **Seint Symoun:** Haskell (1971:218–24) claims that Thomas's oath refers to Simon Magus, whose story is told in the apocryphal *Acts of Peter* (ed. James 1924:307–33) and who, as an Antichrist figure, would be brought to mind by *SumT*'s several mentions of the devil and fire, and the parallelism between the flight and fall of Simon and the ascent and fall of Friar John. She also notes that in the play of *Antichrist* thunder accompanies the destruction of Simon Magus, and wonders whether Chaucer had that thunder in mind when he described Thomas's "earbreaking cataclysm of the 'soun'" (Haskell 1971:224). Richardson (RI) suggests that this Simon may be Saint Simon the disciple (Mark 3.18) or, as Haskell argues, Simon Magus.

2095   Richardson (RI) compares *ParsT* 1006.

shryven: Ross (1972:204) notes that *shrift* meant copulation in Shakespeare's day, but detects no obscene meaning here.

I have hym toold hooly al myn estat;
Nedeth namore to speke of it, seith he,
But if me list, of myn humylitee."
   "Yif me thanne of thy gold to make oure cloystre,"
Quod he, "for many a muscle and many an oystre,   2100
Whan othere men han been ful wel at eyse,
Hath been oure foode oure cloystre for to reyse,
And yet, God woot, unnethe the fundement

   2096   **hym toold**} t. h. Pw+ TH¹–SP³   **hooly al**} al h. Ad³ Cp Gg He La Pw+
CX²–PN² UR TR SK; al (Ii+) CX¹ TH¹–SP¹; h. (Ha³+) SP²,³   **estat**} hert He+ CX¹
   2097   **Nedeth**} It n. Cp Dd He La Pw+ CX¹–UR; N. it Gg   **to speke of it**} s. of
it Ad³ Cp La+   **seith**} sayde Cp He La Pw+ CX¹–PN²; quoth (Cn+) UR
   2098   **me list**} it l. He+ CX¹–PN²
   2099   **thanne**} *om.* Gg+   **thy**} ȝore Gg Pw+   **gold**} good Dd Ha⁴ He+ CX¹–
PN² WR   **oure**} o Pw (Pw₁ *corr.*)
   2100   **Quod**} Seid He+ CX¹–PN²   **many an**} *om.* ~ WN
   2101   *Lines 2101–02 trans.* Cp Ha⁴ La+ WR
   2102   **Hath**} Have He+ CX¹–PN² UR   **for**} *om.* Ha⁴+ WR   **to**} *om.* He
reyse} arreyse Ha⁴ WR
   2103   **yet**} *om.* Pw+   **the**} our He+ CX¹–PN²

   2096   **hooly al**: MR do not report the He reading *al hooly*, though it is correctly
reported on their collation card. The variant in SP²,³ is supported in effect only by Ma; the
variant occurs in Ha³, but that manuscript corrects the omission.
   2097   Though other modern editions punctuate this line to close the quotation after
"it," attributing "seith he" to the narrator (parallel to "quod the sike man"), "seith he" is
more likely to refer to the curate. *Seith* is rarely used to tag direct discourse in *SumT*; *quod* is
the preferred form, with *seyde* coming a distant second. The idea of the testimony of the
curate being adduced by Thomas to counter the importunings of the friar is attractive, and
the text as punctuated here means "there is no need to speak of it more, the curate tells me."
   2099–2106   Warton (1774:2.258) feels that this passage was inspired by the scene in
Piers Plowman B 3.47 in which Meed confesses to a friar.
   2099   **thanne**: Fleming (1983:16) notes the ease with which the friar shifts from
exhorting shrift to demanding gold, *thanne* signalling his considering the latter a suitable
alternative to the former.
      oure: MR ignore the error and correction in Pw.
   2100   **muscle . . . oystre**: According to Havely (1975:145), "mussels and oysters do
not seem to have been thought such delicacies in Chaucer's time as they are now. Friar John is
citing them here as examples of very cheap and simple food, such as would be fitting for poor
and abstemious friars. (Compare with this, though, the actual meal that he orders [lines
1839–43])." Bowden (1964:120) and Rowland also feel that "such shellfish was regarded as
poor fare" (Rowland 1971:89).
   2101   **at eyse**: Hg reads *ateyse*.
   2103   **fundement**: Though the friar is speaking of a literal foundation, Baum (1956:

Parfourned is, ne of oure pavement
[N]ys nat a tyle yet withinne oure wones.   84v   2105
By God, we owen fourty pound for stones.

2104 **ne of oure**] and of o. Pw+; ne of o. ful He+; ne of o. chirche ful (Tc[2]) CX[1]–PN[2]   **pavement**] pament He Pw (Pw *corr.*) CX[1,2] WN PN[2]
    2105 **Nys nat a tyle yet**] ys n. a t. y. Hg (N *eaten away*) Dd Ha[4]+ TH[1]–SP[3] WR; Ther is n. a t. He+ CX[1]–PN[2]; Is n. a t. Pw+; There is n. y. a t. ~ UR   **wones**] house He+
    2106 **owen**] o. ȝit Ha[4]+ WR   **fourty**] fifty He+ CX[1]–PN[2]

---

237), seconded by Richardson (1970:155), Ross (1972:90), and Elliott (1974:221), detects a pun, adding that "the other meaning, with the same spelling, is in [*PardT*] C 950": "Though it were with thy *fundement* depeint." Fleming (1966:698) agrees, noting that the friar is anticipating money, and that "the comic (as opposed to the merely farcical) element in the disappointing gift which he receives lies in the background of the rather peculiar view which St. Francis and his closest disciples took toward money. Francis considered the mere touching of coins a major offense for a friar, and he constantly likened money to dust, vipers, stones, and . . . excrement." Levy (1966:49) feels that the pun points both back to the image in *SumP* of the *develes ers*, and forward to Thomas's gift.
    2104 **pavement:** Though *pament* is ignored by MR as only a spelling variant of *pavement* (see s.v., *MED*), it is included in the collations here because it seems likely that the *b* MSS reading *ful pament* was taken by CX[1] to mean "full payment" (see *MED*, s.v. *paiement*, with the spelling *pament*), leading to the addition of *church*, with the passage then meaning "and yet, God knows, hardly the foundation / completed is, nor of our church full payment [completed is]." This reading would have been encouraged by the fact that in the *b* MSS, line 2105 begins with "There is," which looks like (and indeed can be) a new clause rather than the completion of "of our pavement / is not a tile." Finally, it is worth noting that Pw reads *payment*, with a correction to *payvement*, *ve* being added above the line and signaled by a caret below.
    2105–06 Fleming (1966:696), echoed by Giaccherini (1980:144), sees in the friar's appeal for building money an echo of contemporary antifraternal sentiment directed against the splendor of fraternal churches, citing Richard de Bury to the effect that "the aspirations of the mendicants have degenerated into excesses of 'the belly, clothes, and buildings.' In the light of the widespread antifraternal literature of the fourteenth century, practically every word in the friar's building appeal obliquely condemns him and his order." Fleming adds that "according to the *Speculum Perfectionis*, Saint Francis had insisted that the friars' churches be small, and their buildings made of wood and mud." Richardson (RI) notes criticism of fraternal building in Wyclif (ed. Matthew 1880:5, 14) and *Rom* 6571.
    2105 **tyle:** WR notes that "the pavements were made of encaustic tiles, and therefore must have been rather costly," while Jephson (Bell 1855:2.117) adds that "churches and public buildings were usually floored with tiles of various colours and patterns, in the arrangement of which exquisite taste was displayed."
    2106 **fourty pound:** Havely (1975:145) points out that fourty pounds was a good deal of money in Chaucer's day: "It was, for example, four times the annual salary that

Now help, Thomas, for Hym that harwed helle,
Or ellis mote we oure bookes selle;
And if yow lakke oure predicacioun,
Thanne gooth the world al to destruccioun. 2110

2108   Or] For El Ad³ Pw+ TH¹–TR SK RB¹ RB² RI   ellis] *om.* La   mote
we] moste we El Gg He+ CX¹–PN² SK RB¹ RB² RI; we most La+   **oure bookes]**
needs al o. b. ~ SP²,³; alle o. b. ~ UR
   2109   yow] ye El+ TR SK; we Cp La+; þu Dd He+; men (Tc²) CX¹–PN² UR
lakke] take He+
   2110   the] þis Pw+ TH¹–TR

Chaucer himself earned (between 1374 and 1386) as controller of customs in the Port of London."
   2107–10   Birney (1960:215) notes that "the hoarding of manuscripts bought from the profits of begging forms an item in the long list of complaints made against the friars by the antimendicant Archbishop, Fitzralph of Armagh." Fleming (1966:697) comments that "it is somewhat startling to discover that in the fourteenth century there was a considerable and vocal party which maintained that the friars *should* sell their books," opulent as they often were, in the spirit of absolute poverty. Thus, he continues (1966:697–98), "Chaucer was able to allude to a body of general antifraternal literature from within the friar's own camp, as it were, with an apparently harmless reference to books." Pratt (1966:639), demonstrating the importance to preaching friars of commonplace books like John of Wales's *Communiloquium*, from which Chaucer apparently took the exempla of Friar John's sermon on wrath (see note 2017), writes that "the wheedling friar appears to be proud of his sermon books, and he considers them to be most valuable. . . . Clearly the friar knew that without such books he could not preach!"
   2107   **Hym that harwed helle:** Christ. As SK, RB and RI note, the story of Christ's harrowing of hell, based on the apocryphal *Gospel of Nicodemus* (ed. Kim 1973, trans. James 1924:116–46), was extremely popular.
   2108   Lawler (1980:189 n.2) feels that "one of the funniest lines in this brilliant tale is [the friar's] attempt to extract a donation from Thomas with [this] threat—as if Thomas cared."
   Or: MR write that "in view of the fact that El is here derived from a *d**¹ MS, the evidence is in favor of 'or' as the reading of O¹" (3.467).
   mote we: MS support for the El *moste* is even slimmer, though it is interesting perhaps to note that the two El variants in this line associate it with two separate groups of MSS, which would tend to diminish the classificatory value of either variant, both of which are easy scribal slips.
   2109–13   Koeppel (1911:180–81) notes the parallelism of this passage to Cicero's *De Amicitia* 13.47, "Solem enim e mundo tollere videntur qui amicitiam e vita tollunt" ("They would appear to take the sun from the world who remove friendship from life"), though he thinks it more likely that Chaucer found the passage in a book like Peraldus's *Summa de virtutibus*, which contains it, than in Cicero's text. Pratt (1966:631) indeed reveals that the line is found in John of Wales's *Communiloquium*, twenty-five lines earlier than the verses quoted from Proverbs in lines 2086–88. Levitan (1971:237) suggests a parallel to *Rom*

For who so fro this world wolde us bireve,
So God me save, Thomas, by youre leve,
He wolde bireve out of the world the sonne.
For who kan teche and werchen as we konne?
And that is nat of litel tyme," quod he,   2115
"But sith Elie was, or Elize,

2111   **who so**] whos Cp+; w. La+   **fro this world wolde us**] wolde vs f. t. w.
El+ SK RB¹ RB² RI; wolde f. t. w. vs Cp La Pw+; wold vs f. þe w. Ha⁴ WR; wold f. t. w.
He; wol f. t. w. us (Ne+) CX¹–SP³; woll us f. the w. (Bo²) UR
    2113   **He**] Ye Ad³+   **of the**] o. this El Ad³ Dd Gg Ha⁴ He+ CX¹–RI
    2114   **who**] w. so Ad³+
    2115   **that**] þis Ha⁴ WR   **litel tyme**] lytyme Gg
    2116   **sith**] s. þat Gg SK   **Elie**] Ennok El+   **was**] w. her Ha⁴ WR   **or**]
and Ad³ Dd He+ TR   **Elize**] ele Ha⁴

7113–21, where Fals-Semblant speaks of the Joachimites' fondness for "making fantastic
comparisons to their own credit; as the sun is greater than the moon, . . . so their new 'gospel'
was better than the word of any evangelist." Olson (1986:230) suggests that Friar John is
offering a "'Joachimite' prophecy to promote building friar libraries to forestall the Johan-
nine world's end and Christ's return."
    2111   **fro this world wolde us:** The El reading printed by SK, RB and RI is
supported only by Ha³ and Hk, two MSS quite unrelated to one another or El (Ha³ is from
the *b** group, Hk from *d*¹); the inference may be drawn that all three MSS have edited or
slipped independently.
    2113   **the:** The MSS divide equally on *the* versus *this*, *d*¹ and *cd*² supporting the
former, *a*, *b*, and the Gg group the latter.
    2116   **Elie was or Elize:** "The friars claimed Elijah and Elisha, who, it appears [3
Kings (AV 1 Kings) 18.19–40], were supported on the voluntary principle, as examples of
their mode of life," Jephson (Bell 1855:2.118). Hertzberg (1866:584) states that the Car-
melites traced their origin to Elias and Elijah; Düring (1883–86:3.375) adds that they did so
because those prophets spent time on Mount Carmel, and cites further 4 Kings (AV 2 Kings)
2.25. SK writes that "there was great strife among the four orders of friars as to the priority of
their order. The Carmelites . . . actually pretended that their order was founded by the
prophet Elijah when he retired to mount Carmel to escape the wrath of Ahab; and by this
unsurpassable fiction secured to themselves the credit of priority to the rest. It is therefore
clear that the friar of Chaucer's story was a *Carmelite*, as *no other* friar would have alluded to
this story." Olson (1986:215), however, writes that Bonaventura claimed on behalf of Francis-
cans that mendicancy began with Elijah (see "Apologia Pauperum" 12.24 [ed. 1898:324]).
Manly (1926*b*:104) argues that "the point of the tale depends upon his being a member of
the same order as the Friar with whom the Summoner was quarreling, and whom the
scurrilous anecdote of the Summoner's prologue certainly proves to have been a Franciscan,"
but he offers no evidence regarding that point, nor does Bowden (1964:59), who writes that
the friar "is described as a Franciscan." Manly further notes that there was only one Franciscan
house in the district of Holderness, at Beverley, and that "Chaucer's readers would have

Han freres been—that fynde I of record—
In charitee, thonked be oure Lord.
Now Thomas help, for Seinte Charitee,"
And down anon he set hym on his knee.   2120
   This sike man weex wel neigh wood for ire;
He wolde that the frere hadde been afire

2117   that] *om.* Ha⁴ WR
2118   thonked] þon kidde Pw
2119   help] h. us ~ UR; *om.* Pw+ TH¹–SP¹
2120   And down] A d. Cp Ha⁴ La+ WR; Haue done Pw+   anon he set hym]
he s. h. a. Ha⁴ WR; a. he sittith He+ CX¹–SP³; a. he sit h. ~ UR   on his] on h. on h. La
(La₁ *corr.*)
2121   weex wel] wex Dd Gg He La Pw+ CX¹–SP¹; waxeth ~ SP²,³; woxin ~ UR
2122   wolde] woldin ~ UR   that] *om.* (Fi+) TH¹–SP³   afire] on a fire ~
SP²,³

---

understood him to have that one in mind," a claim that Fleming (1967:100) finds "shocking
from an historical point of view and obtuse from a literary one." Fleming argues here and
elsewhere (1966:689) that the anecdote of the nest of friars in hell is based upon the story of
Maria Misericordia, which was as often used by Carmelites as Franciscans, but that in any
case "it is quite unjustified to identify [the friar] as a Minorite or as a member of any other
particular order on the basis of the story," an argument seconded by Giaccherini (1980:157).
See further in notes to lines 1675–99, 1710, and 2128. Williams (1953:510) demonstrates
that such claims of antiquity were regularly attacked by the friars' antagonists, while, in an
article demonstrating the ubiquity of Carmelite propaganda in writing and the visual arts,
Koch (1959:548) notes that "so much was written by promoters of the cause that Chaucer
would have had little difficulty in finding the matter 'of record.'" Richardson (RI) notes that
"the Carmelites received their first rule in 1209 or 1210 and were endorsed by the papacy in
1226."
   Elize: WR observes that Ha⁴'s *Ele* is "an evident corruption by the scribe."
   2118   **thonked:** The spelling *y-thanked*, as found in all printed editions, is not a
variant, but it may be worth signalling that the Lydgate line found in Hg and others, and as
printed here, is perhaps more authentically Chaucerian metrically.
   2120   **on his:** MR ignore the dittography and correction in La.
   2121–30   Zietlow (1966:9–10) argues that the friar shows a characteristic obtuseness
here in not recognizing the peculiarity of Thomas's change of heart. "In a single action
Thomas, and through him the Summoner, has revealed two aspects of the friar: his obtuse-
ness and the essential grossness beneath his 'curteis' exterior."
   2121   Tupper (1914:113) cites this image in support of his reading *SumT* as an exem-
plum of Wrath. See further under "Thematic Issues" in Critical Commentary, pp. 37–38,
above.
   2122   **afire:** Some MSS (viz. El En² Fi Ha² Ha⁴ Hk Ii La Mc Ps Ra² Sl¹) read *on fire*,
which MR report as a variant of *a fire*. But as Mustanoja (1960:399) notes, *a* is a "weakened
denasalized form" of *on*, and "not uncommon before a consonant." *On fire* is accordingly not
counted a variant in these collations.   §   Szittya (1976:26) suggests that "Thomas' wish is

With his false dissimulacioun.
"Swich thyng as is in my possessioun,"
Quod he, "that may I yeve and noon oother;   2125
Ye sey me thus, how that I am youre brother?"
    "Ye certes," quod the frere, "trusteth wel;
I took oure dame oure lettre with oure sel."

2123   **his**} al h. He UR
2124   **thyng as is**} t. as is her Cp La+; tithis as is He+; thingis as ben (Tc²+) CX¹–
UR
2125   **that**} *om.* Gg   **may I**} I m. Cp He+   **and**} ʒow a. Dd Ha⁴ He+ CX¹
UR–WR RB¹ RB²
2126   **me thus**} me þis Gg+; t. He   **how**} *om.* El Cp La+
2127   **the**} this Ad³ Pw+ TH¹–TR   **trusteth**} ye t. Ad³+; t. me Cp La+ TH¹–
UR; t. me right He+ CX¹–PN²
2128   **oure lettre**} the l. Ad³ Dd Ha⁴ Pw+ TR WR; o. lettres Cp La+   **with**} and
El Ad³ He+ CX¹–UR; of Dd Pw+ TR; vnder Ha⁴+ WR

---

a reversal of the alighting of spiritual fire upon the apostles in Acts II. In one sense, Thomas gets his wish, for the friar departs from the Pentecostal *flatus* filled with the fire of rage, not like the apostles, with the fire of 'seinte charitee,' sent by the Holy Spirit." See further in note 1981–82.

2125   **and:** RB¹,² print the metrically smooth reading of Dd and Ha⁴, though the El spelling of *yeuen* for *yeve* would have accomplished the same metrical result. RI takes note of the El reading but prints as here.

2126   **youre brother:** Birney (1960:215–16) argues that Thomas's evocation of his fraternal relationship (see note 2128) with John as he prepares his revenge is a particularly deft touch: "by alluding directly to the relationship as he prepares to lure the friar's greedy hand under the bedclothes, [Thomas] easily tricks Brother John into thinking that an especially valuable gift . . . is about to be his for the grasping."

2128   **lettre with oure sel:** A letter of confraternity. TR (n. 7710) and Furnivall (1868:51) cite a document of 1347 as an example: "*Fratres Prædicatores,* Warwicc. *admittunt* Thomam Cannings et uxorem ejus Agnetem *ad participationem omnium bonorum operum conventus ejusdem*" ("The Friars Preachers, Warwick, admit Thomas Cannings and his wife Agnes into participation in all good works of the same convent"). WR, seconded by Hertzberg (1866:625) and SK, explains that "it was a common practice to grant under the conventual seal to benefactors and others a brotherly participation in the spiritual good works of the convent, and in their expected reward after death." Jephson (Bell 1855:2.118) points to *Jacke Upland*: " 'Why aske ye no letters of bretherhead of other men's praiers, as ye desire that other men aske letters of you?' [ed. Heyworth 1968:62; SK 7.193 § 17]. And again 'Why be ye so hardie to grant by *letters of fraternitie* to men and women, that they shall have part and merit of all your goode deeds?' [ed. Heyworth 1968:68; SK 7.198 § 49]." SK also cites *Jacke Upland,* and argues that "a benefactor could even thus belong to *all* the orders of friars at once," which "gives point to the question in l. 1955 above." Fleming (1967:101) writes that "the lay confraternities were probably the most important spiritual phenomenon of the late

"Now wel," quod he, "and somwhat shal I yeve
Unto youre holy covent whil I lyve, 2130
And in thyn hand thow shalt it han anon,
On this condicioun and oother noon,
That thow departe it so, my deere brother,
That every frere have as muche as oother;
This shaltow swere on thy professioun, 2135
With outen fraude or cavelacioun."
"I swere it," quod this frere, "upon my feith."

2129 **wel quod he}** q. he w. Pw+ TH¹–UR   **shal}** wil La+
2130 **whil}** w. þat Ha⁴+ WR
2131 **han}** hald Gg
2132 **On}** vp Cp Pw+; Vpon La+   **and}** an He
2133 **deere}** leeue El+ TH¹–UR; owne d. Cp La+; derere Gg
2134 **as muche}** also m. El La SK RB¹ RB² RI   **oother}** another (Fi+) SP²,³
2135 **This}** Thus Dd+; Thy Ha⁴
2137 **this}** the Dd Gg He Pw+ CX¹–TR   **upon}** by El Pw+ TH¹–UR RB¹ RB²
RI

Middle Ages" and says (p. 102) that as many as half the laymen of England probably belonged to some such confraternity in 1400. Richardson (RI) notes that Philippa Chaucer had herself received a letter of fraternity from Lincoln Cathedral in 1386. There is a "hidden barb," Fleming argues (1967:104) in this allusion to the confraternal *seal*, for the image of the Maria Misericordia, ironically inverted in *SumP*, was a common device on such seals; and Fleming finds it "amusing to speculate that the seal may well have looked much like one now in the Musée Cluny, from a Parisian confraternity, on which the members of the brotherhood are shown kneeling in security beneath the mantle of the Mother of Mercy" (pp. 104–05). Richardson (RI) also notes that these letters were severely criticized by Wycliffites; see, e.g. Arnold ed. 1869–1871:3.377–78, 3.420–29.

2130   **covent:** Levitan (1971:245–46 n. 19) holds that Chaucer is punning on OF *vent* here, so that "the friars' *covent* is both a religious house and a common wind," an argument accepted as possible by Giaccherini (1980:157). Levitan notes further that *SumT* "is not Chaucer's first irreverent jest on flatulence in a divine context," and cites Leyerle, who in turn argues that the eagle's speech on sound in *HF* is an "elaborate joke on flatulence" (Leyerle 1971:255). See further in note 2234.

2131   **in thyn hand:** "In a more concrete sense than he might have imagined," remarks Giaccherini (1980:157).

2134   **as muche:** *also m.*, found in El and La, and printed by SK, RB and RI, makes for a smooth line, but is supported by no other MSS. The pronunciation of final -e on *frere* produces an equally iambic line.

2136:   **cavelacioun:** "This is probably the earliest recorded use of the word *cavillacioun* in English, though it occurs also in *Sir Gawain and the Green Knight* (l. 2275), and must be 'in the air' at the time" (Brewer 1984c:214).

2137–52   Coghill (1966:129–30) remarks on the way Chaucer in this passage "swings

And therwithal his hand in his he leith.
"Lo, here my feith; in me shal be no lak."
"Now, thanne, put thyn hand down by my bak,"   2140

2138   therwithal] þer with Ha⁴+ WR
2139   here] by Ad³   feith] fey Ad³+; hond Ha⁴ WR
2140   Now] *om.* Cp Dd He La+ CX¹–TR   thanne put] t. p. in El+ RB¹ RB²
RI; p. t. Gg+   thyn hand down] t. h. a doun right Dd He+ CX¹–PN² UR TR; t. h.
adowne ~ SP²,³   by] at Ha⁴+ WR

---

forward on the rhymes, as on stepping-stones, from one swift narrative-thought to another."
He adds (p. 130) that "every rhyme here has peculiar importance, ease and force, and carries
the story along from one climax of gratified expectation to another."

2137   **upon:** El's *by* is also the reading of all 13 *d*∗¹ MSS (and only Ps otherwise), but
MR apparently regard the El–*d*∗¹ convergence as accidental here, since they do not list this
agreement as evidence for a common ancestor (2.241); that ancestor, in MR's reconstruction,
also sired Gg Ad³+, which agree with the present edition in what is usually taken to be the
authentic reading.

2138   Benson (1980:75) remarks that this "rather insignificant gesture fixes our atten-
tion on the friar's hand, the hand which will become so important within the next few lines."

2140–48   For comments on the ironic anticipation of this moment, see note 1817.
Zietlow (1966:18) remarks that for the Summoner, Friar John's groping "symbolizes the
activity of all friars; their pretensions, their gentility, their oratory all are aimed at the
culminating moment when the hand grasps the loot." Richardson (1970:156–57) adds that
Chaucer deflates the friar "by showing to what vulgar and ludicrous lengths his true 'grop-
ing' is willing to go"; Ross (1972:51) similarly finds the scene rich in poetic justice. Giac-
cherini (1980:158) remarks that Friar John shows that "he is not like those negligent curates
whom he accused of being 'slow / To grope tendrely . . . ,'" and Peltola (1968:567) finds in
the Summoner's "morbid interest in anal manipulations" a reinforcement of suggestions of
sexual deviancy in his *GP* portrait.

Clark (1976*a*:171) argues that this groping scene (lines 2119–51) parodies
the story of Doubting Thomas's handling of Christ's wounds in John 20.26–30. He points
out that in homilies, hagiography, poetry and drama, medieval English writers used *grope* for
Doubting Thomas's action (e.g., *Piers Plowman* B 19.165, "And toke Thomas by the hand
and taughte hym to *grope*"). Haskell (1976:62) also sees an "up-so-doun" version of the
Doubting Thomas story in this scene. Alford (1984:201–03) argues for the relevance of
another scriptural story, Genesis 24.1–4, which tells of Abraham requiring his servant Eliezer
to swear to seek a wife for Isaac not among the Canaanites but in his native land. "Put thy
hand under my thigh," Abraham orders. Alford notes that exegetical commentary on this
oath-taking "could hardly be a more exact indictment of the Friar" (1984:203), because in
such commentary Abraham was taken to stand for God the Father, Isaac for Christ, and the
bride-to-be for the Church. The servant was understood as a type of the good prelate or
preacher, and the daughters of Canaan as Churchmen who live soft lives in this world.
Lancashire sees yet another biblical parody operating here, a combination of the imagery of
the theophanies accorded Moses and Elijah: "Moses sees God's back parts from the cleft rock
where God's hand put him and covered him," and "the loud broken wind from Thomas'

188

Seyde this man, "and grope wel bihynde;
Bynethe my buttok there shaltow fynde
A thyng that I have hyd in pryvetee."
"A," thoghte this frere, "that shal go with me."
And down his hand he launcheth to the clifte,   85r   2145
In hope for to fynde there a yifte,

2142   **shaltow**] þou shalt Pw+ TH¹–SP³ TR
2144   **this**] the Ad³ Pw+ TH¹–SP³   **that**] this El Ad³+ SK
2145   **And down**] A d. Ad³ Pw+ TH¹–UR   **his hand he launcheth**] his h. he
launched Dd Ha⁴ He+ PN²; he shofth his h. ~ TH¹–UR   **to**] vnto Cp+ UR; into La+
2146   **In hope**] he hoped Cp La+; I h. Pw+   **for to fynde there**] þere forto f. Cp
La+; to f. t. (En¹+) PN²–UR   **a yifte**] som good y. (Tc²) CX¹–UR

'cleft'" distorts either "the thunder and trumpet call announcing God's first descents on
Sinai" to Moses or "the great godless wind that shatters the rocks when God passes by
another 'cleft,' Elijah's cave" (Lancashire 1981:24–25). Olson (1986:231–32) suggests a pa-
rodic inversion of the action depicted in Giotto's Bardi Chapel picture of St. Francis, "which
shows the saint on his deathbed while a friar, modeled after St. Thomas, reaches into the
wound in his side to experience Francis's spirit." O'Brien (1990:4) notes that alchemists
referred to their alembics in metaphors of the human body; fluids were heated in the "body"
until they condensed in the "head" and flowed out the "nose." In Thomas we have perhaps a
parody of such imagery. Whereas in *CYT* the gull is invited to "put in thyn hand and grope"
(G 1236) and does indeed find the (planted) silver, the groping here is rewarded only by the
"explosion" of the alembic Thomas.

2140   **thanne put:** The El reading of *thanne put In*, printed by RB and RI is shared
with only two MSS, En³ and Ad¹. These are members of *d*¹ (see note 2137), but the
connection may well be by coincidence here.

2141   See note 1817, above.

2143   **pryvetee:** Whittock (1968:140–41) is reminded both of Nicholas's claims in
MilT to knowledge of "Goddes pryvetee" and the devil's "privitee" experienced by the sum-
moner in *FrT*. Ross (1972:171) sees a double meaning in the words, "secret" and "private
parts." See further note to *Cristes secree thynges* in line 1871.

2144   **that shal go with me:** Hanning (1985:13) writes: "given his general hypoc-
risy, I believe we are justified in considering this an elliptical utterance, of which the unstated
conclusion is something like 'and not be shared with anyone else'—despite the fact that the
limiter has just sworn to share the gift equally with his entire convent."

2145   **launcheth:** Benson (1980:75) remarks that in 1426 Lydgate used this word to
mean "to lance, to release infection," and that perhaps "the friar's hand might also be re-
garded as a lance draining the infection of Thomas' ire and giving him some relief at last,"
but he adds that 1426 may be too late to support the suggestion.

2146   **yifte:** In arguing for Pentecostal allusions throughout *SumT*, Szittya (1974:27)
notes that the Holy Spirit was often referred to as God's Gift in Pentecostal liturgy. "Hence,
Thomas' mock 'yifte' of wind is a parodic reversal of the gift bestowed by God at Pentecost,
which also appeared in a wind."

And whan this sike man felte this frere
Aboute his tuwel grope there and heere,
Amydde his hand he leet the frere a fart,
Ther is no capul drawyng in a cart 2150
That myghte han late a fart of swich a sown.
    The frere up stirte as dooth a wood leoun;

2147   **whan this sike man**] þanne ful besy Cp La+   **felte**] was Cp La+
2148   **tuwel**] trwel Pw+   **grope**] gropyng Cp He La+ CX¹–UR   **there and heere**] t. a. there Ad³; h. a. t. Cp Dd He La Pw+ CX¹–UR
2150   **is**] nys El Ad³ Gg Pw+ TH¹–TR SK–RI   **a**] þe Cp La+
2152   **as dooth**] as it were Cp La+   **wood**] fers Cp La+; *om.* Pw+

2148   **tuwel:** SP²,³ and UR gloss "[the] tail"; literally, the word means a chimney [*OED*, s.v. *tewel*], though as Ross (1972:227) points out, it is here metaphorical for Thomas's "nether chimney."

    grope: Benson (1980:75) notes that the *OED* records a 1590 use of *grope* to mean "to handle (poultry) in order to find whether they have eggs"; he notes further that the word is used in describing the Summoner's ignorance in *GP* 644. See note 1817, above.

2149–51   Fleming (1966:699), reminding us of St. Francis's attitude that money was as filthy as excrement (see note 2103), writes that "according to the ideals of mendicancy, the friar gets precisely what he is looking for."

2149   Rowland (1971) and Wentersdorf (1980:251–53 and 1984:7) argue that passing gas was popularly regarded as a repellent against Satan: "This homeopathic cure was one which Luther advocated all his life, and he relates the story of a young lady acquaintance who followed his advice with success" (Rowland 1971:72). Thomas's act is thus seen as an attempt to rid himself of the importunings of the diabolic friar. Lawler (1980:189 n. 2) feels that "the fart satirizes preaching in the same way that Chauntecleer's 'chuk' or the inarticulate cries of both humans and animals in the chase scene in NPT satirize Chauntecleer's ample rhetoric."

2150   **is:** Hg shares this reading with 38 other MSS, and these are evenly distributed among the MR genetic groups, with the exception of their Gg–Si group, which (excepting Si) shares the El reading *nys*, printed by all modern editions. Tenuously, then—for the *nys / ys* variation is highly likely to follow scribal habits—this line may be taken to bear out part of MR's analysis of the El affiliation from line 1991 on. See note 2137.

    capul: According to Brewer (1984c:213), "some acquaintance with draught horses is necessary to realise the thunderous effect of the comparison."

2151   According to Ruggiers (1965:106), "the Summoner is at this juncture all too clearly the speaker, and the trumpet blast by which Chaucer characterizes him in the *General Prologue* [674] is echoed in the language" of the line. See also note 2226, below.

2152–68   Makarewicz (1953:223–24) suggests that Chaucer's "description of the Friar, who so ably denounced the sin of wrath and gave such an eminent example of it in his own person," might have been inspired by Augustine's *Enarratio in Psalmum* 96.5 (*PL* 37.1241). Huppé (1964:208) also feels that the friar "illustrate[s] his own sermon." Benson (1980:76), in studying Chaucer's use of gestures, remarks that this passage is "notable for its reliance on rage gestures. [The friar's] leaping up 'as dooth a wood leoun' not only expresses his outrage, but also serves to get him off his knees and on his way out of the house."

"A false cherl," quod he, "for Goddes bones,
This hastow for despit doon for the nones.
Thow shalt abye this fart if that I may." 2155
His meynee, which that herden this affray,
Cam lepyng in and chaced out the frere,
And forth he gooth with a ful angry cheere,
And fette his felawe ther as lay his stoor.
He looked as he were a wilde boor; 2160

2153 **quod he]** he seyde Gg; q. þe frere Pw+ TH¹–UR **Goddes]** cokkes Cp He
La+ CX¹–PN²

2154 **This hastow for despit doon]** T. h. in d. d. Ha⁴+ CX¹–WR; Thowe doist t.
in d. He; T. h. f. spite d. La; T. despite þou hast d. Pw+

2155 **this]** þi Cp **that]** *om.* Ad³ Dd Pw+ TH¹–SP³

2156 **which]** with (Gl+) CX¹–PN²; *om.* Gg Pw+ TH¹–SP³ **herden]** h. of Ha⁴
TH¹–UR WR **this]** swich Dd He+ CX¹–PN² **affray]** aray He+ CX¹–PN²

2157 **lepyng]** lepand Ha⁴ WR **chaced]** cachede Gg

2158 **ful]** foul Ha⁴+ WR; *om.* He+ **angry]** hevy He+ CX¹–PN²

2159 **And]** An La **ther as]** ther t. as Ad³; t. Ha⁴ WR **lay his stoor]** hadde
h. s. Gg; l. here s. La *Spur. line:* He ne had nat ellis for his sermoun Pw+

2160 **he]** it El Ad³ Cp Gg Ha⁴ La+ TR–RI *Spur. line:* To parten amonge his
breþeren whan he come home Pw+

2152 **wood leoun:** Birney (1960:216), Richardson (1970:151), and Giaccherini
(1980:154) note that Chaucer foreshadows this image in line 1989 ("Withinne thyn hous ne
be thow no leoun"), during the friar's sermon against the very wrath he now exhibits.
Richardson (RI) notes the parallel in *WBP* 794 and in Whiting (1968:L326 and L327).

2153–55 Fleming remarks (1983:17) that "even when he is farthest in spirit from
penitence, the friar is still the master of those outward forms of penitential expertise which
make him such an excellent groper of consciences. Analyzing the fart as a sin, he immediately
applies the appropriate categories of the confessional manuals. Was the act committed invol-
untarily or in malice? How many times was the act committed?"

2157 Craik (1964:129) notes that "the servants farcically come leaping *in* and chase
out the friar in a single line," and adds (p. 129 n. 1) that "this is the first and the last that we
hear of these servants, who are wanted to speed the friar away and prevent his attacking
Thomas. The contrast between his deliberate arrival and his unceremonious departure is very
amusing."

2158 "The remainder of this tale is omitted in Mss. B. G. and Bod. β [Ry², Sl¹, Ld²]
and instead of it they give us the following *lame and impotent conclusion.* He ne had nozt ellis
for his sermon / To part among his brethren when he cam home. / And thus is this tale idon. /
For we were almost att the toun. I only mention this to shew what liberties some Copyists
have taken with our author" (TR n. 7740; quoted in WR).

2159 At this point Pw and other *d**¹ MSS break off the tale, omitting the concluding
episode of Jankyn's division of Thomas's gift. See further "The Textual Tradition," above.

2160–61 Root (1906:252) comments of these lines that "the only thing [the friar]

He grynt with his teeth, so was he wrooth.

2161 **He**] And Dd Ha⁴ He+ CX¹–PN² WR **grynt**] grynded Cp; gruntid He+;
grenteþ La+ CX¹–WN; grynneth ~ PN²; grynted (Ad²+) TH¹–UR **with**] *om.* Cp La+
TH¹–SP³ **his**] the Dd+ CX¹–WN *Spur. line:* And þus is þis tale ydoun Pw+

---

forgets is, that for a preacher who has so ably denounced the sin of wrath, it is hardly
consistent to give such an eminent example of the sin in his own person." As Ruggiers
(1965:106) puts it, "the friar who preached continence, the spiritual life, and the perils of
wrath has fallen into the sin himself"; Giaccherini (1980:158) makes the same point. Flem-
ing (1966:699) adds that the friar forgets "the injunction of Saint Francis that friars should
welcome insults and injuries as opportunities to practice humble forgiveness." Whittock
remarks (1968:141) that the "coarse cunning of the trick at last breaks down the friar's poise
and smoothness." He also feels we are intended to remember here that *SumT* is itself a
product of the Summoner's rage expressed in lines 1665–68, while Richardson (1975:232),
in arguing that *SumT* and *FrT* are similar in showing the narrators as perceptive and also self-
revelatory, remarks that the friar's anger here reflects the Summoner's "quaking like an aspen
leaf" (line 1667) more than Huberd's "louryng chiere" in *FrT* 1266.

2160 **as he were:** Six of the nine base-group MSS that have this line read *as it were*, as
do all editions since TR. The remainder of the MSS are split exactly evenly; *a*–Ln (excepting
Ma) and *b** read *he*, with Hg, while *cd**² and the Gg–Si group read *it*, with El. One might
argue that *as it were* is the more difficult reading, but the consistency with which it is
recorded in *NPT* B² 4369, "He looketh as it were a grym leoun," where *it* is found in all
texts except *Ne* and Ra², suggests it was not *very* difficult. In any case, there is nothing wrong
with the Hg reading, and, following the principles of this edition, the Hg reading has with
no great enthusiasm been allowed to stand.

wilde boor: Tupper (1914:113) cites this image along with those in lines 1667
and 2121 in arguing that the tale is "directed against Wrath." Rowland (1971:73) notes that
Thomas is compared to the domestic boar in line 1829, an animal also associated with wrath,
but that the friar's porcine metaphor is suggestive of considerably greater anger. Haskell
(1976:59) makes a similar point, contrasting John's boar-like to Thomas's ant-like anger (line
1825). She notes that "the wild boar was eventually adopted in Christian symbolism as the
icon for wrath in the context of the Seven Deadly Sins," and that in Seneca's *De Ira* one finds
the image "wild boars foam at the mouth and sharpen their tusks by friction." See further
note 1825 and under "Thematic Issues" in Critical Commentary, pp. 37–38.

2161 **grynt:** Except SK, all modern glossators follow TR's interpretation (5.90),
"*ground* or *gnashed*." SK (6.117) glosses "grinned. . . . For *grente*, from M.E. *grennen*; pt. t.
grennede, grente." TR reports that *grinte* represents the preterite of the strong verb *grind*. RB
(glossary) and Davis et al. (1979, s.v. *grinte*) identify it as a preterite form of the weak verb
grynten, which, Davis suggests, is imative, based on the verb *grind*. *OED* (s.v. *grind*, v.¹) and
MED (s.v. *grinden*, v.[1]) indicate that *grind* developed a weak preterite, *grinded* (16th c.,
according to *OED*; "late," according to *MED*). MR report that only Cp reads *grynded* here. It
is noteworthy that *MED* presents the form *grynt*, the spelling of Hg Ad³ Dd Gg Pw (and
MR), as the 3d pers. sing. pres. ind. of the strong verb *grinden* (v.[1]) and quotes, in 2.(b), the
Hg+ version of this passage. *MED*, s.v. *grinten* v.(c), quotes the same passage from La to
illustrate the weak verb *grinten* (with preterites *grinte* and *grinted*). *OED*, on the other hand,

A sturdy paas doun to the court he gooth,
Wher as ther woned a man of greet honour,
To whom that he was alwey confessour;
This worthy man was lord of that village.   2165
This frere cam as he were in a rage

2162   **to]** *om.* Ad³   **the]** t. lordes El+   *Spur. line:* ffor we were almost at þe
toun. Pw+
2163   **ther]** *om.* El+ SP²,³   **woned]** woneth ~ PN²   *Out:* Pw (2163–*end*)
2165   **that]** al t. ~ WN
2166   **he]** þough it Cp La+

---

quotes the present passage s.v. *Grint*, and shows *grint* as one of the preterite forms of that
verb. The spelling *grynte* (in El Ha⁴ TR–RB¹ RB² PR RI) improves the meter. On these
variant spellings of the weak preterite, see further the note to line 1886, *Fasted*.

MR's CV distinguishes between the forms *grynted* (Ad²+) and *grunted* (He+)
and between the forms *grintith* (CX¹+) and *grunteth* (Ha²+), listing La (which spells *grenteþ*)
with Ha². This treatment of forms, apparently not MR's original intention, seems to be the
result of confusion introduced by a change in the lemma. MR's collation card employs the
lemma *He grinte* and distinguishes He from Ad² and CX¹ from Ha² because He and CX¹
read *And* for *He*, not because they spell their variant verbs differently. For the CV, MR made
separate lemmata of *He* and *grynt* but did not make the necessary adjustments in the record of
verb forms on their collation card. The card makes clear that the editors wished to distin-
guish between -*nd* and -*nt* forms and between the inflectional endings -*ed* and -*eth*, but not
between -*t* and -*te* or between -*in*-, -*yn*-, -*en*-, and -*un*- forms.

2162   **court:** The manor-house, as RB notes. WR, followed by SK, explains that "the
larger country-houses consisted generally of an inclosed court, from which circumstance this
name was usually given to the manorial residence," but Jephson (Bell 1855:2.119) suggests
that "the residence of the lord of the manor was sometimes called 'the court,' from the
manorial and other courts held there." Havely prefers the architectural explanation, and notes
that "the word is still used in the names of some buildings of this kind—notably Hampton
Court" (1975:146). Whitmore (1937:9–10) writes that this is Chaucer's only explicit allu-
sion to a manorial court.

2163   **a man of greet honour:** For suggestions about the identity of this man, see
note to line 1710, *Holdernesse*; Richardson (RI) adduces only the suggestion of Manly
(1926*b*). Shelly (1940:254) calls our attention to the characterization of the lord: "He is a
village Sir Thomas Browne. On a small scale he is possessed of the curiosity and tenacity of
mind, the interest in the difficult and the occult, which characterized the great physician of
Norwich." Havely (1975:22) sees in his "puzzled but scholarly approach" more of Walter
Shandy.

2164   Suggesting that the friar would have taken pride in being assigned to such a
lord, SK cites Wyclif, "Of ech sich privat seete, by licence of the pope, ben maad, some
chapeleyns of houshold, summe chapeleyns of honour" (ed. Arnold 1869–71:3.511) and another
of Wyclif's works (ed. Matthew 1880:333); also *Jacke Upland* § 37 [incorrectly for § 25? ed.
Heyworth 1968:64; SK 7.194] and *Piers Plowman* B 5.136–42 and 20.341–45.

2166–75   Craik (1964:129) writes that Chaucer "brilliantly avoids an anti-climax of

Where as this lord sat etyng at his boord.
Unnethe myghte the frere speke a woord,
Til atte laste he seyde, "God yow see."
    This lord gan looke and seyde, "Benedicitee.   2170
What, Frere John, what manere world is this?
I se wel that som thyng ther is amys;
Ye looken as the wode were ful of thevys.
Sit doun anon and tel me what youre grief is,

2167   **as]** þat Ha[4] WR   **sat]** sit Gg   **his]** the (Ii+) PN[1]
2168   **the]** this (Se) UR   **speke]** to s. ~ SP[2,3]   **a woord]** o w. He CX[1]–TR
2169   **atte]** at (Ad[1]+) WN PN[2]
2170   **gan]** bigan to El+; g. to Ad[3] Gg+
2171   **What]** Quod he Cp La+   **world]** a w. ~ TH[2]
2172   **se wel]** trowe El; se right w. ~ UR   **that]** om. El He+ CX[1]–PN[2]   **som]**
s. maner El+   **ther]** om. Cp Ha[4] La+ TH[1]–UR WR
2173   **Ye]** Y Ad[3]   **as]** as thogh Ad[3] Gg Ha[4] He+ CX[1]–UR WR
2174   **Sit doun]** Sitteþ La   **anon]** om. He+ CX[1]–SP[3]   **me]** vs Gg; om. He+
what] w. þat He   **youre]** ȝowe He+; ȝoure (re *del.*) La   **grief is]** fgref is Gg; grevis
He La+

---

his own by devising an anti-climax for the friar, whose calculated entrance falls completely flat." He adds that the friar never ate the meal he ordered at Thomas's house, "and so is still hungry when he arrives at the lord's house—where he finds the company at dinner." Havely (1975:21) feels that "there cannot be many comic 'entrances,' except in the theatre itself, that are as dramatically effective as this."

    2168–71   Lawlor (1968:121) sees "a nice revenge for the actual narrator in the speechless rage of his friar." He adds that "with an exact timing, the narrator pauses [between lines 2169 and 2170]. Can this be our eloquent friend? The point must be taken by the audience just one moment before the lord of the manor raises his head in astonishment." Szittya (1974:27) sees in the speechlessness a reversal of the Pentecostal gift of tongues. Lancashire (1981:26), who argues that John and Thomas have acted out a parodic version of God and Moses (respectively) on Sinai, wonders whether John's fearsome visage is meant to echo the terrifyingly radiant or "horned" face (*facies cornuta*) of Moses in Exodus 34.29–35.

    2168 **a woord:** MR do not record *o* (= *one*) as a variant of *a*.

    2169 **God yow see:** "A laconic form of salutation, characteristic of an angry man, and meaning, May God look upon you," Jephson (Bell 1855:2.119).

    2171 **John:** Levitan (1971:238) suggests that the friar's name may be intended to remind us of the Joachimites, who, in *Rom* 7165–86 are associated with that name; and Lancashire (1981:26–27) suggests that the name implies that John "considered himself a new Elijah, because Christ identified the 'second' Elijah as *John* the Baptist (Matt. 17.10–13)."

    2173   RB suggests that the phrase was a proverbial expression.

    2174 **what youre grief is:** He, Ne, and La among others have a verbal ("what you grieves") as opposed to the nominal ("what your grief is") form of the line. This transformation was perhaps instigated by pressure to have a more perfect rhyme than *thevys / grief is.*

And it shal been amended if I may."   2175
"I have," quod he, "had a despit today,
God yelde yow, adown in youre village,
That in this world ther nys so poure a page
That he nolde have abhomynacioun
Of that I have receyved in youre toun.   2180
And yet ne greveth me no thyng so soore
As that this olde cherl with lokkes hoore
Blasphemed hath oure hooly covent eke."
"Now maister," quod this lord, "I yow biseke—"

2175   if} if that El Cp Ha⁴ La+ PN¹ TH¹–SP³ WR
2176   had a} a La; haue a ~ CX²   today} this day El+ SK RB¹ RB² RI
2177   yow} it y. Dd He+ CX¹–UR   youre} ȝoue La
2178   ther nys} is noon El Cp Ha⁴+ TH¹–SP³ WR–RB¹ RB² RI; n. non Gg+; t. n.
no He+; t. is none La+   so poure a} that p. Ad³; p. He+
2180   youre} þis Cp; the Dd He+ CX¹–PN²
2181   yet} *om.* Ad³   ne greveth me} g. me El+; me g. Cp La+ TH¹–SP³; ne g. it
me Dd+; it g. me nat He+; it g. not me (Ne+) CX¹   no thyng} half Dd He+ CX¹
2182   this} the Dd He+ CX¹–TR   lokkes} his l. (En²+) PN²
2184   this} þe Gg He+ CX¹–PN² UR

2176–80   Williams (1953:509), seconded by Fleming (1983:17), notes that Friar
John's condemnation of Thomas parallels William of St. Amour's complaints that friars
"sojourn in courts of princes and magistrates . . . that they procure themselves friends in this
world, and that they use their influence with the powerful to make trouble for their
enemies."
2176   **today:** Because the ten MSS which share the El reading of *this day* are scattered
in their affiliations (excepting Cn, Ma, En³ and Ad¹, which MR group in lines 2159–2294
with *a*), the variant is more probably scribal than genetic.
2177–80   Hertzberg (1866:625) notes the free variation between *village* and *toun* here,
explaining that with the exception of episcopal cities and some mercantile centers the dis-
tinction between town and country was in England much less sharply conceived than on the
continent.
2178   **ther nys:** Nine of the eleven MSS supporting the El reading *is noon* (including
Cp) are from *cd*². RI provides a notice of some MS readings for this lemma, but prints
as RB².
2184–88   Jephson (Bell 1855:2.120) remarks that "this is an admirable picture of an
angry man; nothing pleases him, not even the courtesy of his patron the great man." Root
(1906:251–52) takes a different if no less admiring view: "At the shameless hypocrisy of the
friar, one knows not whether to laugh or to weep. So complete a master is [the friar] of the art
of shamming that, even in his transport of rage, he remembers to protest at the title of
'master' which the lord bestows on him . . . a disclaimer which is careful to specify that the
title is not at all inappropriate." SK, seconded by Adams (1962:126–27), Severs (1964),
Szittya (1974:34), Giaccherini (1980:159–60), Mann (1973:39–40) and others, remarks that

"No maister, sire," quod he, "but servytour,   85v   2185
Thogh I have had in scole that honour;
God liketh nat that Raby men us calle,

2185   **sire quod he]** q. h. El Cp La+; q. he s. Gg; s. seid he He   **but]** b. a Cp+
2186   **scole]** scholis ~ UR   **that]** swich El Ha⁴ WR SK RB¹
2187   **nat]** *om.* He+   **Raby men us]** m. vs R. Cp La+ TH¹–TR

"the hypocrite here declines to be called 'master' though he had allowed the good wife to call him so twice [at lines 1800, 1836] without reproof." Severs (1964) notes that Thomas also calls John "master" in line 1781, and adds that "the full import of the Friar's hypocritical disclaimer of the title 'maister' is apparent only to the reader who recalls the Biblical passage [Matthew 23] which the Friar has in mind as he makes his disclaimer. It occurs in the sermon in which Christ attacks the scribes and the Pharisees for their hypocrisy." Lawlor (1968:122) remarks on the way the friar's "automatic eloquence once again settles into its habitual track. . . . It passes belief; but it is precisely true. The automatic response, the practised assertion of humility, the mechanical allusion to the Master which blandly links scriptural market-place with actual manor-house—all take the breath away." Giaccherini (1980:159) reminds us of the parallel pretensions of Huberd, "lyk a maister or a pope" in *GP* 261. Szittya (1974:41) notes that the association of friars with the Pharisees "is one of the most conventional of antifraternal conventions," and offers evidence that it almost always pivots upon an allusion to Matthew 23. He adds (p. 43) that "it is highly ironic that the very biblical verses [the friar] cites to support his denial are those chiefly associated by the anti-fraternal critics with what he is trying to dissociate himself from." See further note 2187.
     Arguing that Chaucer is playing with scholastic *insolubilia* in the conclud-ing scene (see note 2231), Pearcy (1967:323) writes that "a general connexion with the university is first established by the friar, whose mock-modest rejection of the title 'master' is used to remind the lord of the village that he is, nevertheless, a university graduate. . . . This connexion is reinforced when, throughout the ensuing scene, characters show that penchant for polysyllabic technical terms (*reverberacioun, perturbynge*), or stilted periphrasis (*parfournen up the nombre*), which in all ages is used to stigmatize pedantry." Richardson (RI) observes that "Friar John has a Master of Arts degree (required at Oxford by a statute of 1251 for those seeking subsequent graduation in theology)."
   2186 **that:** Only El and Ha⁴ have *swich*, and this is one of 6 lines altered in RB² from RB¹ in *SumT* under the influence of the MS data collected by MR.
   2187 **Raby:** As Jephson (Bell 1855:2.120) and all subsequent commentators point out, the injunction forbidding the disciples to be known as master (rabi) is in Matthew 23.8 (by typographic error Matt. 13.8 in Jephson); the injunction is also suggested, as RB notes, in Mark 12.30–40. Landrum (1924:90) argues that though *RR* offered Chaucer the parallel passage "Et aiment que l'en les salue / Quant il trespassent par la rue; / Et veulent estre apelé *maistre* / Ce qu'il ne devraient pas estre" ("And they like to be greeted as they walk along the street, and they want to be called master, which they should not be") [cited from Michel ed. 1864, lines 12570–573; in Langlois ed., 1914–24, lines 11631–634], his use of *Raby* sug-gests rather that he has the Vulgate itself in mind: "Vos autem nolite vocari Rabbi" ("But do not wish that you be called Rabbi").

Neither in market nyn youre large halle."
"No force," quod he, "but tel me al youre grief."
"Sire," quod this frere, "an odious meschief   2190
This day bityd is to myn ordre and me,
And so *par consequens* to ech degree
Of Holy Chirche, God amende it soone."
"Sire," quod the lord, "Ye woot what is to doone;
Distempre yow noght, ye be my confessour;   2195
Ye been the salt of th'erthe and the savour;

2188   nyn} n. in Gg; neyther in Ha⁴ He+ WR   youre} our (Ne+) CX¹; other ~
PN¹   large} *om.* Cp La+
2189   but} *om.* Ad³ Ha⁴+ WR   tel} tellith Ha⁴ WR   al} of Cp La+ TH¹–SP³
2190   Sire quod this frere} S. q. he El; T. f. sayd s. Ha⁴ WR; S. q. þe f. La+   an}
in He+ CX¹   odious} ydious Cp+; hydous La+
2191   bityd is} is betid Gg+ TH¹–SP³; b. (Bo¹+) UR   to} *om.* Dd He+ CX¹
me} to me Cp Ha⁴ La+ TH¹–SP³ WR
2192   consequens} consequece ~ PN²   to} in El Dd He+ CX¹–PN²
2194   Ye} we ~ PN¹ UR
2195   Distempre} Distemperyth Gg+
2196   th'erthe} þe cherche Gg+   the savour} sauyour Ha⁴ WR

2188   **large halle:** Whitmore (1937:9–10) suggests that the friar means the whole
house—not just the great hall.
2189   **tel:** Following their conventions, MR do not record the variant imperative form
of Ha⁴; see note to line 1671, *suffreth*.
2190   **odious:** Ross (1972:152) suggests the possibility of a pun on *odorous*, and notes
Bottom's parallel malapropism in *A Midsummer Night's Dream*: "Thisby, the flowers of odious
savors sweet."
2192   **par consequens:** Giaccherini (1980:160) remarks that the Summoner ridi-
cules the Friar John's habit of parading learning: "even in such a situation he does not give up
the Latin citation."
2194–99   Craik (1964:130) writes that "the lord's remarks, without his intending it,
are a rebuke to his confessor (and Thomas's) for not practising the self-control he preaches,"
and Giaccherini (1980:160) notes that the calm civility of the lord underlines the intensity of
and lack of justification for the friar's wrath.
2196   **salt of th'erthe and the savour:** Jephson (Bell 1855:2.120) and all subse-
quent editors adduce Matthew 5.13. Kaske (1972:123) sees this allusion to Matthew as part
of a pattern of contrast in *SumT* between the friar's actual activities and the pattern of
perfection established by Christ's instructions to his apostles and disciples, while Reiss
(1984:59) similarly notes that the remainder of Matthew 5.13 warns that the salt that has
lost its savor is of no use "except to be thrown out and trodden under foot by men." Ames
(1984:46) comments that "it is clear that the lord and his lady perceive the lack of Christly
savor in this friar." Haskell (1971:223) claims that the *Seint Symoun* of line 2094 (see note,
above) is Simon Magus, who claimed divinity equal to Christ, and that "this is possibly a

For Goddes love youre pacience ye holde.
Tel me youre grief," and he anon hym tolde
As ye han herd biforn, ye woot wel what.
The lady of the hous ay stille sat   2200
Til she hadde herd what the frere sayde.
  "Ey Goddes moder," quod she, "blisful mayde,
Is ther aught ellis? tel me feithfully."
  "Madame," quod he "how thynketh yow therby?"

    2197   ye} now Dd He+ CX¹–TR
    2198   **Tel}** Telleþ Cp La TH¹–SP³
    2199   **As}** Ais La
    2200   **the hous}** þat h. Ha⁴+ WR   **ay}** al El+
    2201   **hadde herd}** herd La+; hadde h. fully ~ SP²,³; had h. al (Ad¹+) SK
sayde} had s. (Sl²) CX²–PN² UR
    2202   **blisful mayde}** blessid m. He+; the blissid m. (Ne+) CX¹,² WN PN²; this
blissed m. ~ PN¹; and b. m. (Ad²₁+) TH¹–SP³
    2203   **aught}** nouȝt Cp Gg La+ TH¹–UR; ony thing He   **tel}** telleþ Cp La
    2204   **thynketh}** lykyth Gg   **yow}** ye El He+ CX¹–UR RB¹ RB² RI
therby} her by El Gg He+ SK RB¹ RB² RI

---

play on the word *Saviour.*" Ha⁴ actually reads *savyour.* The more prominent word play, which
Alford (1984:201) calls "the cruelest *double-entendre* of all," is of course on *savor* as meaning
"taste" and "smell" (see line 2226). On the latter sense, see Levy (1966:59–60) in note 2226,
below.
    2198   **Tel:** MR do not record such variations of imperative forms; see note to line
1671, *suffreth.*
    2200   Ewald (1911:31) and Birney (1960:217) feel that the silence of the lady and of
her husband (line 2216) during the friar's story suggests suppressed amusement, an effort to
forestall their bursting out in laughter. Benson (1980:76) notes that such composure is often
used as a gesture symbolic of virtue in saints' lives, and here shows at least that the lady has
"a degree of equanimity far beyond the reach of the friar."
    2201   SK's emendation is drawn expressly from Ad¹'s *all* (SK 4.386); Ad¹ replaces Pw
(which lacks lines 2159–2294) in the Six-Text transcription (Furnivall 1868–77) consulted
by Skeat for his edition, hence the erroneous reference to Pw in RB's textual note. RB
suggests that the reading with *all* may be correct "since it improves the meter," but RB also
suggests reading *hered* for *herd* or *what that* for *what.*
    2203   **Is ther aught ellis:** Eliason (1972:107–08 and n. 78) takes the lady's calm
words here as evidence that Chaucer's original audience would have not taken offence at the
language and subject of *SumT.* He notes further that the same "imperturbable question"
occurs again in *FranT* F 1469, where Arveragus asks it of Dorigen. Lawler (1980:50) argues
that this is the real confession scene, as the friar responds to the "gropings" of the lady and
her husband (e.g., "tel me al" in line 2189).
         tel: MR do not record the variant forms of the imperative; see note to line
1671, *suffreth.*
    2204   **yow:** The distinction *you / ye* is parallel to that between *me thinketh* and *I think.*

"How that me thynketh," quod she, "so God me spede,   2205
I seye a cherl hath doon a cherles dede.
What sholde I seye? God lat hym nevere thee.
His sike heed is ful of vanytee;
I holde hym in a manere frenesye."
"Madame," quod he, "by God I shal nat lye;   2210
But I on oother wise may be wreke,
I shal diffame hym over al wher I speke,

2205   that] *om.* ~ UR   quod she] *om.* (En[1]+) WN TH[1]–SP[3]
2208   ful] alle f. ~ UR
2209   a] *om.* (Lc) PN[2]   manere] m. of Gg+ TH[1]–UR; m. of a He+ CX[1]–PN[2]
2210   quod he] *om.* Gg   by God] I wis Ha[4] WR
2211   on oother wise may] on him o. weyes El; in o. w. m. Ha[4]+ UR–WR; in ony w. m. on hym He+ CX[1]–PN[2]; in any w. m. ~ TH[1]–SP[3]; on o. weyes m. ~ SK   be wreke] ben awreke Cp La+ UR TR; a vrech He; a wreke (Ii+) CX[1]–PN[2]; ben on him awreke ~ TH[1]–SP[3]
2212   diffame] disclaundre El RB[1] RB[2] RI; sclaundre Cp La+ TH[1]–SP[3]   wher I speke] ther I s. El Ad[3] Gg+ TR SK RB[1] RB[2] RI; w. I prech He

---

Chaucer meant the former, as line 2205 makes clear, but the degeneration of such forms was widespread by the 15th century (Visser 1970:1.20–35) and about a dozen—mostly late—MSS share the reading of El.

2205   **thynketh:** SK recommends pronouncing *thynketh* as a single syllable, which would make the line metrically regular.

2206   Root (1906:251) sees the lady's comment on Thomas's action as perhaps softening an audience's reaction to the coarseness of the deed, dismissing it as no more than can be expected of a churl. Lawrence (1950:74) reads the interchange as suggesting that Chaucer's audience would have found the story less offensive than many modern critics: "The lady of the house listens calmly. The friar does not hesitate to describe a coarse bodily function in her presence, and she takes no offense. Her comment is illuminating: 'What can you expect of a yokel?'"

2210–15   Ruggiers (1965:107) comments on this passage that "the revenge that has been wrought on [the friar] gives rise to his own desire for revenge expressed in his self-consuming anger," and Havely (1975:22) adds that "these violent threats, appropriately enough, are the last that we hear from the previously genteel and subtle friar."

2211   **wise:** Though often assiduous in recording spelling differences among Ha[4] (Furnivall 1885) and the Six-Text transcriptions (in which here Ad[1] replaces Pw; Furnivall 1868–77), SK ignores the distinction between El's and Ad[1]'s *weyes* and the spellings of Hg Cp Gg Ha[4] La. MR do not always record the difference as truly variant (see Baker 1990:222), but do so in this line.

2212   **diffame:** The El reading *disclaundre* is unique, and the RI editors, though following RB in printing it, write that *diffame* is "more likely correct" (p. 1127).

wher: *Wher* and *ther* are such easy substitutions for one another that little can be inferred from the MS evidence, but MR take the variant as evidence for El's affiliation with

199

The false blasphemour that charged me
To parte that wol nat departed be,
To every man yliche, with meschaunce."   2215
　　The lord sat stille as he were in a traunce,

　　2213　　**The**} This El Ad³ Gg+ TR SK RB¹ RB² RI; That He+ CX¹–UR　　**that**}
þa La; which t. ~ CX²–PN² UR
　　2214　　**parte**} depart Ad³ Gg+　　**that**} it t. ~ CX²–UR　　**wol nat**} might n. Cp
La+ TH¹–SP³　　**departed**} partid He+
　　2215　　**To**} What Gg+　　**man**} *om.* He+　　CX¹–PN²　　**yliche**} alych He+
with} meche w. Gg+ CX¹–PN² UR
　　2216　　**were**} lay Cp La+

---

the Gg–Si *Ad³* group, part of their argument that El was using the ancestor of *cd*²* after line 2158. They incorrectly report (2.241) that El shares 2 variants with the group in this line, apparently counting the unique El *disclaundre*.

　　2213–14　　Levy (1966:50–51) notes that the friar "seems to be more humiliated by the fact that Thomas has presented him with what seems to be an insoluble problem than by the insulting nature of the gift itself," and Carruthers (1972:212–13) agrees, adding that it is the "literal-minded objection of the friar that opens the way for Jankyn's brilliant, and equally literal, solution." Allen and Moritz (1981:171 n. 33) remark that the friar's problem "resembles the difficulty of the disciples in Matthew 14.17; they must divide the five loaves and two fishes to distribute to the multitude." Giaccherini (1980:159) feels that the friar adds the accusation of blasphemy here because the initial reaction of his audience to the affront was luke-warm. Alford (1984:201) finds humor in the misplaced literalness of both friar and manor court: "Immediately everyone puts his mind to thinking how to divide the gift and thus help the Friar to keep his promise. This, of course, is not what the Friar meant at all. But once again it is the letter and not the intent that predominates."

　　2213　　**The:** The remarks on *wher* versus *ther* in note 2212 apply to *the* versus *this* in this line. El is, for the most part, with the same MSS.

　　2215　　**with meschaunce:** RB suggests "an imprecation," parallel to *with harde grace* in line 2228. Richardson (RI) directs attention to Chaucer's other uses of the phrase, noting that as an imprecation it "varies considerably in forcefulness."

　　2216–26　　Ewald (1911:31) notes the humor that arises from taking the "problem" seriously. Adams (1962:128) sees the lord's consideration of the problem as "mock-serious," arguing that he "turns the quasi-problem of division and distribution into a metaphysical quiddity," while Craik (1964:130) notes that "his treatment of it as a scholastic 'question,' ideally capable of 'demonstracion,' prepares us for Jankyn's solution of it by natural science," and Ruggiers (1965:107) comments on the "comic invention consisting of treating what has been a comic gift as a serious problem requiring the utmost scientific sobriety." Knight (1973:74–75) notes that the lord is amused rather than shocked by the friar's discomfiture, and he contrasts the lord's style with the friar's: both speak in an elevated way, but the lord's style is "educated, thoughtful and pausing . . . whereas the friar's style was a froth of hypocrisy." O'Brien (1990) feels that Chaucer's main interest here is the dispute between authority-based versus experience-based science: "What Chaucer calls attention to here is not the lord's cleverness, not the characters in the scene, but the discourse itself and the values that adhere

And in his herte he rolled up and down
"How hadde this cherl ymaginacioun
To shewe swich a probleme to the frere?
Nevere erst er now herde I swich matere;   2220
I trowe the devel putte it in his mynde.

2217   **rolled}** rolleth Dd+; rolle La
2218   **hadde this cherl}** h. the c. El; that t. c. had Ad³ Dd He+ CX¹ TH¹–SP³; that t. c. hath ~ CX²–PN²; that his c. had ~ UR   **ymaginacioun}** this y. El Gg+; abominacioun He+; dilectacion (Tc²) CX¹
2219   **swich a}** þis Gg   **the}** a El Ad³ Gg+
2220   **erst}** eft Ha⁴+ WR   **er}** to (Tc²) CX¹   **herde}** ne h. Dd+ TH¹–SP¹ TR   **swich}** of s. El Cp Gg Ha⁴ He La+ WR–RI; s. a Ad³+ TH¹–SP³; of s. a (Bw+) CX¹–PN²

---

to it" (p. 15). The lord represents the older *via rationis*, which sought to arrive at truth by beginning with authority and proceeding with strict logic. The Squire represents the new *via experientiae*, which follows Bacon in attributing final authority to the senses (p. 18). See further note 2231.

2218–28   This edition follows others since TR in placing this passage in quotation marks, but it should be noted that the lord is not speaking, but rather sitting still, "rolling up and down in his heart" the following matter. As Havely (1975:23) puts it, the lord's words are a good example of "thinking aloud" or soliloquizing. The decision to treat lines 2218 through 2228 as (silent) dialogue requires a question mark at the end of line 2219, but if the whole passage is considered interior, the question mark could be suppressed, and understood as follows: "The lord . . . rolled up and down in his heart how the churl had the imagination to . . . ," as is suggested by the reading of Ad³, Dd, and He+ in line 2218. The lord's first spoken words would then be "Lo sires" in line 2228.

2219   **shewe:** As SK suggests, the word here means to "propose" or "propound."

2220   **erst:** Though MR record *eft* in Ad¹, they do not report it in Ha⁴. WR allows that *erst* is the reading of "some" manuscripts.

    swich: The decision here not to follow all modern editors since WR in printing *of s.* is based not upon any notion of the superiority of sense or metrics of the Hg reading but simply on the conservative principles of emendation used in this edition. With or without *of* the sense of the line is the same; only the meter changes. Presuming *Nevere erst* to be an iambic foot in either case, the El+ line is iambic pentameter, and the Hg+ version forms a Lydgate line (by omitting the unstressed syllable at the caesura between the second foot and the third). Manuscript evidence tends to favor El+, but not decisively. While 30 MSS read with *of* and only 15 without, and while omission is an easy error, nevertheless it is clear that some scribes who inherited a "short" line felt a need to add an extra syllable somewhere: *ne h.* Dd+; *s. a* Ad³+. The variant in Ad³+ perhaps is owing to the influence of *swich a* in line 2219. So too the majority reading *of s.* may anticipate *of swich* in line 2223. It is noteworthy that the manuscripts of MR's group *a* (Dd+), normally quite consistent in their sharing of variants, contrive to produce a metrically regular line, but in three different ways.

In Arsmetrik shal ther no man fynde
Bifore this day of swich a questioun.
Who sholde make a demonstracioun
That every man sholde han ylike his part   86r   2225
As of a soun or savour of a fart?
O nyce prowde cherl, I shrewe his face.

2222   **In**] In al (Mc) TH[1]–TR   **Arsmetrik**] arte methrice He   **shal ther**]
coude t. Gg+; t. s. (Tc[1]) TH[1]–UR   **no**] nevir He
2223   **of**] *om.* Ad[3] Gg+   **swich**] schuld Gg (Gg[2] *corr.*)
2224   **make**] have He+   **a**] such He   *Spur. line*: Certes it was a shrewed con-
clusioun El+
2225   **sholde**] schul Gg+   **ylike**] lyke Dd He+ CX[1]; a lyk Ha[4] WR
2226   **As**] *om.* Cp La+ TH[1]–SP[3]   **a soun**] the s. El Gg+ UR SK RB[1] RB[2] RI
or] or of a Cp Dd Ha[4] La+ CX[1] WN PN[2]; or a He+; or of (En[1]+) CX[2] PN[1]
2227   **nyce**] vile El+   **shrewe**] beshrew (Py) SP[2,3]   **his**] thi Ad[3]+ TH[1]–UR

2222   **Arsmetrik:** MR do not record the He reading *arte methrice* as a variant; it is
interesting as perhaps a minor bowdlerization, eliminating the pun on *Ars*.   § Thomas
(UR) soberly glosses "Arithmetick," literally (says RI [footnote]) "art of measurement." Kö-
keritz (1954:952) takes this to be a pun on arse, and Baum (1956:231), seconded by Ross
(1972: 37–38), notes that "the context leaves no doubt," while Adams (1962:130) calls the
pun a "specific needle jab at this friar's piddling occupation with refined speculations and
sophistry."
      shal: In Gg the variant *coude* is followed by a blank space caused by an erasure;
as noted on MR's collation card, the erased word probably was *coude* (MR do not report this
information in their CV).
2224   Brusendorff (1925:84) considers that the El version of this line is the most
significant of its errors.
      demonstracioun: O'Brien (1990:18), who sees in this scene a critique of new
Baconian scientific methods, detects a hint of the demonic in *demon*stracioun, *demon*stratif
(line 2272), and *demon*yak (line 2240). Accusations of demonism were common among the
opponents of experience-based science.
2225/2230   According to Patterson (1987:488), the lord understands Thomas's in-
junction that the fart be divided equally as a covert demand for social justice: "At issue . . . is
the burning peasant demand for equality."
2226   In arguing that the (later) proposal for dividing the fart involves a parody of the
iconography of Pentecost (see note to line 2255, below), Levy (1966:59–60) points to the
medieval custom of releasing a shower of red roses from the church rooftop and sounding a
trumpet during Pentecost Sunday services: "Such a celebration suggests the two thematic
sensory images of 'soun' and 'savour' echoed in the *Summoner's Tale*." Levy is reminded too of
another trumpet, "one that would also link the sound as of a mighty wind with the *develes
ers*" in *Inferno* 21.139, and notes the prominence of sensory imagery in Confirmation, deriv-
ing from Pentecost. Cf. notes to lines 2151 and 2196, above.
      a soun: Only Nl Ps Si Tc[2] support the reading of El Gg.
2227–38   In arguing that Chaucer is involved in a sophistical scholastic joke in this

Lo sires," quod the lord, "with harde grace,
Who evere herde of swich a thyng er now?
To every man ylike, tel me how.   2230
It is an inpossible, it may nat be;

2228   **the]** þis La
2229   **evere herde]** h. e. El Cp Gg+   *Lines 2229–30 trans.* Dd (Dd₁ *corr.*)
Out: [*Spur. line bef.* 2231] He+ CX¹
2230   **man]** *om.* (Ne+) CX¹   **tel]** telleþ Dd
2231   *Spur. line bef.* 2231 That a fart shuld be partid (departid CX¹) nowe He+
CX¹   **It]** This ~ PN¹   **an]** *om.* Ha⁴+ UR WR

---

scene (see note 2231), Pearcy (1967:324) writes that the lord's descriptions of Thomas as shrewd (2238), subtle (2290), foolish (2227, 2232), and proud (2227) "are noteworthy in identifying him with the sophist's part, for they are just the terms used to condemn sophists by those critics of the excesses of thirteenth- and fourteenth-century scholasticism who considered such frivolous intellectual ingenuity a perversion of the proper ends of logic." Lawler (1980:189 n. 2) remarks that "Thomas and Jankyn are finally the best scholars in the tale."

    2227   **nyce:** Havely (1975:147–48) suggests that the word here and in line 2232 "is used in the sense of 'academically precise,' as a term of high praise for the way in which Thomas has posed the problem. . . . like 'nice distinctions,' or 'a nice sense of timing.'"

    2228   **with harde grace:** SK closes the quotation marks after *sires* and does not open them again until the beginning of line 2229, taking *with harde g.* as the narrator's voice. So punctuated, the passage means the lord spoke "with bitterness." RB and RI reopen the quotation marks before *with*, as here, taking the phrase as the lord's speech. So punctuated the phrase means something like "with bad luck to him." Richardson (RI) refers to the phrase as a "common imprecation," citing *CYT* G 1189 and *MED*, s.v. *grace* 3 (b) (d).

    2229   Dd transposes lines 2229–30, Dd₁ marking them in the left margin for correction. MR report it as "*L. over eras. after* 2230 Dd (Dd₁ *corr.*)." It would appear that the scribe skipped line 2229, wrote lines 2230 and 2231, but caught the error before he wrote line 2232. He then erased line 2231, wrote line 2229, and marked the transposition before continuing.

    2230   SK and RB place a question mark after *how*; RI does not.

    every man ylike: See note 2225/2230.

    tel: MR do not report such variants in imperative forms; see note to line 1671, *suffreth*.

    2231   **an inpossible:** RB notes the parallel in *WBP* 688. Pearcy (1967:322) remarks that Chaucer "is the first English writer known to have used the word *impossible* as a noun," and argues that he intended his audience to see the statement and solution of the problem of the division of the fart as a parodic version of "*impossibilia* . . . a class of exercises used in late medieval scholastic teaching." The *impossibile* is a "proposition, advanced by a self-acknowledged sophist, which violates the dictates of common sense or is clearly incapable of demonstration, but which is nevertheless vigorously defended or 'proved' by a series of such paralogical arguments as the sophist's ingenuity can devise" (pp. 322–23). "The lord" (see lines 2216–26) he continues, "is responsible for reflecting the expected reaction to the sophist's statements, wonderment at the ingenuity which devised so outlandish an assertion, and

Ey, nyce cherl, God lat hym nevere thee.
The rumblyng of a fart and every soun
Nys but of eyr reverberacioun,
And ther it wasteth lite and lite awey. 2235

2232   **Ey}** O Cp+; A La+   **hym}** thee El; hem ~ ST–SP³
2233   **The}** This He+   **rumblyng}** rublyng Cp+
2234   **Nys}** n. nat He+   **but of eyr}** b. an e. Ha⁴; bot bot of e. La; b. of the e. (Ha²+) PN¹   **reverberacioun}** revellacioun Cp La+
    2235   **ther}** euere El Ad³ Gg Ha⁴+ CX²–SP³ TR–RB¹ RB² RI; þer wiþ Cp La+; ay ~ UR   **it}** *om.* Cp La+   **lite and lite}** litel a. litel El Cp Dd+ CX¹ TH¹–SP³ RB¹ RB² RI; littl He+; lytel a. lite La   **awey}** al wey He+

---

incredulity that its validity should be susceptible of proof. The role of sophist is shared by Thomas . . . and his representative, the squire, who offers the unexpected and sophistical proof of the initial assertion" (p. 324). The prominence of such *sophismata physicalia* among a group of mathematicians at Merton College, Oxford, in the first half of the 14th century suggests the real possibility that Chaucer was familiar with the form (p. 325). O'Brien (1990:13) also sees scholastic activity here, the question of "what in God's kingdom is and is not divisible. The answer, of course, is that God is the only indivisible thing; hence it is the friar, not Thomas, who commits blasphemy by claiming that a fart, like God, cannot be divided." See further notes 2184–88, 2227–38, and 2272.

    2234   **of eyr reverberacioun:** SK, RB, Richardson (RI), Ross (1972:206), and Giaccherini (1980:161–62) note Chaucer's similar explanation of sounds in *HF* 765–821, SK—seconded by Wright (1988)—adding that "he seems to have taken it from Boethius, *De Musica*, i.14." As SK's note (3.259–60) to *HF* 765 ("Soun is noght but air y-broken") points out, the conception of sound as vibrating air was also treated in Vincent of Beauvais' *Speculum Naturale*, 4.14: "Sonus est aeris percussio indissoluta, usque ad auditum" ("Sound is a striking of air which comes undissolved to the hearing"). Grennan (1967:42) suggests that the *HF* definition is not of sound per se but a deliberately garbled version of the definition of an echo available to Chaucer in such texts as Grosseteste's commentary on Aristotle's *Posterior Analytics*. Pratt (1978:267–68) suggests that, since the ancient scientists' theories covered only sound, Chaucer's ideas (and Jankyn's) might have come from Albertus Magnus' *De sensu et sensato*, wherein is declared that not only sound but smell and sight propagate radially. Albertus argued that the "sensible essence" is divided in such an event, but "while all these things are thus separated, they are the same perceptible thing in kind, and in this way many people see and hear and smell the same thing at the same time." See further note to line 2130; also Boitani (1984:212–14), and Irvine (1985). In commenting on Chaucer's concreteness, Preston (1952:246) notes that "*curtesye* or no, Chaucer got the 'thing' down on paper straight from the *reverberacioun* of air impinging on his ear-drums."

    2235   RI reports MS information on the two El readings in a textual note, but prints as RB². The two El variants show only partially overlapping MS support: *euer* is found in all but one of the Gg–Si *Ad³* affiliated MSS and about one third of *cd*²*, while *litel and litel* is shared with the *a*–Ln group, most of *b**, and twelve of the eighteen *cd*²* MSS.

Ther nys no man kan deme, by my fey,
If that it were departed equally.
What, lo, my cherl; lo, yet how shrewedly
Unto my confessour to day he spak.
I holde hym certeynly demonyak.   2240
Now ete youre mete, and lat the cherl go pleye;
Lat hym go hange hymself a devel weye."

2236   **nys**} is El Cp Gg He La+ CX^1–UR SK RB^1 RB^2 RI
2237   **If**} Thogh Ad^3
2238   **my**} this (Bo^2+) CX^1 **lo yet**} lo Gg+ CX^1 SP^{2,3}; what lo Ha^4 He+ WR
shrewedly} shrewley He
2239   **Unto**} Vp to Gg
2240   **certeynly**} certeyn a El Cp Dd He La+ CX^1–TR SK–RI; c. a Ad^3+
2241   **ete**} eteþ Cp Ha^4 La TH^1–SP^3 WR   **lat**} leteþ Cp   **the cherl**} him Cp
La+
2242   **a**} on Ha^4 WR

2236 **nys**: Though MR, PR and the present edition follow Hg in printing *nys*, the support for the El reading *is* is impressive: one half of *a* (though not Dd), all of *b**, most of *cd*^{2}*, and Gg. In the case of such an easy variation, however, these groupings provide little help in deciding what Chaucer wrote.

2238 **my cherl**: Jephson (Bell 1855:2.122) takes the phrase to indicate that Thomas was in villeinage to the lord of the manor, and SK assumes that the phrase "probably implies vassalage," but it need not in this context. *OED*, s.v. *my* offers a more likely sense: "2. Used vocatively. a. Prefixed . . . in a jocular or merely familiar tone, to certain designations which are otherwise rarely used vocatively, as in *my man, my boy, my good fellow, my poor man*."

    shrewedly: MR do not report He's *shrewley* as a variant. *OED* lists it separately from *shrewedly*, but notes that it may be the same word with a syllable lapsed. *MED* lists *shreueli*, adv., from *shreue*, n., meaning "in a shrewish manner, sharply."

2240 **certeynly**: *Certeyn a* is perhaps a more difficult reading than *certeynly*, but the MS evidence is mixed, and the evidence is that El has been separated since line 1991 from the excellent exemplar with which it began the tale. The testimony of *cd*^{2}* is mixed, though numerically on the side of *certeyn a*. That this group is mixed at all suggests the presence of editing; *a* and *b* solidly back the El reading, but the independent (and untrustworthy) Ha^4 and the entire Gg–Si Ad^3 group read as Hg (except that Ad^3+ reads *certeynly a*). Though the evidence leans against the Hg reading here, it is deficient in neither sense nor meter, and is, without zeal, retained.

    demonyak: Baker (1961:36), followed by Jungmann (1980), argues that the use of this word here and in line 2292, coupled with "the devel putte it in his mynde" in line 2221 is an attempt on the Summoner's part to associate the friar with "witchcraft and the language of sorcery." These phrases are, however, all applied to Thomas, not the friar.

2241 **ete . . . lat**: MR do not report the different imperative forms; see note to line 1671, *suffreth*.

Now stood the lordes squyer at the boord,
That carf his mete and herde word by woord
Of alle thyng of which I have yow sayd.   2245
    "My lord," quod he, "be ye nat yvele apayd,
I koude telle for a gowne clooth
To yow, sire frere, so ye be nat wrooth,
How that this fart sholde evene ydeled be

2243   **stood the]** s. t. the ~ SP²   **at the]** at his Dd He+ CX¹–PN²
2244   **carf]** carued ~ PN¹ PN² UR   **his]** here Cp La+   **by]** for Cp La+
2245   **thyng]** thynges El SK RB¹ RB² RI; this t. Dd Ha⁴ He+ CX¹–PN² UR–
WR   **of which I have]** w. that I h. El; w. I h. Gg+ RB¹ RB² RI; w. þat I of h. Ha⁴
WR   **yow]** *om.* El Ha⁴+ WR
2246   **be ye nat]** beþ n. El Cp; be n. Dd (Dd₁ *corr.*) He La+ CX¹ TH¹–SP¹; be not
not ~ SP²   **yvele]** ill ~ UR   **apayd]** payd Cp Ha⁴+ WR
2247   **I]** ffor I He+ CX¹–PN² UR   **clooth]** of c. ~ UR
2248   **so]** be so Gg; so þat Ha⁴ He+ CX¹ TH¹–WR
2249   **fart]** *om.* La   **sholde evene ydeled]** e. delt shal El; e. departed s. Ha⁴ WR

2243   *Heading:* The wordes of the lordes Squier and his keru*e*re / for (f. the Tc²)
departynge of the (t. *om.* Tc²) fart on (in Tc²) twelue (t. partes Tc²) El(*in text before l.* 2243)
Ad³ Tc² RB¹–RI.
      Adams (1962:127) argues that the solution of the squire represents a "gloss" on
the "text" of Friar John's adventures, such that "the lord's carver, playing a friar's role, solves
the dilemma."
      the lordes squyer: SK remarks that "although the squire was not above win-
ning 'a new gown,' he was probably a young man of (future) equal rank with the lord of the
manor. In fact, his scornful boldness proves it."
2244   **carf:** The reading *carued* in PN¹ PN² UR (the latter two spell *carft*) probably
represents a "correction" of a strong past tense form which was no longer recognized. Since
MR do not distinguish between strong and weak forms, MR provide no information about
MS distribution of the forms.   §   Richardson (RI) compares *GP* 100 and *MerT* E 1773.
2245   RB and RI print the unique El *thynges* but reject its unique *w. that I h.* in favor
of the Gg reading *w. I h.*; they thereby avoid a second *of* in the line, and if *thynges* is
pronounced as two syllables, achieve metrical regularity as well.
2246   **be ye:** Because they do not report differing forms of the imperative (see note to
line 1671, *suffreth*), MR conflate the two reports given here on *be ye.*
2247   **gowne clooth:** WR, seconded by SK, notes that "in the middle ages, the most
common rewards, and even those given by the feudal land-holders to their dependants and
retainers, were articles of apparel, especially the gown or outer robe. . . . Money was compara-
tively very scarce in the middle ages; and as the household retainers were lodged and fed,
clothing was almost the only article they wanted." Andreas (1990:147) wonders whether, in
the context of this poem's "multiple parody" with its "relentless deflation of the most sacred
of Christian doctrines and rituals," we are not meant to think here of the robe divided at the
foot of the cross, and the wagon wheel as the cross.
2249–50   Fleming (1966:699) notes that Jankyn's solution of the problem of division

Among youre covent if it liked me." 2250
"Tel," quod the lord, "and thow shalt have anon
A gowne clooth, by God and by Seint John."
"My lord," quod he, "whan that the weder is fair,
Withouten wynd or perturbynge of air,
Lat brynge a cartwheel heere into this halle, 2255

2250   it] I Ha⁴ WR   liked] like Cp Gg He+ CX¹–PN²; comaunded Ha⁴ WR;
likeþ La+ TH¹–UR   me] the me Dd (Dd *corr.*); be Ha⁴ WR; the He+ TH¹–TR; sithee
(Tc²) CX¹–PN²
2251   Tel] T. on Cp La+ TH¹–SP³
2252   clooth] of c. ~ UR   God and by] g. a. be god & be La (La *corr.*)
2253   that] *om.* La+ SP²–UR   the] þis La
2254   *Spur. line:* Right her be forn ȝowe sitting in a cheyr He+ CX¹
2255   cartwheel] large whel Ha⁴ WR   heere] right He+ CX¹–PN²; *om.* El
Ha⁴+ WR

"carefully follows the principles for the division of communal property outlined in the fourth
clause of the brief Carmelite Rule written by Albert of Vercelli."
2250   me: MR fail to record Cp among manuscripts reading *like* for *liked*, and report
the error but not the correction in Dd.
2252   MR ignore the dittography and its correction in La.
2255   cartwheel: Fleming (1966:699–700) suggests the possibility that the wheel
alludes to the frequent accusations that friars were wanderers (*girovagi*) or the defense by
Archbishop of Canterbury Friar John Pecham that the friars were not to be called *girovagi* but
rather *rote Domini*; Fleming also notes that Erasmus makes a joke about friars as "wagon
wheels" of the Church, but Giaccherini (1980:165) finds the evidence thin. Levy (1966) and
Levitan (1971)—Levitan actually making the initial discovery—see in the image of the friars
assembled around the rim of the cartwheel and Thomas's placement upon the hub to "lete a
fart" a parodic allusion to the descent of the Holy Spirit upon the Apostles at Pentecost as it
is described in Acts 2.1–11 and as it is depicted in medieval representations and celebrations
of Pentecost. Most pointedly, the biblical account begins with a great wind: "And when the
days of Pentecost were drawing to a close, they were all together in one place. And suddenly
there came a sound from heaven, as of a violent wind blowing, and it filled the whole house
where they were sitting." Szittya (1974:23) notes that the Old Latin version of Acts, with
which Chaucer might well have been acquainted, has instead of the Vulgate "tamquam
advenientis spiritus vehementis" the even more suggestive phrase "quasi ferretur *flatus* vehe-
mens." "Of course it is quite a different kind of wind," writes Levy (1966:54), but the
common representation of Pentecost in the cupola of churches underlines the parallel, "with
the *Hetoimasia*, the prepared throne of the divinity—the source of inspiration—at the zenith
of the cupola, and with the parting tongues of fire descending from the center upon the heads
of the twelve Apostles, who are seated about the outer edge of the circle of the cupola, at
equal distances from one another." Furthermore, Levy continues, "in some representations of
this scene, particularly one that Chaucer may have been familiar with from personal experi-
ence, the Pentecost cupola of St. Mark's in Venice, the central iconographic image is a wheel."

But looke that it have his spokes alle;
Twelf spokes hath a cartwheel comunly.
And brynge me thanne twelf freres, woot ye why?
For thrittene is a covent, as I gesse.

2256   **looke}** so (Ne+) CX¹–PN²; l. well ~ SP²,³; l. to ~ UR; *om.* Ha⁴   **that}** *om.*
La+ TH¹–SP¹   **it}** he Cp La+ TH¹–SP³   **his}** the (Ps) PN¹
2257   **cartwheel}** carte Ad³+   **comunly}** I (*eras.*) trowe I Gg
2258   **thanne}** *om.* Dd (Dd₁ *corr.*) Ha⁴ He+ CX¹ WR
2259   **thrittene}** twelue El La+

He suggests another connection between Pentecost and a wheel in the medieval custom of imitating the violent wind of Acts in church on Pentecost Sunday with trumpets, hissing, humming, and pressing windbags, while from the ceiling through an opening called the "Holy Ghost Hole" appeared a wheel bearing the figure of a white dove which descended into the church (Levy 1966:55). Szittya (1974:29) adds that Saint Francis was reputed to have enjoyed referring to his friars as knights of the Round Table, and that Jankyn's wheel "may be a parody of Francis' spiritual round table." Levitan argues for a literary connection, which Giaccherini (1980:165) finds unpersuasive, between friars and wheels in Dante's *Paradiso* 10–12, noting in particular the chariot wheel of Canto 12, of which Jankyn's cartwheel may be a parody (1971:241–42). He provides instances and reproductions of several depictions of Pentecost in which the grouping of the apostles is circular, adding that "if Chaucer and his listeners were acquainted with such depictions, the ironic force of Thomas's gift emanating from the anus rather than from the mouth of the dispenser would be all the greater as a literal reversal of the corrupted spirit's source" (1971:243). Wentersdorf (1980: 254) suggests that Chaucer might also have had in mind the common representation of the twelve winds of heaven, "sometimes represented iconographically as a cartwheel, with each wind depicted as a face blowing along one of the spokes towards the hub," and cites an example from a twelfth-century English manuscript of Bede's *De natura rerum* printed in Howard (1976:204, fig. 11). Cooper (1989:177–78) suggests that Hugo de Folieto's 12th-century tract on the religious life, *De rota verae et falsae religionis*, "presented the monastic vices and virtues in diagram form as a twelve-spoked wheel, with the influence of the head of the house, for good or ill, at the hub." Particular versions are reminiscent of traditional depictions of the Wheel of Fortune, which "fits the tale well." See further in note 2259.

2257   **comunly:** MR's CV reports an erasure in Gg, as indicated in the collation above; the erased *I* does not show on the film used for the present edition. MR's CV also suggests tentatively that the second *I*, which mends the rhyme, may have been added later.

2259   **thrittene is a covent:** WR—echoed by Jephson (Bell 1855:2.122–23), Hertzberg (1866:625), SK, and RI—notes that "the regular number of monks or friars in a convent had been fixed at twelve, with their superior; in imitation, it is said, of the number of twelve apostles and their divine master. The larger religious houses were considered as consisting of a certain number of convents." Havely adds that "here we have another reminder of the friars' claims to be living the life of the Apostles" (1975:148). Fleming (1983: 18–19) argues that the elaborate Pentecostal parody of these lines must be correlated with the image of the Maria Misericordia of *SumP* for its full effect: "[I]n the Gothic iconography of Pentecost there is also a thirteenth and most worthy member around whom the twelve

Youre confessour heere, for his worthynesse,   2260
Shal parfourne up the nombre of this covent.
Thanne shal they knele adown by oon assent,
And to every spokes ende in this manere,
Ful sadly leye his nose shal a frere.
[Y]oure noble confessour, ther God hym save,   86v   2265
Shal holde his nose up right under the nave.
Thanne shal this cherl, with baly stif and toght
As any tabour, hider been ybrought;
And sette hym on the wheel right of this cart,
Upon the nave, and make hym lete a fart,   2270

2260   Youre] The El Gg+ SK; Y. noble Ha⁴ WR   heere] hede Cp La+   for
his worthynesse] god him blesse Ha⁴ WR; f. h. wordynesse (Ma+) CX¹˙
2261   this] his El Cp Gg He La+ CX¹–TR SK RB¹ RB² RI
2262   they] yee He+   adown] doun El Ad³ Cp Gg Ha⁴+ CX¹–PN² WR–RB¹
RB² RI
2263   this] his Gg
2264   leye his nose shal] scholden l. her n. La   a] þe Cp; iche a La
2266   nose] *om.* La   under] vnto Cp+; in to La+ UR   nave] caue (*del.*) n. He
2267   stif] sterne Gg   toght] stout Gg He+; strouȝt ~ WN
2268   hider been] b. h. El Gg+   ybrought] brought out Gg₂
2269   right] *om.* Ha⁴+ WR   of] on Cp La+
2270   make hym lete] l. h. m. La+

---

apostles are reverently gathered. The thirteenth 'apostle' is the Virgin Mary." *SumT* thus ends as it began, "with a jarring iconographic burlesque. In the first the Blessed Virgin has been replaced by Satan, in the second by Fr. John: the implied equation is not without force."

Noting that friars were frequently accused of witchcraft by their enemies because of their supposed talents for divination and exorcism, Rowland (1971:71) remarks that "a convent of Friars was of the same number as a coven of witches," and Jungman (1980:20–22), though admitting there is no evidence that *covent* had associations of witchcraft this early, argues that Chaucer does intend the Summoner to suggest a connection between friars, witches, and demons. See further note to line 2240, *demonyak*.

2261   **this:** No argument for *this* or *his* on grounds of style or sense would be conclusive, and the MS evidence is, not surprisingly, divided.

2262   **adown:** Though reported by MR and in the present collations, the *adown / doun* variant can make no difference in the line's sense (or even its sound, since the pronunciation of the final -e on *knele* will replace the first syllable of *adown*). The reading suggests, however, that El is still with the Gg–Si group at this point.

2267–68   Holley (1980:42) writes that "the distended body of Thomas . . . is a travesty (like the well-fed, belching friars John had described) of the friar's earlier statements of his own function: anyone who wishes truly to participate in the association with the divine must 'fatte his soule, and make his body lene.'"

2270–74   Braddy (1964:220) feels that "with these lines Chaucer probably shocked

And ye shal seen, [up] peril of my lyf,
By prove which that is demonstratyf,
That equally the soun of it wol wende,
And eek the stynk, unto the spokes ende,
Save that this worthy man youre confessour,   2275
By cause he is a man of greet honour,
Shal han the firste fruyt as reson is.
The noble usage of freres yet is this,
The worthy men of hem shul first be served,
And certeynly he hath it wel disserved.   2280

2271   up] on Hg+; vpon (Ad²+) PN¹
2272   By] By verray Ha⁴ TR WR; The He+ CX¹; By good ~ SP²,³; And by ~ UR
which] *om.* Ha⁴+ TR WR   that] *om.* (Cn+) TH¹–SP³
2274   And] Ad Dd   unto the] out atte He+ CX¹,² WN PN²; to t. La+; out of t.
~ PN¹   spokes] þokis He
2275   youre] þis Cp Gg He La+
2277   fruyt] fruytes Cp+ TH¹–UR   reson] worthy Gg
2278   The] As yet t. El; And as t. Gg+   of freres yet is this] of f. is El; of f. y. it
is Ad³ He+ CX¹ TR; ȝit of f. is Gg+; of f. is t. Ha⁴+ UR WR
2279   worthy men] worthiest man He+ CX¹–PN² UR; worthest man ~ TH¹–
SP³   shul first] f. s. Ha⁴ WR
2280   And] As Ha⁴

------

the sensibilities of his audience," and hence sought from them "lenience or understanding"
(1964: 221) in *GP* 725–36 and *MilT* A 3172–75.
2271   **up**: MS support of *up peril* against the Hg *on p.* is overwhelming.
2272   **prove which that is demonstratyf**: Pearcy (1967:324) connects this pseudo-
academic language with his argument that the problem and solution of fart division is a
jocular instance of the sophistic academic *impossibile*. The proof is "triumphantly furnished by
the squire, to complete the pattern and confirm identification with the conventional and
familiar type of school exercise." See notes 2184–88, 2227–38, and 2231.
2277   **firste fruyt**: Szittya (1974:24) suggests that Chaucer alludes in Jankyn's words
to the tradition of associating Pentecost with *primitiae* or first fruits, noting that the Jewish
Pentecost, described in Leviticus 23.15–22 and Numbers 28.26–31, used sacrifices consist-
ing of the first fruits of the harvest. "Sweet-smelling holocausts were to be offered to the
Lord," he notes, adding that "it is to this biblical description of Pentecost, particularly to the
first fruits and the *odor suavissimus*, that the squire no doubt alludes." Clark (1976*b*:49) notes
that in ecclesiastical and feudal practice the term meant a one-time payment made to the
benefactor by a new tenant of a benefice or feudal gift, and Olson (1986:233) seems to
suggest that an allusion to the "English subsidy to the pope, sometimes collected by the
friars" is intended.
2280–84   SK notes that "this implies that the squire, with the rest, had heard the friar
preach in church that morning, and had been greatly bored by the sermon." Richardson

He hath to day taught us so muchel good
With prechyng in the pulput ther he stood,
That I may vouche sauf, I seye for me,
He hadde the firste smel of fartes thre,
And so wolde al his covent hardily,   2285
He bereth hym so faire and holily."
    The lord, the lady, [and] ech man save the frere,
Seyden that Jankyn spak in this matere
As wel as Euclyde or [elles Ptholomee].

2285   **al**} *om.* Ad³+   **his**} the El+   **covent**} brethren ~ CX²–TR   *Out:* Gg
(2285–*end*)
2286   **and**} a. so Dd He La+ CX¹–PN²
2287   **and ech**} e. Hg+; and alle El   **man**} men El
2288   **that**} þan Ha⁴
2289   **Euclyde**} Ouyde (Gl+) CX¹–PN²; Ouyde did (Ii) TH¹–SP¹; E. did (Ry¹) SP²,³
RB¹ RB² RI; E. cou'de ~ UR   **or elles**} or Hg El Ad³ Cp Dd He La+ CX¹–UR RB¹–
RB² RI; or as ~ SK PR   **Ptholomee**} Protholomee Hg El Ad³ Cp Dd Ha⁴ He+ PN¹
MR; Plholome La

(1975:234) links Jankyn's insulting tone to his impatience with the "empty self-interest" he has perceived in the friar's preaching.

2281   **muchel**: MR record *much* as a variant on *muchel* here, though they do not do so in line 2011. Because the two forms are common substitutes for one another they are not included in these collations. The base-group MSS with *much* are El, Gg, He and La; all printed editions read *much*.

2285   Gg is Out here and for the remainder of the tale because of missing leaves.

2287   **and ech**: Tempting though it would be to retain the Hg reading, which is deficient in neither sense nor meter, the MS evidence in favor of the inclusion of *and* in the line is incontrovertible: only Hg, Bo² and Py omit.

2288   **Jankyn**: Havely (1975:149) notes that "'Jankin' (Jack) is often the name of a clever lad or cunning lover in popular literature of this time. Both the apprentice that the Wife of Bath goes out with and her fifth husband are given this name [*WBP* D 303–07, 627–31]. In a 15th-century lyric there is a clerical seducer called Jankin [in Robbins 1952:21, no. 27]." See also Morris (ed. 1872:188): "theos prude maidens that luuieth Ianekin." Hanning writes (1985:13) that Jankyn, whose name means "little John," in winning his new gown and solving the textual puzzle of the fart division, "bests the friar at begging as well as at glossing—no small disgrace to a mendicant."

2289   Citing Euclid and Ptolemy as examples of Chaucer's use of exemplary figures, Baker (1962:40) writes that "since both were not only mathematicians but were identified in the medieval mind with music, the irony is quite apparent and the tribute richly deserved." Ruggiers (1965:107 n. 7) writes that "Chaucer's knowledge of these ancients may well have come to him from his reading of the arithmetical treatises of Boethius, in particular *De Musica*. The problem of division posed by the tale is suggested by the precise and meticulous reasoning that went into the sectioning or dividing of the monochord, a scientific investigation into which, according to Boethius, Ptolemy and Euclid made their ample contribution."

Touchynge the cherl, they seyde subtiltee   2290

2290   **Touchynge**] Touchand Ha⁴ WR   **the**] this El+   **cherl**] cherles Dd
He+ CX¹–SP³; clerk Ha⁴   **they seyde**] t. s. þat Ha⁴+ UR WR; s. (Se) TH¹–SP³; *om.* He
La+

Euclyde: SP¹'s "Annotations, with some Corrections," states "Ouide, *read* Eu-
clide." MR (3.468) observe: "'Euclide' was unknown to several of the scribes [and] five
misspelled his name; [nine] substitute 'Ouyde.'"

Ptholomee: It is easy to understand what happened to the spelling of this
name: "the occurrence of an unpronounceable *P* at the beginning of *Ptolomee* made the scribes
think something must be *omitted*. Hence several of them introduced a stroke through the *p*,
which stood as an abbreviation for 'ro,' and this turned into *Protholomee*, which looked right,
but made the second *as* superfluous" (SK 5.341). It is, however, less easy to guess what the
reading for the entire line should be. The line is, as SK pointed out, a syllable short if
Ptholomee is restored. Three solutions have been offered by modern editors. SK, followed by
PR, emends by adding (in square brackets) an *as* not found in the MSS: "I supply the word
as, which is plainly wanted. MS [Ha⁴] supplies *elles*, but I believe *as* to be right" (SK 5.341).
RB and RI print *E. did* (in textual notes RB gives TH¹ as the source of *did*; RI cites Ii, Ld¹,
Ry¹, and Si, but of these only Ry¹ reads *E. did*); and MR print the line as found in Hg. RB
(textual note) allows that *Protholome*, "the corrupt form, . . . would make the extra word
metrically unnecessary." MR take *Protholome* to be the intended reading, noting that "the line
lacks a syllable unless the summoner is made to pronounce 'protholome' as most of the MSS
spell it" (3.468). RB² takes note of the MR interpretation (also registered in a textual note in
RI) and makes more explicit ("meant . . . humorously as a blunder of the Summoner") MR's
apparent understanding. Knight (1973:76) also argues that the line is meant to be read as in
most of the manuscripts, and that the mispronunciation "Protholome" is the Summoner's,
and is "meant to re-create his rather crude personality, to bring us back to the drama of The
Canterbury Tales." But transmitting a mispronunciation in a manuscript tradition is a tricky
business, as Chaucer must have recognized; he would have had no more assurance of the
error's being "accurately" transmitted than he would of a correct spelling being preserved.
The number of MSS which record *Ptholomee* correctly in the other two instances of its use in
CT (*WBP* 182 and *WBP* 324), where the line is metrically correct when the name is
pronounced correctly, is analogous to the case for this line, and in fact *Ptholomee* is spelled
correctly in a specific small number: Sl¹, Lc, Mg, Mc, and Py in all three instances, En², Ha²,
Pw, Ph³, Cp, Ra¹, To, Ne, CX¹, and Tc² twice. The most straightforward interpretation of
the evidence would seem to be that most of the earliest MSS contained the misspelling and
had consequently dropped a monosyllable, and that only scribes and editors aware of the
correct spelling corrected. Because the *as* supplied by SK and PR is not in the MSS, and
because the MSS supplying *did* are of such feeble authority and furthermore in all but one
case have quite corrupt readings of the line, the reading offered here is based, not without
misgivings, on the ever-suspect Ha⁴, with the following reasoning: Ha⁴, being early, could
have preserved the original, missing monosyllable (*elles*); the Ha⁴ scribe is notoriously med-
dlesome, but not notoriously inaccurate; the Ha⁴ line uses the abbreviated form of the name.
If the scribe accurately recorded what was before him it may be that *elles* is genuine, and he
did not drop it because he did not load the *ro* abbreviation with syllabic value. Because Ha⁴

And hy wit made hym speke as he spak;
He nys no fool ne no demonyak.
And Jankyn hath ywonne a newe gowne;
My tale is doon, we been almoost at towne.

Here endeth the Somnours tale

2291   **And**} An(d *eras.*) Dd; An Ha⁴+   **hy**} by heyh Cp La+; by He+   **wit**}
om. La+   **made**} make Cp La+
2292   **nys**} is Cp He La+; nas Ha⁴+ WR   **ne**} he is He+   **no**} *om.* (Ne+) CX¹
2293   **Jankyn**} Ianky La
2294   **doon**} doun Ad³   **at**} at the (Bo¹+) PN¹   *Out:* Gg (*lines* 2285–94); Pw
(*lines* 2159–2294)

Explicit: **Here endeth the Somnours tale**} Hic finit*ur* fabula sum*m*onitoris Dd; H.
e. t. Sompnour his t. He; Explicit fabula Ap*ar*itoris La; Thus e. t. S. t. Pw; *om.* Ad³ CX¹
SP²,³ TR WR   *Out:* Gg

---

tends to regularize lines (see line 1768), it seems unlikely that he would have added *elles* to a
line he saw as containing a sufficient number of syllables.

2291   **made:** MR do not report *make* in Cp, a reading that appears only in the *c* group
MSS.

2294   *Marginal gloss:* quod Wyttoun Dd.

For the spurious ending found in the *d**¹ MSS see the collations to lines 2259–
62, the notes to lines 2158 and 2159, and the description of Pw in "Descriptions of the
Manuscripts."   §   Arguing that the tales of the D Group show a "steady debasement on all
fronts," Cooper (1983:133–34) suggests that Chaucer might have had difficulty in following
on *SumT*; the last line "sounds like a deliberate signing off on Chaucer's part."

towne: The "town" is very commonly assumed to be Sittingbourne, based on
the Summoner's earlier threat, in *FrT* 847, to tell two or three tales of friars before he comes
to Sittingbourne. But if this town is Sittingbourne, the later (in the Ellesmere order) mention
of Rochester in *MkP* (B² 3116) is problematic, since Rochester stands about ten miles closer
to London than Sittingbourne. Hence of course the arguments about the Ellesmere, Brad-
shaw, and "1400 order" of tales. Greenfield (1953:52) rejects the identification of the "town"
with Sittingbourne, pointing out that "in the last couplet the 'gown' is the important thing;
it is what has been promised to Jankyn for his remarkable scheme of division. 'Town' is the
tag-word and not a deliberate reference to the particular town, Sittingbourne, of l. 847," an
argument with which Eliason (1972:200 n. 96) agrees. Owen (1951:824) argues that the
pilgrims are at this point on their return journey to London, and that "the 'town' refers to
[the Summoner's] earlier threat rather than an over-night stopping-place. They could hardly
have reached Sittingbourne, some distance away when the Summoner speaks, and ridden on
to Rochester (or in the other direction to Ospring) during the three tales of III (D), ll. 847 to
2294." He argues further that the Summoner's threat to tell three tales has been carried
through: "The Summoner's three tales are the one about friars in hell, the one about the
Friar's disappointment and anger, and the mechanically connected one of the way to divide a
'gift' among friars" (Owen 1951:824), an idea Greenfield rejects (1953:52). The argument
that the *towne* is by no means necessarily Sittingbourne is raised again by Olson (1984).

Bibliographical Index

Adams, John F.   1962. The Structure of Irony in the *Summoner's Tale*. *EIC* 12:126–32.

Aers, David   1986*a*. *Chaucer*. Harvester New Readings. Atlantic Highlands, N.J.: Humanities Press International.

———   1986*b*. Reflections on the "Allegory of the Theologians," Ideology, and *Piers Plowman*. In David Aers, ed., *Medieval Literature: Criticism, Ideology, and History*, pp. 58–73. New York: Saint Martin's Press.

Alderson, William L.   1984. John Urry (1666–1715). In Ruggiers, ed. 1984, pp. 93–115. (Abridged version of chapter in Alderson and Henderson 1970, pp. 80–129.)

———, and Arnold C. Henderson   1970. *Chaucer and Augustan Scholarship*. University of California Publications, English ser., 35. Berkeley, Los Angeles, and London: University of California Press.

Alford, John A.   1984. Scriptural Testament in *The Canterbury Tales*: The Letter Takes its Revenge. In Jeffrey, ed. 1984, pp. 197–203.

Allen, David G.   1987. Death and Staleness in the "Son-Less" World of the Summoner's Tale. *SSF* 24:1–14.

Allen, Judson Boyce, and Theresa Anne Moritz   1981. *A Distinction of Stories: The Medieval Unity of Chaucer's Fair Chain of Narratives for Canterbury*. Columbus: Ohio State University Press.

Ames, Ruth   1984. *God's Plenty: Chaucer's Christian Humanism*. A Campion Book. Chicago: Loyola University Press.

Andreas, James   1990. "Newe Science" from "Olde Bokes": A Bakhtinian Approach to the *Summoner's Tale*. *ChauR* 25:138–51.

Andrew, Malcolm   1993. Explanatory Notes. *The General Prologue. A Variorum Edition of the Works of Geoffrey Chaucer*, vol. 2, part 1B. Norman: University of Oklahoma Press. See also Ransom 1993.

Arber, Edward, ed.   1869. *The Revelation to the Monk of Evesham, 1196*. London. Reprint. New York: AMS Press, 1966.

Arnold, Thomas, ed.   1869–71. *Select English Works of John Wyclif*. 3 vols. Oxford: Clarendon Press.

Baird, Joseph L.   1969. The Devil's *Privetee*. *NM* 70:104–06.

Baker, Donald C.   1961. Witchcraft in the Dispute Between Chaucer's Friar and Summoner. *The South Central Bulletin* (Tulsa, Okla.) 21:33–36.

———   1962. Exemplary Figures as Characterizing Devices in the Friar's Tale and the Summoner's Tale. *University of Mississippi Studies in English* 3:35–41.

———, ed.   1984. *The Manciple's Tale. A Variorum Edition of the Works of Geoffrey Chaucer*, vol. 2, part 10. Norman: University of Oklahoma Press.

———   1986. William Thynne's Printing of the *Squire's Tale*: Manuscript and Printer's Copy. *SB* 39:125–132.

———, ed.   1990. *The Squire's Tale. A Variorum Edition of the Works of Geoffrey Chaucer*, vol. 2, part 12. Norman: University of Oklahoma Press.

Bandello, Matteo   1974. *Novelle*. Ed. Giuseppe Guido Ferrero. Turin: Unione Tipografico-Editrice.

Baugh, Albert C., ed.   1963. *Chaucer's Major Poetry*. New York: Appleton-Century-Crofts.

Baum, Paull F.   1956. Chaucer's Puns. *PMLA* 71:225–46.

——— 1958. Chaucer's Puns: A Supplementary List. *PMLA* 73:167–70.

Beichner, Paul E.   1956. Non Alleluia Ructare. *MS* 18:135–44.

——— 1961. Baiting the Summoner. *MLQ* 22:367–76.

Bell, Robert, ed.   1854–56. *Poetical Works of Geoffrey Chaucer*. 8 vols. Annotated Edition of the English Poets. London: John W. Parker and Son. [Notes by John Mountenay Jephson.]

Bennett, H. S.   1947. *Chaucer and the Fifteenth Century*. Oxford History of English Literature, vol. 2, part 1. Oxford: Clarendon Press. Reprint. 1958.

Benson, Larry D.   1981. The Order of *The Canterbury Tales*. *SAC* 3:77–117.

———, and Theodore M. Andersson   1971. *The Literary Context of Chaucer's Fabliaux: Texts and Translations*. New York: Bobbs-Merrill.

———, et al., eds.   1987. *The Riverside Chaucer*. Boston: Houghton Mifflin.

Benson, Robert G.   1980. *Medieval Body Language: A Study of the Use of Gesture in Chaucer's Poetry*. Anglistica 21. Copenhagen: Rosenkilde and Bagger.

Besserman, Lawrence   1984. *Glosynge is a Glorious Thyng:* Chaucer's Biblical Exegesis. In Jeffrey, ed. 1984, pp. 65–73. Originally published in *RUO* 53 (1983), 327–35.

Bevins, Lloyd Edward   1951. Chaucer's *Monk's Tale*: A Study of the Manuscript Texts. Ph.D. diss., University of Virginia.

Birney, Earle   1960. Structural Irony within the *Summoner's Tale*. *Anglia* 78:204–18. Reprinted in Birney 1985, pp. 109–23.

——— 1985. *Essays on Chaucerian Irony*, ed., with an essay on irony, by Beryl Rowland. Toronto, Buffalo, London: University of Toronto Press.

Bishop, Ian   1987. *The Narrative Art of the* Canterbury Tales: *A Critical Study of the Major Poems*. London and Melbourne: Everyman's University Library.

Blake, Norman F.   1977. *The English Language in Medieval Literature*. Towata, N.J.: Rowman and Littlefield.

——— 1979. The Relationship Between the Hengwrt and Ellesmere Manuscripts of the *Canterbury Tales*. *E&S* 32:1–18.

——— ed.   1980. *The Canterbury Tales by Geoffrey Chaucer. Edited from the Hengwrt Manuscript*. York Medieval Texts, 2d ser. London: Edward Arnold.

——— 1983. The Editorial Assumptions in the Manly-Rickert Edition of *The Canterbury Tales*. *ES* 64:385–400.

——— 1985. *The Textual Tradition of the Canterbury Tales*. London, Baltimore: Edward Arnold.

Blodgett, James E.   1984. William Thynne (d. 1546). In Ruggiers, ed. 1984, pp. 35–52.

Bloomfield, Morton W.   1958. Symbolism in Medieval Literature. *MP* 56:73–81.

Boitani, Piero   1984. *Chaucer and the Imaginary World of Fame*. Chaucer Studies, 10. Cambridge: D. S. Brewer; Totowa, N.J.: Barnes and Noble.

Bonventura, St.   [1898.] *Doctoris Seraphici S. Bonaventurae . . . Opera Omnia*, vol. 8. Quaracchi: Collegium S. Bonaventurae.

Boucher, Holly Wallace   1986. Nominalism: The Difference for Chaucer and Boccaccio. *ChauR* 20:213–20.

Bowden, Betsy   1987. *Chaucer Aloud: The Varieties of Textual Interpretation*. Philadelphia: University of Pennsylvania Press.

Bowden, Muriel   1964. *A Reader's Guide to Geoffrey Chaucer*. New York: Farrar, Strauss and Giroux; Toronto: Ambassador Books; London: Thames and Hudson, 1965.

Bowen, Robert O.   1959. The Flatus Symbol in Chaucer. *Inland* (Salt Lake City), Spring, 1959:19–22.

Boyd, Beverly   1967. *Chaucer and the Liturgy*. Philadelphia: Dorrance.

———— 1984. William Caxton (1422?–1491). In Ruggiers, ed. 1984, pp. 13–34.

Braddy, Haldeen 1966. Chaucer's Bawdy Tongue. *SFQ* 30:214–22. Reprinted in Braddy 1971, pp. 131–39.

———— 1969. Chaucer—Realism or Obscenity? *Arlington Quarterly* 2.i:121–38. Reprinted in Braddy 1971, pp. 146–58.

———— 1971. *Geoffrey Chaucer: Literary and Historical Studies.* Port Washington, N.Y., and London: Kennikat.

Brewer, Derek S. 1953. *Chaucer.* London and New York: Longman. 2d ed., 1960. 3d, rev. ed., 1973.

————, ed. 1966. *Chaucer and Chaucerians: Critical Studies in Middle English Literature.* University: University of Alabama Press.

———— 1984*a*. Chaucer and Arithmetic. In Wolf-Dietrich Bald and Horst Weinstock, eds., *Medieval Studies Conference Aachen 1983: Language and Literature*, pp. 111–19. Bamberger Beiträge zur Englischen Sprachwissenschaft, 15. Frankfurt am Main: Peter Lang.

———— 1984*b*. *Chaucer: The Poet as Storyteller.* London: Macmillan.

———— 1984*c*. *An Introduction to Chaucer.* London and New York: Longman.

Brink, Bernhard ten 1883–96. *History of English Literature.* Trans. Horace M. Kennedy, William Clarke Robinson, and L. Dora Schmitz. 2 vols. in 3. London: G. Bell and Sons; New York: Holt. Reprint. New York: AMS, 1974. [Contains revisions not in original *Geschichte der Englischen Literatur* (cf. Hammond 1908:555).]

Brunet, Gustave 1858. *Le violier des histoires romaines: Ancienne traduction françoise des "Gesta Romanorum."* Paris: P. Jannet.

Brusendorff, Aage 1925. *The Chaucer Tradition.* Copenhagen: Branner; London: Oxford University Press.

Bryan, W. F., and Germaine Dempster, eds. 1941. *Sources and Analogues of Chaucer's Canterbury Tales.* Chicago: University of Chicago Press. Reprint. Atlantic Highlands, N.J.: Humanities Press, 1958.

Burlin, Robert B. 1977. *Chaucerian Fiction.* Princeton: Princeton University Press.

Butler, Alban 1956. *Butler's Lives of the Saints.* Edited, rev., and supplemented by Herbert Thurston and Donald Attwater. New York: Kenedy.

Caldwell, Robert A. 1944. The Scribe of the Chaucer MS, Cambridge University Library Gg 4. 27. *MLQ* 5:33–44.

Carruthers, Mary 1972. Letter and Gloss in the Friar's and Summoner's Tales. *JNT* 2:208–14.

Cavendish, Richard 1977. *Visions of Heaven and Hell.* London: Orbis Publishing.

Chapman, C. O. 1929. Chaucer on Preachers and Preaching. *PMLA* 44:178–85.

Child, F. J., ed. 1892–98. *The English and Scottish Popular Ballads.* 5 vols. in 10. Boston and New York: Houghton Mifflin; London: Henry Stevens, Son and Stiles. Reprint. New York: Dover, 1965.

Chute, Marchette 1946. *Geoffrey Chaucer of England.* New York: E.P. Dutton.

Clark, Roy Peter 1976*a*. Doubting Thomas in Chaucer's *Summoner's Tale. ChauR* 11:164–78.

———— 1976*b*. Wit and Witsunday in Chaucer's *Summoner's Tale. AnM* 17:48–57.

Cline, Ruth H. 1945. Four Chaucer Saints. *MLN* 60:480–82.

Coghill, Nevill 1949. *The Poet Chaucer.* Home University Library of Modern Knowledge. London, New York, Toronto: Geoffrey Cumberlege/Oxford University Press. 2d ed. London, New York: Oxford University Press, 1967. Reprint. 1968.

———— 1966. Chaucer's Narrative Art in *The Canterbury Tales.* In Brewer, ed. 1966, pp. 114–39.

Colgrave, Bertram, ed. and trans. 1956. *Felix's Life of Saint Guthlac*. Cambridge: Cambridge University Press.

Cooper, Helen 1983. *The Structure of* The Canterbury Tales. London: Duckworth; Athens: University of Georgia Press, 1984.

———— 1989. *The Canterbury Tales*. Oxford Guides to Chaucer. New York: Oxford University Press.

Correale, Robert M. 1965. St. Jerome and the Conclusion of the *Friar's Tale*. ELN 2:171–74.

Corsa, Helen Storm 1964. *Chaucer: Poet of Mirth and Morality*. Notre Dame: University of Notre Dame Press.

Costa, C. D. N., ed. 1973. *Seneca: Medea*. Oxford: Clarendon Press.

Cotgrave, Randle 1611. *A Dictionarie of the French and English Tongues*. London: Adam Islip. Reproduction. Columbia: University of South Carolina Press, 1950. Reprint. 1966.

Cowling, George H. 1927. *Chaucer*. London: Methuen; New York: E. P. Dutton.

Craik, T. W. 1964. *The Comic Tales of Chaucer*. London: Methuen.

Cross, F. L., and E. A. Livingston, eds. 1974. *Oxford Dictionary of the Christian Church*. 2d ed. Oxford: Oxford University Press. Reprint. 1983.

Crowther, J. D. W. 1980. The *Summoner's Tale*: 1955–69. ChauN 2.i:12–13.

Curry, Walter Clyde 1923. The Bottom of Hell. *MLN* 38:253.

———— 1926. *Chaucer and the Mediaeval Sciences*. New York and London: Oxford University Press. 2d, rev., ed., New York: Barnes and Noble; London: Allen and Unwin, 1960.

Dahlberg, Charles, trans. 1971. *The Romance of the Rose by Guillaume de Lorris and Jean de Meun*. Princeton: Princeton University Press. Reprint. Hanover and London: University Press of New England, 1983.

Davis, Norman, et al., eds. 1979. *A Chaucer Glossary*. Oxford: Clarendon Press.

Dearing, Vinton, ed. 1974. *John Gay: Poetry and Prose*. 2 vols. Oxford: Clarendon Press.

Dempster, Germaine 1932. *Dramatic Irony in Chaucer*. Stanford University Publications, University ser., Language and Literature, vol. 4, no. 3. Stanford: Stanford University Press. Reprint. New York: Humanities Press, 1959.

D'Evelyn, Charlotte, and Anna J. Mill, eds. 1956–1959. *The South English Legendary*. 3 vols. EETS, o.s. 235, 236 and 244. London: Oxford University Press.

Diekstra, F. 1974. *Chaucer's Quizzical Mode of Exemplification*. Nijmegen: Dekker & Van de Vegt. [No date, but text based on lecture delivered 15 February 1974.]

Donaldson, E. Talbot, ed. 1958. *Chaucer's Poetry: An Anthology for the Modern Reader*. New York: Ronald Press. 2d ed., 1975.

Doyle, A. I., and Parkes, M. B. 1978. The Production of Copies of the *Canterbury Tales* and the *Confessio Amantis* in the Early Fifteenth Century. In M. B. Parkes and Andrew G. Watson, eds., *Medieval Scribes, Manuscripts & Libraries: Essays Presented to N. R. Ker*, pp. 163–210. London: Scolar Press.

———— 1979. Paleographical Introduction. In Ruggiers, ed. 1979, pp. xix–xlix.

Du Cange, Charles Du Fresne 1710. *Glossarium ad scriptores mediae & infimae latinitatis . . . .* 3 vols. Frankfurt am Main: J. A. Jungium.

Düring, Adolf von, trans. 1883–86. *Geoffrey Chaucers Werke*. 3 vols. Strassburg: Karl J. Trübner.

Dunn, Thomas F. 1940. *The Manuscript Source of Caxton's Second Edition of the Canterbury Tales*. Chicago: University of Chicago Press. [Part of University of Chicago diss.]

East, W. G. 1977. "By Preeve Which That Is Demonstratif." ChauR 12:78–82.

Eccles, Mark, ed. 1969. *The Macro Plays*. EETS, o.s. 262. London: Oxford University Press.

Edwards, A. S. G. 1984. Walter Skeat (1835–1912). In Ruggiers, ed. 1984, pp. 171–89.

Eliason, Norman E.   1972. *The Language of Chaucer's Poetry: An Appraisal of the Verse, Style, and Structure.* Anglistica 17. Copenhagen: Rosenkilde and Bagger.

Elliott, Ralph W. V.   1974. *Chaucer's English.* The Language Library. London: André Deutsch.

Engel, Hildegard   1931. *Structure and Plot in Chaucer's Canterbury Tales.* Inaugural dissertation, Rheinischen Friedrich-Wilhelms-Universität. Bonn: L. Neuendorff.

Everett, Dorothy   1955. *Essays on Middle English Literature,* ed. Patricia Kean. London: Oxford University Press.

Ewald, W.   1911. *Der Humor in Chaucers* Canterbury Tales. Halle: Niemeyer.

Fansler, Dean S.   1914. *Chaucer and the Roman de la Rose.* Columbia University Studies in English and Comparative Literature. New York: Columbia University Press. Reprint. Gloucester, Mass.: Peter Smith, 1965.

Fisher, John H., ed.   1977. *The Complete Poetry and Prose of Geoffrey Chaucer.* New York: Holt, Rinehart and Winston.

Fleming, John   1965. Chaucer's "Syngeth Placebo" and the *Roman de Fauvel. N&Q* 210: 17–18.

———   1966. The Antifraternalism of the *Summoner's Tale. JEGP* 65:688–700.

———   1967. The Summoner's Prologue: An Iconographic Adjustment. *ChauR* 2:95–107.

———   1983. Anticlerical Satire as Theological Essay: Chaucer's *Summoner's Tale. Thalia* 6.i:5–22.

———   1984. Gospel Asceticism: Some Chaucerian Images of Perfection. In Jeffrey, ed. 1984, pp. 183–95. [Originally published in *RUO* 53 (1983), 445–57.]

Fleming, Martha H.   1984. "Glosynge Is a Glorious Thing, Certyn": A Reconsideration of *The Summoner's Tale.* In Peter Cocozzella, ed., *The Late Middle Ages,* pp. 89–101. Center for Medieval and Early Renaissance Studies. ACTA, vol. 8. Binghamton, N.Y.: State University of New York Press.

Friedel, V.-H., and Kuno Meyer, eds.   1907. *La Vision de Tondale.* Paris: H. Champion.

Furnivall, Frederick J.   1868. *A Temporary Preface to the Six-Text Edition of Chaucer's Canterbury Tales: Part I.* Chaucer Society, 2d ser., 3. London: Trübner.

———, ed.   1868–77. *A Six-Text Print of Chaucer's Canterbury Tales in Parallel Columns.* 8 vols. Chaucer Society, 1st ser., 1, 14, 15, 25, 30, 31, 37, 49. London: Trübner.

———, ed.   1875. See Kingsley, ed. 1865.

———, ed.   1885. *The Harleian MS 7334 of Chaucer's Canterbury Tales.* Chaucer Society, 1st ser., 73. London: Trübner.

———, ed.   1902. *The Cambridge MS. Dd. 4.24 of Chaucer's Canterbury Tales, Completed by the Egerton MS. 2726.* 2 vols. Chaucer Society, 1st ser., 95, 96. London: Kegan Paul, Trench, Trübner.

———, ed.   1903. *Political, Religious, and Love Poems.* EETS, o.s. 15. London: Kegan Paul, Trench, and Trübner. First published 1866; re-edited 1903. Reprint. 1965.

———, et al., eds.   1872–87. *Originals and Analogues of Some of Chaucer's Canterbury Tales.* 5 vols. Chaucer Society, 2d Ser., 7, 10, 15, 20, 22. London: Trübner.

Gallacher, Patrick J.   1986. The *Summoner's Tale* and Medieval Attitudes Towards Sickness. *ChauR* 21:200–12.

Gardner, John   1977. *The Poetry of Chaucer.* Carbondale: Southern Illinois University Press.

Gerould, Gordon Hall   1952. *Chaucerian Essays.* Princeton: Princeton University Press. Reprint. New York: Russell and Russell, 1968.

Giaccherini, Enrico   1980. *I "Fabliaux" di Chaucer: Tradizione e innovazione nella narrativa comica chauceriana.* Pisa: ETS Università 12.

Godley, A. D., ed. and trans. 1920–30. *Herodotus*. 4 vols. Loeb Classical Library. London: William Heineman.

Godwin, William 1804. *Life of Geoffrey Chaucer*. 4 vols. London: T. Davison, White-Friars; for Richard Phillips. [Originally published in 2 vols., London, 1803.]

Graesse, [Johann Georg] Th[eodor], ed. 1850. *Jacobi a Voragine Legenda Aurea*. 2d ed. Leipzig: Libraria Arnoldiana. Reprint. Osnabrück: Otto Zeller, 1969.

Gray, Douglas 1990. Notes on Some Medieval Mystical, Magical, and Moral Cats. In Helen Phillips, ed. *Langland, the Mystics and the English Religious Tradition: Essays in Honour of S. S. Hussey*, pp. 185–202. Cambridge: D. S. Brewer.

Green, Richard Firth 1987. A Possible Source for Chaucer's Summoner's Tale. *ELN* 24.iv:24–27.

Greenfield, Stanley B. 1953. Sittingbourne and the Order of the *Canterbury Tales*. *MLR* 48:51–2.

Greg, W. W. 1924. The Early Printed Editions of the *Canterbury Tales*. *PMLA* 39:737–61.

Grennan, Joseph E. 1967. Science and Poetry in Chaucer's *House of Fame*. *AnM* 8:38–45.

Grosvenor, Mr. (Eustace Budgell) 1741. The Farmer and the Fryar: or the *Sumner's Tale*. In Ogle, ed. 1741:3.133–42.

Haeckel, Willi 1890. *Das Sprichwort bei Chaucer*. Erlangen and Leipzig: Georg Böhme. Reprint. Amsterdam: Rodopi, 1970.

Hamelius, P., ed. 1919–1923. *Mandeville's Travels, Translated from the French of Jean d'Outremeuse*. . . . 2 vols. EETS, o.s. 153, 154. London: Kegan Paul, Trench, Trübner. Reprint. London, New York, Toronto: Oxford University Press, 1961.

Hamilton, Marie P. 1942. The Summoner's "Psalm of Davit." *MLN* 57:655–57.

Hammond, Eleanor P. 1908. *Chaucer: A Bibliographical Manual*. New York: Macmillan. Reprint. New York: Peter Smith, 1933.

Hanning, R. W. 1985. Roasting a Friar, Mis-taking a Wife, and Other Acts of Textual Harassment in Chaucer's *Canterbury Tales*. *SAC* 7:3–21.

Harrison, Thomas P. 1956. *They Tell of Birds*. Austin: University of Texas Press.

Hart, Walter M. 1941. The Summoner's Tale. In Bryan and Dempster, eds. 1941, pp. 275–87.

Hartung, Albert E. 1967. Two Notes on the *Summoner's Tale: Hosts and Swans*. *ELN* 4:175–80.

Haskell, Ann S. 1971. St. Simon in the *Summoner's Tale*. *ChauR* 5:218–24.

——— 1976. Attributes of Anger in the Summoner's Tale. In *Essays on Chaucer's Saints*, pp. 58–63. Studies in English Literature, 107. The Hague and Paris: Mouton.

Havely, N. R., ed. 1975. *Geoffrey Chaucer: The Friar's, Summoner's and Pardoner's Tales from the Canterbury Tales*. London: University of London Press.

——— 1983. Chaucer, Boccaccio and the Friars. In Piero Boitani, ed., *Chaucer and the Italian Trecento*, pp. 249–68. Cambridge, London, New York, New Rochelle, Melbourne, Sydney: Cambridge University Press.

Heist, William W. 1950. Folklore Study and Chaucer's Fabliau-Like Tales. *Papers of the Michigan Academy of Science, Arts, and Letters* 36:251–58.

Hench, Atcheson L. 1950. Printer's Copy for Tyrwhitt's Chaucer. *SB* 3:265–66.

Hertzberg, Wilhelm, trans. 1866. *Geoffrey Chaucer's Canterbury-Geschichten*. Hildburghausen: Verlag des Bibliographischen Institut. Rev. J. Koch as *Geoffrey Chaucer's Canterbury-Erzählungen*. Berlin: Stubenrauch, 1925.

Heyworth, P. L., ed. 1968. *Jack Upland, Friar Daw's Reply, and Upland's Rejoinder*. London: Oxford University Press.

Higuchi, Masayuki 1990. On the Construction "I Was Go Walked." *Studies in Medieval English Language and Literature* 5: 13–26

Holley, Linda Tarte   1980. The Function of Language in Three Canterbury Churchmen. *Parergon* 28:36–44.

———   1990. *Chaucer's Measuring Eye*. Houston: Rice University Press.

Holme, Randle   1688. *The Academy of Armory, or a Storehouse of Armory and Blazon*. Chester: Printed for the Author. Reprint. Menston, England: The Scolar Press, 1972.

Homann, Elizabeth R.   1954. Chaucer's Use of 'Gan.' *JEGP* 53:389–98.

Hornsby, Joseph Allen   1988. *Chaucer and the Law*. Norman, Okla.: Pilgrim Books.

Horstmann, Carl, ed.   1887. *The Early South-English Legendary or Lives of Saints*. EETS, o.s. 87. London: Trübner. Reprint. Millwood, N. Y.: Kraus, 1973.

Howard, Donald R.   1976. *The Idea of the Canterbury Tales*. Berkeley, Los Angeles, and London: University of California Press.

Howard, Edwin   1964. *Geoffrey Chaucer*. Twayne's English Authors ser., 1. New York: Twayne. Griffin Authors ser. London: Macmillan, 1976.

Hudson, Anne   1984. John Stow (1525?–1605). In Ruggiers, ed. 1984, pp. 53–70.

Hughes, Robert   1968. *Heaven and Hell in Western Art*. New York: Stein and Day.

Huppé, Bernard F.   1964. *A Reading of the* Canterbury Tales. Albany: State University of New York Press. Rev. ed. 1967.

Irvine, Martin   1985. Medieval Grammatical Theory and Chaucer's *House of Fame*. *Speculum* 60:850–76.

Isaacs, Neil D.   1961. "Furlong Wey" in Chaucer. *N&Q* 206:328–29.

James, M. R., trans.   1924. *The Apocryphal New Testament*. Oxford: Clarendon Press. Reprinted with corrections, 1953. Reprint. 1969.

Jeffrey, David L., ed.   1984. *Chaucer and scriptural tradition*. Ottawa: University of Ottawa Press.

Jungman, Robert E.   1980. 'Covent' in the *Summoner's Tale*. *MissFR* 14:20–23.

Kaluza, Max   1893. *Chaucer und der Rosenroman: Eine litterargeschichtliche Studie*. Berlin: Emil Felber.

Kane, George   1984. John M. Manly (1865–1940) and Edith Rickert (1871–1938). In Ruggiers, ed. 1984, pp. 207–29.

Kaske, R. E.   1972. Horn and Ivory in the *Summoner's Tale*. *NM* 73:122–26.

Kazantzakis, Nikos   1941. *England: A Travel Journal*. Trans. Amy Mims. New York: Simon and Schuster, 1965.

———   1954. *The Fratricides*. Trans. Athena G. Dallas. New York: Simon and Schuster, 1964.

Kean, P. M.   1972. *Chaucer and the Making of English Poetry*. 2 vols. London and Boston: Routledge and Kegan Paul. Abridged ed., 1 vol., London, Boston and Henley-on-Thames: Routledge and Kegan Paul, 1982.

Kellogg, Alfred L.   1953. The Fraternal Kiss in Chaucer's Summoner's Tale. *Scriptorium* 7:115. Reprinted in *Chaucer, Langland, Arthur: Essays in Middle English Literature*, pp. 273–75. New Brunswick, N.J.: Rutgers University Press, 1972.

Kelly, J. N. D.   1986. *The Oxford Dictionary of Popes*. Oxford: Oxford University Press.

Kendrick, Laura   1988. *Chaucerian Play: Comedy and Control in the* Canterbury Tales. Berkeley: University of California Press.

Kennard, J. S.   1923. *The Friar in Fiction*. New York: Brentano's.

Kerkhof, J.   1982. *Studies in the Language of Geoffrey Chaucer*. 2d, revised and enlarged, ed. Leiden: E. J. Brill/Leiden University Press.

Kilian, Cornelius [alias Kiel]   1599. *Etymologicum Teutonicae linguae, sive dictionarium Teutonico-Latinum*. 3rd ed. Antwerp: I. Moretus.

Killough, George B.   1982. Punctuation and Caesura in Chaucer. *SAC* 4:87–107.

Kim, H. C., ed. 1973. *The Gospel of Nicodemus: Gesta Salvatoris*. Toronto: Pontifical Institute.

King, J. E., ed. and trans. 1930. *Baedae Opera Historica*. 2 vols. Loeb Classical Library. London: William Heinemann.

Kingsley, G. H., ed. 1865. *Francis Thynne's Animadversions upon Speght's First (1598 A.D.) Edition of Chaucer's Workes*. EETS, o.s. 9. London: Oxford University Press. Rev. F. J. Furnivall, 1875. Also published by Chaucer Society, 2d ser., 13. London: Trübner.

Kirby, Thomas A. 1953. Theodore Roosevelt on Chaucer and a Chaucerian. *MLN* 68:34–37.

Kittredge, G[eorge] L[yman] 1892. The Authorship of the English Romaunt of the Rose. [*Harvard*] *Studies and Notes in Philology and Literature* 1:1–65.

——— 1915. *Chaucer and his Poetry*. Cambridge, Mass.: Harvard University Press.

Knapp, Peggy 1990. *Chaucer and the Social Contest*. New York and London: Routledge.

Knight, Stephen 1973. *The Poetry of the Canterbury Tales*. Sydney: Angus and Robertson.

——— 1986. *Geoffrey Chaucer*. Oxford: Basil Blackwell.

Koch, John 1890. *The Chronology of Chaucer's Writings*. Chaucer Society, 2d ser., 27. London: Kegan Paul, Trench, Trübner.

——— 1902. *The Pardoner's Prologue and Tale by Geoffrey Chaucer: A Critical Edition*. Chaucer Society, 2d ser., 35. Oxford: Oxford University Press. Reprint. 1928.

Koch, Robert A. 1959. Elijah the Prophet, Founder of the Carmelite Order. *Speculum* 34:547–60.

Kökeritz, Helge 1954. Rhetorical Word-Play in Chaucer. *PMLA* 69:937–52.

Koeppel, Emil 1891*a*. Chauceriana. *Anglia* 13:174–86.

——— 1891*b*. Über das Verhältnis von Chaucers Prosawerken zu seinen Dichtungen und die Echtheit der "Parson's Tale." *Archiv* 87:33–54.

——— 1892. Chauceriana. *Anglia* 14:227–67.

——— 1911. Chaucer und Ciceros "Laelius de amicitia." *Archiv* 126:180–82.

Kolve, V.A. 1984. *Chaucer and the Imagery of Narrative: The First Five Canterbury Tales*. Stanford: Stanford University Press; London: Edward Arnold.

Kuhl, Ernest P. 1923. Chaucer's "My Maistre Bukton." *PMLA* 38:115–31.

——— 1925. Chaucer and the Church. *MLN* 40:321–38.

Kynaston, [Sir] Francis 1635. *Amorvm Troili et Creseidae. Libri duo priores Anglico-Latini*. Oxford: John Lichfield.

Lancashire, Ian 1981. Moses, Elijah and the Back Parts of God: Satiric Scatology in Chaucer's *Summoner's Tale*. *Mosaic* 14.iii:17–30.

Landrum, Grace 1924. Chaucer's Use of the Vulgate. *PMLA* 39:75–100.

Lange, Hugo 1938. Chaucer und Mandeville's Travels. *Archiv* 174:79–81.

Långfors, Arthur, ed. 1914–1919. *Le Roman de Fauvel*. SATF. Paris: Librairie de Firmin Didot.

Langlois, Ernest, ed. 1914–1924. *Le Roman de la Rose par Guillaume de Lorris et Jean de Meun . . .* 5 vols. SATF. Paris: Librairie de Firmin-Didot (vols. 1-2), de Honoré Champion (vol. 3), de Édouard Champion (vols. 4-5).

Lawler, Traugott 1980. *The One and the Many in the Canterbury Tales*. Hamden, Conn.: Archon Books.

Lawlor, John 1968. *Chaucer*. Hutchinson University Library. London: Hutchinson; New York: Harper and Row, 1969.

Lawrence, W. W. 1950. *Chaucer and the Canterbury Tales*. New York: Columbia University Press. Reprint. 1951.

Lawton, David 1985. *Chaucer's Narrators*. Chaucer Studies, 13. Cambridge: D. S. Brewer.

Le Grand d'Aussy, Pierre Jean Baptiste, ed.   1829. *Fabliaux ou Contes, Fables et Romans du xiie et du xiiie siècles*. 3rd ed. 5 vols. Paris: J. Renouard.

Legouis, Emile   1910. *Geoffrey Chaucer*. Les Grands Ecrivains Etrangers. Paris: Bloud. Trans. by L. Lailavoix. London: J. M. Dent and Sons; New York: E. P. Dutton, 1913. Reprint. New York: Russell and Russell, 1961.

Levitan, Alan   1971. The Parody of Pentecost in Chaucer's *Summoner's Tale*. UTQ 40:236–46.

Levy, Bernard S.   1966. Biblical Parody in the *Summoner's Tale*. TSL 11:45–60.

Leyerle, John   1971. Chaucer's Windy Eagle. UTQ 40:247–63.

Lindahl, Carl   1987. *Earnest Games: Folkloric Patterns in the Canterbury Tales*. Bloomington: Indiana University Press.

Lindner, F.   1888. Die englische Übersetzung des Romans von der Rose. *Englische Studien* 11:163–73.

Livingston, Charles H.   1925. Middle English "Askances." MLR 20:71–72.

Lobineau, Gui Alexis   1707. *Histoire de Bretagne . . .* 2 vols. Paris: Nicolas Simart.

Lounsbury, Thomas R.   1892. *Studies in Chaucer: His Life and Writings*. 3 vols. New York: Harper; London: James R. Osgood, McIlvaine. Reprint. New York: Russell and Russell, 1962.

Lowell, James Russell   1870. Chaucer. *North American Review* 111:154–98. Reprinted in *The Complete Writings of James Russell Lowell*, vol. 2, *My Study Windows*, pp. 183–269. Boston and New York: Houghton, Mifflin, 1904. Reprint. New York: AMS, 1966.

Lowes, John Livingston   1915. Chaucer and the Seven Deadly Sins. PMLA 30:237–371.

———   1934. *Geoffrey Chaucer and the Development of His Genius*. Boston: Houghton Mifflin. Also published as *Geoffrey Chaucer*. Oxford: Clarendon Press. Reprint. Bloomington: Indiana University Press, 1958.

Luard, Henry Richards, ed.   1872–83. *Matthaei Parisiensis, monachi Sancti Albani, Chronica Majora*. London: Longmans.

Lumiansky, R. M.   1955. *Of Sondry Folk: The Dramatic Principle in the Canterbury Tales*. Austin: University of Texas Press.

Macaulay, G. C., ed.   1899–1902. *The Complete Works of John Gower*. 4 vols. Oxford: Clarendon Press.

MacDonald, Donald   1966. Proverbs, *Sententiae*, and *Exempla* in Chaucer's Comic Tales: The Function of Comic Misapplication. *Speculum* 41:453–65.

McPeek, James A. S.   1951. Chaucer and the Goliards. *Speculum* 26:332–36.

Magoun, Francis P., Jr.   1953. Chaucer's Ancient and Biblical World. MS 15:107–36. Incorporated into Magoun 1961.

———   1961. *A Chaucer Gazetteer*. Chicago: University of Chicago Press; Uppsala: Almqvist & Wiksell.

Makarewicz, Sister Mary Raynelda   1953. *The Patristic Influence on Chaucer*. Washington, D.C.: Catholic University of America Press.

Mâle, Emile   1913. *The Gothic Image*. Trans. Dora Nussey. London: J. P. Dent; New York: E. P. Dutton. Reprint. New York: Harper and Row, 1958.

Malone, Edward A.   1989. Chaucer's *Summoner's Tale*. Expl 47:4–5.

Manly, John M.   1926a. Chaucer and the Rhetoricians. Warton Lecture on English Poetry, 17. PBA 12:95–113. Also printed separately. Reprinted in Schoeck and Taylor, eds. 1960, pp. 268–90.

———   1926b. *Some New Light on Chaucer: Lectures Delivered at the Lowell Institute*. New York: Holt; London: Bell. Reprint. New York: Peter Smith, 1951.

———, ed.   1928. *Canterbury Tales by Geoffrey Chaucer*. New York: H. Holt; London, Calcutta, and Sydney: Harrap.

————, and Edith Rickert, eds.   1940. *The Text of the Canterbury Tales: Studied on the Basis of All Known Manuscripts*. 8 vols. Chicago: University of Chicago Press.

Mann, Jill   1973. *Chaucer and Medieval Estates Satire: The Literature of Social Classes and the "General Prologue" to the "Canterbury Tales."* Cambridge: Cambridge University Press.

Martin, Daniel, and Margaret Wright   1990. A Further Note on "Hostes Man," *Canterbury Tales* D 1755. *ChauR* 24:271–73.

Matthew, F. D., ed.   1880. *The English Works of Wyclif Hitherto Unprinted*. EETS, o.s. 74. London: Trübner. 2d, rev., ed. 1902. Reprint. Millwood, N.Y.: Kraus, 1973.

Mehl, Dieter   1973. *Geoffrey Chaucer: Eine Einführung in seine erzählenden Dichtungen*. Grundlagen der Anglistik und Amerikanistik, 7. Berlin: Erich Schmidt. Rev. and trans. as *Geoffrey Chaucer: An Introduction to his Narrative Poetry*. Cambridge and New York: Cambridge University Press, 1986.

Méon, M., ed.   1814. *Le Roman de la Rose par Guillaume de Lorris et Jean de Meung*. . . . 4 vols. Paris: P. Didot l'Aîné.

Merrill, Thomas F.   1962. Wrath and Rhetoric in the *Summoner's Tale*. *TSLL* 4:341–50.

Meyer, Emil   1913. *Die Charackterzeichnung bei Chaucer*. Studien zur englischen Philologie, 48. Halle a.S.: Max Niemeyer Verlag.

Michel, Francisque, ed.   1864. *Le Roman de la Rose, par Guillaume de Lorris et Jean de Meung*. 2 vols. Paris: Firmin Didot.

Morris, Edward P., ed.   1911. *Horace: The Epistles*. New York, Cincinnati: American Book Co. Reprinted in *Horace: Satires and Epistles*. Norman: University of Oklahoma Press, 1968.

Morris, Richard, ed.   1863. *Pricke of Conscience*. Berlin: Philological Society.

————, ed.   1866a. *Dan Michel's Ayenbite of Inwyt*. EETS, o.s. 23. London: Trübner.

————, ed.   1866b. *The Poetical Works of Geoffrey Chaucer*. The Aldine Edition. 6 vols. London: Bell and Daldy; rev. ed. 1872, reprinted London: George Bell & Sons, 1902.

————, ed.   1872. *An Old English Miscellany*. EETS, o.s. 49. London: Trübner.

————, ed.   1874. *Cursor Mundi*. EETS, o.s. 57, 59, 62, 66, 68, 99, 101. London: K. Paul, Trench, Trübner.

Muscatine, Charles   1957. *Chaucer and the French Tradition: A Study in Style and Meaning*. Berkeley and Los Angeles: University of California Press.

————   1966. *The Canterbury Tales*: Style of the Man and Style of the Work. In Brewer, ed. 1966, pp. 88–113.

Mustanoja, Tauno F.   1960. *A Middle English Syntax*, part 1: *Parts of Speech*. Mémoires de la Société Néophilologique de Helsinki, 23. Helsinki: Société Néophilologique.

O'Brien, Timothy D.   1990. "Ars-Metrick": Science, Satire, and Chaucer's Summoner. *Mosaic* 23.iv:1–22.

Oesterley, Hermann, ed.   1872. *Gesta Romanorum*. Berlin: Weidmann. Reprint. Hildesheim: G. Olms, 1963.

Ogle, George, ed.   1741. *The Canterbury Tales of Chaucer, Modernis'd by several Hands*. 3 vols. London: J. & R. Tonson. [Vol. 3, pp. 127–42 applies.]

Olson, Glending   1984. The Terrain of Chaucer's Sittingbourne. *SAC* 6:103–19.

Olson, Paul A.   1986. *The Canterbury Tales and the Good Society*. Princeton: Princeton University Press.

Owen, Charles A., Jr.   1955. Morality as a Comic Motif in the *Canterbury Tales*. *CE* 16:226–32.

————   1966. "Thy Drasty Rymyng. . . ." *SP* 63:533–64.

————   1977. *Pilgrimage and Storytelling in the Canterbury Tales: The Dialectic of "Ernest" and "Game."* Norman: University of Oklahoma Press.

Page, William, ed.   1913. *The Victoria History of the County of York*. 3 vols. London: A. Constable. Reprint. Folkstone [Kent] & London: Dawsons of Pall Mall, 1974.

Parkes, M. B., and Richard Beadle, eds. 1979. *Poetical Works: Geoffrey Chaucer. A Facsimile of Cambridge University Library MS Gg.4.27*. 3 vols. Norman, Okla.: Pilgrim Books; Cambridge: D. S. Brewer, 1979–80.

——— *See also* A. I. Doyle and M. B. Parkes 1978, 1979.

Patch, Howard Rollin 1939. *On Rereading Chaucer*. Cambridge, Mass.: Harvard University Press; London: Oxford University Press.

Patterson, Lee W. 1978. The "Parson's Tale" and the Quitting of the "Canterbury Tales." *Traditio* 34:332–80.

——— 1987. "No Man His Reson Herde": Peasant Consciousness, Chaucer's Miller, and the Structure of the *Canterbury Tales. SAQ* 86:457–95. Reprinted in Lee Patterson, ed. *Literary Practice and Social Change in Britain, 1380–1530*, pp. 113–55. Berkeley: University of California Press, 1990.

Pearcy, Roy J. 1967. Chaucer's "An Impossible" ("Summoner's Tale" III, 2231). *N&Q* 212:322–25.

——— 1974. Structural Models for the Fabliaux and the *Summoner's Tale* Analogues. *Fabula* 15:103–13.

Pearsall, Derek, ed. 1984a. *The Nun's Priest's Tale. A Variorum Edition of the Works of Geoffrey Chaucer*, vol. 2, part 9. Norman: University of Oklahoma Press.

——— 1984b. Thomas Speght (ca. 1550–?). In Ruggiers, ed. 1984, pp. 71–92.

——— 1985. *The Canterbury Tales*. Unwin Critical Library. London, Boston, Sydney: George Allen & Unwin. Reprint. 1986.

——— 1986. The *Canterbury Tales* II: Comedy. In Piero Boitani and Jill Mann, eds., *The Cambridge Chaucer Companion*, pp. 125–42. Cambridge: Cambridge University Press.

Peltola, Niilo 1968. Chaucer's Summoner: "Fyr-Reed Cherubynnes Face." *NM* 69:560–68.

Pollard, Alfred W., ed. 1894. *Chaucer's Canterbury Tales*. 2 vols. London and New York: Macmillan.

———, et al., eds. 1898. *The Works of Geoffrey Chaucer*. The Globe Edition. London: Macmillan. Reprint. 1913.

Pratt, Robert A. 1966. Chaucer and the Hand That Fed Him. *Speculum* 41:619–42.

———, ed. 1974. *The Tales of Canterbury, Complete: Geoffrey Chaucer*. Boston: Houghton Mifflin.

——— 1978. Albertus Magnus and the Problem of Sound and Odor in the *Summoner's Tale. PQ* 57:267–68.

Preston, Raymond 1952. *Chaucer*. London and New York: Sheed and Ward. Reprint. New York: Greenwood Press, 1969.

Raizis, M. Byron 1969. Nikos Kazantzakis and Chaucer. *CLS* 6:141–47.

Ramsey, Roy Vance 1982. The Hengwrt and Ellesmere Manuscripts of the *Canterbury Tales*: Different Scribes. *SB* 35:133–54.

——— 1986. Paleography and Scribes of Shared Training. *SAC* 8:107–44.

Ransom, Daniel J. 1993. Textual Notes. In Malcolm Andrew, Charles Moorman, and Daniel J. Ransom, eds., *The General Prologue. A Variorum Edition of the Works of Geoffrey Chaucer*, vol. 2, part 1A. Norman: University of Oklahoma Press.

Reinecke, George F. 1984. F. N. Robinson (1872–1967). In Ruggiers, ed. 1984, pp. 231–51.

Reiss, Edmund 1984. Biblical Parody: Chaucer's "Distortions" of Scripture. In Jeffrey, ed. 1984, pp. 47–61.

Rennhard, Siegfried 1962. *Das Demonstrativum im Mittelenglischen, 1200–1500*. Keller: Winterthur.

Richardson, Janette 1970. *Blameth Nat Me: A Study of Imagery in Chaucer's Fabliaux*. Studies in English Literature, 58. The Hague and Paris: Mouton.

————— 1975. Friar and Summoner: The Art of Balance. *ChauR* 9:227–36.

Robbins, Rossell Hope, ed. 1952. *Secular Lyrics of the XIVth and XVth Centuries*. Oxford: Clarendon Press. 2d ed., 1955.

Robertson, D. W., Jr. 1962. *A Preface to Chaucer: Studies in Medieval Perspectives*. Princeton, N. J.: Princeton University Press.

Robinson, F. N., ed. 1933. *The Complete Works of Geoffrey Chaucer*. Boston: Houghton Mifflin.

—————, ed. 1957. *The Works of Geoffrey Chaucer*. 2d ed. Boston: Houghton Mifflin; London: Oxford University Press.

Rogers, William E. 1986. *Upon the Ways: The Structure of The Canterbury Tales*. English Literary Studies Monograph Series, 36. Victoria [B.C.]: University of Victoria Press.

Root, Robert K. 1906. *The Poetry of Chaucer: A Guide to Its Study and Appreciation*. Boston and New York: Houghton Mifflin. 2d, rev., ed., 1922. Reprint. Gloucester, Mass.: Peter Smith, 1957.

Ross, Thomas W. 1972. *Chaucer's Bawdy*. New York: Dutton; Toronto and Vancouver: Clarke, Irwin.

—————, ed. 1983. *The Miller's Tale. A Variorum Edition of the Works of Geoffrey Chaucer*, vol. 2, part 3. Norman: University of Oklahoma Press.

————— 1984. Thomas Wright (1810–1877). In Ruggiers, ed. 1984, pp. 145–56.

Rowland, Beryl 1971. *Blind Beasts: Chaucer's Animal World*. Kent, Ohio: Kent State University Press.

Ruggiers, Paul G. 1965. *The Art of The Canterbury Tales*. Madison: University of Wisconsin Press. Reprint. 1967.

————— 1976. A Vocabulary for Chaucerian Comedy: A Preliminary Sketch. In Jess B. Bessinger, Jr., and Robert Raymo, eds., *Medieval Studies in Honor of Lillian Herlands Hornstein*, pp. 193–225. New York: New York University Press.

—————, ed. 1979. *The Canterbury Tales, Geoffrey Chaucer: A Facsimile and Transcription of the Hengwrt Manuscript, with Variants from the Ellesmere Manuscript*. [A Variorum Edition of the Works of Geoffrey Chaucer, vol. 1.] Norman: University of Oklahoma Press; Folkestone: Wm. Dawson and Son.

—————, ed. 1984. *Editing Chaucer: The Great Tradition*. Norman, Okla.: Pilgrim Books.

Rutledge, Sheryl P. 1973. Chaucer's Zodiac of Tales. *Costerus* 9:117–43.

Ryan, Granger, and Helmut Ripperger, trans. 1941. *The Golden Legend of Jacobus de Voragine*. 2 vols. New York, London, Toronto: Longmans, Green.

Samuels, M. L. 1983. The Scribe of the Hengwrt and Ellesmere Manuscripts of *The Canterbury Tales*. *SAC* 5:49–65.

Sandras, E.-G. 1859. *Etude sur G. Chaucer considéré comme imitateur des trouvères*. Paris: Auguste Durand.

Schaar, Claes 1955. *The Golden Mirror: Studies in Chaucer's Descriptive Technique and its Literary Background*. Lund: C. W. K. Gleerup.

Schlauch, Margaret 1956. *English Medieval Literature and Its Social Foundations*. Warsaw: Panstwowe Wydawnictwo Naukowe.

Schless, Howard H. 1984. *Chaucer and Dante: A Revaluation*. Norman, Okla.: Pilgrim Books.

Schoeck, Richard J., and Jerome Taylor, eds. 1960. *Chaucer Criticism*, vol. 1, *The Canterbury Tales*. Notre Dame and London: University of Notre Dame Press.

Scott, H. von E., and C. C. Swinton Bland, trans. 1929. *The Dialogue on Miracles [by] Caesarius of Heisterbach*. 2 vols. London: G. Routledge & Sons.

Sedgwick, Henry Dwight 1934. *Dan Chaucer*. New York: Bobbs-Merrill.

Severs, J. Burke 1964. Chaucer's *Summoner's Tale* D 2148–88. *Explicator* 23, Item 20.

Shain, Charles E. 1955. Pulpit Rhetoric in Three Canterbury Tales. *MLN* 70:235–45.

Shaw, Judith   1984. Wrath in the Canterbury Pilgrims. *ELN* 21.iii:7–10.

Shelly, Percy Van Dyke   1940. *The Living Chaucer*. Philadelphia: University of Pennsylvania Press. Reprint. New York: Russell and Russell, 1968.

Silvia, Daniel S., Jr.   1964. Chaucer's Friars: Swans or Swains? *Summoner's Tale*, D 1930. *ELN* 1:248–50.

Skeat, Walter W., ed.   1894. *The Complete Works of Geoffrey Chaucer*. 6 vols. Oxford: Clarendon Press. Vol. 7, *Chaucerian and Other Pieces: Being a Supplement to the Complete Works of Geoffrey Chaucer*, published in 1897.

————   1905. Introduction. In *The Works of Geoffrey Chaucer and Others, Being a Reproduction in Facsimile of the First Collected Edition 1532 from the Copy in the British Museum*. London: Alexander Moring/De La More Press; Henry Frowde/Oxford University Press.

Skinner, Stephen   1671. *Etymologicon Linguae Anglicanae*. . . . London: Roycroft.

Smith, J. J.   1988. The Trinity Gower D-Scribe and His Work on Two Early *Canterbury Tales* Manuscripts. In J. J. Smith, ed., *The English of Chaucer and His Contemporaries: Essays by M. L. Samuels and J. J. Smith*, pp. 51–69. Aberdeen: Aberdeen University Press.

Smith, [Joshua] Toulmin   1870. *English Gilds: The Original Ordinances of More than One Hundred Early English Gilds*. . . . EETS, o.s. 40. London: N. Trübner. Reprint. London: Humphrey Milford/Oxford University Press, 1924.

Smyser, H. M.   1967. Chaucer's Use of *Gin* and *Do. Speculum* 42:68–83.

Southworth, James G.   1953. Chaucer's *The Canterbury Tales*, D.1746–53. *Explicator* 11, Item 29.

Speirs, John   1951. *Chaucer the Maker*. London: Faber and Faber. 2d, rev., ed. 1960. Reprint. 1967.

Spencer, Theodore   1927. Chaucer's Hell: A Study in Mediaeval Convention. *Speculum* 2:177–200.

Spitzer, Leo   1945. Anglo-French Etymologies. *PQ* 24:20–32.

Spurgeon, Caroline F. E.   1925. *Five Hundred Years of Chaucer Criticism and Allusion, 1357–1900*. 3 vols. Cambridge: Cambridge University Press. Reprint. New York: Russell and Russell, 1961. Originally published as Chaucer Society, 2d ser., 48–50, 52–56. London: Trübner, 1908–17.

Stanford, Mabel A.   1920. The Sumner's Tale and Saint Patrick's Purgatory. *JEGP* 19:377–81.

Strange, Joseph, ed.   1851. *Caesarii Heisterbacensis Monachi Ordinis Cisterciensis Dialogus Miraculorum*. Cologne: J. M. Heberele.

Szittya, Penn R.   1974. The Friar as False Apostle: Antifraternal Exegesis and the *Summoner's Tale*. *SP* 71:19–46.

————   1986. *The Antifraternal Tradition in Medieval Literature*. Princeton: Princeton University Press.

Tatlock, John S. P.   1914. Notes on Chaucer: The Canterbury Tales. *MLN* 29:140–44.

————   1916. Puns in Chaucer. In H. Rushton Fairclough, Karl G. Rendtorff, and William Dinsmore Briggs, eds., *Flügel Memorial Volume: containing an unpublished paper by Professor Ewald Flügel, and contributions in his memory by his colleagues and students*, pp. 228–32. Leland Stanford Junior University Publications, University ser., 21. Stanford: Stanford University Press.

————   1935. The *Canterbury Tales* in 1400. *PMLA* 50:100–39.

————, and Arthur G. Kennedy   1927. *A Concordance to the Complete Works of Geoffrey Chaucer and to the Romaunt of the Rose*. The Carnegie Institution of Washington.

Thro, A. Booker   1970. Chaucer's Creative Comedy: A Study of the *Miller's Tale* and the *Shipman's Tale*. *ChauR* 5:97–111.

Thynne, Francis   1599. See G. H. Kingsley, ed. 1865.

Tupper, Frederick   1914. Chaucer and the Seven Deadly Sins. *PMLA* 29:93–128.
———   1915*a*. Anent Jerome and the Summoner's Friar. *MLN* 30:63.
———   1915*b*. Chaucer's Bed's Head. *MLN* 30:5–12.
———   1915*c*. The Quarrels of the Canterbury Pilgrims. *JEGP* 14:256–70.
———   1916. Chaucer's Sinners and Sins. *JEGP* 15:56–106.
———   1940. Chaucer and the Cambridge Edition. *JEGP* 39:503–26.
[Tyrwhitt, Thomas, ed.]   1775. *The Canterbury Tales of Chaucer*. 4 vols. Additional 5th vol., containing glossary, 1778. London: T. Payne. Reprint. New York: AMS Press, 1972. 2d ed. 2 vols. Oxford: Clarendon Press, 1798.
Urry, John, ed.   1721. *The Works of Geoffrey Chaucer*. London: Bernard Lintot. [Glossary by Timothy Thomas, with the assistance of William Thomas.]
Visser, Fredericus Theodorus   1970. *An Historical Syntax of the English Language*. Leiden: E. J. Brill.
Voss, A. E.   1985. Thematic Unity and Parallel Structure in Fragment III of *The Canterbury Tales*. *UMS* (Pretoria) 2:11–17.
Wagenknecht, Edward   1968. *The Personality of Chaucer*. Norman: University of Oklahoma Press.
Wallace, David   1990. Chaucer's Body Politic: Social and Narrative Self-Regulation. *Exemplaria* 2:221–40.
Warton, Thomas   1774. *The History of English Poetry, from the Close of the Eleventh to the Commencement of the Eighteenth Century*, vol. 1. London. Rev. ed., *History of English Poetry from the Twelfth to the Close of the Sixteenth Century*, ed. W. Carew Hazlitt, vol. 2. London: Reeves and Turner, 1871. Reprint of rev. ed. New York: Haskell House, 1970.
Wasserman, Julian N.   1982. The Ideal and the Actual: The Philosophical Unity of *Canterbury Tales*, MS. Group III. *Allegorica* 7.ii:65–99.
Wentersdorf, Karl P.   1980. The Motif of Exorcism in the *Summoner's Tale*. *SSF* 17:249–54.
———   1984. The Symbolic Significance of *Figurae Scatologicae* in Gothic Manuscripts. In Clifford Davidson, ed., *Word, Picture, and Spectacle*, pp. 1–19. Kalamazoo, Mich.: Medieval Institute Publications.
Wenzel, Siegfried   1970. Two Notes on Chaucer and Grosseteste. *N&Q* 215:449–51.
Wetherbee, Winthrop 1989. *Geoffrey Chaucer: The Canterbury Tales*. Landmarks of World Literature. Cambridge: Cambridge University Press.
White, Beatrice   1965. Medieval Beasts. *E&S* 18:34–44.
Whitesell, J. Edwin   1956. Chaucer's Lisping Friar. *MLN* 71:160–61.
Whiting, Bartlett Jere   1968. *Proverbs, Sentences, and Proverbial Phrases from English Writings Mainly Before 1500*. (With the collaboration of Helen Wescott Whiting.) Cambridge, Mass.: Belknap Press/Harvard University Press; London: Oxford University Press.
Whitmore, Sister Mary Ernestine   1937. *Medieval English Domestic Life and Amusements in the Works of Chaucer: A Dissertation*. Washington, D.C.: Catholic University of America Press. Reprint. New York: Cooper Square, 1972.
Whittock, Trevor   1968. *A Reading of The Canterbury Tales*. Cambridge: Cambridge University Press.
Williams, Arnold   1953. Chaucer and the Friars. *Speculum* 28:499–513. Reprinted in Schoeck and Taylor, eds. 1960, pp. 63–83.
———   1960. Relations Between the Mendicant Friars and the Regular Clergy in England in the Later Fourteenth Century. *AnM* 1:22–95.
Windeatt, B. A.   1984. Thomas Tyrwhitt (1730–1786). In Ruggiers, ed. 1984, pp. 117–43.
Wlislocki, Heinrich von   1889. Vergleichende Beiträge des Chaucers Canterbury-geschichten. *Zeitschrift für vergleichende Literaturgeschichte und Renaissance-Literatur*, Neue Folge, 2:194–99.

Wood, Chauncey   1984. Artistic Intention and Chaucer's Use of Scriptural Allusion. In Jeffrey, ed. 1984, pp. 35–46.

Wright, Joseph   1928. *An Elementary Middle English Grammar.* 2d ed. London: Oxford University Press.

Wright, Stephen K.   1988. Jankyn's Boethian Learning in the *Summoner's Tale. ELN* 26:4–7.

Wright, Thomas   1844. *St. Patrick's Purgatory.* London: John Russell Smith.

———, ed.   1847–51. *The Canterbury Tales of Geoffrey Chaucer: A New Text with Illustrative Notes.* 3 vols. Percy Society, 24–26. London: Percy Society.

Zanden, Cornelius Mattheus van der   1927. *Etude sur le Purgatoire de Saint Patrice accompagnée du texte latin d'Utrecht et du text anglo-normand de Cambridge.* Amsterdam: H. J. Paris.

Zietlow, Paul N.   1966. In Defense of the Summoner. *ChauR* 1:4–19.

Zupitza, Julius, ed.   1893. *Specimens of All the Accessible Unprinted Manuscripts of the Canterbury Tales: The Doctor-Pardoner Link, and Pardoner's Prologue and Tale.* Part III. Chaucer Society, 1st ser., 86. London: Kegan Paul, Trench, Trübner.

General Index

Adams, John F.: 36, 114, 122, 133, 155, 161, 170, 195, 200, 202, 206
Aeneas: *See* Virgil
Aers, David: 34, 41, 125
Aesop: 161
Agrippa, Cornelius, 144
Albert of Vercelli: 207
Albertus Magnus: *De sensu et sensato*, 204
Alderson, William L.: 87–88, 104, 120, 145
Alford, John A.: 12, 20, 30, 39, 130, 188, 200
Allen, David G.: 52, 134
Allen, Judson Boyce: 27, 200
Ames, Ruth: 196
Andersson, Theodore M.: 8–10
Andreas, James: 43–44, 109, 125, 131, 206
Andrew, Malcolm: 111
Anger: *See* Seven Deadly Sins
Anne, Queen of Richard II: 110
Antichrist, play of: 180
Antwerp: 9
Aquinas, Saint Thomas: 47, 125, 141
Arber, Edward: 5
Aristotle: 44; *Posterior Analytics*, 204
Armagh: 44
Arnold, Thomas: 180, 187, 193
Artes praedicandi: 168
Augustine, Saint: 16, 44, 141; *Enarratio in Psalmum*, 190
Ayenbite of Inwit: 177

Bacon, Roger: 29, 201–02
Baird, Joseph L.: 6–7, 105
Baisieux, Jacques de: *Le dis de le vescie a prestre*, 9–11, 13, 15, 19, 21, 35, 110
Baker, Donald C.: 25, 32, 35, 42, 80, 85, 199, 205, 211
Baker, Henry (pseudonym for Henry Stonecastle): 17
Bakhtin, Mikhail: 40, 43
Bandello, Matteo: 11
Bartello, Tadello di: 6

Bath: 110
Baugh, Albert C.: 120–22
Baum, Paull F.: 109, 122, 133, 151, 160, 166–67, 181–82, 202
Beadle, Richard: 70–71
Bede: *Ecclesiastical History*, 5, 141; *De natura rerum*, 14, 208
Bee, or Universal Weekly Pamphlet, The: 17
Beichner, Paul E.: 24, 103, 155
Bell, Robert: 175; *see also* Jephson, John M.
Bennett, H. S.: 126, 130–31
Benson, Larry D.: 8–10, 59; general editor of *The Riverside Chaucer* (RI), 66, 94, 97, 121–22, 124, 128, 132, 138, 153, 165, 167, 174, 184, 186–87, 189, 193, 195, 202–03, 206, 212
Benson, Robert G.: 43, 103, 115, 117, 126, 128, 140, 188–90, 198
Berkeley, Bishop: 40
Besserman, Lawrence: 39, 48, 129
Beverley Minster: 111, 184–85
Bevins, Lloyd Edward: 75
Bible: 15, 47–48, 129, 139, 152; Beatitudes, 152; Douay, 155, 165; English Bibles, 145; New Testament, 43, 45, 46, 134; Old Testament, 45, 46, 147; Old Latin version of, 207; Translation of, 48, 152; Vulgate, 16, 130, 196, 207
Bible (and Apocrypha), citations of: Genesis, 12, 13, 178, 188; Exodus, 12, 146, 148, 156, 194; Leviticus, 148, 210; Numbers, 210; Isaiah, 8; Ecclesiasticus, 165; 3 (AV 1) Kings, 12, 119, 141, 147, 184; 4 (AV 2) Kings, 184; Job, 139; Psalms, 40, 16, 155, 177; Proverbs, 178, 183; Matthew, 133–34, 139, 152, 194, 196–97, 200; Mark, 180, 196; Luke, 115–17, 120, 125, 133, 138, 145, 161–62; John, 139, 162, 188; Acts, 47, 186, 207–08; Ephesians, 38; 1 Timothy, 16, 146; 2 Timothy, 116; James, 16, 156; 1 Corinthians, 139; 2

231